Max Arthur was born in Shoreham, Sussex, in 1939. After completing his National Service with the RAF, he qualified as a teacher and taught in primary, secondary and special schools. He also teaches military technique to the Royal Academy of Dramatic Art and has been a professional actor himself since 1976, appearing in a number of television productions. His first play, 'Above All, Courage', is a dramatised adaptation of this book which received its premiere at the Northcott Theatre, Exeter, on 12 June 1985. He is the author of *The Manchester United Aircrash: A 25th Anniversary Tribute to the Busby Babes* (1983).

Above All, Courage

First-hand accounts from the Falklands
front line

MAX ARTHUR

SPHERE BOOKS LIMITED

First published in Great Britain by
Sidgwick and Jackson Limited 1985
Copyright © 1985 by Max Arthur
Published by Sphere Books Ltd 1986
27 Wright's Lane, London W8 5SW

Map pp. xiv–xv by Neil Hyslop

To my brother, Adrian

Set in 10 on 11pt Linotron Plantin

Printed and bound in Great Britain by
Collins, Glasgow

Author's Acknowledgements

I wish to put on record my thanks to all the men and women of the Task Force who gave me their time and stories, and to the Ministry of Defence for granting me permission to interview them.

I would like to thank in particular the following: Major-General Julian Thompson, for introductions to 3 Brigade; Major Graham Langford and Captain Rod Boswell, both formerly with the Royal Marines' Department of Public Relations, who arranged many of the interviews; Captain Isla Ferrier RM, who organized my stay in Arbroath; and Colonel David Chaundler, who gave me every help when I interviewed 2 Para, and on innumerable subsequent occasions. Thanks are also due to the officers and men of the Scots Guards; the Welsh Guards; 2 Para; 3 Para; 3 Brigade Air Squadron; HMS *Ardent*; 42 and 45 Royal Marine Commando; the Royal Marine Mountain and Artic Warfare Cadre; and to the Matron and staff of Queen Alexandra's Royal Navy Nursing Service.

I would also like to thank Jane Heller and Robert Allen, for their invaluable assistance in preparing the book for publication; Don McClen, for his advice and encouragement; and Maureen Davenport, for her constant support. Jenny Robson, Janice Sheridan, Yvonne Mitchell, and Grey Garnet typed every word.

Finally, I would like to thank Diana Martin, who throughout brought me colour, love, and laughter.

M. A.

Contents

The Battle for Darwin and Goose Green, 28/29 May
Attack on Wireless Ridge, 13/14 June

Attack on Mount Longdon, 11/12 June

Attack on Mount Harriet, 11/12 June

Assault on Two Sisters, 11/12 June

Assault on Tumbledown Mountain, 13/14 June

Command at Sea

Preface

The fight to recover the Falkland Islands was an extremely harsh and violent one, and every battle hard fought. The bleak terrain, savage weather and sub-zero temperatures made life very uncomfortable and taxed even the toughest. It was a short war, the casualties amounting to no more than those suffered during the first five minutes of the Battle of the Somme. But it was, and remains, a significant war, and one which has made a profound impression on the British people.

In October 1982, four months after the campaign, the *London Gazette* published the names of the men and women who were to be decorated for their part in the conflict. The citations for the awards gave only brief outlines of what had happened and I realized that behind those bare facts must be some remarkable individual stories. I asked the Ministry of Defence for permission to talk to the men and women listed, and over a period of two years interviewed more than 200. It is my regret that I cannot include all of them in this book.

By nature most servicemen seldom discuss anything as personal as their actions in war, and tend to be particularly reticent with an outsider. However, once I had assured them that I had no particular axe to grind they described their experiences with frankness and modesty, humour and sadness. For many it was the first time they had spoken so comprehensively, in such depth and at such length. Some had not communicated their feelings even to their families or those who fought alongside them.

They talked to me in small rooms, quiet corners of the mess, over supper; by the banks of the Isis; at the Ministry of Defence; in Plymouth, Arbroath, Portland, the Brecons, Aldershot; in Berne, Höhne and Bahrain. I found their stories utterly compelling. I heard accounts of aggression and tenacity from the Marines and Paras; of compassion for the wounded from Sam Drennan, Pierre Naya and Brian Faulkner; of surgery under fire from Steve Hughes; of dignity amidst appalling suffering from Charles Bremner and Hilarian Roberts of the Welsh Guards; of technical expertise supported by wry humour from Willie McCracken and Alan Swan. John Coward exemplified the great traditions of the Royal Navy, and David Morgan the élan of the Royal Air Force. The company commanders all impressed me with their leadership and concern for their men, and Admiral Woodward told of how he managed the pressures of command at the highest level. I was especially moved by the bravery of Bob Lawrence and his astonishing determination to overcome the severe injuries he sustained.

The twenty-nine men and one woman I have selected each gave me their story without knowing what the others had said. Their accounts were transcribed from the taped interviews, edited and then returned to them so they could change anything they wished. Most added extra, richer material, and the few changes they made were often to protect the dead in order that the next of kin should not be caused more grief. As was always my intention, apart from the occasional interlinking sentence, their stories are entirely in their own words.

Each account is a chapter in itself, and I have arranged them in an approximate chronological order; because they are personal experiences, not cold histories, that order is necessarily imperfect. Most begin from when they were told of the crisis; others at the start line of battle; a few select only the most affecting moments. Many accounts are prefaced with the citation for the award won. Some are not, because the individuals were not decorated. All equally deserve a place in the book because, as in every war, many courageous actions passed unnoticed and unrecognized. Excluded for reasons of security are members of the SAS and SBS, whose acts of courage throughout the campaign were in the highest traditions of both those elite organizations.

The ranks given throughout the book are those held at the time of the campaign.

Throughout the last two years it has been my privilege to meet so many fine men and women. I believe that their words not only provide a unique chronicle of almost every facet of the Falklands campaign, but also illustrate the indomitable spirit of the British soldier at war. I have been but a catalyst. These are their stories – they speak for themselves.

Max Arthur
Keats Grove, Hampstead, London
February 1985

Chronology

2 April	Argentine invasion of the Falkland Islands
25 April	South Georgia recaptured by British forces
2 May	*General Belgrano* sunk
4 May	*Sheffield* sunk
15 May	SAS raid on Pebble Island
21 May	D-Day – San Carlos landings begin
	Ardent sunk
23 May	*Antelope* sunk
25 May	*Coventry* and *Atlantic Conveyor* sunk
28/29 May	Battle for Darwin and Goose Green
8 June	*Sir Galahad* and *Sir Tristram* bombed
11/12 June	Mt Longdon, Two Sisters, Mt Harriet taken
13/14 June	Tumbledown Mountain and Wireless Ridge taken
	White flags fly over Stanley
14 June	Formal surrender of Argentine forces

SOUTH   ATLANTIC

(25 May)
COVENTRY
×
Pebble Island

Keppel
Island

Saunders
Island

Byron Sound

Port How

Mt Maria

King George
Bay

Swan

Queen Charlotte
Bay

W E S T   F A L K L A N D

Fox
Bay

Falkland Sound

Weddell Island

Eagle

Speedwell
Island

George
Island

0   5   10   20 km

Introduction

In March 1984, the Adjutant of 2 Para rang me and asked if I'd go and talk to yet another author about the Falklands War. Since the conflict, the battalion had been approached by a number of prospective authors and not many had been that prepossessing. A date was arranged and I met with Max Arthur. I was impressed by his technique and his declared intention that he wanted no gloss but simply to reproduce the story as it came from us. He had already spent some considerable time interviewing people and quite clearly was becoming hooked on the book, not out of what it might mean for him but rather because of the human qualities that illuminated each individual's story. Since then he has become even more involved in, and absorbed by, the humanity and depths of experience disclosed by individuals' accounts of the time they spent in the Falklands campaign.

As one reads these accounts it is not difficult to see why they are so appealing. It is not because the individuals are not aware of the courage that they were displaying, but rather because we are able to see so clearly the inside story of men under stress, in fear of their lives and yet, despite their fear, prepared to risk their lives. What also stands out is that the cause for which they were prepared to lose their lives wasn't written in heroic terms. It wasn't for Queen and country, it wasn't for the Government, it wasn't even for the Falkland Islanders; it was for their comrades, who depended upon them. Perhaps when all is said and done this is what unit pride boils down to.

There is nothing attractive about war; war is a dung heap. But it is a dung heap upon which grow some remarkable blooms. What this book does is to enable us to see some of these blooms, not as outsiders, but through the innermost thoughts of some of the individuals who were involved in the Falklands conflict.

Ultimately, for the serviceman and particularly the soldier, war is a battle of will. Perhaps it is a battle of will at all levels. America lost the war in Vietnam when the will of the population in the United States was no longer sufficient to sustain the effort, not because the American soldier gave up. Equally, however, it must be clear that if the fighting man does give up, then no amount of enthusiasm on the part of the public back at home will produce a battlefield victory.

This book is about the fighting man and those in immediate support of him, and their will. No system is stronger than its weakest part, and this is true of the military system. It does not matter how well a force is equipped if the person himself is unable to withstand the pressures on him. If the man is the weak link then his side will fail. The side that wins is the side whose will is the stronger. This book is about willpower and what motivates it. It is often concerned with men whose willpower is stronger than the average, for the will to continue despite fear is in large part the content of courage. Courage is a basic human feeling, perhaps the most basic, for if one considers any other human attribute, be it hope, honesty or sense of justice, without courage to employ it, it might as well not exist, and this is why these accounts are important. Although these experiences are based on historical events that can be dated to a specific point in history, the feelings described and the human values disclosed are not. They are timeless. Although they are described in a particular situation, that of war, they are fundamental to human beings, and I believe they are to be found wherever you find human beings. Indeed, the continuing existence of our society depends upon the will of our society to maintain it. Once that will fails, then the entire system will begin to decay. What you read in this book, therefore, is of relevance to everyday life. If the values and courage displayed seem to be too stark to be relevant, too remote from everyday existence to be applicable, then perhaps the time has come to evaluate our attitude to life and society. The catalyst that produced all these insights into human nature was death and its imminence. That that catalyst is, for us, still in a distant future should not blind us to the relevance of what is being said here.

There is a common attitude that considers the serviceman to be a different kind of creature from the civilian. Whilst in part this has some truth, for he does submit himself to a more demanding discipline than his civilian counterpart, at the core he is a human being with much the same hopes and fears as every other human being. It is probably true that the Falklands War was the first since the Boer War to be started and finished by professional servicemen; however, it is also true that all servicemen are civilians first. The qualities that they display, recorded here, are qualities that life in the services has fostered and developed. The foundations of these qualities were laid before the men ever put on a uniform.

Sometimes the original motivation for these qualities appears to be somewhat startling. Thus Able Seaman Dillon can trace his tenaciousness back to the comics he used to read. It might surprise some to discover that Spiderman was as great an influence as the uniform he wore. On the other hand, Lieutenant Sheldon's account reveals an attitude that is rather more expected, but nevertheless impressive in its professionalism and integrity.

The late Lord Moran described courage in terms of a bank balance. Each person has his credits on which he draws when necessary. Sometimes these withdrawals are in large quantities, sometimes they are in a steady trickle. If too many demands are made, a person will become bankrupt. The point at which this happens is determined by the size of the account and how able the individual is to replace those credits when not drawing on them. A significant number of contributors to this book remark upon the effectiveness of their earlier training, basically saying that their courage was a product of training. Not unexpectedly, other factors were also important, not least the friendships that existed between individuals and units.

This was a great factor for Major Drennan of the Army Air Corps and his old regiment, the Scots Guards, and in a different way for Major Kiszely and 2 Para. What is paramount is that all these men, when tested, were able to put the work that they had to do above the desire for personal survival.

It is my belief that the courage a man will show on the battlefield is related to his peacetime nature. War requires very little from a man. The requirements are clearly seen and it is quite obvious to those on the battlefield whether an individual meets those requirements. In simple terms, all that is required is that a person be prepared to risk his life. Whether he is or is not seems very largely to be determined by his qualities of unselfishness, and this can be seen in peace as well as war. The man who is self-centred in peace is very unlikely to become unselfish in war. If he thinks of himself first when the going is easy, it is almost inconceivable that he will think of others first and risk his life for them during war.

To a great extent, therefore, the training a man undergoes to build up his 'bank account', to use Lord Moran's analogy, teaches him to be unselfish; it trains him to put his unit and its objectives above his own life. Other things contribute as well: pride is one, and of course the friendships that develop within units in the services, the feeling of belonging.

What Max Arthur has done here is to bring together a wide variety of accounts and experiences from the Task Force that sailed in 1982 and present us with a picture, a very personal picture, of the men who sailed. He allows these individuals to show how they felt and allows us to draw our conclusions about the origins of their courage.

Soldiers do not like cameras on the battlefield. War, for them, is too personal an event. Death and injury is something that they feel should not be trivialized by public exhibition. Glory does not exist on a battlefield; it grows in time and distance from the event.

This book does more than any camera ever could. It shows us the inside of men and the springs of their courage.

D. Cooper
Eton College, February 1985

4

2 April

Invasion of the Falklands

Major Michael Norman

Royal Marines

Mention in Despatches

I was quite looking forward to going to the Falklands because I'd been down there on *Endurance* in 1971 for seven months. The detachment were all volunteers for the posting. I was to train my detachment, Naval Party 8901, during the winter and the Falklands Islands Defence Force in the summer. That was the general plan. I don't think anyone thought the Argentinians would ever invade; I don't think anyone thought that until the day they came. When I went for my final briefing at the Foreign Office in London in March 1982, the briefer gave me the lowdown on the latest talks, which had broken down, and told me that things would get very uncomfortable out there in six months' time because the Argentinians might cut off the supply line. By this stage the Falklands were dependent on two aircraft from the Argentine and that was their only regular link with the mainland, and the outside world, other than a quarterly visit from a UK-based ship. The briefer finally said that the Argentinians could also take the military option, but they'd never do that. Then he covered himself by saying that they were very unpredictable people!

All went well and we were planning to go on 26 March but the day before we were due to leave a phone call came from the MoD saying that our departure might be delayed indefinitely. Major Bob Bruce told us that *Endurance* had gone down to South Georgia to sort out the naughty scrap dealers, and therefore there was no definite way of getting us across from Montevideo to the Falklands. They wanted us to wait in the UK, but I argued the case, saying that it was bad for morale because everyone had said their goodbyes and were all keyed up and ready, so they let us go.

We arrived in Montevideo, expecting to wait there for at least eight days but we were met by the agent who told us we were going straight to the ship, the *John Biscoe*, a British Antarctic Survey ship. We left for the Falklands at six o'clock the same day – no eight days' holiday! We'd had no news for a few days, but as far as we knew, *Endurance* had sorted out the scrap dealers. However, as we approached Stanley, an Argentinian Hercules flew past us several times, so low that we could see the pilot. The Captain and I waved from the bridge, the engineering officer tried to fix up a hose to squirt at him and the Marines and the sailors were waving in their own peculiar fashion – one even showed his arse, 'mooning' from the rear of the ship – but the pilot ignored us! That was the first hint of trouble.

The Argentinians did a lot of things in the Falklands that they shouldn't have; they knew the islanders could do nothing about it. In fact, one plane had actually landed at Stanley; the pilot didn't ask for permission, he just landed! There were a lot of similar incidents prior to the actual invasion.

It had taken us three days to get to the Falklands. We'd had a sweepstake as to how long it would take us to get through the Narrows, and I'd won £50 with which I planned to buy a horse as my mode of transport. When we arrived, we started the handover, which normally takes about five days. We had to go to a party most nights and meet all the local dignitaries, because the Major over there was treated very much as a local squire – everyone had to meet him.

On Thursday, 1 April, at 9.00 a.m. I took over Operational Command from Major Garry Noott. The previous morning I had received a signal saying that an Argentinian submarine was nearby, probably to carry out a surface recce of the Stanley area to look for a likely landing beach. We put out observation posts to watch for the submarine but nobody took it as a serious threat and certainly not as a prelude to an invasion! It was put into the category of 'yet another incident' which the Argentinians were going to use to raise the temperature. The orders from the Governor, Rex Hunt, were that if the Argentinians landed, we were to arrest them – not to shoot them, just to arrest them. For this I had my forty incoming Marines plus about thirty of Garry's outgoing Marines, but only enough equipment for one group. Although I'd taken over the administrative command, my men still didn't have any equipment, so they had to borrow weapons from the Falkland Islands Defence Force (FIDF).

At 3.00 p.m. on 1 April the Governor summoned Garry and myself and showed me another signal which said: 'An Argentinian invasion force will be off Cape Pembroke at first light tomorrow morning and it is highly likely they will invade and you are to take up appropriate positions.' The Governor said, 'What do you think about that?' All I could say was, 'Well!' He said, 'We've called their bluff for twenty years and it looks like you and I are the poor buggers who're going to have to force it through.' Although the Governor had summoned both Garry and myself, the signal had a high-level clearance, only to be read by the people who had been named, and for reasons unknown to us it was addressed to the Governor and Major Norman, thus excluding Garry. So I had to go outside and brief Garry.

My detachment were barracked at Moody Brook and Garry's were billeted out in Stanley, three miles from Moody Brook. We called them all together and briefed them about what was happening. During an earlier briefing in the UK one of the Marines had asked what we would do if the Argentinians mounted a fullscale invasion. I replied, 'The best thing we can do is go fishing and politely offer the señors a cup of tea!' So the big joke amongst my detachment was that we were all going to the Falklands to hunt, shoot and fish; I had to break the news to them gently!

We didn't have very much time because it was already four o'clock and would be dark by six, but we did have a contingency plan. There are only two beaches around Stanley where the Argentinians could land, and Garry and I had to decide which beach to defend as we couldn't defend more than one – we didn't have sufficient defence stores, let alone men.

I think it's fair to say that at this stage the intelligence available was very bad. I'd read everything that was available to read in the MoD; I'd spoken to all sorts of people about the job and nobody had ever briefed me; nor did I read anywhere the capabilities of the Argentinian forces. For example, I was under the impression, as was Garry, that if they carried out an amphibious assault they would do it the same way as us. I expected them to come in landing craft, which influenced our decision about which beach to defend. One beach was shallow, the other deep. In our traditional way, a shallow beach means a long wade which is the last thing you want if you're going into a defended beach. So we'd elected to defend the deep beach. It transpired that the Argentinians had American amtracks which are much more suited to a shallow beach. So we selected the wrong beach through lack of intelligence. We also hadn't anticipated any special forces operations against us, because we didn't appreciate that they had them. I've since spoken to numerous previous OCs who have been in the Falklands, none of whom were any wiser than I was about the Argentinian tactics; so all the people who had been down there and made defence plans based them on the wrong assumptions.

When we'd finished laying out the defensive positions we returned to the Brook and I gave my orders at about 23:00. The Governor had been quite clear that we weren't to fight in Stanley. We assumed that after the enemy landed at Cape Pembroke they would take control of the airport, then bring helicopters and aircraft into the airfield, and from there advance up the peninsula towards Stanley. We knew we didn't have a cat in hell's chance of stopping them. We laid our defences only to try and delay the Argentinians; delay and cause casualties. Delay, delay, that was my thinking, hoping that while the enemy were being held up somebody would take some initiative and start talking and have a ceasefire or a truce.

We laid out our defences as a long line of sections along the narrow peninsula approaching Stanley from the area of the airfield. One section, the local fire section, would make the enemy deploy, causing as many casualties as they could. As soon as the enemy had deployed, the fire section would withdraw through the next section behind. Then, as the enemy got up to move, within about half a mile they'd be hit by that next section, who would make them deploy again. We would do this all the way back to the edge of Stanley, where the four sections would be regrouped. Bill Trollope, my Second-in-Command, would then do exactly the same, only this time much harder, as a twenty-eight-man position. Hopefully we would have inflicted sufficient casualties to make them think again and perhaps negotiate.

Corporal Carr's section was detached to the Murray Heights to watch other likely areas of approach from the north and give us early warning. Corporal York's section was on the Narrows in Stanley Harbour with our 84mm anti-tank gun in case the Argentinians decided to steam a fleet into Stanley Harbour. The section's orders were quite simple: sink the first naval ship that came in through the Narrows. Lieutenant Keith Mills did the same thing in South Georgia and almost covered himself in glory by nearly sinking a patrol boat with an anti-tank gun. His 84mm fell short of the ship and continued like a torpedo, striking the target below the water line.

I put two men with a GPMG (general-purpose machine gun) in the sand-dunes overlooking what we thought would be the landing beach, with orders to open fire at the disembarking troops as the first wave of landing craft hit the beach. This way we hoped that any subsequent waves of landing craft coming in behind them would stand off, thinking it was an opposed landing, and the two lads, Milne and Wilcox, would make their getaway on two of the detachment's three motorbikes. One of Garry's men, Marine Berry, came up to me and said, 'I think it would be a good idea if someone went up on Sapper Hill.' I agreed, but couldn't spare anybody to go. He said he would. All these three men were incredibly brave. Berry went with the third motorcycle to the top of Sapper Hill, all by himself. It broke all the principles of deploying people; it was a very bad thing for me to do, but we needed to occupy Sapper Hill, because potentially it gave us a very good view and an early warning.

Our final *pièce de résistance* was to switch the light off in the lighthouse at Cape Pembroke, and pray for bad weather. The weather in the Falklands has to be seen to be believed. You can get all four seasons in one day, so we switched the light off and hoped it would blow a hoolie. Our prayers went unanswered: it was a lovely, calm, moonlit night!

Ours was a self-administrating unit which broke down into about two-thirds fighting and one-third administration. The latter included vehicle mechanics, cooks, drivers, clerks, butchers, etc., so a lot of the people who opposed the invasion were not young, fighting Marines from a Commando rifle company. The admin section, as they became, were to defend Government House. My Sergeant-Major, Colour-Sergeant Bill Muir, and my RQMS, Warrant Officer 2 Bill Aspinall, were put in command of these men. We hadn't had time to site a defensive position around Government House because it was not in our original plan. The original plan had been that we would try to delay an invasion and then Garry and the Governor would go into the hinterland, but the Governor rejected this idea. He was going to stay, and that tied us completely because the role of Naval Party 8901 wasn't to defend the Falkland Islands – it was to defend the seat of Government. My interpretation of that was that where the Governor was, the detachment should be. So we made a compromise: my detachment was going to stay with the Governor and Garry would go with his men into the country. They knew the land, they had the kit, and we had drawn the short straw! My blokes had rifles but they hadn't got sleeping bags, or rations.

12

Apart from ourselves there were 100 men of the Falkland Islands Defence Force, which was like a territorial army. There was also the settlement reserve volunteers who were similar to the old Home Guard and operated from their settlements. I was under the command of the Governor and so was the OC of the Defence Force, but they had their own tasks, which were to defend vulnerable points, like the Town Hall and the power station. Twenty-three of the FIDF actually turned out to assist in the defence of Stanley.

My favourite story about the FIDF happened in the battle for Stanley. The Governor's phone rang and it was the Commanding Officer of the Defence Force. He said, 'We're all in the Town Hall, and there are lots of Argentinians outside.' So the Governor said, 'Well, shoot them.' And this chap said, 'There are lots and lots of Argentinians outside.' So the Governor said, 'Well, shoot some of them.' To which the CO replied, 'My men are all very young, Sir, and they're frightened,' which was probably very true, because we were as well. The Governor said, 'Okay. Get your men, put all their weapons at one end of the room and you sit at the other end, so it's quite obvious when the Argentinians come in that you're not armed soldiers, and that you're not in an aggressive mood.' The CO replied, 'We've done that. We've done that already!' They were very young lads; they weren't trained soldiers.

One of the sad things about the whole situation was that the media had built up this myth that, come the day of an invasion, every man and his dog would be there, fighting in the streets. I think the Falkland Islanders themselves had come to believe it but it's just not their way. They're very nice, placid people, not unlike the Western Islanders of Scotland. If the Russians landed in the Orkneys the Orcadians wouldn't grab their shotguns and start fighting. They certainly wouldn't co-operate with them in any way whatsoever, but they wouldn't go on the streets and fight them, and I don't think we'd expect them to fight because it would be a *fait accompli*. I suppose we had expected the

Falkland Islanders to help and we were disappointed that they didn't. There are over 1,000 people in Stanley and we could have used the men, but it was clear that the Governor quite rightly wanted to avoid endangering the civilian population as far as possible. But I still thought people would come out on the streets; Garry Noott didn't.

We had a ship, *The Forest*, on charter to us which I sent out to sit in Port William, which is the outer harbour, with two Royal Navy officers, Lieutenants Ball and Todd-Hunter, to keep a radar watch and tell us when the Argentinians were arriving. They radioed in about 3:00 a.m. and said they'd had a radar contact on two unidentified ships, showing no lights, which were steaming very slowly round to the south, so we knew the invasion was definitely on. I told *The Forest* to come in again. By 4:00 a.m. we'd heard nothing at all, so I asked *The Forest* to go out again and see what was going on. Jack Solace, the Master, refused, because he could see an aircraft carrier sitting in Surf Bay. I went shooting down to Hooker's Point by Land-Rover to see my section and told them there was an aircraft carrier in the bay. It turned out to be the silhouette of the wreck of the *Lady Elizabeth* with the stars behind her! But Jack was like everybody else that night, a bit twitchy and making substance out of shadows.

We had deployed at 2:00 a.m. and we were as ready as we could be; we couldn't do any more until first light. I was never convinced that they were going to land, but I was sure they were going to be there in the morning, just to show the Falkland Islanders how vulnerable they really were. I think, with hindsight, they could have achieved much more by not landing; they'd have just made us, the British Government, and the Falkland Islanders look stupid. That would have been far more effective than what they did.

Although we all knew we were pathetically equipped to deal with an invasion force, we all went out determined to fight. I know it sounds very melodramatic, but I made my orders quite clear to them: we were there to defend the seat of Government. I spelt it out that it meant that we would fight until the Governor gave in or we were overrun, and that would probably mean dying. Most of us probably would have died because we had every intention of fighting all the way through; none of the lads would've stopped and surrendered. They were all quite determined and everybody's attitude, including mine, was exactly the same: 'Just who the bloody hell do they think they are? Okay, there're only seventy of us here, but we're trained men. We belong to an elite corps of the Royal Marines. If they're going to land here, they're going to get more of a bloody shock than they thought!' The final word of encouragement I gave to the lads about the next day was, 'Forget the Falkland Islands, we can't save them. Tomorrow, when they come, we're fighting for ourselves: each and every one of us. We're fighting for what we stand for, and then we're fighting for each one of us. If you survive tomorrow, it's because you've fought better and been lucky.' The lads took that incredibly well; to my surprise, they were raring to go. I'd been in Aden in 1966 as a new 2nd Lieutenant but this was the first time I'd had to give orders when I expected to lose. I'd always been with a fairly big gang who were going to win. So this was new to me, giving orders to people, knowing you're going to lose.

About five o'clock I was sitting in my vehicle at Look-out Rocks, talking to the driver, Patterson, with Farnworth, my radio operator, behind in the back. Radio operators are notorious for making a lot of noise because once they put the headset on and start talking to everyone on the radio, you can't shut them up. As I was sitting there, out of the corner of my eye I saw a patrol coming up the road, fully armed! I knew it wasn't one of ours by their equipment, so Patterson and I were trying quietly to sneak out of the vehicle and drag our weapons out, which were in their holders behind us. Farnworth, however, decided to do a radio check at this moment and say 'Hello' to everybody. I hissed at him, 'Farnworth, shut up.' He was oblivious. He couldn't understand why we'd stopped talking, and why we were going through these strange motions of trying to sneak out. I must admit my heart came right up into my mouth. I thought, 'The first casualty in this battle is going to be me. I'm going to get shot and I'm not even holding a rifle!' All this time Farnworth was still doing his Forces' Favourite bit! But, thank God, it turned out to be an FIDF patrol who were leaving a pumping station and going back to the Town Hall. Because they weren't under my command, I didn't know that. Fortunately, Patterson, who'd been there for a year, recognized one of them.

An hour later there was a fantastic amount of fire and explosions from Moody Brook. You didn't have to be a military genius to realize that things weren't proceeding as we'd thought they would. We'd been completely wrong-footed: all our defences were facing the wrong way, all committed to a beach assault and they'd come in behind us. They'd split their force: one went to neutralize Moody Brook, expecting us to be there, and the other went to capture Government House. They had a very good plan and it was well co-ordinated, but, of course, we weren't at the Brook, thank goodness, and when they got to Government House they came across my Headquarter Section, who opened fire on them.

I ordered my sections to get to Government House as fast as possible, and I shot back in my vehicle to arrive just before the Argentinians attacked. I was just getting a brief from Garry when they opened fire from the back of the house. They came down the only covered approach there is. It's Sod's Law that the back of Government House is the only covered approach in Stanley: there are trees and bushes and there's high ground, so it was a perfect position for them. They attacked with about eighty men initially, then later in the day their other company came down from Moody Brook. Incredibly quickly they got very, very close, putting in a lot of firepower. Government House has a three-foot stone garden wall round it, enclosing about twenty yards of lawn in the front and about ten yards in the back. We were literally on one side of the wall and they were on the other. We numbered about thirty men at the most, most of whom were administrators or sailors.

The Argentinians had silencers on SMGs (submachine guns), which made a very peculiar noise – a noise I'd never heard before. They had very effective flash eliminators which meant there was nothing to fire back at; we just had to fire into the blackness. The explosions going on around us were quite horrific. Garry shouted out, 'What is it?' Being a mortar officer by trade I shouted back, 'I think we're being mortared' – and we were protecting a weatherboard house! Then I thought it was grenades, but there was something missing, and I suddenly twigged that there was no shrapnel flying around at all. None of us were getting injured from all these explosions that were going on amongst us. That was when I realized it was stun grenades, which our SAS use, and I realized we were up against their special forces. They were obviously a snatch team. Their job was to come into Government House, thinking that no one was going to be there, and snatch the Governor. They sent in a group of six and we badly wounded three of them. It was a sort of murky half-light, but we could see what was happening. The routine was simple: as a black figure climbed over the stone wall, we would shoot at him. This seemed to go on for quite a long time, but I suppose it was only about five or ten minutes. While they were attacking they carried out psychological warfare at the same time. They were shouting at us in English the whole time, 'Come out, Mr Hunt,' or 'Time to give up, Mr Hunt.' But the Marines shouted back, 'Go away. Mr Hunt is not going to come out,' or words to that effect!

There was a lull in the firing and they went away. It was a bit like cowboys and indians: they went away, but you knew they were going to come back. That was the most frightening moment because we suddenly realized that they had a phenomenal amount of firepower, and therefore had a lot of men there. They had a lot more firepower than we had and these were only their special forces, so there was bound to be a conventional landing

17

coming along at first light. I was lying behind an old-fashioned cannon outside the entrance to Government House and was shaking uncontrollably from head to foot. Chris Todd-Hunter was lying on the other side of the cannon and I actually never told him he was lying on the wrong side – there wasn't room on mine for both of us!

There was absolute quiet. There weren't any Marines shouting to each other; the Sergeant-Major wasn't shouting; and I wasn't shouting. Everyone was thinking the same thought: we suddenly realized we were going to die. There was no doubt in my mind that they were going to come back, and there was no way we could keep all these people away for any length of time, and we would surely die. It was really quite frightening. As I lay there shaking I gave myself a quiet but strong talking-to: 'Get a grip on yourself, Norman; you knew it would come to this, you told all the others it would. For God's sake, if somebody climbs over the wall now, in this state you'll be pushed to hit the wall, let alone him.' But once I'd said that to myself, once I'd accepted it and come to terms with it, it disappeared and the physical shaking stopped. Suddenly I shouted out to the Sergeant-Major, the Sergeant-Major shouted back, and all the Marines started talking to each other. I said to Todd-Hunter, 'Are you married?' and he said, 'No, it's easier for me.' So he was thinking exactly the same thing as I was.

We got on with our job as if it was a thing we did every day of our lives. Colour-Sergeant Muir was incredibly brave during this time. There was all this sniper fire going on and it was getting light and they were still sniping at us but he just ran around the detachment, checking up on ammunition, checking up with people, moving people around – completely as if he was bullet-proof. No. 2 Aspinall, my RQMS, was doing the same in the front garden.

When the Argentinians withdrew, they left three blokes behind, outside the back door of the kitchen, very badly wounded, one of whom subsequently died. They were dressed just like the SAS who went into the Iranian Embassy – all black, balaclavas, the lot. It was a bit unreal.

18

I thought the Argentinians were just going to sort themselves out and report that there were more of us than they thought. They were still sniping at us the whole time but they didn't attack Government House again. They didn't have to. They knew there were another 2,000 coming up the beach, and so did we! Marine Berry, who was on Sapper Hill, reported at 6:30 that two amtracks had landed; by 6:45 there were twenty and helicopters were landing on the airfield. The only saving grace for Garry Noott and me was that they actually did come ashore in landing craft and helicopters eventually. So we got it half right. But we had got the wrong beach!

I was very worried about the two men on the motorcycles because we hadn't heard from them at all – their radio had gone duff – but in fact they got away. As soon as they saw the Argentinians land on the other beach, they'd got on their motorcycles and joined up with the first section they could find. I didn't know this until long after the surrender. We still had Bill Trollope with his HQ at Look-out Rocks, and the infamous Stefan York at Naval Point, waiting to sink the first battleship that came into the Narrows! Bill had got hold of Corporal Johnson's section, so we still had them as well, and they'd moved back to Headquarters and waited for the amtracks to move into range and carry out the original plan of engaging them. As soon as the landings had started, Garry had recalled Corporal Carr's section back to Government House, so they were on the move, and I had ordered Corporals Duff and Armour to abandon their airfield positions and reinforce Government House.

To illustrate the absurdity of the whole situation, at about 7:00 a.m. our clerk, Turner, was looking down the road towards Moody Brook where there were some bungalows. All of a sudden he sees a bloke walking along the road carrying a white flag while bullets overshooting the house were bouncing off the tarmac. Turner shouted to Mr Aspinall, 'There's a civvy coming down the road.' So Mr Aspinall said, 'Well, tell him to eff off, then. Tell him not to be so bloody stupid and go home.' Turner sticks his head through the hedge and says, 'Oi! Push off! Get back to your house.' This bloke replies in a broad Jock accent, 'It's all right for you, but some of us have to go to work' – as if we were having an exercise and playing around, being a nuisance! Eventually he was persuaded to go home.

The other problem we had, apart from being hopelessly outnumbered, was that we didn't know the place very well. Corporal Johnson was moving back from Stanley when the Governor came up to me and said, 'Mike, they've just taken the power station, but I understand there's only two or three of them, and it would be very good for morale if we took it back.' So I got on to Corporal Johnson and told him to take the power station out. He replied, 'Roger. Wilko.' Then there was a pause and he came back and said, 'Where is the power station?' And I said, 'I dunno. I'll find you another job.' There were no street maps of Stanley.

Before that incident, the amtracks were working their way up the road towards Bill Trollope. Unfortunately, we hadn't got round to zeroing our anti-tank weapons. When one got within range of the 84mm Bill told Marine Brown to engage it. He fired, and the round hit the ground about 100 yards short. Brown loaded again, readjusted his aim and fired; he got closer to the amtrack but he didn't hit it. The amtracks completely ignored these two warning shots and continued to accelerate up the road. Amid much encouragement from the rest of the section, Brown loaded for the third time. Meanwhile, Gibbs with the 66mm, whose range is only about 100 metres, also opened fire and hit the passenger compartment of the first amtrack, which stopped. Brown now fired again at the stationary target and scored a direct hit, straight on the nose! Black smoke came from it, but nobody got out. The other amtracks halted out of range and disembarked ten men each and returned fire.

The Governor was getting rather worried, as we all were at this stage. I reckoned there was a battalion ashore by now and they had helicopters, fixed-wing aircraft, support weapons, 81mm mortars, the lot. I think they intended to win! Hunt never panicked but he was sitting under his table, contemplating. What we did in Government House was to close all the curtains, then walk around as if we were in a concrete bunker! We'd crawl around outside, rush into the house, and then just walk about as if we were totally protected. There were bullet holes in the walls on either side of the corridor, but once we were inside, we seemed to think we were safe. I told the Governor that I didn't think they were trying to kill us now; they were quite happy to keep us pinned down where we were.

Garry had been running the Ops Room and I think he was a bit fed up with this. His adrenalin was pumping and he said to me, 'Will you take over the Ops Room for a while and let me go on the outside?' So out he went, and came straight back in. 'Have you anybody upstairs?' he asked. I'd done a tour of the upstairs, and said, 'I've got Corporal Armour's section in the west wing.' 'No,' he said, 'have you got anybody above the kitchen?' I said, 'No.' He said, 'Right. I'm going to take two men and go up there. Is that all right?' I said, 'Fine. Why, what's the problem?' He said, 'There's somebody up there.' To my amazement he came down with three prisoners, all in their black balaclava outfits, festooned with machine pistols and grenades all over them. And they'd been there for three hours. Garry had heard them muttering to each other.

If their task was to snatch the Governor, they had failed. They could have done so easily at any time, because we only had one Marine outside the Governor's Ops Room as protection; the rest of our attention was concentrated outside. They could have killed the Governor any time, but they didn't. I think I can now understand why the rest didn't come back for a second attack. They'd come down in one attack and six men had not returned. None of the six seemed to have radios so their commander could never have been quite sure what they were facing.

During the whole battle I never fired my weapon – I was too busy. But at one point I spotted a man lying on top of some rocks. I was in the wooden storm porch and was leaning out of the door to try and get a big enough angle to get my rifle to my shoulder to beam onto this bloke when I decided that I would have to expose far too much of myself. I was trying to adjust my position when Farnworth, our ever-talking radio operator, appeared again in my life. 'What are you doing, boss?' he said. 'Look up there,' I said. 'Got him, got him!' he said, and fired a couple of shots which went right across the entrance of my storm porch. Now, you get a fantastic explosion from the end of a rifle barrel and it was very painful. So I said to Farnworth, 'For Christ's sake, stop shooting at him. It's making my ears hurt. Don't shoot at him again.' Reluctantly he said, 'All right then.' I began shouting across to the Sergeant-Major when all of a sudden there was another great bang and my ears were ringing. I turned round angrily to Farnworth and said to him, 'If you fire that rifle again, I'll wrap it round your bloody neck!' A shocked Farnworth pointed to a large hole in the weatherboard inches above my head – it had been an incoming round!

Meanwhile, one of my sniper teams, Corporals Pares and Gill, were doing an excellent job. Gill would look through his sniper scope and tell Pares where the enemy were and Pares would fire ten rounds rapid, and as soon as that got them on the move, Gill would take them out with the sniper rifle. They took out four or five this way and all the time they were giving the rest of us a running commentary.

It was very confusing and the battle was going on all around; I didn't know if we'd taken any casualties. I had a rough idea of what each section was doing. I knew about the success with the amtrack and I knew that Corporal Carr's section had got away from Murray Heights and had reached *The Forest*, hoping Jack Solace, the Master, would take him further, but this was not possible.

Garry Noott came to me and said, 'It's time you did some straight talking to the Governor and told him what's going on.' I went in to him and told him there was a war going on; that amtracks were coming through the town and that they were flying more things in all the time – by this time Hercules were arriving. We had actually tried to improve our defences and push out and try to get up onto the higher ground but the enemy were well enough ensconced to stop us doing that. It seemed to me that we had three options. One was for the Governor and us to break out while we still could. We would take casualties, but we could have got away and taken the Governor with us. By taking the Governor we'd be with the seat of Government so the Falklands would still be British territory and the Argentinians would have to come and fight us. The second one was to remain exactly as we were and carry on fighting. I told him that we were quite happy to do that, but with their numbers and firepower it wouldn't be very long before we were defeated. The third option was to try and negotiate a truce. Nobody, least of all the Governor, was talking about surrendering, but I thought we might be able to get negotiations going. We were fighting and winning locally, it was obvious that we weren't going to give up, and if we got in quickly with the negotiations while we were still killing them it would be better than in half an hour's time when they were killing us. So if we were going to get a truce, now was the time to get it.

By using Patrick Watts on the civilian radio, we managed to get in contact with the Argentine forces and also the Argentinian military air service, LADE, which used to fly civilian aircraft from the Argentine to the Falklands. There had just been a changeover at LADE so there was a new man there, almost as new as I was. But the previous commander, Hector Gilbert, had returned to sort out some administration. He'd told the Governor the day before that he didn't know anything about the invasion. But I noticed at their victory celebrations after the surrender that he was all dressed up in his best uniform, so I think he did. The Governor asked Hector to come down and negotiate with the commander of the invasion forces. Hector appeared, walking down the road with a white flag, and there was a temporary ceasefire. Then the

Argentinians all started moving their positions around, which isn't quite the rules of the game, so we said, 'Okay, carry on firing!' As this poor devil approached the door of Government House his face was deathly white, as white as the flag he was carrying. He was about five yards from me and I was encouraging him: 'Come on. Come on, Hector, this way!' Then, *bang*, and he went flat down. I thought, 'God, they've shot their own man,' but he'd only been frightened by the bang, and had reacted by falling over.

After he'd recovered his composure he went off with Dick Baker, the Chief Secretary, to find the invasion force's leader. They came back with a deputy commander, Admiral Carlos Busser. Busser was a very tall, elegant man, in American-type fatigues and baseball hat who spoke impeccable English and wanted to shake everybody by the hand. Before Busser could say anything, the Governor, this little, dapper man in his pinstripe suit, pulled himself up to his full five feet six, looked at Busser and said, 'This is British property. You are not invited. We don't want you here. I want you to leave and to take all your men with you.' I looked across to Garry and thought, 'Only an Englishman could say that, but it might work.' Busser looked at him, smiled, and said, 'I've got 800 men ashore at the moment. I've got another 2,000 about to land. The only sensible thing you can do is tell these brave men to stop fighting. They've put up a magnificent battle. We didn't expect any resistance here at all. I came with such great numbers because I thought if I came this way there'd be no fighting at all – we'd be able to have a peaceful annexation.'

Busser was a professional soldier, he wasn't a politician. After we'd surrendered, he couldn't have been nicer. Neither could the officer who was in command of their special forces; he was also a very professional serviceman.

The Governor didn't confer with me at this point, nor should he have done. I'd given my military advice, the three options, and he'd decided to go for the truce, but the Argentinians weren't interested. They knew how many there were of us, they knew how many they'd got, so why have a truce? Their reaction was, 'If you don't want to stop fighting, carry on fighting; it's entirely up to you.'

Busser was obviously a compassionate man and he spoke again to the Governor. 'I don't want to damage civilians and I don't want to kill these men. If we continue, that's what you're asking me to do, because we're not going to stop. Your Marines are not going to win either.' The Governor thought about it for a while and then said, 'You've given me no option. I will order my men to lay down their arms.'

As a professional soldier, inwardly I reacted strongly to that – it was against all my training. I didn't like it. And when I went round telling my Marines to lay down their arms, they were very angry and some of them wanted to continue the fight, but it was out of my hands. As a military man, I couldn't have come to that decision; I'd have fought. It is not our job to surrender. We have deep and unfashionable feelings of responsibility for the traditions of our corps, rather like the Paras. We've both got a very strong tradition as a fighting force, and that's what we were there to do.

At the time I was aware that we'd done all we could. But it had not been enough and in a way we were letting down lots of people. We were letting down the Falkland Islanders; they didn't do a lot to help themselves, but we were there to help them and we felt, when we left, that we'd let these people down. We were an inadequate force, but I still felt that perhaps we could have done something else. I kept thinking throughout the battle, 'I've got seventy men here and they're going to die, and there's nothing that I can do about it.' That was a real feeling of helplessness. So when the decision was taken away from me and the Governor ordered the surrender, professionally I didn't like it; but as a human being and as a commander I was relieved that somebody else was making that decision. I was also very, very relieved that at least all those around me were not going to die for an unnecessary reason, because if we'd fought to the end, the Argentinians would still have taken the islands and we would all be dead. I'd given the Governor fair advice and he had said to me, 'So I've got to make the decision.' I said, 'That's the perks of being in command. I'll give you all the advice you like, and I can tell you the options that I favour, but it's got to be your decision, Sir.' I'm sure that uppermost in the Governor's mind was the safety of the civilians and the need to avoid unnecessary damage to property in Stanley. If we'd started fighting in the streets of Stanley, we could've lasted out for a longer time, but there would have been many civilian casualties and the end result would have been the same.

Sergeant Short on the radio told those that were still out on the hills to stay where they were, to unload their weapons and lay them down. Bill Trollope broke his up so nobody else could use it. Corporal Johnson, who had by now reached Sapper Hill, was angry because he felt he could do more, but I told him to just stay where he was. Corporal York had gone into the hills rather than surrender. That's the sort of guy York is. He's a tremendous leader of men at that level. But he'd ditched all the heavy kit so he could move quickly and hadn't taken his radio with him. The last message he sent to me was, 'Boss, we're going fishing!' He got away in a rubber boat, which showed fantastic initiative – all power to him. He and his men stayed out for four or five days, living in caves without any food, sopping wet. Then they were captured, interrogated, and finally despatched via Montevideo to England. They eventually rejoined us on board *Canberra* a few days before our landings began.

So the reason why many of the lads were upset when the surrender came was that, locally, we were doing quite well. And they were upset for the same reason I was.

Then we went through the indignity of having to lie in the road and be searched. After that the Argentinians put us in a field and took our weapons, and we just sat there. I kept walking round, talking to people out of the corner of my mouth, giving them briefings as to what I thought was going on. We didn't know how many men were safe, so as each section of Marines came marching down the road to surrender, you could see everybody counting and when they'd got the right number, a great cheer would go up around the field!

Garry and I were taken off to witness the raising of the Argentine flag outside Government House. They had known they were going to win; they'd come along with a choir, a guard of honour and a band. They all sang their national anthem and they had this huge, great flag – the biggest I'd ever seen. With the band playing its head off and the choir singing away, they began to raise their bloody flag. It got half-way up and the rope snapped – to an almighty cheer from our field! In reaction, an Argentine corporal who was marching a section of my men down the road made them put their hands on their heads. The Argentinian officer who was with me told the corporal, 'Let those men take their hands off their heads. If you've searched them, let them walk down the road normally, please.' Another lot were lying down on the ground, being searched, and I saw Carlos Busser saying, 'Let those men stand up.'

They told us they were going to fly us out. Everyone came down to see us off – the Argentinians even offered us a guard of honour but I didn't know what the lads would do. No one could believe we were all there, that any of us were left alive after all that fighting. We didn't have a single casualty, not one – it was incredible.

Even on the aircraft the Argentinians were incredibly frightened of us. There was one guard, as tired as we were, who insisted on standing the whole way. He stood guarding us with a submachine gun with his finger over the trigger, and his eyes kept drooping and his head kept nodding. I sat there awake the whole time because I was petrified he was going to shoot half my blokes in his sleep.

The thing that amazed me was how quickly we became conditioned to being prisoners and not doing what we wanted to do. My seat broke, and myself and the chap next to me ended up on the floor. Normally you'd get straight up and fix it, but my first reaction was to sit there and look at the sentry until he said I could stand up.

27

We were told we'd be taken to Buenos Aires. I was more than a little perturbed. I guessed there would be some kind of PR show and I knew the Argentinians' reputation for crowd control was none too good. I fully expected that we'd spend the next few months, at least, as prisoners at Patagonia. It was a surly and defensive OC that disembarked on the Argentinian mainland.

At Comodoro Rivadavia we transferred to a Boeing 707. We went through a tunnel of guards lined up from one aircraft to the other in two ranks, which amused us. By that stage, we weren't showing any emotions – we were just looking. We were tired, unshaven, fed up and, I suppose, in a state of shock. They were just staring at us and we just looked back at them. We felt like a load of cattle being herded around. But amongst ourselves there was lots of humour. I can't remember any particular jokes but there was a lot of laughing and joking to keep our morale up.

We then landed at what I took to be Buenos Aires: that's where they'd said we were going. But I thought it was a bit strange when they took us into Immigration and this bloke asked for my passport. I told him I didn't have a passport, and he said, 'Why not?' I told this little dago exactly why I didn't have a passport, and exactly who he should go and see about it. As I was in the middle of this tirade, I happened to glance at the big badge on his shoulder and it read, 'Airport Control, Montevideo, Uruguay.' So there was this guy opening his country to us as prisoners of war and getting harangued for it because he'd had the audacity to ask for a passport.

They took us to a very nice hotel and put us under 'hotel' arrest; we were not allowed out of it. None of us had any money but our RQMS, WO2 Bill Aspinall, who could fix anything, went up to negotiate. He came back and told me, 'They're going to allow us to sign chits at the bar and they will send us the bills later. All you've got to do is print your name.' So I said, 'Fine. Any particular name?' and he said, 'All they want is a printed name.' So I got all the lads together and told them they could use the bar, all they had to do was print their names on the chits so the Foreign Office could forward the bills to us later. I looked at the chits later and I think Mrs Thatcher and Queen Victoria have some fairly big bar bills coming their way!

After two days we were flown back to England and were home for two weeks before we were re-equipped and told to report for duty at some ridiculous hour like three o'clock in the morning. I made a great promise to Colonel David-Storrie that we'd look after the weapons this time. We flew to Ascension Island and the next morning the *Canberra* came steaming in. We hadn't got a job; we'd gone back mainly because a politician had stood up and amid great roars of applause in the House had said that Naval Party 8901 was going back. What I had originally been told was we would go back as volunteers and when we'd recaptured the island, we would be re-established as the detachment. The detachment did volunteer to return.

After much manoeuvring I eventually found myself in charge of Juliet Company and we went ashore at San Carlos. We fought with 42 Commando RM throughout the campaign.

When the Argentinians surrendered we were given the task of disarming the prisoners at Stanley Airport. With some very mixed feelings I marched my company of 100 men through Stanley, and escorted by only two Argentinian policemen we passed through hundreds of still armed Argentinians. When we arrived we found 900 waiting to hand over their weapons. It was remarkable; it just showed how much they'd lost their will to fight. I compared their attitude to my own men, who when called on to surrender a couple of months before had been so angry. These blokes couldn't wait to give you their weapons.

We were 48 days from our surrender to landing again at San Carlos and then there were 28 days that the Task Force was ashore, making a total of 76 days from the surrender to walking back into Government House.

Walking into Government House was quite something.

I looked at it, nodded, and went to walk in. The Marine sentry, who'd been given his orders, told me to wipe my feet, because Stanley was very muddy. I said, 'They didn't make a fuss about what state my feet were in three months ago. They were only too delighted for me to go in there!' But I wiped my feet and walked in.

When I looked out at Stanley my feelings were surprising, really; there was no feeling of revenge, just satisfaction, and also great sorrow for the people of Stanley. Stanley is very attractive in a Western Isles sort of way. It's grey slate, but always prim and proper, always well cared for, and there it was now, filthy, mud everywhere, broken up, in a disgusting state. I felt very sorry for the people of Stanley, seeing what a mess the Argentinians had made of their home, but it was satisfying to be back – particularly because we had actually said to the Governor, 'We will be back.' I didn't in fact meet him again.

Marine Urand, our butcher, had an interesting reunion. He had been one of Corporal York's party. After the Argentine surrender Urand was standing at a checkpoint and heard an Argentinian officer shout at somebody. Urand strolled over and tapped him on the shoulder and said, 'I'd recognize that voice anywhere.' The Argentinian turned round and paled – he was the fellow who'd interrogated Urand.

One night while my company was processing their prisoners I got a message that one of the ships could take another 300 Argentinians, so I went off in search of an Argentinian officer – I was walking around amongst thousands of prisoners, armed with only a rifle. I asked a soldier to take me to a Marine officer. He took me to a Marine unit and I told the officer to pack off 300 of his men. When I got back to my tent Corporal Armour came up and said, 'Sir, there's a chap on the checkpoint asking for you by name.' I asked what he was complaining about. He said, 'No, he's not complaining at all.' I put my wellies on and went down to the checkpoint. This chap saluted and said, 'Good morning, Major Norman. Nice to see you.

How are you?' I said I was fine. Then he asked, 'How are all your men? Did they all get through okay?' I told him I had three injured on the day before the final surrender, one quite badly. 'Ah,' he said, 'I'm very pleased to hear that your casualties are so light. Do you know who I am?' I said, 'No.' He said, 'I'm the Second-in-Command of the company that attacked you on 2 April and the Company Commander would very much like to say goodbye to you before he goes.' So I went down to see him and he introduced me to all his officers, saying, 'This is Major Norman who was defending when we attacked. His men were very brave.' It was very strange, very strange indeed. We had come full circle, and more.

And that was it. That was my war over and done with. Inevitably there are many not mentioned: Mr Bill Curtis and Jim Fairfield, the only two civilians to actively assist us; Mrs Mavis Hunt, who was brave and kind; David Welles and the girl on the telephone exchange who remained at her post all night; and all my lads, whose bravery I will never forget.

21 May

Bomb Attack on
HMS *Ardent*

Able Seaman (Radar) John Dillon

Royal Navy

George Medal

On 21 May 1982 Able Seaman (Radar) Dillon was in the After Damage Control Party on board HMS Ardent *in Falkland Sound. Following a bomb attack on the ship he was assisting in the control of flooding in the dining hall when the area sustained further major bomb damage and he was rendered unconscious. On regaining consciousness he found that he was pinned to the deck by heavy debris in the dimly-lit devastated compartment. A fire was raging and the area was rapidly filling with thick smoke.*

He extricated himself and despite pain from a large shrapnel wound in his back attempted unsuccessfully to free a man pinned down by a girder across his neck. He then made his way through the smoke towards a further man calling for help, whom he found trapped under heavy metal girders, bleeding from head and face wounds and with his left hand severely damaged. After several attempts, between which he had to drop to the deck to get breathable air, AB(R) Dillon succeeded in raising the debris sufficiently to allow the man to drag himself free. AB(R) Dillon's anti-flash hood had been ripped off in the explosion, so afforded him no protection from the heat, and his left ear was burned. In their search for an escape route, the man, who was heavily built, fell into a hole in the deck, but was dragged out by the much slighter AB(R) Dillon to a hole in the ship's side where, although the man was able to inflate his own life-jacket, AB(R) Dillon was unable to follow suit, due to the pain in his throat caused by the smoke. Despite this, fearing that the weakened man would be dragged beneath the ship, AB(R) Dillon followed him into the water and pulled him away from the ship's side. By this time his exertions, pain and the cold of the sea had weakened AB(R) Dillon until he could do little to support himself in the water. Realizing that there was a danger of him pushing the man under the water if he continued to hold on to him, he moved away, and appreciating that he could no longer swim or grasp the strop lowered to him from a helicopter, slipped beneath the surface. He and the man were then rescued by a helicopter crewman.

There is little doubt that but for Able Seaman (Radar) Dillon's selfless acts with complete disregard for his personal safety the other man would not have escaped from the ship which was then being abandoned and sinking.

I'm not really into reading books. I used to read comics a lot when I was small. My favourite comic man was probably Spiderman. I used to collect comics as well. I've got hundreds at home, they're all stored in boxes. I used to be really into them. They're a kind of mixture, like Silver Surfer and stuff like that. He's a guy who rides around on a board – he rides around in the skies and that, he's got cosmic power, stuff like that. On the ship it all came to mind, you know; it all kind of worked together.

I was interested in sport, but not the sort of sport you could do at school. I used to do karate, and I practised a lot at home. I think what karate gave me was something – I don't know what – it's just a feeling inside. I used to go to the pictures every weekend with my brother. I used to take him down there because I was so interested in Kung Fu. I think it could have been one of the things that saved me on the *Ardent*. When I was trapped in the *Ardent* all these things were flashing through my mind, it was just like a big screen in front of me and it had all these blokes that I used to see in the pictures. They were the sort of blokes that never seem to give up. They just sort of kept trying and kept pushing forward – didn't mess anything up. I always used to be fascinated by them; they never seemed to give up and always seemed to push themselves forward – I think that's what saved me. I should have died. I should have died about three times.

Before the bomb fell, everyone was laughing and joking. The ship had already been under attack and we'd had to keep taking cover, which after a while was getting a bit boring. Then, at around four o'clock, we got an order to take cover and we just thought it was another false alarm. We all lay on the floor and the next thing we heard was this big bang and everything went quiet. It just seemed like a dream, we couldn't believe that we'd actually been hit. I think the flight deck was hit and as I was in the Damage Control Team I got up with my mates to tackle the problem of one of the pipes that had broken and was starting to spray water everywhere. The dining hall was starting to fill up with water so we got some buckets and started bailing out water. At the time it felt really good, you know, that we'd been hit; we could go home and tell all our mates. The next minute we were told to take cover again, which we did. The worst thing about being below deck is that you can't really hear or know what is going on outside. You can hear all the gunfire but you don't actually know what is happening. Then there was a loud bang. We all got up to assess the damage, then we were told to take cover again. There was another loud explosion and all I remember was waking up with all this black smoke around me and all these people screaming and groaning. Most of the blokes down there had been killed. I was trapped under all this wreckage with all these people screaming to get out. I thought, 'What's going on here?' It was just like a nightmare. Everything started flashing through my mind; I got this image of my Mum at home doing the cooking in the kitchen, I imagined my sisters there and my brothers at school.

I was dying; it was weird. I thought someone was just going to open a big curtain and there'd be a crowd of people watching us, like being on a stage. It all seemed so unreal – there was a pain in my arm, the smoke, just everything together, you know. I was trapped, there seemed no way out. I was actually dying. I was just going to say 'Forget it' and wait there to die.

It was then the images of my heroes Bruce Lee and

Silver Surfer started flashing through my mind. That really was strange, but that seemed to change things. Although I was hit in the back and it was difficult to move my right arm, which I was using most of the time, and all this thick, black smoke kept pouring into my lungs, I thought, 'I can't just lie here and die – I've got to do something. They wouldn't give up. They'd have the will to survive and somehow get out in the end. They wouldn't give up until they were dead.' So I just kept pushing and somehow I got out. I don't know how, but I did it. I got the girder off me and somehow crawled out.

I tried to stand up but there was so much smoke about that I just kept close to the deck. It was then that I realized that I'd shrapnel in my back but I soon forgot my own pain because there was someone lying beside me with a girder right across his head. I thought, 'I've got to get him out.' He was screaming for help. Water was pouring into the ship, I knew I was fighting time, but however hard I tried I couldn't lift the girder off. It really was tremendously heavy so I had to leave him. I felt bad about it because I knew he must have died. I don't know to this day who he was.

I could hear a lot of other people screaming but I couldn't see anything because of the dense smoke. There was a small emergency light on the ship but even that was being covered up because the smoke was so thick; you could almost touch it. I thought to myself, 'I've got to get out – I can't hack it in here.' As I was going down aft to find a way out I heard this voice in the corner shouting, 'Get me out, mate.' I looked over and saw a man trapped in the wreckage. I thought, 'I've got to try and help him.' So I crawled over to where he was under all this rubble and said, 'Are you all right?' He said, 'Get this girder off me,' so I put my shoulder underneath and slowly managed to lift it so he could crawl out a bit. I could just see his hand coming out. He said, 'Go on, keep lifting it.' But because the air was so bad, I had to keep stopping to get my breath. I'd managed to lift it and he'd crawl out a bit, until gradually he managed to crawl free. He looked a mess but I didn't realize how badly he was hurt.

The smoke seemed to be getting worse so that I could hardly see anything. We crawled about a bit trying to find a way out. I looked down aft and it was all black. Then I looked for'ard and there was a fire up there. I thought, 'I'd better try down aft.' I got half-way down there but the smoke was so thick I couldn't go any further. So I went back to the middle of the dining hall and just sat there. I thought, 'This is it. I'm going to die.' Then I looked over at this Chief and I think he was praying, he was kneeling there, praying. I thought, 'We can't die now.' I'd seen the fire up front and realized that if there's a fire then there's got to be air somewhere. So I crawled up towards the for'ard a little bit; the fire looked bad from a distance but all it was was some wires on fire. So I called the Chief over and said, 'Look, we can get out of here.' When I got closer to the fire, I saw this big hole in the bulkhead which I couldn't believe – a big hole like that and yet there was so much smoke inside the ship. I thought, 'Oh great! At last some fresh air.' So I just stood as near as I could to the edge and started taking deep breaths. The Chief just followed me as I climbed up some steps because I didn't fancy jumping into the oggin – you know, the sea. We could've jumped in but I didn't know if anyone would have seen us. I suppose we were about twenty feet above the sea. We were used to jumps like that from training, but I thought, 'I don't fancy going in there because I'm bound to drown' – I was so weak from exhaustion.

I started looking for a way out. The Chief was inflating his life jacket so I thought he must want to jump or something. So I tried to open the hatch but it was all buckled. I tried to use my other arm, but I couldn't do it because of my back, so I let that go, and I just climbed down. I'd seen him inflate his life jacket, so I tried to inflate mine, but I couldn't because my throat was all burnt. So I just thought, 'Forget it – I'll jump in without the life jacket.'

The Chief then started walking across the bulkhead and I followed him. Suddenly he began to sway and because he was so dazed he fell into a hole in the deck. It was then that

I realized how bad he was; one of his fingers was hanging off and he had a big split all the way down his face. I thought, 'Oh God, this bloke's going to die.' I'd never seen anything like that before. He didn't seem to know what he was doing, so I bent over the hole and said, 'Here you are, mate.' He grabbed my hand, and I pulled him up. That took some time as I was feeling pretty weak. He then stood upright, walked over towards the edge and jumped into the water. I knew he was trying to get away from the ship. He was calm though; it was surprising. He just jumped into the water. I looked down and I could see him, he was just drifting away. I thought, 'He's going to die unless I do something.' So I just jumped in beside him and got my injured arm and kind of hooked it around him; I couldn't move it any other way, I just hooked it round him and started swimming. We were swimming away from the ship, but I knew I couldn't last long, because I'm not a very good swimmer. I'm surprised at what I did in the water; I did all right. I don't know how long I was in the water, probably about ten minutes but that's a long time in the cold. It was a relief to jump in there though, it felt really cool to start with. But I had my boots on, and they're pretty heavy when you're trying to swim. To make it worse they had steel toecaps as well. As I was swimming away from the ship I knew I wouldn't be able to keep it up for long. I kept shouting at the Chief to kick his legs hard because I was starting to go under. So 100 yards away from the ship I just turned round and there was a warship. I think it was the *Glamorgan*, or something like that. I thought, 'Oh great! It's going to pull us out of the water.'

At that moment I looked at the *Ardent* and all the back end was just full of smoke – it was a right mess. I looked up for'ard and saw these blokes all lined along it in their red suits. I couldn't believe it because I thought everyone on the whole ship had been killed. I just couldn't believe that one half of the ship was all right and the other half was smashed to pieces. It was mostly the dining hall that had been smashed up. Just seeing all those people up there . . . I couldn't believe it. They were all shouting because they were trying to direct someone down towards us. I looked up and it was getting closer. I started swimming pretty fast this time. I don't know where I found the strength from but I really swam hard and then I looked up again and the ship seemed to be further away! I thought I would never make it. The blokes on the ship were telling me to move away from it in case I got caught up in the props or something. But I didn't care at this time, I was just trying to get onto some dry land. But I was so tired and my arm was killing me. I couldn't hold on to the Chief any longer – I was slipping under the water and dragging him down as well. I thought, 'I'll let him go because at least he's got a life jacket so he'll be all right for a while.' So I let him go and he just started drifting away but he was almost unconscious by then. I started swimming by myself but I was really tired now. Then I looked up and saw this helicopter and it was lowering this strop. I tried to reach the strop but I couldn't. They lowered it down a little bit more, and I was just about to reach it, and they flew off. I thought, 'Oh no, this is it. After all that I've been through, I'm just going to finally die,' and I just started going under. I began to sink – all I could see above was water. I didn't feel any pain or anything, just kind of relaxed. I wasn't even frightened as I quietly waited for myself to go right to the bottom. It was all over.

The next minute this hand grabbed me from behind and it just lifted me out of the water. It was magic! This bloke had come down the hawser; he wasn't supposed to, but he did. He just picked me up and grabbed me. I thought, 'What a relief.' He just lifted me out of that water. He was a really good bloke, he was. I owe him my life. He was Surgeon Commander Rick Jolly. It was a very brave thing to do. I couldn't believe it; I was safe. Then he went down again for the Chief as well. He told me later how he'd seen me going down under the water, and wanted to try and save me. I was totally exhausted when he returned with the Chief and pulled him in beside me.

They flew us to the *Canberra*, and wrapped me up in

this blanket because of hypothermia. As they were carrying me down to the sick bay, I heard the tannoy call out 'Air Raid Warning Red, Air Raid Warning Red. Enemy aircraft on the starboard side and closing.' I thought, 'Oh God! I can't go through that again.' I just cried; I couldn't believe it. 'Not again, don't say I have to go through that lot again.' Everyone was running around with these life jackets. I've never been so scared in my life. I was lying on the stretcher on the deck. They all took cover beside me. One of the blokes got all these pillows and he covered me with them. All this within a couple of hours of them fishing me out of the sea. Thank God it all came to nothing.

Slowly I recovered; my back's all right now. It was sore for a couple of months but now it's all right. I think the smoke had a much longer-lasting effect. I keep getting colds and sometimes a smoky room triggers off memories – that's going to take a few years to get out of my system. What I do feel bad about was meeting Commander Jolly at Buckingham Palace. He came up and offered me his congratulations, but I didn't even know who he was. I felt really bad about that – he's a good bloke.

Although I'm not a strong Roman Catholic, I think what I went through has changed my ideas about God. I think about it a lot. I'm not even sure we've got a soul. If I had died I wouldn't have gone anywhere, I'd have just been in a relaxed state. I'd be nothing, you know, nothing, as if you weren't there. You'd just fade away. I don't know what helped me out there – I suppose I never will.

MEA(M)1 Kenneth Enticknap

Royal Navy

Queen's Gallantry Medal

On 21 May 1982, HMS Ardent was on station in San Carlos Water, East Falkland Island, providing a defensive cover against air attack from Argentine forces as land forces equipment and supplies were being put ashore. The ship was first straddled by two bombs with little damage caused, but a subsequent aircraft in the same wave hit the ship port aft, destroying the Seacat missile launcher.

HMS Ardent was then attacked by eight aircraft resulting in eight further hits and very severe damage. The Damage Control parties, working in exposed positions, suffered the most serious casualties. There was widespread flooding of major spaces and a list developed.

Marine Engineering Artificer (M) 1st Class Enticknap was in charge of the After Damage Control Party. Although the area was wrecked by the first bomb hits and he slightly injured, he led his team successfully in fire fighting and damage control. Then, in the second wave of attacks, further bombs hit his team, killing all except two of his men. Now seriously injured, MEA (M)1 Enticknap continued to fight the fire with one other man until a further bomb felled him, trapping him in the wreckage. Despite his own serious injuries MEA(M)1 Enticknap showed dedication to duty under constant enemy attack in the best traditions of the service in placing the safety of other lives above his own.

We went into the Falklands under cover of darkness. We were very aware that the Argentinians might have mined the seaway. We thought they'd mined the main approaches so it was decided to go between the mainland and a little island where there were some shallows. We went through as fast as we could, probably 30 knots or so. It was terrifying because we'd never been through anything like this before. We were down in the dining hall and were all lying on deck in case we had an explosion. The water was so shallow you could actually hear the gravel being thrown up by the propellers and hitting the ship's bottom. Once we were through – it seemed like an age – and came out into the main channel the ship went back to the usual sound that we were used to.

We went past San Carlos, down into Grantham Sound, and took up station on a gun line there. We spent most of our time on the floor because if you stand up and you get a shock, it's going to be jarred straight up through your legs and probably break them. So we were lying flat and face down, with our hands covering our ears.

Action-working dress for Damage Control parties is cotton overalls, trousers tucked into woollen socks, and anti-flash hoods and gloves. In this case we were instructed to wear warm clothing under our 'ovies'. Only the two people designated as 'fire fighters' were dressed in fear-naught suits. We had our anti-flash hoods on our heads, but we could breathe normally. They are stuffy but not really restrictive. Knowing now how many people were saved from serious burns, wearing these is quite a sensible way to go into battle.

While we were going up and down the gun lines during the night, awaiting our call for fire, some of the lads were lying on the floor playing Ukkers. It's like Ludo, a highly technical game which you play with two dice.

I'm a Marine Engineering Artificer so during action stations I was in charge of a Damage Control Section. I was to control the repair parties for any action damage – fire, flood, that sort of thing. There was also a First Aid Party attached down aft, because the surgery had been set up down there in the dining hall. Normally it's the technical branches who man these positions but on board Type 21 frigates the Damage Control parties are supplemented by ratings of the seaman specialization and some chefs. It's my job to organize these people when damage occurs. We'd had plenty of rehearsals in the past, with large holes shown in chalk – but of course we'd no experience of the real thing. But this time we had heard of HMS *Sheffield* going, so we knew that we were in for something.

We went past San Carlos, then we waited and waited. We were still in the bottom of the ship, not really knowing if it was night or day. I am told 21 May was a glorious, bright and perfect day – it was to be a day I shall never forget.

The Chief Chef had been detailed as a member of a gun's crew, so to relieve the tension I helped cook breakfast. The First Lieutenant announced it over the tannoy: 'Good morning, chaps, I have an action breakfast for you.' Which was an egg and bacon butty. Shortly after breakfast we heard the aircraft coming over. There we were in our metal box, we could hear the whoosh, bangs and the sounds of gunfire and explosions, but down there we were totally impotent. It was very, very frightening.

We were lying on a cold, steel deck and I can tell you that the call of nature comes quite quickly under these circumstances. Of course we couldn't go to the toilets because the rest of the ship was sealed off. So I had a bucket put behind one of the watertight doors and the lads could nip through there and have a wee. Anyone that upset me had to empty the bucket!

I was frightened; I don't mind admitting it. We were still very apprehensive about what was happening. Very early, after the first couple of attacks, even in our small company people started muttering and there were so many people shouting out 'Take Cover' after the air raid warning that I took it on myself to get close to my communications man. I told him that instead of shouting out, to tell me quietly, then I'd decide what to say. Now, of course, people say that all they can remember is me shouting it out all the time!

The *Ardent* was certainly giving the Argentinian aircraft

plenty to worry about. We started counting the rounds, as you do, but we lost count at about thirty. It seemed to be going on for ever. We'd fire a dozen rounds and they'd come back again and give us a few more. All the time the aircraft were flying over us. During all the action we were stuck in our little hole, hardly believing what was going on.

As the *Ardent* moved towards Falkland Sound the First Lieutenant did a walkaround. He was looking white as a sheet and told us, 'I saw those bastards! The bombs actually straddled us. I saw these big green things with red strips.' We realized then that we were getting a bit of stick. Shortly after, we were hit for the first time. I ordered my teams into action. The water was coming through the deck head. This was unusual, as you would normally expect water to come from below, but this was split pipes and things. I waited for reports to come back, as we do in training, but people were very much involved in the first aid action, so I wasn't getting any reports at all. I could see through the open watertight door what was going on. I thought, 'If I don't look, I'll never find out.' I went through the door and there was absolute chaos: water, smoke and very limited light. I isolated a few systems, organized a portable pump and got buckets into action to bail out. Meanwhile, the Marine Engineering Officer, who is the Action Officer, was standing at the door of HQ One, which was where the damage had occurred, shouting, 'What's going on? What's going on?' He needed to tell the Captain the extent of the damage as soon as possible. So I told him the best I could of what I'd seen – all the chaos and a hole in the bulkhead, a nice, neat bomb-sized hole. The bomb had gone through the bulkhead, through the deck head, had rattled its way round what we call the auxiliary machinery room, taken a diesel with it and finally gone through the after bulkhead but thank God had not exploded. So we were collating all this information which I suppose took a quarter of an hour. I think, given another twenty minutes, we'd have had everything under control and been off, away again.

Meanwhile, I went back to my section base and started filling in my report. Some people went aft to see the damage there, and just as they were coming back to me, a very worried voice on the tannoy said, 'Take cover.' We all went flat out where we were. After that I don't remember anything else. When I came round, the air was black – thick, acrid, black. I couldn't see and I could hardly breathe. The first thing I noticed was that my left hand was damaged, there was one finger hanging off. I then thought I'd better see what else was wrong with me. I started at my head where I pulled a piece of formica out that was six, seven inches long which left a fair-sized gash in my head. I had a quick feel elsewhere and I was bleeding in other places, including the back of my neck where there was a long gash. Then I tried to get up; I could get up onto all fours but there was something stopping me from crawling free. All the while I was struggling I could hear the horrifying cries of the injured. One chap I remember crawling around was young Able Seaman John Dillon – I think he was checking all the others. He came to me and I said, 'Get this thing off my back.' He slowly pulled it off me and picked me up. I then found a ten-inch gash on my back. I felt quite weak because I'd lost an awful lot of blood. I don't know how long it took him to get the obstruction off me. I think it must have been caught because I just couldn't free myself. I was entangled in it rather then weighted down by it. It had embedded itself into my skin but I was numb all over and couldn't feel any pain.

As there was more ship for'ard than there was aft it was more sensible to go for'ard. The bomb had gone off in the galley and blasted everywhere so there was just debris as far as we could see and there was also a raging fire going on to our left. I realized afterwards that it was aviation fuel burning – dangerous stuff! John was trying to help me for'ard. I don't know if I stumbled, but I remember sitting down somewhere. Both of us were gasping for breath. At that moment of despair I certainly had a little cry and I prayed. I thought of my family and of my wife who was

47

pregnant and that I would never see the baby. I most certainly thought that I'd had it. I don't know what happened next, either the bulkhead melted or the ship caught a breath of wind, but suddenly we saw some light in the smoke and felt the marvellous, sweet taste of fresh air. It was then that I found a second strength. I thought, 'We can get out of here.'

We struggled down aft again, through the door behind which we'd had the pee bucket; the door wasn't on its hinges any more, it was lying on its side. There was no bulkheads, no roof. What bulkhead there was, was all tangled up over this winch which was still on its mountings. We couldn't crawl over it because I thought we'd get tangled up in all the steel and whatever; it wasn't a clear way out. I elected to crawl underneath the winch which had a gap of about two square feet and was our only way out. I suppose I was still numb because I couldn't feel my injuries at all. I went first, with John pushing me, and somehow we both managed to crawl through to the other side, even though we both had bulky life jackets around our waists. There was no deck and we had to walk on the edges of the bulkheads. I lost my balance and stumbled into what must have been the tiller flat, which is the steering gear machinery room and where the rudder sticks up into the ship, but somehow John managed to pull me out.

We got onto the quarterdeck, put on and inflated our life jackets. John was having difficulties with his. I said to him, 'Don't put your Once Only suit on because we haven't got time.' I was also anxious about hypothermia but I took a gamble, hoping we wouldn't be in the water too long. It was, after all, the safest place. Once in the water, John dragged me clear of the props area since I wasn't feeling particularly good at the time. It was then that we saw HMS *Yarmouth*. I thought, 'Great! They're going to pick us up.' I was thinking about the rest of the Damage Control teams fighting the fire and wished I was there helping them. Just when I thought we were safe, the *Yarmouth* went straight past us and John started swimming after it. I looked back to *Ardent*. Everybody was on the upper deck, in their orange survival suits. I thought, 'Lord, we've lost her – we've lost her.' The anchor cable was down, her gun was pointing right up in the air, and deep, black smoke was billowing from aft; she was indeed a sad sight. The Captain of the *Yarmouth* had quite rightly ignored us in order to pick up her survivors.

There we were in the water and people on the *Ardent* were pointing to us. But the ship seemed so far away and everything was becoming hazy. Then, to my great relief, a helicopter came along and someone came down and picked up John who had looked as if he was drowning. Because he was in such a bad state the guy had to hold John in his arms, all the way up to the helicopter. By this time I was shouting, 'Help, helicopter, help – come over here!' which was totally pointless really because helicopters are so damned noisy. But the guy did come down again and just hooked onto the blue tag that came out of the front of my life jacket. His rank tag was hanging on the front of him. I thought, 'Oh no, it's a Commander.' Every Commander I had known was old, and I thought, 'I've had it; he won't have the strength to get me into the helicopter.' But I'd underestimated this Commander. He just hooked onto the tab, wrapped his legs round me and hauled me up into the helicopter. I've since done a survival course and the instructor said that no way should you hook onto the life jacket. The man I owe my life to turned out to be Surgeon Commander Rick Jolly who told me later that bringing John up in his arms had knackered him, so when he came down for me, he'd just hooked me on and hoped for the best!

The last thing I remember was Jolly telling someone to get us to the *Canberra*, double quick. I woke up on the floor of the *Canberra* wrapped in blankets and peering out from an awful lot of field dressings. I was a bit confused! I knew *Canberra* was a friendly ship, but I couldn't picture what she was like. When I was moved into surgery, I had a finger amputated and later another – both of them from my left hand. My head injuries were patched and stitched up. In fact, the doctor who put five stitches in my head called them 'homeward bounders' – they looked awful. They've faded now but I'm still in and out of hospital, two years after the event, but there are many people far worse off than I am.

War's the thing we're all being trained for, and the training is all useful experience, but you still think, 'Will I be able to do it?' I was very grateful for the experience of having the responsibility of taking charge and doing the job in that situation. I always worried deep down that I could be the one who was going to crack up so I was very pleased when I didn't, but I still went through a range of emotions which I'd never felt before in my life. We were very lucky that it turned out to be the last attack of the day because if the planes had come round again, the hundred and twenty-odd people up on the deck, in their bright orange suits, would have been sitting targets. I'll never know why the Argentinian air force didn't come back, but I have every admiration for them.

When I think about comradeship and moving moments, I think of the one on the *Canberra* with Rick Jolly who had come along to ask if I was all right. I'd heard that all survivors got a tot so I rather cheekily asked him where my tot was. He happened to have his in his hand and asked the nurse if I could be given a tot. She replied that, due to the condition I was in, it would be inadvisable. So Rick Jolly dipped his finger in his rum and rubbed it all over my lips.

Although we had lost our ship and twenty-one shipmates, we Ardents are very proud that we were instrumental in ensuring that all the landing forces were able to put ashore without loss. There was a lot of heroism at the time. But the one lad I remember later was young Lieutenant Bob Lawrence of the Scots Guards. We have a close association with the Scots Guards as they are the affiliated regiment to us and their colours went down on the *Ardent*. I met him at the investiture at Buckingham Palace when he'd only been out of hospital a few days. He was two or three in front of me. Like all of us, when he received his Military Cross from the Queen he had to step back four paces – which were absolute agony for him because he was almost paralysed down one side. We all felt for him; it was marvellous to see his absolute determination to take those four paces. He was not going to be deterred, and he did it. What a brave lad!

But, of course, without John Dillon there would be no story to tell.

Petty Officer John Leake

Royal Navy

Distinguished Service Medal

Petty Officer Leake originally joined HMS Ardent *as a civilian NAAFI Canteen Manager. On the declaration of Active Service he volunteered to enrol as a Petty Officer on 15 May 1982.*

On 21 May 1982 HMS Ardent *came under heavy attack by Argentine aircraft. Using his previous Army training, Petty Officer Leake was stationed as a machine gunner. Throughout the air attacks he remained cool and calm even though the ship was being hit by bombs and cannon fire. He fired large quantities of accurate tracer at the attackers and inflicted damage on a Skyhawk. His courage, steadfastness and total disregard for his own safety was an inspiration to all those in the vicinity.*

After I left the Army at twenty-four, I worked with security firms, including Securicor at Birmingham Airport. Then, in 1977, I saw an advertisement in the local paper for people to work for NAAFI on the warships. It was the best of both worlds, like being a civilian in the services: you could have your independence but there was still some sense of discipline. I've been with them ever since.

On HMS *Ardent* I worked in the shop, selling toiletries, sweets, souvenirs, stereos, all that sort of thing. I used to order the provisions and the duty-free beer and cigarettes. I originally started as Grade 4 Manager in the POs' Mess, and as the grades went up I went to the Chiefs' Mess. It wasn't very often, but sometimes I felt I wasn't really part of the ship's company, although I knew I was an essential part of the crew, especially at action stations, when my job would be the Medical Co-ordinator in the sick bay.

We'd just got to Ascension Island when I went up on deck to get some fresh air and saw a Petty Officer sitting on the deck with a manual, trying to work out how to use a general-purpose machine gun. I said to him, 'Ah, the good old GPMG.' He said, 'Oh, you know about it?' I said, 'Yes, I used to be an instructor on it in the Army.' He said, 'Well, you can have a go if you want to.' But I said I couldn't because as a civilian I wasn't entitled to carry arms. Later he had a word with the Captain, who said only if active service had been declared and I'd actually signed on in the Navy would I be able to use it. After we'd sailed from Ascension, active service was declared and we were then given the option of signing on with the Navy or getting off the ship and having NAAFI fly us back to England. I had no hesitation – I signed on in the Navy as a Petty Officer. It had to be done under the Articles of the Geneva Convention, stating that I was a combatant; otherwise, had I been captured, I would have been treated as a civilian and not covered by the Convention. But all the time I thought, 'We'll just get near the islands, rattle our sabres and that will be it.'

Then, as we approached the Falklands, and the *Belgrano* and the *Sheffield* were sunk, we realized we were close to war and that we were not invincible. The *Sheffield* was a much bigger boat than the *Ardent*. When the news came, everybody went quiet. It was then that we started reflecting on actually going into combat and for a couple of days the ship was subdued. But everyone realized they had a job to do and things soon got back to normal. Every day Captain West would visit each mess in turn and give us a situation report, which was good for morale. I always think the *Ardent* was a one-off ship anyway; such a happy ship.

We were on defence watches when we were told that the *Ardent* was going to lead the ships through the passage between the two islands. The Captain said he didn't know if the channel was mined, but we were going to chance it, and find out. We knew then that we were going to war – the talking was over. But I don't remember having any fears.

We took up station in Falkland Sound to bombard Goose Green. It was there that a funny thing happened. We were about 500 yards off the coast of East Falkland when somebody said, 'There are vehicles along the coastline and men are getting out of them.' It was just as the false dawn was starting and we were all peering into semi-darkness. I cocked the gun ready and waited for the word to fire. The figures seemed to be moving very slowly, and as the light gradually got better they turned out to be a herd of cows! I've often thought we could have been the first people to shoot cows on the Falklands.

Then we did the bombardment at Goose Green, and a message came through that aircraft were approaching from the mainland. We were ordered into the middle of Falkland Sound to take station to break up the air attacks as they came in. We got into a position where they had to overfly us before attacking the men ashore.

Their first attack came from a Pucará, but when we fired the Seacat at it, it veered off. I then went on to the GPMG. For me, taking hold of that gun was the most natural thing in the world. I'd lugged that gun thousands of miles; I'd taken it apart in daylight, darkness, rain and snow. I had such an affinity with it; I'd fired it under so many conditions. But when I left the Army I never expected to use it again, yet here I was, in action again, on a ship.

Then their aircraft really started coming. It was one big mass attack all day. The first few, probably Skyhawks and Mirages, came in from the port side, low and fast. I remember the bows of the ship being straddled by bombs but fortunately she wasn't hit. There were explosions about fifty yards in front of me, where the bombs had missed. But in one of the next few attacks we were hit by a plane that flew over the length of the ship. I could feel further attacks hitting other parts of the ship, but I was so preoccupied that I didn't have time to find out the extent of the damage. It seemed that I was in action all through the day. At one point a couple of lads came up from the aft end, which they told me had been badly hit. They were in a bad state of shock so I got them to sit down by my side and gave them some Nutty bars. Then somebody shouted to us, 'Aircraft bearing green 90.' I looked over our starboard side and there were two aircraft coming in low. I opened fire on them, but they both dropped their bombs on the ship. Then two more turned up, and this time I hit one. I could see bits coming off his wing and underneath fuselage.

Then more came over and the ship was hit again. At one point I ran out of ammunition. One of the lads had gone to get more but we were under heavy attack and there was nothing else to do but hit the deck. While I was lying there I looked up and there was a Skyhawk coming across. I watched his bombs leave the aircraft and they passed so close to the ship's mast that I thought, 'Christ, this is it.' I felt fear then, because I knew the ship was being badly hit. Then PO Chef Goldfinch, who'd brought me ammunition throughout the attack, shouted, 'Come on, John. We've got the stuff,' and back we went. I could keep going. It's in moments like that when fear seems to spur you on, as long as it is not unreasonable fear, which makes you not know what you're doing. But I did know, so I got back and could keep on firing.

Then, suddenly, the aft end of the ship was covered with one big pall of smoke. I couldn't see anything, couldn't see anything at all, so I moved over to the other side of the ship with my GPMG. It was only then that I realized how much of a tilt the ship was at. She was settling over to starboard. I stood there for a while and

54

watched all the lads coming up from below decks. Then the *Yarmouth* came alongside and we stepped off. I took the gun with me because I was hoping they would give it to me as a souvenir – but I was out of luck, I had to hand it over on the *Yarmouth*. But, even then, there was more to fear, because when we were down below decks on the *Yarmouth*, 'Air Raid Warning Red' came over the tannoy. I realized that there was absolutely nothing we could do stuck down below, having spent a day with everything to do. Eventually the *Yarmouth* took us into one of the bays where the *Canberra* was and we were taken in a landing craft to her.

I found out afterwards that the *Ardent* had been hit by seventeen bombs and missiles, plus rockets and cannon fire. I think that with all they threw at us that day it was a miracle we only lost twenty-two men. I thought of the *Coventry*, a big destroyer, which was hit by five bombs and went down in minutes, yet we'd been there all that afternoon being hit, hit and hit, and all at the aft end – I've never worked out how. I often think, 'Why did they sink the *Ardent*?' She wasn't a significant ship, especially when you take into account all the others that were there, like the *Canberra*. Perhaps they were actually out for a kill, and with our main armaments out they knew it was an easy thing. Because there wasn't a lot of fire coming from us, they had a sitting duck.

I suppose if it hadn't been for my affinity with the old GPMG, there wouldn't be a story to tell. I did what I could. I never thought when I left the Army that I'd ever see action again, let alone get involved with it, but I wouldn't have wanted to do anything else in the circumstances.

Those boys on the ship were like a family to me. I remember when I was walking down on the jetty, before the *Ardent* sailed, and saw some of the lads painting the ship. One of them shouted, 'Are you coming with us, John?' I stopped and said, 'Of course I'm bloody coming with you. I'm like a father to all you lads. I wouldn't be able to sleep if I didn't come with you.' Just before we came under attack I brought up stacks of Mars Bars and Nutty and a crate of Gotters, because I thought we might need them. So whenever I could, while the action was on, I'd throw them a Mars Bar or a tin of drink and say, 'I'll be round tomorrow for the money.' I took some movie film of the lads on the way down. I've only played it back twice since. It's wonderful to see all those faces laughing – then suddenly you'll see one of the lads who was killed.

On a happier note, a year after the sinking I got a phone call to say that I had been credited with shooting down a Skyhawk. The pilot had bailed out and they picked him up and took him to Stanley; he said he'd had his fuel tanks hit while attacking the *Ardent*.

I suppose if there is one example that summed up the spirit of the *Ardent* it was the courage of Lieutenant-Commander John Sephton and the flight crew. After the Argentinian aircraft had put out our Seacat missile system, he organized all the small arms he could and fought a last-ditch defence. He was on the flight deck firing up at the Skyhawk with a submachine gun – he was totally exposed, just him against a Skyhawk. He and the flight crew were still firing into the belly of the plane when its bombs killed him. But he showed them we weren't going to give in. He was a good officer and a very good man.

Sea, Air and Ground Support

Captain John Coward

Royal Navy

Distinguished Service Order

As the Commanding Officer of HMS Brilliant Captain Coward was involved in many of the significant incidents during Operation Corporate. This was not coincidence, but a reflection on the outstanding initiative, determination and bravery which he displayed at every stage of the operation. He took HMS Brilliant to South Georgia to join in the final stages of Operation Paraquat and contributed markedly to the success of the operation, particularly with regard to the determined and professional handling of his ship which led to the attack on and subsequent capture of the Argentinian submarine Santa Fe. After South Georgia he rejoined the remainder of the battle group as quickly as possible and upon entering the Total Exclusion Zone he showed tremendous initiative and capacity to engage the enemy on every conceivable occasion.

With HMS Brilliant he encouraged enemy air attack on several occasions by forming a gun line off Port Stanley with a Type 42 destroyer and shot down several enemy aircraft. He seized every opportunity to volunteer his ship for dangerous night raids through the Falkland Sound and assisted with several difficult missions to infiltrate Special Forces. He escorted the amphibious group into the Amphibious Operations Area and was in the thick of the action during heavy air raids for the whole of D-Day. Despite damage to his ship which effectively put most of his weapons system out of action, he was determined to stay in the area for the second day and quite prepared to take on the enemy with whatever means remained at his disposal. Even on retiring from the Amphibious Operations Area after the second day for essential defect repair, he managed to engage the Monsoonen, a resupply

vessel, and caused it to run aground after giving it suitable
warning.

Captain Coward showed exceptional professional ability,
stamina, leadership, initiative and personal bravery in every
aspect of his duties, and the high performance of his ship and
the men he commanded reflects this.

In late March 1982 *Brilliant* was sailing quietly off the
coast of Morocco on an exercise with Admiral Sandy
Woodward. We went into Gibraltar for a week and on
Sunday the 29th at lunchtime I was in the next berth to the
Admiral. He sent for me and said, 'It's the squadron's
Sports Day today. However, we've had to send a
submarine from the UK towards the South Atlantic as a
precaution. The cover story is that it's exercising with
somebody and that somebody had better be you. So get
out of here this afternoon and meet it.' So I ran in the
veterans race and believe it or not I won; but I hadn't time
to wait for the prize and ran on down to the jetty where my
crew had the boat waiting. As I climbed up the side the
First Lieutenant let go and we were off. Sandy Woodward
had cut the sports and stood on the bridge of *Antrim* to see
me off. 'See you in South Georgia,' we joked; and indeed it
was prophetic. So I steamed 200 miles straight out into the
Atlantic.

I teamed up with the Admiral and his frigates when they
left Gibraltar on 2 April and we steamed down together to
Ascension Island, except that we were far from together.
He told us to spread out and avoid being seen by passing
ships, fuel when we could, and see him there. It was a
shrewd precaution. We hung around for a couple of days
gathering stores. At that stage the Government was
deciding whether or not to re-invade South Georgia and
trying to get the Task Force together back home. Then
Antrim, *Plymouth* and *Fort Austin* were sent to South
Georgia, and my force – *Brilliant*, *Glasgow*, *Sheffield*,
Coventry, *Arrow* and *Appleleaf* – was ordered to steam off
south towards the Falklands: go as fast and as far as we
could until we ran out of fuel and then wait for the tanker

to catch up with us, in order to establish a British presence as far south as possible.

Going south as spearhead of the force in this very bracing South Atlantic weather was exciting, probably the most exhilarating part of the campaign. Type 22 frigates are exceptionally good at going fast into weather and *Brilliant* averaged around twenty-four knots. The other ships didn't like it; *Arrow* was starting to crack and I had to send them a message, 'If you break down, don't worry – we'll leave you behind!' I used to get all the Captains on board at nine o'clock each day to talk over what we were going to do. We thought we'd be in action as a group of six against the Argentinian navy a month before a carrier arrived on the scene, so there was quite an atmosphere. We practised Exocet attacks until we were blue in the face, targeting from our helicopters all the way down. I had a Royal Marine detachment on board and had them practising against the *Glasgow* and the *Sheffield* all the time. I told them we might get the chance to take or burn or capture an Argentinian Type 42; they thought I was mad!

We'd hardly settled down to that task when the South Georgia operation went wrong, in that the assault force lost their helicopters before they even started. I was signalled to take the troop-carrying helicopters from the *Coventry* and the *Sheffield* and rush off on my own. It was blowing like hell, and in running fast to South Georgia *Brilliant* rode the gales exceptionally well. Until the Falklands conflict the Admiralty had tended to dismiss Type 22s as little more than expensive yachts, but they emerged as one of the successes of the campaign both for their missile capability and simply because they would go so fast in bad weather.

When I arrived at South Georgia our ships were well off the coast because they'd heard the night before that there was an Argentinian submarine, the *Santa Fe*, in the area. Our helicopters joined up with those from *Antrim*, *Plymouth* and *Endurance* to range along the coast and found the submarine almost at once, just diving on his way out of Grytviken at dawn, having landed some commandos overnight to bolster the Argentinian base headed by Captain Astiz. The boys dropped bombs and torpedoes and damaged it quite badly, and the Captain, shaken, turned back to the harbour and rammed it against the old base jetty.

The Argentinians in South Georgia capitulated when the firing really laid itself down on their heads, and the next morning the Army asked me to get the submarine off the jetty in case it sank and blocked the harbour. The British Force Commander, Brian Young, had instructions to salvage it because of its supposedly high intelligence value, and decided it should be put with the old whaling wrecks up beside the whaling station. It really was a horrible, old-fashioned piece of junk, in a terrible state, and I realized I'd have to use the Argentinian crew to help move it. So we gathered them up and I was given some Marines to guard them. I was worried they might try to scuttle it, which would have been a bold stroke for Argentina, blocking the harbour beautifully, but in retrospect they didn't have the fight left in them – they were crushed, poor chaps, absolutely crushed.

I stood on the bridge as we moved off, the Captain giving orders in Spanish, and then suddenly he realized it was going to sink on us, and ordered the crew down below to blow out the tanks to keep the boat on the surface. The trouble was, down below it was dark and drippy, and the Marines thought the crew were trying to scuttle it so a fight started. The first thing I knew there were shots in the air and an Argentinian was killed. Boats started coming out from the shore. The Captain, I think, understood the situation and the Argentinian crewman was buried with full military honours. It seemed it was going to be rather an odd war – up to then nobody had been killed.

Almost immediately I embarked Cedric Delves and his SAS men and some Marines and rushed off to get them up to the Falklands. I joined up with Sandy Woodward and the main Task Force who at that point were starting to move into the Total Exclusion Zone. The Argentinians had a lot of Exocets spread around their fleet and we were convinced we had to win the initial Exocet encounter. Both sides were firing the same weapon from their ships which was a bit worrying since Exocet is quite a successful fire-and-forget weapon if the right person fires it first. We weren't sure then if they were going to be as incompetent as we hoped, particularly their Type 42 Exocet ships, because we'd trained those ourselves at Portland and we knew they weren't that bad. So we were much more concerned about their surface force than anything else; wrongly, as it turned out. The Total Exclusion Zone was dominated by the Argentine air force and there was bound to be trouble, and the trouble descended on *Sheffield*. From then on, as far as we were concerned, it was very much a shooting match.

Brilliant's principal job throughout the Falklands episode was bodyguarding HMS *Invincible* during daylight hours every day. Whatever else I was doing, I had to flash back and fall in dead astern of the *Invincible* by first light, and HMS *Broadsword* did the same job for *Hermes*. Everyone was worried that an Exocet would flash out of the sky, and the Sea Wolf missile system on board the Type 22 frigates was the only weapon available that had a chance of shooting one down. Every dawn they thought they were about to be attacked, but in the event dusk became a much more dangerous time. We would close up at action stations an hour or so before dusk and wait anxiously while we heard the reconnaissance flights for the Exocet coming up. Then, when it was nearly dark, I would say to the ship's company, 'Right, that's it for the night, chaps, we hope!' and two minutes later the bloody alarm would go. The crew got sick of that!

On many nights we ran into the islands to drop off SAS, SBS and Marines or to collect them after daring deeds ashore. I had a marvellous boatman, Leading Seaman Gould, who really liked getting wet and cold – a tough character, the sort of bloke you'd normally find running a boxing booth. I gave him a wireless, and our fast boat used to flash him into the night, often on his own, to land or pick up the Marines. Once close inshore we'd direct him like a helicopter and tell him where the rocks were from the radar. His principal interest was the bottle of rum I'd leave for him in my pantry for when he got back, but we all thought Gould was pretty noble and he was mentioned in despatches. He is the sort of seaman Nelson relied on and just as good.

We had a great rapport with the SAS; they really were wonderful chaps and we regarded them as our special army. They were outstandingly brave. One night about twenty-five were being transferred across to *Fearless* when their helicopter fell in the water. About five SAS men were clinging to a small life raft that had inflated automatically and we brought *Brilliant* up alongside them. It was cold, dark, rough and horrible, and they were in a terrible state, with broken arms and legs and collarbones, and weren't wearing life jackets. One of my young Marines, Neat, dived in and prised them off the raft they were hanging onto and swam them back to the ladder – he was also mentioned in despatches. I remember packing one of the survivors, an Army sergeant in Delves's squadron, into our helicopter to send him back to *Hermes*. His arms and legs and neck were all bandaged up. 'You know,' he said, 'this is the fourth helicopter ride I've had in the last fortnight, courtesy of the Royal Navy. The first one fell on the glacier at Fortuna on South Georgia. The second one rescued me and then fell in the bleedin' Fortuna glacier again. Then I got in the one that fell in the water! I hope yours is under guarantee.' Quite tough lads.

The anti-aircraft requirements in the anchorage by day, running in SBS or Marines to the islands at night, and rushing back for the dawn action stations in the Task Force was tiring. But I had very good young officers and could safely go to bed and let them get on with it; they were totally capable. I never had a moment of worry over the ship's company. I'd talk to them every day to keep them informed of all I knew of the situation and I'd arranged beforehand a signals link via our sister ship *Battleaxe* in the UK which kept our wives in the picture.

In a very modern ship like *Brilliant* you are remarkably detached; it's lovely and warm inside and you know everything that's going on because you've got better radio and monitoring equipment than anybody else. It's a slightly unreal world. Even action stations didn't quite break that, but it certainly got the adrenalin moving when you heard that general alarm – it really is the most hideous, horrible sound.

One night *Brilliant* went chasing submarines, which proved rather less than successful. I had received a typical Woodward signal: 'An aircraft has reported sighting a submarine twenty miles north of Port Stanley. Go find him and bring me back his hat.' I knew if we found him he'd be on the bottom and the whole place was littered with old whaling ships. We would find something, ping on it and it would look about the size of a small submarine, so we'd fly a helicopter with a magnetic detector over it and, yes, it would say it's metal. But I didn't have enough bombs to cover each wreck, and very few helicopters with metal detectors on them. The place was also full of whales, which gave enormous echoes on the sonar. Every so often a whale would come up, give a little blow, and a flock of seagulls would gather round, appearing as a quick flash on the radar. Everybody would say, 'Christ, it must be a submarine,' and we launched a few torpedoes at things like that. All in all, it was a total frustration but, looking back, I've a feeling that one of those wrecks was the *San Luis* and I think that eventually the analysis boys will confirm it.

On 12 May Sandy Woodward sent us in to bodyguard the *Glasgow* with the Sea Wolf whilst he shot up Port Stanley. The aim was also to bait their aircraft out to try and shoot a few down – nobody had shot anything down then. After *Glasgow* had been banging away for about half an hour it was quite obvious that somebody was going to be called out to thump us and on the radar we picked up two squadrons of their aircraft flying down over the mountains. Four of them then peeled out from the coast and started skimming out towards us in a tightly-packed group, right down on the water. I said to the *Glasgow*, 'You steer over here and I'll keep between you and them. Watch the Sea Wolf go!' and turned it on. The Sea Wolf is an entirely automatic system designed to shoot down missiles fired at you at close range – as long as it's switched to FIRE it'll go on its own. It went on its own and shot down three of the four aircraft with two missiles: the first missile took the first aircraft, the second took the second, and the bits from the second aircraft knocked out the third one, which flew into the sea. The fourth one dropped some bombs, which bounced over us. We didn't mind that.

Then the second squadron came at us, more spread out, and I said to the *Glasgow*, who'd started firing his gun, 'Relax, don't fire – the Sea Wolf might think it's a missile. We'll do the same trick again.' The Sea Wolf looked at this lot, said, 'That is not a missile,' and went back to park. Things happened quite fast then and they dropped bombs everywhere. Fortunately, they nearly all bounced over us again, but one went straight through the *Glasgow*'s engine room and out the other side – it didn't explode, but it knocked out an awful lot of pipes and mucked up her fuel and compressed-air systems. We then thought that maybe this wasn't such a good idea – fifty per cent probability by the Sea Wolf wasn't what we'd expected. So I called up *Hermes* and said we'd come back out and try to persuade the Sea Wolf it had to do better. The problem was that the Sea Wolf is controlled by its surveillance computer system which was originally designed to recognize missiles not aircraft. In order to see a projectile approaching against the background it was programmed to pick out something less than a football in size and to reject clutter and big things. So the things the Sea Wolf discriminated against had included these four aircraft flying in loose formation. The system was still in the experimental stage and I had on board an electronics engineer from Marconi, David Breen, who'd been with us on Operation Spring Train off Africa in March. On the way south I'd received repeated orders to send him back to the UK because he was a civilian. So very reluctantly I'd transferred him to a tanker going north, asking him to pack his bags of spares and fly down to meet us in Ascension, which he did. He was absolutely first class. He kept the Sea Wolf going, and being strafed by Mirages and the like didn't put him off at all! Once he had identified the problem he got on the telex to the team working on the computer at Portsmouth and by the next morning they came up with a change in the software, telling the Sea Wolf that once it had seen one target it should engage it, and not take notice of any other distractions. We put that into the system. The *Glasgow* went back to find the support ship *Stena Inspector*, to have a patch put over her side. But the bomb had done her a lot of damage and because at that stage Sandy Woodward thought there might be a stalemate lasting many weeks, he sent her back home to be repaired.

Brilliant's next big job was bodyguarding the Task Force at San Carlos. That morning, 21 May, I took up position out in the Sound on the gun line with *Broadsword*, *Ardent*, *Argonaut* and *Alacrity*. When things really started to get nasty and the *Antrim* was bombed I moved in to be close to the *Fearless* and *Intrepid*. The aerial attacks were very, very fierce and we found ourselves virtually defenceless because the Sea Wolf wouldn't go at all. It had been all right in the Sound but in San Carlos Water, which is virtually a creek, its radar was seeing so much clutter and putting so many inputs into the computer that it was overwhelmed: the computer could handle thirty or forty inputs but not hundreds all at once. We felt absolutely frustrated and infuriated because we knew bloody well that if we could get the missiles away they were going to knock the Mirages down. The only other firepower we had on this almost brand-new ship were two absolutely useless Bofors, built in Canada in 1942! The only modification they'd had since then were electrical firing circuits instead of old springs, which virtually ensured that they hardly ever worked.

But it was well worth staying there because half way through the morning it suddenly became clear that all the ships with fighter direction capability were miles too far away to do anything about the Argentinian aircraft, who were over San Carlos Water; the *Antrim* could have hacked the problem but got bombed. Our Sea Wolf computerized radar was seeing them all right and my First Lieutenant, Lee Hulme, who'd been a fighter direction instructor back in the great days of the Fleet Air Arm, picked up the fighters coming in off the carrier and guided them in. Although the computer wasn't designed for this task, by reading off its print-out numbers he managed to intercept seven Mirages and Skyhawks during the day. That evening I was handed a smashing message from the carrier saying, 'All our pilots here are talking with great admiration about your First Lieutenant, who really made the day.' That was nice and Lee Hulme was mentioned in despatches.

On the second day of San Carlos, *Brilliant* was hit, the first and only time during the campaign. A Mirage shot a string of 35mm cannon shells through our side which exploded inside. We weren't badly hit by many poor chaps' standards, just three men injured, but it was disastrous for our weapons system. It came in from the water line right up to the Ops Room, through the Sea Wolf office, through the for'ard Sea Wolf launcher and peppered the wiring to all the electronics. In our wisdom we'd run the computer's myriad input channels right up the ship's side, and the whole system was firmly out of action. We tried to fix it up as best we could, using everything we had on board, but it definitely didn't work so Sandy Woodward called us out to the repair ship. That night about thirty-five electrical engineers descended from the *Stena Inspector*, and under the guidance of David Breen they bypassed the whole mess with a load of new wiring and got it working again, virtually overnight.

The chap at San Carlos who stuck out in my mind as a very tough egg was Pentreath in the *Plymouth*. That first morning it became obvious that the *Plymouth* was more or less useless to the event, being an ancient ship with ancient radar and no very modern weapons. Pentreath's answer to

68

that was to steam in defiant circles round and round *Fearless* and *Intrepid* just to show he was there, blazing away with his gun. About a week later I flew over the anchorage and he was still doing this – it was perfectly clear that sooner or later he was bound to be bombed, which he was, quite badly. It was magnificent defiance, quite preposterous really, and very good stuff I thought.

Next night, the Commander of the Amphibious Force asked me to bring in the *Monsoonen*, a supply ship for the islands, which the Argentinians had taken from the islanders and were now using to run their supplies. He wanted it intact for his own use. We nipped down through Falkland Sound and found it, about twenty miles away, steaming east towards Stanley. He saw us coming from behind, and although we called on the radio to him to stop or we'd blow him out of the water, he turned north and ran it into the shore, through the rocks, through the kelp and up the beach. That was a bit disappointing, but I didn't want to gun it to ruination. It seemed possible the war might be over pretty soon and as well as the Amphibious Force the Falkland Islanders would want it back, so I didn't think they'd thank me for smashing it up. The islanders got it off later and it is back in use round the islands. If I'd known that it was carrying howitzers for the defence of Stanley I would have changed my mind, but *Invincible* was calling me to get back out to the Task Force because dawn was coming up.

We continued bodyguarding *Invincible*, but of course after San Carlos the Navy's role as a fighting force diminished. On the basis of first in, first out, *Brilliant* steamed up north soon after the Argentinian surrender.

Looking back, the ship and everybody in it had behaved exactly as expected, and the things that went wrong had done so for entirely predictable reasons. On the way north, the weather was very similar to when we went down, big sea, bright sky, lots of cloud, the same albatrosses – very South Atlantic. I fell the crew in, in their best uniforms, and we had prayers for the dead, particularly for the *Sheffield* and the *Coventry*. Both ships had been part of my little squadron coming down from Ascension. Now we were going back without them and it seemed almost incredible that those fine ships had disappeared.

Major Peter Cameron

Royal Marines

Military Cross

Major Cameron is the Commanding Officer of 3 Commando Brigade Air Squadron. From the first day of operations his squadron of Gazelle and Scout helicopters rendered outstanding service in support of the Brigade, often flying in appalling weather conditions by day and night, having to evade Argentine fighters and anti-aircraft fire.

During these operations three helicopters were shot down with the loss of four lives. Nonetheless, the squadron continued to provide extremely valuable support to the ground forces, ferrying urgently needed ammunition and evacuating wounded during the battle for Darwin and Goose Green, amongst other actions.

Throughout this most demanding period, Major Cameron led his squadron with humour and compassion both on the ground and in the air. His fine example of courage and determination, in the face of severe losses, was an inspiration to all and his leadership ensured that no call for help went unanswered.

I had decided to take an early Easter skiing holiday in France with my family. I wanted to get away from the squadron, then come back during leave, when there would be a bit of peace, to work on various reports on my own, with my Staff Officer and clerk. I'd said to my Staff

Officer, Lieutenant Warren, 'Listen, Richard, I'm going to give you, and you only, my address, and I am not to be disturbed unless we're either going to war, which is highly unlikely, or we have a crunch (crash).' I'd been out there a week and was just about to go off for a picnic with the family up the mountain, when the phone rang. I picked it up and this French bloke said, 'Are you Major Cameron? We have a call for you from Plymouth.' I immediately thought someone had crunched and my heart came out of my mouth. One of my Flight Commanders came on the line and said, 'Hello, boss. It's Andy Newcombe. You'd better get back – we're getting ready for something big.' So I told him not to be so bloody neurotic and he said, 'Well, you know our little lot down south, well, they're in trouble and they want all of us.' You can imagine my relief that no one in the squadron was hurt and that we were only going to war!

I flew out of Geneva on the midday flight the next day, and by that stage we'd read about it in the press. I certainly didn't believe we were going to war and I don't think my wife Carol did either. I was met at Heathrow, ushered through, bypassing Customs, and on the way my gunner driver told me all about it, and what was going on. I met my senior pilot, Andrew Eames, at his home, found out what he'd done and made one or two decisions, like taking all the aircrew. Originally, Andrew had decided that we could leave some chaps who were on courses, and chaps who were on draft, studying for staff college, etc., but I said, 'No bloody way. If we're going, we take every bugger we can.' I spent that evening with my Brigadier, Julian Thompson, and his staff sorting out what to take; there was a shipping space problem and they only wanted us to take nine out of our twelve Gazelles and four of our six Scouts.

I went to the squadron where everyone was beavering around and at 1 a.m. I called an O Group, and with my Flight Commanders and Engineer Officer sat down and discussed the whole thing through and swapped ideas. I followed it up with a telephone call to an Army Air Corps

Staff Officer, Tug Wilson, who happened to be on leave. I got him out of bed about three o'clock and said, 'Look, Tug, sorry to bother you.' He wasn't exactly pleased to hear me. He said, 'I'm on leave.' So I said, 'Well, so was I!' and gave him my shopping list, all the kit I wanted – armour plate, goggles, machine guns, all sorts of things. Tug said, 'Don't worry, mate. I'll do everything I can for you. Leave it to me.' By 8:15 the following morning he phoned and told me there was a Hercules on its way with all the kit I wanted! We flew the six Scouts out to Yeovilton that day to marry up with the kit and do all the fitting out. Everyone had been fantastic – couldn't have been more helpful. By Monday evening all were embarked, less three Scouts. On Tuesday, 6 April, the last three Scouts flew onto *Fearless* in the Solent and the squadron departed UK waters.

After the excitements of the weekend I must say it was something of a relief to get to sea and somehow we had managed to squeeze an extra two Scouts on board, much to the *Fearless*'s wrath! Our nine Gazelles and six Scouts were divided between the LSLs *Geraint*, *Galahad*, *Percival*, *Lancelot*, *Tristram*, and HMS *Fearless* but the overall lack of shipping space meant we had to leave about a third of our men behind (less one, Gunner Bird, who managed to stow away on *Galahad* to go to war with us) and almost all our vehicles. Gunner Bird's Flight Commander, Lieutenant-Commander Gervais Coryton, was not quite sure how to handle this so I told him to charge Bird with being absent from place of parade, namely RM Coypool in Plymouth, fine him £20.00 and then congratulate him on his initiative!

The journey south was spent in preparation and planning. Overall, the squadron was well prepared for war. We had spent many years supporting our brigade and we were a well worked-up team. I now first wanted to ensure everyone was absolutely ready – in particular that the aircrew were at their peak in flying proficiency by day and night and confident in themselves as to what I would be asking them to do. So we flew every day, we flew by night, we fired our newly-fixed SNEB rockets and machine guns at splash targets and we worked up all our ground crews to a peak of efficiency in deck handling. At times it was hair-raising taking off and landing from pitching and rolling decks in the South Atlantic, but by 19 May, two days before we went in, I had given my orders and personally spoken to every man in the squadron and the 656 Army Air Corps Scout detachment under my command. Despite the difficulties of commanding a team split between seven ships overall, I knew in my mind the squadron was ready; I had also prepared them and myself for the worst.

Our war started well before dawn on 21 May. Gazelles and Scouts took off to make way for the first waves of Sea Kings that were off-loading the guns and Rapiers. Aircraft that were placed in direct support of the Commandos and Paras married up with their respective units and two Gazelles of C Flight braved no-man's land to clear landing sites. Our tasks were all closely tied in and related to the brigade landing plan. We had a job to do and we were getting on with it. All seemed to be running smoothly. However, while the battle for Fanning Head was going on supported by two Gazelles of A Flight we suffered our first tragedy. A Gazelle and a Sea King carrying mortar ammunition in an underslung load were heading for Port San Carlos to land near the settlement. Unfortunately, both aircraft had got ahead of 3 Para, who'd been delayed and who were supposed to clear the settlement. So these two aircraft came into the area where forty Argies were resting up. The Argies had heard the Naval gunfire support going on in Fanning Head and so they had bugged out and were now in a gorse area to the east. When they saw the Sea King and Gazelle, they opened fire with automatic rifles.

The Sea King heard the firing and saw the tracer bullets go past, but what he had not appreciated was that the Gazelle behind him had been hit and Sergeant Evans, the pilot, had been seriously wounded. Evans obviously thought, 'Well, what the hell do I do? I'm in a hell of a state.' But he managed to flutter down and ditch his aircraft in the water. Both Sergeant Evans and his aircrewman, Sergeant Candlish, managed to get out of the helicopter but only after Candlish had cut himself free of his harness. Candlish inflated his Mae West life jacket and turned to his pilot to give him a hand when Evans said, 'Help me, Eddy, I'm bloody hurt.' As he did so the Argies opened up on them in the water from the bank some 200 metres away. To get to the settlement and safety they had to swim about 600 metres in ice-cold water. Thank God they had their immersion suits on because they wouldn't have survived at all without them. Whilst they swam, for about twenty minutes they were under constant fire.

They got to the shore and by that stage we'd got the report from the Sea King that it had been fired upon. The Brigadier, myself and the command team then got together and asked ourselves the question, 'Who the hell is this enemy?' We'd received earlier reports that there were no enemy in Port San Carlos. So we were confused. 3 Para hadn't even started advancing properly, they were only just landing, so they couldn't give us any information at that stage and we had to make the decision that despite the risks we must find out what this enemy was and what they were doing.

We elected to send two Gazelles forward to find out, to sum up the situation and report. But as so often happens, the reported grid reference of the original firing was 2,000 metres away from where it actually happened. We didn't know that at the time. One Gazelle only went up there initially; we will never know why. Sergeant Candlish had just made it to the beach with Sergeant Evans when he looked up and was absolutely dumbstruck to see this Gazelle flying along slowly above him at eighty knots towards the enemy. As it circled it was shot out of the air by the same people who had shot down Sergeant Evans and himself. Sergeant Candlish knew, no matter who it was, that two of his friends had just died and when, twenty minutes later, after much effort to save him, Sergeant Andy Evans also died, Sergeant Candlish's whole world seemed to collapse. Even at this stage we did not know in Brigade Headquarters that these aircraft had been hit.

The second Gazelle came up and did his stuff, probed a bit on the south side, wasn't happy, came back and went up the other side. 3 Para were also now moving up. It was all terribly confusing; the fog and confusion of war was proving an even greater factor than we had expected. And to cap it all, this third Gazelle, piloted by Robin Makeig-Jones, rounded a point further east and came under fire from the same bunch! He lost a blade off his tail rotor, had twelve shots all the way down his tail boom and one through the cockpit as well but managed, remarkably, to struggle back to *Galahad*, vibrating like hell, to give us our first, very good and accurate, contact report. By this time 3 Para's report also arrived to say there was about a platoon strength of enemy seemingly moving east and that one or two Gazelles had been shot down, a pilot was dying, would we send a casevac helicopter and would we stop flying in their area. For hours after that we never flew anywhere near that area! We banned flying completely up there until the area was declared free of enemy.

It was a very sad day, very tragic. The end result was that we had lost three very good friends and comrades in arms: Lieutenant Ken Francis, Sergeant Andy Evans, and Lance-Corporal Bret Griffin. The whole squadron was exceedingly cut up. I'd prepared them for this sort of occurrence, I'd gone round and said to them, 'For better or worse, if we have casualties, we've got to knuckle down and get on with the job.' But it was very hard to take. Very hard.

That evening I went on board the *Galahad* for a memorial service for the three men. It was a very moving service and as the men all came from the same flight, everyone of that flight was there and most of Squadron Headquarters. After the service we listened to the World Service and we heard the landing had been successful, but we'd lost two Gazelles. What really got through to me and, indeed, the others, was that all my Gazelle pilots were married. We knew that if it had been announced on the

World News it would've been announced on the nine o'clock news back home and the wives would know and be worrying themselves sick. At that point we didn't know who'd actually been killed so we couldn't release any names. The chaps had all been casevac'd back to the *Canberra*, including Sergeant Candlish, and because of the subsequent air raids we had that day the Navy command, quite rightly, told every civilian ship to get out of San Carlos Water. So there was no way of getting hold of *Canberra* except by signal.

We knew the four that had been shot down; we knew that three had been killed but we didn't know which one had survived. It wasn't until two hours later that we learnt that Candlish had survived, and we got the signal away. Of course Candlish was the only one who knew what had really happened. I picked up information from 3 Para and from talking to Robin Makeig-Jones. But we couldn't really put the pieces together until three or four days later, when I managed to get a signal away to the squadron back in Plymouth and give them and the wives a rough idea of what had happened. It was very difficult, a very trying time. The original signal just said bluntly that they'd been killed in the initial landing and their wives were told as soon as possible in the morning. That was all – we couldn't tell them anything more and I was desperate to try and tell them, to keep them informed, because we're quite a close-knit unit.

Back home the wives were all getting together that Saturday morning for a video show, to make a video for us; they'd brought their new babies along, and their dogs and their teddies and everything else. Of course the bereaved didn't turn up, but the rest of the squadron's families didn't know. My wife, Carol, had to go along and tell them what had happened. They were shocked and stunned into silence and there was much weeping.

I was very cut up about the deaths, but I pulled myself together. It's not the first time I've lost aircrew in my flying history. It is a strange thing, but once you get over the initial remorse and sadness, you tend to say to yourself, 'How would they expect us to behave?' and the last thing that anybody within our outfit would have expected from the disaster was a lot of weeping.

That night the officers were asked by my Sergeant-Major, WO2 Gilbert, to go and join the men in the canteen: 'You must come down, Sir. The men need you.' When I got there all the officers and senior NCOs and Marines and corporals sat round in an enormous circle. Crates and crates of beer were provided. Not by us or my men, but by the *Galahad* ship's company, the Chinese on board and all the other units. It was remarkable. Again, there was a lot of weeping, particularly among the chaps that had lost good, close friends. But once they had got over that, and the anger and everything else, we ended up very happy, singing songs they would've sung, and when the last can of beer was finished we went to bed. That was midnight and we were up an hour later and away, not quite knowing what to expect on our second day in the Falklands.

It was obvious we should get moving. We got warnings of approaching enemy aircraft over the radio, and as soon as we got those we would keep out of the way of the ships and get into the re-entrants around San Carlos Water and sit tight. The Brigadier and myself at one time were sitting in the back of a Gazelle en route to Port San Carlos waiting for the Skyhawks to go away when our burly Royal Navy and Combined Services rugby player pilot, Colour-Sergeant Pulford, turned to us both and said, 'What I wouldn't do now, Sirs, to be walking my dog in Tavistock!' Roars of laughter all round, and we moved off.

As soon as we landed in the Falklands and had set up our Headquarters, I met up with Ewen Southby-Tailyour, a good friend of mine, and he put me on to Pat Shore, the San Carlos Settlement Manager, who gave me a shed for maintenance work when we required it. I slept with my Headquarters staff in tents literally in his back garden and then he suggested we use his garage so we stayed there for ten days. He subsequently took pity on me, because I was up all night, and he gave me a bed in his son's bedroom.

That was good – things like baths and actually being able to go to the loo.

That first week we were completely on our own. We only had five Wessex and my remaining seven Gazelles and six Scouts. That was all. I had a chat with everyone once or twice a day. My job was to command my squadron and keep in the Brigadier's pocket; in fact, whenever the Brigadier flew anywhere, I would throw out the pilot and jump in and fly him around. This way, I generally knew what was going on in the different areas.

One of the things that came out of this campaign was that all the procedures which had been practised in Norway and been revised over the years worked a treat, though we had to break the normal rules and go beyond our usual defence umbrella.

About that time we heard the tragic news that the *Atlantic Conveyor* had been sunk, so we suddenly realized that although we'd got one Chinook off it, we'd lost three more and twelve Wessex. It was a hell of a blow as the few helicopters we had ashore were working overtime. We depended on our helicopters so much. I had double Gazelle crews who basically were working for a day, resting for a day. But I only had one Scout crew and they were absolutely bushed by the end of the war; they were flying three and a half to four times the normal rate. It wasn't so much the flying hours that was crippling them but the long day, sitting strapped in, not always flying, but just the strain, and of course eating spasmodically, or just getting a brew on when, blow me down, you're taking off again.

The other interesting thing was that the Sea Kings also were limited on crews, and they did all sorts of things, like every single aviator on *Fearless* who was not on a current flying tour flew second dickie. The Commander was a pilot at one time; all these sort of people helped out. But the fact of the matter was that to fly all these insertion operations at night, the Sea Kings had to rest their crews by day. So in effect we only had about six Sea Kings by day out of the eleven we had ashore, which meant that there was no way we could support a major move-up. That was the limitation of the helicopters we had at that stage, so the fact that we lost the *Atlantic Conveyor* was a real blow. I remember telling my senior pilot, Andrew Eames, that I reckoned it was going to be a Dunkirk if we went on losing ships at this rate. We were losing a ship a day, and we were all bloody worried that we weren't going to pull it off.

For 2 Para's battle at Goose Green we had to support them some way. Quite understandably, the Sea Kings, it was decided, would not fly over Sussex Mountain and outside the defence umbrella by day. They were prepared to use them to fly by night but even then they were not to do more than three sorties. So what happened was that when we set this whole thing up, with the Brigadier's agreement, we gave 2 Para two Scouts and the Gazelles in direct support, to be used as they wished. But in order to exercise a bit of control over how they were used, I put my senior pilot down with them in their Battalion Main Headquarters. He didn't work in the Tactical Headquarters, but back in the Main HQ with Major Chris Keeble. That was a very, very wise decision as it transpired.

I stayed back in Brigade HQ and I co-ordinated the whole effort with my Ops Officer, Paul Bancroft. We followed the normal battle procedures and Andrew Eames and the two Flight Commanders, Jeff Niblett and Nick Pounds, went to the O Group on Sussex Mountain, walked forward, saw the ground, got the plan and made the decisions as to how best to support 2 Para. I also told both Flight Commanders that they were to keep the same crews throughout so that they really could get to know the ground and the battalion, and support them to the best of their ability.

That night, 2 Para shot off down the Camilla Creek. The next night we flew in the artillery and mortar, and throughout that day and the day after my Gazelles and Scouts were rushing backwards and forwards keeping the battalion topped up.

What we did was to set up a Forward Arming and Refuelling Post at Camilla Creek House, and with Andrew Eames forward and the Battalion HQ and me back, the whole thing was tied up. This was an interesting performance, because it was the first time that we'd actually been involved in a conventional battle with the helicopters supporting a battalion that was fighting a desperate battle. Basically, our routine was ammunition in and casualties out. We didn't use underslung loads because if we had, we'd have been too high up and would have been shot at. The other important fact that came out of it was that most of my crews were Royal Marines. I had a few Army pilots and one Naval pilot, but the Royal Marines had all been infantry section commanders, troop sergeants or troop commanders in commandos so they understood the battle procedures, knew what the battalion was doing on the ground and could talk sensibly on the radio. This is where the military helicopter, flown by the military in support of the military, proved its worth; that was why we were able to get right forward and give the battalion its ammunition and support.

We'd been flying for about three and a half hours during the battle for Darwin when H. (Lieutenant-Colonel H. Jones, 2 Para's Commanding Officer) and his team were gunned down. Two Scouts were tasked to go forward and pick them up from Camilla Creek. Barely five minutes after taking off from Camilla Creek two Pucarás appeared out of the 300-foot cloud base. They were going to attack the companies on the ground but when they saw the two Scouts, they went for them. Jeff Niblett, my Scout Flight Commander, with his aircrewman Sergeant Glaze, and Richard Nunn with Sergeant Belcher as his aircrewman immediately spotted the Pucarás and broke. The Pucarás took one each. Jeff somehow or other managed to evade every attack in quite the most remarkable bit of flying and co-operation, with Sergeant Glaze darting around the back of the Scout literally ordering Jeff which way to fly – 'He's coming in now. Stand by to break. Right, break now!' Richard Nunn survived one attack but on the second one

80

he was hit and a rocket went straight through Belcher's leg, so he was unable thereafter to help Richard as a look-out.

The Pucarás then realized that the Scouts weren't armed. They could have climbed through the cloud but the Pucarás had radar and in any event there was no way to recover back to the ground without ground radar assistance. We'd discussed all sorts of tactics on the way down as to how the bloody hell we'd combat this threat, but there was nothing to do but just fly our normal fighter-evasion procedures and hope to God that by flying by the seat of your pants you'd shake them off. But it was very difficult to shake these chaps off.

On the third run, the Pucará machine-gunned Richard and unfortunately he was killed instantly. Sergeant Belcher was wounded again, in his other leg. The aircraft just crashed to the ground and then, quite remarkably, it swung through 180 degrees and Sergeant Belcher was thrown out. The aircraft caught fire and Belcher was sitting on the ground unable to move, one leg nearly severed and the other one pretty badly shot up. But, as calm as a cucumber, he got out his morphine and inserted it into his good leg, having decided the other one was a write-off.

At Camilla Creek House the Gazelles, which were also churning around, had seen Richard being shot down and Nick Pounds immediately went down there. Sergeant Wood and Sergeant Priest jumped out of the aircraft, saw that there was no hope of saving Richard, but managed to get to Belcher. They gave him every assistance they could and radioed back to Camilla Creek House that they must have a Scout forward to do the casevac as Belcher was a stretcher case. They used a doorpost off the crashed Scout to make a splint for his leg. Jeff Niblett had by that stage got back to Camilla Creek House. The Pucarás had been frightened off by the Blowpipes and small-arms fire. Jeff carried out his fastest shut-down ever, almost beating his aircrewmen to the nearest foxhole, and then had to get airborne again to go down and get Sergeant Belcher. They got him into the aircraft and had him back in Ajax Bay within fifteen minutes. If they hadn't got him to Rick Jolly's set-up he wouldn't have survived.

The next day Jeff Niblett and Sergeant Glaze picked up Richard Nunn, which must have been hard for them both, and took him back to Ajax Bay where later we had a funeral service which was very moving. Myself and his close mates from his flight carried Richard in. We were very shaken up. As with the others lost at Port San Carlos, Richard was a very tragic loss to the Royal Marines and the squadron. To my dying day I'll never forget Jeff coming up on the radio: 'Hello Zero, this is 29. Am returning to Ajax Bay with serious casevac. Over.' And I came up on the air and said, 'Hello 29. This is 9 speaking. Request sitrep. What's going on?' And he came back, absolutely calm, and said, 'Very much regret to inform you 29 Alpha has been killed, shot down by Pucará, but I have his assistant with me and although he's been severely injured in the legs we hope he will survive.' As calm as that; just remarkable.

For us Goose Green was a success. Every single bomb and bullet that was fired in that action, except those which were carried in on 2 Para's belts or flown in by the Sea Kings at night, was flown into battle by the squadron helicopters. Every single casualty, both British and Argentinian, was flown out the same way. The light helicopters really proved their worth at that stage, because the only other way of getting across country was by Volvo or on foot.

We had a very alarming moment with John Greenhalgh of 656 Squadron Army Air Corps, under command, who was on his way back from Goose Green. We had no homing facility on the Scout; we had homing facilities on the Gazelle, but not on the Scout. So this aircraft was flying around above the cloud, and in the end I had to rush out of my garage and tell him on the radio which way to fly. As soon as I heard him overhead, I told him where he was and eventually he leapt down through the cloud. But it was dark, pitch-black dark. I was fearful because the ships would fire at anything that was above fifty feet. We managed to stop the ships firing on him and got him down, thank God. Otherwise we'd have lost John, his aircrewman and his three casevacs.

We were using the Scout, where you can put a stretcher in the back, for lying casualties, and were using the Gazelles for sitting casualties. We carried some casualties outside on stretcher pods. We were aware that we might be carrying injured men who were unconscious when they were put outside on the pods. In order to reassure them should they wake up in mid-flight and think they were en route to the Pearly Gates, we had written on the inside of the pods: 'Don't be concerned. You are in a helicopter – you are being casevac'd!' The trouble is it's not possible to look after the casualty or administer a drip if he is outside in the pod. We preferred to put them in the back of the aircraft whenever possible.

It was a remarkable three days, really. We wiped our feet after that, and had a bit of a lull. Time for maintenance and a sort-out. We then moved forward first to Teal and then to Mount Kent and established my HQ there. 45 Commando were yomping, 3 Para were tabbing and we were supporting them. We moved quite a lot of supplies, acted as courier and delivered messages. We tried where possible to fly in pairs across no-man's land, to keep a good look-out. So we screamed over the ground at 120 knots at five feet, across the awful open and exposed prairie, and all the time we knew the festering Skyhawks were coming in that way. So one had to keep a bloody good look-out. We tried to do it in pairs but in the end I had to accept that single helicopters had to have a go. It was a bit of an anxious time. But it was impressive watching both the commando and the battalion moving, because in a helicopter you have a unique viewpoint of the whole thing, even from five feet!

Having learnt from the past experiences of Darwin and Goose Green, for the final battles I basically put a Gazelle flight in direct support of each of the fighting units, so 3 Para, 42 Commando and 45 Commando each had two

Gazelles in direct support. I kept the Scouts in reserve. I told the flights to have liaison officers forward so that they worked out in advance exactly how we were going to do the casevac procedures, ammunition forward, and where we were going to fly it to. In the battles we had discovered that because the Marines and Paras were so young and fit, every single casualty we took out survived! If a chap was without a leg, or had a stomach wound, the important thing was to get him off the battlefield fast. Important also was to give the injured a little hope. The chap on the ground would say, 'Don't worry, mate, there will be a chopper here for you in fifteen minutes.' As soon as it arrived we would load the injured on, just get them on – there was no place or time for stretchers. Everyone where possible would help themselves. Men with only one arm were holding drips for people with no legs and someone was probably holding a drip to him. Even in these conditions there was a great sense of camaraderie. The aircrewmen were also corporals and sergeants with basic experience of infantry work, so they were able to appreciate what these lads had been through. 'Don't worry, lads, we'll have you in the dressing station within ten minutes,' they would say; then as soon as they got to the dressing station the doctors would get their hands on them and carry out immediate surgery, and were able to say to them, 'Don't worry chaps, you'll be on the *Uganda* by teatime.' I think that factor kept a lot of them alive, it gave them milestones of hope. Some of those lads were very young, just boys, 17, 18 and 19 years old, just young, fit lads, and that is how they survived.

We didn't get terribly involved in the night approach. It was a silent attack on Harriet, Two Sisters, Longdon – they all went on concurrently. We started getting involved in the early hours of the next morning. I must say the aircrew were remarkably brave. I flew forward that day as well and there was artillery falling all round me but quite remarkably we didn't get hit. It was just pure luck, because every time we flew anywhere near the front line, we would immediately draw fire. So the great thing was to get in there quick and get out equally fast. The units had to be really ready with their casevacs or whatever it was they wanted because we never hung about. It was in/out, and if they weren't ready we went away again and called them on the radio, saying, 'For God's sake, get ready – I'm coming in again.' Because every time, except for the reverse slopes of Two Sisters and Harriet, we drew fire. It was very difficult. One of the conclusions we came to after the war was that we must have some sort of protection for the aircrew against small arms and against flak if we're going to be required to fly in a forward area to get the ammunition in or casualties out during or after a battle, or during a counter-attack. We were vital but we are vulnerable.

In the twenty-four-hour period after the battles, we actually casevac'd something like eighty-five casualties and only one died en route. The aircrewman tried mouth-to-mouth but unfortunately we lost him.

We weren't actually unscathed ourselves. We had one of our aircraft and two others sitting outside Brigade HQ; in fact, just outside my tent. We'd been a bit slack, I suppose, because we normally kept helicopters about three or four hundred metres away, but these were sitting quite close and got badly damaged as a result of four Skyhawks coming in.

All the press were standing around outside my little place, waiting for helicopters to take them back to San Carlos, from where they sent their despatches after the battles. They were all standing there and suddenly we heard a whistle blast. I was just climbing into my helicopter with the Brigadier, so we took cover and these bloody Skyhawks came in and although the bombs were falling everywhere, within fifteen metres of us, the only injury was to my driver, Marine Gardner, who was temporarily stunned. We were all extremely jittery and shaken. The press, however, got tangled up in the camouflage netting while taking cover and Andrew Eames, my senior pilot, who was shaving underneath the netting at the time, just said, 'That was a close shave, gentlemen, wasn't it?'

I was exceedingly upset that during an air raid warning on the final position on Mount Kent I was in the

Headquarters and I couldn't leave my post – I was on the radio. Everyone else vamoosed, and some bastard took my old steel helmet which was outside my command tent. I was very glad that somebody had taken a photograph of me in it. Eventually I managed to find a Para helmet on Stanley airport.

After that I could see the squadron's morale getting higher. I think the high point, without a doubt, was the last night – the positive response I got from my lads on that night. We all felt, 'If we keep the pressure up . . .' because we'd had an anxious two days going forward yet again across no-man's land between where we were and where the chaps on Harriet were, flying in exposed territory, and we knew bloody well the Pucarás were still around. But, remarkably, the Harriers from *Invincible* had tossed bombs at Stanley and had actually stopped any of them flying which was quite an amazing bit of luck. So there was a lot of anxiety, but my lads were absolute magic that night. I don't know what it was but everyone felt that we really were on the move, the whole squadron felt it, because we were flying as a squadron in preparation for the battle for Stanley.

I had five helicopters that were beavering away all night doing casevacs from Tumbledown and Wireless Ridge and we also flew shelters to 2 Para, who were very exposed on Wireless Ridge. We had to fly two Gazelles all the way back to San Carlos to pick up what we called Kit Individual Protection, fly them back and eventually move them forward to 2 Para before first light. At the same time we had a casevac, a Welsh Guardsman. They finally got back from that at three o'clock in the bloody morning and immediately took off to go forward to pick up three SAS wounded who were part of a diversionary action, using night goggles to find them. It was quite an alarming sortie because they were so far forward. But then that is what they are noted for!

The conclusion we reached was that it was much easier to work at night because every time we flew by day, we drew artillery fire. At night, maybe we'd be unlucky enough to fly in near an enemy position, but they wouldn't know what the hell was going on, so it was far safer to fly at night.

We worked all that remarkable night. I stayed up co-ordinating and the next day the Brigadier was flown forward to Two Sisters or Harriet to meet up with the other Brigadier and the General and they decided to wait twenty-four hours and then go into Stanley the following night. At that stage, we started getting reports in that there were white flags flying over Stanley.

At TAC HQ (Tactical Headquarters) there was the Brigade Major John Chester, the Colonel of the Artillery Regiment, Mike Holroyd-Smith, the OC Engineer Squadron, Roddy Macdonald, and one or two others, including myself. When we heard that they were flying white flags and they were getting out of their trenches we all said to Brigadier Thompson, 'For God's sake, Sir, we must go. We can't delay any longer or we're going to have another bloody day of taking a risk, exposing our chaps to the elements etc.' Julian Thompson sat there for about half a minute, which seemed an age! 'Yup, we'll go.' He got up, got onto the radio, couldn't get hold of Major-General Jeremy Moore, who by this stage was in overall command of the land forces, but got hold of 5 Brigade's commander, Brigadier Wilson, and he agreed. Eventually General Moore was told, and he said, 'Fine, go.' Brigadier Thompson flew forward to Wireless Ridge to join up with 2 Para, and the last thing I did as he left was say, 'Sir, if we can find a target, can we use SS-11 missiles?' He said, 'Providing 2 Para are happy, yes.' 2 Para, well aware that we had this capability, were a bit exposed on Wireless Ridge. So we sent forward three Scouts with John Greenhalgh leading them, and we fired our missiles and took out three gun positions. The Scouts in their exposed position drew more fire, and the Brigadier, who watched this performance, said they were like three little naughty schoolboys on top of a wall, throwing apples at a farmer, who got very angry and got his shotgun out and fired a few rounds. But these three little boys scurried off down the hill shouting, 'Hee, hee, hee, can't catch me!' It did wonders for my airgunners' morale to fire their SS-11 missiles in action for the first time.

Then everyone started moving into Stanley and we were again supporting them, right up until the last. I got into Stanley about three o'clock that afternoon and the first task was to find a suitable site for General Moore to land on for the surrender. I then had a most interesting evening waiting for him, chatting in pidgin English to two Argie conscripts and an officer. It was an extraordinary thing – I was on my own with these guys. They were delighted the whole thing was over and couldn't wait to get home. It was amazing.

I trotted down with the General. Perhaps I shouldn't have been there, but I decided it was an historic moment, so I barged my way in and stood at the back whilst they signed the surrender.

That was it really. After that, I stopped the Scouts flying and calmed them down; they were bushed. The Gazelles went screaming on and flew just as much as they'd ever done before; it was great to get off the ground and for the first time in three weeks be able to climb up to 1,000 feet. It was such a relief and allowed us to see the beauty of the whole place.

We'd never come back from any exercise, let alone an operation, as a squadron. So I asked the Brigadier if we could go back as a squadron and he said, 'My dear Peter, certainly you can. How do you want to travel back?' And I said, 'I want to get the fucking aeroplanes on a ship and forget about the buggers and I want the whole squadron to be together on the *Canberra*.' I'd sussed out *Canberra* and I realized it would be a very good way to come back, because we'd all gone down in tossing, turning ships. So I managed to get all the aircraft on the great ship *Elk*, and I put a small maintenance team on board. The rest of the squadron, without aeroplanes, without any responsibility apart from a bit of morning PT every day, enjoyed the trip back. And what a trip back! We sang our way back to

Southampton. We were able to unwind in a relaxed atmosphere – we got rid of our real emotions and had time to unwind. It was quite remarkable. We were just happy. There was just a marvellous feeling of happiness. On *Hermes* they didn't have time to unwind because they still had the watches system to cope with. We didn't have watches. Our ship was run by civvies and we were just passengers. It was very noticeable watching *Hermes* come back, and the big ships coming back. I mean, a lot of the sailors were weeping through pent-up emotion, whereas we'd got rid of that – it had gone.

I wouldn't have missed the experience of the Falklands for the world, but I never wish to repeat it. I was so pleased that the squadron had been so highly decorated, receiving, in all, sixteen awards – one for every ten men down there. I don't think of myself as a hero – the award was for my squadron, of whom I am exceptionally proud. The reason I wear my MC with pride is because of those boys and the four fine mates we lost. One of my pilots actually said to me when I got it, 'You'll always be the Master of Ceremonies, boss!'

Flight Lieutenant Alan Swan

Royal Air Force

Queen's Gallantry Medal

Flight Lieutenant Swan is Officer Commanding No. 1 Explosive Ordnance Disposal Unit at the Royal Air Force Armament Support Unit, Royal Air Force Wittering, and commanded the eleven-man bomb disposal unit which served in the Falkland Islands throughout the recent conflict. On 27 May 1982, there was an air attack on the Ajax Bay refrigeration plant, which housed the Commando Logistics

Hospital. The attack resulted in thirty-one casualties, and two unexploded bombs were found adjacent to the operating theatre. The hospital could not be evacuated because of continual operations on the wounded, nor could the bombs be defused. Having advised the hospital staff that it was unlikely that the bombs would detonate if they were not disturbed, although being mindful of the possibility that they might be fitted with long-delay fuses, Flight Lieutenant Swan decided to remain billeted in the hospital to reassure the patients and staff by his presence.

In the same attack, the hospital helicopter landing strip was showered with unexploded ordnance which had been damaged by bomb explosions and fire. With complete disregard for his own safety, Flight Lieutenant Swan personally led the manual clearance of ordnance which was in an extremely dangerous condition and made the strip available for further operations.

At Goose Green settlement, on 4 June 1982, a quantity of napalm had to be removed from the centre of the village. The napalm was weeping and in a dangerous condition. It was stored on steel-runnered sledges with the attendant risk of an explosion should a spark be struck. Undeterred by the obvious danger, Flight Lieutenant Swan, with the assistance of Flight Sergeant Knights, moved the napalm to an area where it could be destroyed safely.

On 6 June 1982, a 1,000 lb unexploded Argentinian bomb of the same type that had previously killed an Army disposal expert was found in the vicinity of Brigade Headquarters at Darwin. The bomb was too close to the headquarters to be dealt with by demolition. Regardless of the imminent danger to his own life, Flight Lieutenant Swan defused the bomb and the headquarters continued in operation without interruption.

Throughout the campaign, Flight Lieutenant Swan displayed qualities of leadership, courage and coolness which were a magnificent example to others.

People hold bomb disposal men in a sort of mythical awe because they're the guys who put their life on a limb, go and sit on a bomb and take it to bits. A lot of the time you do it from pure ignorance, but theoretically you've got a lot going for you. You've done the courses, you basically know what the problems are. You also know, if you go wrong, just what the hell's going to happen. This is why it's always better to work on a big bomb, because, if you've got to go, the best way to go is with a really big one – then it's clean. That's also one of the reasons why you talk to people as you're working on the bomb so they know what stage you were at when you went.

In the RAF, getting posted onto bomb disposal duties, officially known as Explosive Ordnance Disposal or EOD, is purely the luck of the draw. There are few volunteers, just pressed men. If you are an armament tradesman you can be posted onto EOD duties and there is no backing out. You do the training courses and then you are posted to one of the full-time units. The officers and SNCOs do seven weeks' training, the airmen do three. The airmen do the actual locating and digging down to an unexploded bomb (UXB) but only officers and SNCOs are permitted to defuse or explode UXBs. However, what we do sometimes is let the men set the demolition charges, the officer or SNCO connects the detonators, and then the men initiate the explosives. This makes them feel more involved, gives them a greater interest in the job.

We get all sorts of people in our unit. I've seen men terror-stricken on duty, waiting for the phone to ring and as soon as it rings they think, 'Oh God.' They pick it up and they're shaking. They get all the information, put the phone down and they go and do the job perfectly. But they're their own worst enemies, because they think about what they might be called out to do, whereas I find it's pointless thinking about it until I actually get to the bomb.

The definitive bomb disposal man is someone who's fifty per cent afraid all the time, and fifty per cent a hero – a balance between the two. Anyone who's totally afraid is useless; anyone who's totally one hundred per cent bravado is a menace. What it requires is the balance between the two – having a healthy fear and respect. Perhaps being an intellectual would be a bit of a drawback, because if you thought about what you were doing too much, it could prey on your mind. We have people from different backgrounds, different intellects, different intelligence levels – they all handle the job in their own way. I handle the job in my own way. It's just that in part I've been a little bit more successful than some of them have, but others have been more successful than I have – they've done more and they've been on EOD longer. I'd only been on bomb disposal duties for two years before we went south, which is a relatively short time.

I got into bomb disposal due to one of those fortunate coincidences. I had been commissioned from the ranks, having served eighteen years as an armament technician, and was posted to RAF Wittering, 'Home of the Harrier', as the unit Armament Officer. Although in a different command, the RAF bomb disposal units are also located at Wittering, and it just so happened that the OC of No. 1 EOD Unit, Flight Lieutenant Terry 'Mad Harry' Holbrook, was posted to Germany just as my tour was coming to an end. As my wife and children were happy and settled in Stamford, I managed to wangle Mad Harry's job and ensure a second tour at Wittering. His parting words as he handed over the reins, a list of local hospitals and the name of a good insurance agent, were 'Good luck, Al – Christ, you'll need it!'

The lead-up to the journey down south, or Operation Corporate as it was code-named, started when we were put on twenty-four-hour standby. We had our own ideas on how many men we'd take and thought that four two-man teams would suffice. However, on the day, we got a phone call from Wing-Commander Keith Hopkins at the MoD and he said, 'You're on your way. I've offered your services yet again and they've been accepted. I've told him you'll need ten men plus yourself.' So there it was, just an arbitrary figure, eleven men.

I think it had taken a lot of persuasion before the Navy would agree to an RAF EOD team being sent to the Falklands. Perhaps, like a lot of people, they were under the misapprehension that a bomb disposal man is a bomb disposal man *per se*. In fact, each service has its own responsibilities and specialities. Each service has superficial knowledge of each others' specialities but usually only enough to know to leave well alone. The RAF are experts in aerially-delivered ordnance of all nations, and, as the Argentinians had over 200 fixed-wing attack aircraft which they would use to counter our counter-attack, it was apparent to us that it was our expertise that would be needed. We were, therefore, doubly incensed to find that two Royal Engineers bomb disposal men had already sailed on the *Canberra*. There is intense comradeship and rivalry amongst EOD men, and the Engineers had definitely got one up on us by sailing before we had even picked a team.

However, we sat down and started to plan what and who we would take with us when our turn came. I decided that I would need Warrant Officer Dave Trafford, a fifty-year-old prickly Yorkshireman, but a man with a mind like a computer when it came to UXBs, fuses, pistols or other ordnance; he could also take over if anything happened to me. Chief Technician 'Hank' Hankinson was another very experienced man, well balanced and one hundred per cent solid on the job. Sergeant Pete Harrington was the next choice, because he was an expert on bomb types, pistols, and possessed an encyclopaedic knowledge of all types of small arms; plus, he was a very nice, warm human being, just the sort of father figure the young airman could, and did, turn to when the going got rough. Flight Sergeant 'Doc' Knights and Chief Technician Mick Sidwell completed the list. They, like myself, had only been in bomb disposal for two or three years, so we had a balance of experience levels.

The five airmen on the team were selected for their ability to work hard and mix well. Balancing personalities and experience levels is an important part of my job; if you get a bad mix and tensions are created, then you're not going to get the teamwork that is vital when you're trying to concentrate on defusing bombs.

My war orders from MoD UK Air were simply to 'Clear Stanley Airfield of unexploded ordnance'. My

Commanding Officer in the field would be Wing Commander Peter Squires, the OC No. 1 (F) Squadron Harriers. In this case the 'field' turned out to be the flight deck of the *Hermes*. This meant that the officer in overall charge of bomb disposal would be commanding his Harrier squadron in combat! I caught him in his office for five minutes just as he was preparing to leave. I gave him the EOD Handbook and grinned – and so did he.

We assembled everything we thought we might need in the war zone: shafting and shoring equipment pumps, bomb locators, explosives, etc. We were told initially that we would not be armed, but who goes to war unarmed? Fortunately, we had our own unit weapons so we took the required number of SLRs (self-loading rifles) and SMGs.

The unarmed order was later withdrawn, but it showed the turmoil that was occurring above our heads. Next we were refused an issue of arctic clothing, and overboots: however, bomb disposal men are the world's best scroungers, so we were soon kitted out. After assembling all the kit, it was weighed and dimensioned, and a 'tongue in cheek' six tons were loaded into an ancient four-tonner and two Land-Rovers. We didn't know then that there were no roads on the Falklands except for a few miles in Stanley. We finished loading on Saturday night, but on a routine check on Sunday we found to our horror that the four-tonner was unserviceable. The world's best rogues and scroungers came into their own again, and persuaded a bemused RAF Wittering Motor Transport corporal that we were part of the 1 (F) Squadron ground support personnel, and we 'acquired' one of the squadron's serviceable four-tonners. Eventually, when 1 (F) Squadron groundcrew landed in Stanley after the surrender, their Flight Sergeant came up to talk to us, and said, 'That looks like one of our four-tonners.' So I said, 'So it is. Take it, it's all yours. We must have taken it by mistake.'

We said our farewells to our families, travelled down to Southampton on 27 April, loaded everything on the RFA *Sir Bedivere* and settled down for a long sea trip. The following morning, and one hour before we were due to sail, we were ordered to disembark. We were just off-loaded and left on the dockside without so much as a by-your-leave. The *Sir Bedivere* actually sailed with our vehicles, kit and explosives. UKLF Planning Staff had ordered us off.

So there we were, standing on the side of the dock in disbelief with just what we could carry. We phoned up and transport came to take us back to our base at RAF Wittering. It was very upsetting for our families – they'd gone through all the trauma of saying goodbye, and there we were back again. The following day while we were in the office, getting pretty angry, trying to find out from Strike Command what the hell was going on, I got a phone call from West Freugh in Scotland. The office suddenly went quiet: the phone message said a bomb had gone off, killing two of our men and severely injuring two others.

The four-man team had been up in Scotland clearing UXBs from the bombing range. The team leader, Sergeant Ginge Rutter, and one of the airmen, Leading Aircrewman Boothroyd, had been killed instantly. The dead and the injured had been moved from the range but there were still UXBs to be cleared. I was stunned; we hadn't had a fatality since 1956. I rushed home, said goodbye yet again to my family, and went to Birmingham to break the sad news to Mrs Rutter, whilst another officer performed the same sad duty with the Boothroyd family. So, within twenty-four hours of being off-loaded from the *Bedivere*, I'd licked my wounds, got the grim news, comforted the bereaved and was now standing on a bombing range in Scotland trying to understand how some of my best men had been killed and wounded. The Falklands disappeared completely from my mind.

The UXB that killed the men was a bomblet from a BL755 anti-armour bomb. We were subsequently to face over 600 of these UXBs in Goose Green and Stanley. When the service buys a weapon and stores it for long periods, every so often they will select one and check its functioning to ensure it hasn't deteriorated in storage.

Depending on the results, they may decide to extend or reduce its shelf life. Occasionally, when Defence Sales are trying to sell a particularly lethal weapon like a BL755 to a foreign power such as Germany, Yugoslavia or Spain, that power may ask for a weapon demonstration plus the technology in dealing with the UXBs. In either case the result would be a live drop on one of our air/ground ranges, and RAF EOD would clear the UXBs. We'd been doing this for about ten years without incident.

The problem with BL755 is that each bomb contains 147 smaller bomblets. If any of these fail to function they become UXBs, but can fall into one of two categories. Category 1 is when there is no apparent reason for non-functioning and Category 2 is when the reason for non-functioning is evident. Cat. 2 UXBs you can play football with; Cat. 1 will function if you look at them sideways. The trick is knowing which category the bomblet you're dealing with falls into, especially if it's submerged or partially buried. At best it's a bit 'iffy', but we'd been getting away with it for years due to hitherto effective render-safe procedure. When one of these bomblets functions, a plasma jet forms which will burn through about a foot of steel; it also gives off over 2,000 pieces of shrapnel. That's what caused the deaths and injuries to my men.

I questioned the survivors, Griffiths and Wensley, in hospital for hours. Despite that and two official inquiries, no one, to this day, actually knows what caused that bomblet to function. The next day another team arrived from EOD HQ, and, together with our man from the Ministry, Wing Commander Keith Hopkins, I led the team back out onto the range to finish the clearance of the rest of the UXBs. Starting from where the accident had happened, feeling angry, with a knot of fear in my stomach, we finished the clearance in near silence. We all knew that the Harriers on the Task Force would be dropping thousands of these bomblets on the Argentinians and we also knew we would be the ones who would have to clear them up. From that day to this, nearly three years later, not one live drop of that weapon has taken place in this country. After the remaining UXBs were dealt with, we returned to base at Wittering. The atmosphere was doom-laden. The events in Scotland were looked upon as a bad omen. Nothing had gone right since we'd originally set off.

Within four days MoD UK Air had arranged for the team to go to Brize Norton and fly to Ascension Island in a VC10, hopeful that we could intercept the *Bedivere* there and pick up the threads of our interrupted journey. We touched down in Ascension and having found a billet, hitch-hiked into town to find out what we could about the *Bedivere*'s arrival. The Naval Staff at HQ professed to know nothing about the ship. Two days later, with still no information forthcoming from HQ, we retired to a local bar only to find out during a casual conversation with a Marine that not only was the *Bedivere* in and loading Marines, it was sailing the day after. We were at the quayside the next day at the crack of dawn, and by joining the tail end of the line of Marines we at last got on board. If we'd sat back and listened to HQ, we would have missed the boat and the war.

All our kit and vehicles were still intact on the ship; they'd even left the sticker on my cabin door which read, 'Royal Air Force Bomb Disposal Unit'. It was all a bit odd.

If there's one thing I'm not too keen on, it's the thought of being torpedoed. When we left Ascension, we were overflown by a Russian aircraft and our Captain gleefully informed us that two Argentinian submarines were thought to be in the area. This fact, coupled with interminable boat drills, did nothing to reassure me. I was immensely relieved to find a large pair of black flippers in a cupboard, which from that moment on lived under my pillow. We soon got used to ship life, but it took a while to understand that the *Bedivere* was an Army ship, with a Chinese crew and civilian English officers.

There was a Naval clearance diving team on board and we soon realized that they had no equipment with which to render safe UXBs. A common bond was soon established and cemented by a few beers. Their boss, Lieutenant Bernie Bruin, used to play the fiddle. His men, however, were never keen for him to do so. When we arrived in Bomb Alley (San Carlos Water) we found out why. Every time he got the bloody thing out and wound it up, we would get bombed, rocketed or shot at by the Argies. 'Must be a race of music lovers,' mused one unkind Marine.

Until we reached Bomb Alley, everything seemed so unreal. We went round the ship giving UXB lectures to the Marines. I'd taken a dummy BL755 bomblet with me just for this purpose. Everyone was briefed to avoid them like the plague, and they sensed we knew what we were talking about. The unreality of the situation disappeared when we heard about the *Belgrano* and the *Sheffield*. We sailed into Bomb Alley early one morning. As the haze lifted, the two halves of the *Antelope* could be seen burning not 400 metres away. It hit us then. This was it: war. It's frightening to see a ship on fire, to smell it, see it burn. Knowing that one of the Royal Engineers bomb disposal team had been killed and another seriously injured brought back the ghosts of Scotland. What made it worse was the fact that Doc Knights and I had been on the same bomb disposal course as the RE who was killed, Jim Prescott, and we had come to know him well, as you do when you're putting a twelve foot by eight foot shaft down through twenty feet thick of London clay to expose a German UXB. The REs' training makes them experts in Second World War German bombs, whereas we are specialists on English/Allied bombs and fuses. The bomb that had taken out the *Antelope* was a British 1,000 lb fitted with a 78 MKII all-ways acting pistol and a 25-second-delay detonator. We knew this from questioning witnesses and the fact that a book was found open at the page with that particular pistol on it; we also found a pistol of the same type in their cabin, so they'd successfully defused at least one UXB.

The next day it was our turn. At first light the first of

four air attacks came over. The *Bedivere* was missed in the first attack, but other ships were hit. It was like shooting fish in a barrel. All the ships seemed so close together that it was a miracle none was sunk. During the next attack the aircraft came over so low you could see the oil streaks and rivet heads. We watched in disbelief as a bomb was released and went into the *Bedivere*'s sister ship, *Sir Lancelot*. The disbelief was due to the fact that the bomb didn't have a tail on it, and if it was a British 1,000 lb with the 78 tail pistol in it, as the others on the *Antelope* had been, that meant it had been dropped safe, as the 78 pistol needs a tail on the bomb to arm it. Incredibly, on the next attack another bomb with no tail on it hit the *Bedivere*. To watch an aircraft bombing you is terribly unreal – it happens in slow motion. The bomb detached, hit an aerial, went through a crane jib, exited through the fo'c'sle, hit the water and went through the side of *Sir Galahad*. Again we thought it might be safe, like the others. On the last attack that day a Mirage came over the top of us at about 100 feet. The machine guns opened up and stitched the Mirage down its belly. The pilot ejected right in front of us, and although every other ship claimed it, it was credited to the *Bedivere*.

We'd been eating carpet most of the day, but when night fell it was time to earn our pay. Myself and three others readied ourselves to go to the *Lancelot* and *Galahad* respectively to check on the UXBs. Due to a misunderstanding Dave and I were never picked up by the diving team's boat, so Hank checked both bombs and, as suspected, both were safe. A relieved Naval clearance diving team got them off the ship and dumped them over the side. We too felt very relieved, because of all the bomb types the Argies had, they were dropping our own 1,000 lb bombs fitted with pistols we knew like the back of our hands.

After a day or two of repeated air attacks, sanity suddenly reigned and we were told that the *Bedivere* was to join the *Hermes*, some 400 miles away.

The Naval clearance diving team was put ashore at Ajax

Bay and after much wrangling so were we, but at midnight! When daylight dawned the Marines couldn't believe it. There in the middle of the combat zone were a four-tonner and two Land-Rovers. The Land-Rovers had red wings, blue oscillating lights and RAF bomb disposal stickers front and rear. 'Oh my God,' they said, 'it's the Air Force.' We'd landed on a rocky beach which went straight into rocky hills. There were no roads. All that kit we'd agonized over was useless. It would stay where it was. All the reference books on bomb types, pistols, fuses, etc. were too heavy to move. We left with what we could carry and no more. I'd had an inkling this might happen; that's why I had picked SNCOs with memories like computers.

We'd heard that an army of instant experts was appearing nightly on TV at home, giving forth on how the war was going, in particular why there were so many unexploded Argentinian bombs on our ships. The reason supposedly given was that the Argentinian pilots were coming in too fast and too low, therefore the bombs weren't in the air long enough for them to arm. Coincidence or not, two days later we got the Argentinian response when they dropped parachute-retarded bombs. It was time for the evening meal, and there were long queues of men at the rear of the old meat-processing plant, which now, ironically, housed our hospital. I had just got my meal and was walking away when two Skyhawks dropped three bombs each on us. The blast, which had it come seconds earlier would have killed me, blew me down the corridor. All hell broke loose, part of the building collapsed and we were scrabbling at the masonry and twisted girders with our bare hands to free the dead and wounded. The Skyhawks came in so fast and so low that we didn't get an 'Air Raid Red' warning. The bombs they dropped were French 400 kg parachute-retarded. Parachute-retarded means that the bombs can be dropped from low-flying aircraft at higher speeds. There were five dead and about twenty-six injured in that raid. I don't think the pilot knew he had hit the hospital because munitions had been stored alongside it and we'd not put up a red cross, whereas when we got into Stanley, every other building had a red cross on it.

The bomb explosion caused fires which in turn set off munition dumps, and rescuers were showered with exploding mortars, bullets and missiles. RSM George appeared at my side, looking immaculate as ever. 'Excuse me, Sir,' he said, 'but there's a bomb by my bed.' True enough, as he'd been sitting on his bed eating his meal, a 400kg bomb, complete with parachute, had come through the wall and embedded itself in a large refrigeration unit next to his bed. All I could see of the bomb was the parachute. It would take four hours with a welding set to get at it, assuming we had the time, because at that stage we didn't know if some of the bombs had time-delay fuses as well as instantaneous fuses or pistols. There was a hurried evacuation of non-essential personnel.

By now darkness had fallen and the temperature was dropping to its usual −10°C. The surgeons were operating on the wounded with a UXB just thirty feet away. We shored up the intervening walls and made blast corridors with sandbags.

Whilst this was going on, a report of a third UXB came in. This one had gone through the whole length of the roof void and exited through the gable end, having passed over the working surgeons, hit the ground fifty feet in front of the hospital, bounced between two Marines who were having a conversation, and landed up the hill some 500 metres away on our forward perimeter. Defensive positions close to the UXB were evacuated and we were asked to deal with it as a priority so that the defensive perimeter could be reinstated.

Doc Knights and I, plus a radio operator, were guided to the bomb which lay in a hollow on top of the hill. Doc gave it a thorough examination and we decided we didn't have a clue as to the fuse's identity. It was a French Matra type, which no one had ever seen before. We decided to blow it using safety fuse and 1 lb of plastic explosive. I don't like safety fuse, because once you've ignited it, you have no control over the situation. Once you light it, you go, and you don't go back. Doc told the radio operator to go down the hill and wait for us. We lit the fuse and stumbled down the hill in pitch darkness, not daring to show lights or make too much noise as we were on the forward defence lines and we didn't want to attract the enemy. In the darkness we missed the radio operator, and as the seconds ticked by, thinking he was within the danger radius of the blast, we ignored the 'no noise no lights' order and both Doc and I flashed torches and yelled like madmen. A face materialized out of the gloom and said, 'Shut up and lie down! Don't you know there's a bomb going to go off?' It was the radio operator. We had a sense of humour failure and threw him to the ground. With that there was a bloody great explosion and shrapnel showered down on us. In the darkness we thought we'd gone far enough away from the bomb to be safe, but we hadn't.

Doc went back up to the site of the explosion at daybreak and came back grinning from ear to ear. Apparently, after the bang, the Marines had resumed their normal guarding, and one of them, looking for a place to obey the call of nature, couldn't have believed his luck as he tumbled into a six-foot-deep crater which was ten feet wide. Due to the heat of the explosion the bottom of the crater was some sixty degrees warmer than the cold night air. Overcome by the luxurious surroundings, the Marine also overcame three days' constipation. 'The man was an artist,' said Doc, 'there was a turd the size of a bloody python, perfectly coiled, smack in the dead centre of the crater.' Pete Harrington, who had been listening, fascinated, to this conversation, told Doc that he'd been unable to find anything of that description in his EOD Handbook, but Doc could probably render it safe by making a downwind manual approach and using the 'hands on' technique!

We knew there had been two aircraft, each carrying three bombs. One exploded; one was in the fridge; one we'd blown up. That left three. Within minutes of getting back to the hospital after blowing up the bomb on the hill we had several reports of two large splashes in the shallow water in front of the landing stage. That left one bomb to be accounted for.

WO Dave Trafford and I went back to the site of the explosion and started checking around. As I swung the beam of the flashlight round, there, twenty feet above our heads, was a parachute hanging out of the wall. Above it was a perfect bomb-shaped hole. The bomb had gone through the wall side on and was sitting up there waiting for us. The worst part was to get to it. I had to do a balancing act along some four-inch-wide girders. I squeezed through the hole and found myself in the roof void. Some thirty feet away was the bomb. It was directly above the operating theatre area. On examination, it proved to be the twin of the one we'd blown up on the hill; however, we couldn't blow this one up.

The terrible implications of the situation began to dawn on me. It's common practice to mix impact-fused bombs with time-delay-fused bombs. The reasoning is that as the emergency services react to the damage caused by the impact-fused, the time delay goes off and takes them out. As the first bomb had been impact-fused, the chances of this one being time-delay-fused were high. Even worse, it could be fitted with a fuse anti-removal device: as you remove the fuse a second fuse under that one blows the bomb up anyway. What a dilemma! The choice: to defuse or to leave well alone.

Dave Trafford appeared, and we agreed it was a 400kg SAMP fitted with a fuse of an unknown type. We took measurements and details, and gently backed away. Downstairs we briefed Colonel Helberg, the CO, as to the situation, and conferred with Lieutenant Bernie Bruin, the Naval EOD Officer. On being told it was a French bomb and fuse, he triumphantly produced a signal from C-in-C Fleet, detailing render-safe procedures for certain French bombs and fuses. Apart from saying to use special tools, which we didn't have, it referred to documents we hadn't seen, and ended up saying that translation advice on the unseen documents could be obtained by phoning up some bilingual squadron leader back home! Unfortunately, nobody had 10p, or the STD code, so we got back to the real war.

While Doc Knights and the lads were shoring up the roof under the UXB, I had decided not to touch the bomb fuse. It had been there for some hours by now. I was taking a chance, but on balance, it offered the best option. Dave Trafford and Hank Hankinson nodded their agreement. Next, we had to convince everybody else. We decided the best way was to put our money where our mouth was, so we bedded down under the UXB, with fingers, legs and eyes crossed. That broke the tension, and everyone in the hospital went back to what they were doing before the drama started, except the theatre staff, who hadn't stopped working at any time during that post-attack period; brave people.

There was a marked difference after the attack on the hospital and dealing with the bombs. We'd established our identity. Up until then, nobody knew who we were; nobody had command and control over us; nobody was particularly interested if we were there or not; we got food just by joining the queue. So the lads went from being people without identity, who weren't particularly wanted, to people who were needed very much. They became the 'Bomb Disposal Men'. At least they were people, they were known. In the faceless thousands, they were known.

After the raid on the hospital we had to clear up about 200 UXBs, which took us all day. We worked as an eleven-man team to clear that lot. Each bomb was lethal. One bomb had blown up, hit the mortars, which had hit stacks of ammo covered in nylon nets. The nylon had melted, run downhill, puddled underneath more explosives and they'd all gone up – quite a pyrotechnic display. It was also literally feet away from where we lived. So it was a bit warm.

The UXBs had to be cleared urgently as they were all over the heli-pad where supplies, troops and wounded were landed. Because there were tussocks of grass and hillocks it took a while to locate the UXBs and we didn't want to tread on any because we didn't know what we were dealing with. We're not used to dealing with mortars and anti-tank rockets, so we had to examine each one to see what state it was in. We had a vague idea about land service ordnance, but we'd never had hands-on experience. When we saw them, ripped apart with the fuses hanging out, we didn't know if touching them would set them off. With memories of Scotland in our minds we had to pick each one up and walk three or four hundred yards, not knowing if it would go off in our hands. We started off carrying each one like a baby, but as we became more confident, we ended up carrying four at a time until the pad was cleared.

A day or so later, at 3 a.m. in pitch darkness, I was asked to go on board HMS *Argonaut* to look at a UXB that had killed two ratings as it went through the ship's side and ended up in the magazine, below the water-line. I went down with Lieutenant-Commander Dutton, the Naval EOD officer, and peered at the offending bomb which was under two or three feet of water. It was a British 1,000 lb bomb. On past experience I advised the Captain that it was safe to stay on board, as it was unlikely to go off. I agreed to assist in the removal of the bomb, little knowing that we wouldn't be able to fulfil that promise. In the event, Dutton got the bomb out, but it took him seven careful days.

Next day, Goose Green was captured. Goose Green was a major Argentinian air base. It had a grass strip that would be ideal for the Harriers. As my brief was to clear airfields for Harrier operations, we made preparations to move. Later that day the 18 Squadron Chinook brought in some POWs. Amongst them was a Major Tomba, a Pucará pilot. He was the CO of the air base and would know what facilities were intact, UXB density and minefield location. Dave Trafford and I signed Tomba out for the day, and thumbed a lift to Goose Green. There we found extensive minefields, hundreds of UXBs and tons of leaking napalm. The extent of the task was daunting.

HMS *Fearless* gave high priority to airlifting our trailers and kit to Goose Green, but despite the fact that empty Chinooks came from Ajax Bay to backload the POWs from Goose Green, we never got a single item of kit. All we had was what we could carry. Again, because we weren't part of any recognized unit, food was a problem. By rationing what we'd 'acquired' and by shooting geese and sheep, we kept body and soul together. The airmen, Dave Field, Paul Grace, 'Blimp' Thorne, Tony Moreton and Ken Soppet-Moss took it in turns to cook and keep house. Mick Sidwell turned out to be a baker of sorts; so with all that talent and Andrews Liver Salts, we survived.

Life became an endless round of UXBs, mines and ordnance we'd never seen before – like Cobra anti-tank missiles. Some POWs were moving an ammo stack when it blew. Whether it was booby-trapped or not we'll never know. One was killed instantly, another was terribly mutilated. The result was that from that moment on we had to treat every single item we touched as if it were booby-trapped. Life became very difficult.

We then had the job of moving twenty tons of napalm that the Argentinians had left in the centre of the settlement at Goose Green. The containers were punctured, and acetone fumes were leaking out. These fumes are highly dangerous, easily ignited by a spark or a match. The napalm was stored on sledges with steel runners, so we got a tractor and towed it away. The trouble was that we had to tow it over rocks which caused friction and this produced sparks which was a bit nerve-wracking. By now the Gurkhas had taken over from 2 Para, and no amount of cajoling would get them to move away from the napalm. They just grinned and stood their ground; they didn't want to miss the show if things went wrong. We managed to sledge the napalm over to the end of the airfield. We then blew it all up. To our amazement this gigantic fireball just grew and grew. It was huge, about 300 metres across and a quarter of a mile high and climbing – a real mushroom cloud. Those poor settlers at Goose Green had been captured by Argies, liberated by the Paras and now they'd nearly been cremated by RAF bomb disposal. The Gurkhas, however, loved it!

Whilst the rest of the team slogged away at the daily grind of clearing ordnance and stacking it up in neat piles, Doc Knights and I took a bone-jarring trip to Darwin in an ancient tractor. The HQ at Darwin was being menaced by two 1,000 lb UXBs; we were asked to deal with them. The bombs were lying next to the water supply and as they wouldn't evacuate the HQ (there was a war on, someone said), we had no option but to defuse them. Neither Doc nor I had defused anything as big as this before.

The first bomb turned out to have been dropped by a Harrier. The Argies had defused it and then stuffed the fuse pocket with a variety of bits and pieces. We were wary of this bomb: the Argentinians were expert at booby-trapping. We eventually made it safe and turned to the second bomb; it was of the same type that had sunk the *Antelope*. We attached an IGOL (I go on living) to the pistol and paid out the line. An IGOL is a device which will unscrew a fuse/pistol by virtue of a spring-loaded hammer action. The tension is applied and released by means of a rope some 200 feet long. The trick is to find good cover as the end of the rope is paid out. When we got to the end, we were on a patch of ground which was as flat as a billiard table. We lay down, thought small, tugged on the rope and set the hammer action going. Eventually, and probably lubricated by our adrenalin, the pistol came out. Had the bomb gone off we would have been shredded by shrapnel and so would those men running the HQ. That just left the detonator to be removed. As our kit hadn't arrived from Ajax Bay we had no detonator removal tool, so I broke off two twigs from a nearby bush and after five or six attempts, gingerly eased the det out. The nickname 'Twiggy' took some while to live down.

My worst moment of the whole war came when we were clearing the Goose Green schoolhouse. It had been an Argie control post and 2 Para took it out with a Milan. We discovered a cache of explosives and I extracted some soggy brown paper cylinders. On turning one over, I found the word 'GELIGNITE'. In actual fact it was sweating gelignite, which is highly sensitive and extremely dangerous. The team backed off and I slowly walked away from the rest of the explosives, intending to place the gelignite at a point where it could be detonated without setting the explosives off. As I left the shelter of the school, a large pink sow came ambling up out of nowhere and headed for me. Its ribs were showing and it was ravenous. I quickened my pace. I'd heard of how pigs will attack and even eat people. I looked round and saw the grinning faces of the rest of the team. I went a little faster and just as I was about to throw the gelignite and trust in God, the pig found a rotten potato. I adopted a more dignified pace, placed the gelignite gently down, then ran like hell back to the school. EOD humour blossomed. 'Don't worry, boss, we'd have saved your bacon,' said Paul Grace. They then fell about. 'As a render-safe procedure that was sow sow.' As the laughter got worse so did the puns. 'One of the rasher members of the team.'

The laughter dissolved the tension, and the misery of the previous week disappeared. I remember thinking that that was the closest I came to discovering whether adrenalin had lumps in it.

Back at Goose Green settlement we'd picked up over 600 UXBs of the BL755 type that had killed our mates in Scotland. Each one was viewed with suspicion; each one just as dangerous, and in some cases more so, as the second it was dropped. That was a lousy time, picking those damned things up. Every evening the lads would go back to the house, go out back with the Argie weapons they'd put back together and let fly with literally hundreds of rounds at a rock out to sea. It was just like a mini-battle, but it helped to relieve the tension.

The Gurkhas weren't too keen on the minefields, so they asked us to lay some mines in strategic positions. During the previous week we'd been plagued with chopperloads of souvenir hunters off the ships. They were a real problem as they ferreted through piles of guns, helmets, etc., ruining days of painstaking clearance work.

As we laid the last mine along a hedgerow, the bushes parted and another party of Naval tourists headed towards the piles of loot. One of the lads screamed, 'You're in a minefield!' The four-ringer and his v formation stopped instantly and went all thin. The lads ambled slowly towards the statues and stopped some twenty feet away, grinning. I walked carefully up to the Captain and told them to follow me in single file. Their relief at reaching safety was second only to the speed at which Doc Knights relieved them of a sack they were carrying. It contained 4,000 cigarettes, bread, and a couple of *Mayfair*s – a handsome reward. When we drew the minefield map, we realized the mines finished some twenty feet away from where the Naval party had appeared; apparently they were safe all the time. All is fair in love and war. Still, we did give them a goose we'd just shot so they didn't go away empty-handed.

The Paras were fighting their way towards Stanley, so Dave Trafford and I hitched a ride back to Ajax Bay. There we found that Colonel Helberg was preparing to move out. He'd commandeered a ship, the *Elk*, and in return for a promise to clear his allocated billet and HQ area in Stanley of UXBs, booby traps, etc., he readily agreed to ship our vehicles and men to Stanley. Before we arrived the Argentinians had surrendered. It was over. There was no elation for us; the worst was still to come. We knew that. You always lose more EOD men clearing up after a war than during it. Over 4,000 died clearing UXBs after the Second World War; more than 1,000 of these were EOD men.

Dave and I stopped dazed Falkland Islanders in the streets of Stanley and eventually cajoled enough of them into putting up the team when it arrived. Stanley was disgusting. The Argies had fouled everywhere. We got a map of the airfield at Stanley and made plans. The *Elk* arrived and disembarked our men and vehicles. At last the vehicles came into their own. We still had no food, but three Land-Rover loads of mysteriously acquired Argentinian officers' rations soon changed that.

The airfield was a mess, UXBs everywhere: Russian SAM7; American 500 lb MK82 bombs; French Exocet; British Tigercat; Israeli ground equipment; a real international cocktail and, of course, hundreds of those bloody BL755 bomblets. There were thirteen Pucarás, all apparently booby-trapped, plus Cessnas and Aeromacchi, each one taking hours to clear. The Paras had herded all the POWs onto the airfield and left them to their own devices for three days. This gave them the chance to plant hoax and live booby traps. It took nearly four days before we cleared the airfield sufficiently for our C-130 Hercules to land in safety. During the next week the lads worked like Trojans.

We saw the last of the POWs processed and heard a story that the guys who were strip-searching each POW had found a way to relieve their boredom. We all knew that the Argies had been told that we would torture, kill and eat prisoners. On board the processing ship a prisoner was wheeled in, stripped and searched. The guards made great play of pinching the POW's muscles, and this was accompanied by much smacking of lips. They turned him slowly round and there was a table, with a white cloth, salt and pepper, and place settings for two. The Argie fainted.

We were all shipped home, having taken just one casualty: Doc had frostbite in his big toe. In three months we'd dealt with over 900 UXBs, cleared hundreds of plastic mines, tens of thousands of items of ordnance, and tons of napalm. We'd been shot up, rocketed and bombed, and survived.

Seven of the eleven-man team received gallantry or bravery awards.

Flight Lieutenant David Morgan

Royal Air Force

Distinguished Service Cross

The Sea Harrier pilots of 800 and 899 Squadrons embarked on HMS Hermes *showed great courage in the air battle over and around the Falkland Islands which started at the end of April and continued throughout May. They were required to fly sortie after sortie, sometimes as many as four per day, often in appalling weather conditions, but remained steadfast and determined under continuous stress and constant danger. Their contribution enabled the Task Force to gain air superiority and thus almost certainly saved many lives which would otherwise have been lost in enemy air attacks. Flight Lieutenant Morgan flew fifty operational sorties. During one sortie he attacked a Puma helicopter with guns, causing it to crash into a hill, and on a separate occasion he and his wing man attacked and destroyed an entire formation of four Mirages, Flight Lieutenant Morgan himself shooting down two enemy aircraft.*

Beginning in 1982 I began an exchange tour with the Navy, found a house, started the conversion of the Sea Harrier and was half-way through this when one Friday morning I went into work and found everyone sitting around. I walked in and said, 'Hey! Have you guys heard? The bloody Argentinians have invaded the Falklands.' And, to a man, they looked at their watches and said, 'Where have you been for the last four hours?' They'd all been called out at four o'clock in the morning but as I'd only been based there a short time my name wasn't on the call list.

On the Sunday I jumped in an aeroplane and landed on

111

Hermes and on the Monday she sailed. I said goodbye to my wife Carol and my children on Saturday. Then it was all delayed so I went back home again and said, 'I haven't really gone, but I'm going tomorrow.' I'd always explained to the kids while we were in Germany what might happen if ever there was a war. We'd taken them up to Berlin and showed them the other side of the Wall and said, you know, 'That's why we're here, to stop that happening to us. We wouldn't like that, would we?' They couldn't get any chips in East Berlin and the Coke tasted horrible. Communism was way off!

I'd always told Carol if I actually had to go off to war not to expect me back, because in Germany we were operating so close to the front that life expectancy would be pretty short because we would be prime targets. The kids, however, were rather confused that I was going off to war when we were back in England. I'd certainly resolved to do the best I could to stay alive but I didn't really expect to live through the campaign. There was every chance that I was going to get killed. In fact, while I was down south, Carol moved house and I came home to find all my belongings packed in boxes. But that's better than one chap I heard about whose wife said, 'Okay, he's not coming back,' sold their house, bought a smaller one, got rid of all his kit – and then he came back!

When I said goodbye to the kids for the final time my son, Charles, who was five, said, 'Don't worry, Daddy. You'll be all right. They've only got tatty old aeroplanes – you've got brand new ones!'

The landing I made on the *Hermes* was the only deck landing I'd ever done, apart from once in a helicopter. I didn't actually see England to say goodbye to it because by the time I got up on deck, we were out to sea, and England had disappeared. All I saw was the overhead projector screen start to swing in the briefing room. So we rattled off down the Channel with helicopters bringing things on board all the way down.

There was a lot of discussion about what we were actually going to do. We considered ourselves basically as the big

112

stick, the big threat that probably wasn't going to be used because there would be a political solution, and I think a lot of people thought that until we got to Ascension Island. We were anchored off to re-store and bring on kit which had been flown down to us when one of the Royal Fleet Auxiliaries sighted a periscope, so we all upsticked and went very, very quickly and left the Sea Kings tracing this submarine. I don't know whose sub it was to this day, but it wasn't American, it wasn't Argentinian.

While we were heading off south the Admiral came onto the intercom and said, 'Okay, we've actually left earlier than we anticipated. However, we're going now, we aren't going back and you can take it from me that we are going to war. So get settled down, sort out what you've got to do, get your house in order, as things are going to hot up from now on.' We'd already formed planning teams on the way down so we started doing quite a lot of fairly heavy training. There were some pretty heavy sessions for the next ten days or so, to make sure we'd got everything exactly right. A team of us sat down and looked at the ground-attack options. We worked out the best way to attack our first option, which was the airport at Stanley. We also discovered that Goose Green was being used, so we had to plan a secondary attack. Basically, we were trying to use all the aircraft on *Hermes* – we had twelve at the time – nine to attack the airfield and three in reserve to take the place of anyone who was unserviceable. If any two of those three were left at the end of the day, they would go and attack Goose Green. We decided early on never to send 'singletons' because that is a sure way of losing a guy.

It worked itself up gradually, the pitch getting higher and people getting more and more finely-tuned. Our time from normal cruising to action stations went from about twenty-five minutes on the first try, down to a couple of minutes as we approached the zone, so things were getting pretty sharp. We started intercepting an Argentine Boeing 707 which was coming out and snooping around us and finally got clearance to actually fire at him if he came again. That obviously got back through the Argentine channels because they never came again.

113

The evening before 1 May we'd got everything sorted out and there were just the final briefings. Before dawn on 1 May the Vulcan went in and dropped a bomb in the middle of the runway and that was really the most damage they ever did with the Vulcan. We followed that up just before eight o'clock with a raid of twelve Harriers. We hit Stanley just as dawn was breaking. This was the first time we'd really been into action and everyone was very tense beforehand, very much introverted, very quiet, with the odd stupid joke at which everyone sort of cackled aimlessly and then went back into their shells again, everyone walking around, thinking very hard about what they were going to do. We got airborne and were in the air about ten or fifteen minutes before we sighted Stanley. Having had a Vulcan through, the ground defences were very alert. We ran in down the north-east coast and at Berkeley Sound split into two lots – one lot came through between Mount Low and Beagle Ridge, and the boss and I came round the other side of Mount Low to split the fire. As I came up towards the high ground there, I got a radar lock-up because someone had detected me so I descended even lower and then ran in. Meanwhile, the other guys, two of them with cluster bombs, took out the airfield installations and aircraft.

I was the last one across and as I ran in at about fifteen feet high all I could see were just sand-dunes with people firing at me from the top and bombs exploding and missiles going off everywhere; there was a complete umbrella of anti-aircraft fire bursting all over the airfield. The first time I saw it I thought, 'Christ Almighty!' My initial thought was that the cluster bombs that the guys were carrying were going off early but I then realized that that wasn't what it was; it was actually flak. I just hit as low as I possibly could and then saw the boss running in across towards the airport buildings, so I decided I would curve round and come across his path. I pulled up over the sand-dunes and the first thing I saw was a missile go straight across in front of me, chasing one of the guys who'd just gone across at right angles to me. Then I saw a Britten-Norman Islander, the light aircraft which the Falkland Islands Company use for

114

ferrying people around, taxiing across the grass, so I said, 'Okay, you're the first one.' I pickled the first cluster bomb on him and blew him away. Then, as the second bomb came off about one-third of a second later, there was a great bloody explosion just behind me and my aircraft started shaking violently. This made me lift my finger off the 'Release' button and I thought, 'Ah Christ! We're still flying – get this other bomb off.' I dropped the third bomb and that went right over the airport buildings and made a few holes there.

I then dived down, through the smoke, over the airport buildings and past the control tower, still diving down into this great ball of smoke. I thought I was about 50 feet at this stage but I had to pull up to 150 to release the weapons because of 'dudding'. I dived into the smoke and broke left and came out the other side, running down over the sand-dunes, and I must have come bloody close to the hill behind the control tower. I ran out, got locked up again by another fire-control radar, did a quick manoeuvre, dropped a bit of chaff, changed my radio frequency and beetled off.

At that stage we all checked in on the radio and all nine aircraft were up. There were whoops of joy. We were all safe – that was a marvellous feeling. However, I radioed in telling them I'd been hit and might have to eject. I knew we had a search and rescue helicopter somewhere in the region, sitting quietly. If I had had to ditch, I would have been safe, but the sea is bloody cold down there. But I climbed up and slowed down and the discomfort and the rattling became less and I started flying quite smoothly. So I cancelled the call. Later, we had one chap bang out just south of the airfield who was in the water for eight hours before he was picked up. He was a bit cold but he survived!

When I returned to the *Hermes* I held off and let everyone else land first because I didn't know if I was going to be able to land the thing. I later found out there was a bloody great hole in the fin. I wanted to get everyone out of the way so that if I crashed on the deck it wouldn't harm anyone. So I brought it back and rolled it onto the deck. I didn't want to do a vertical landing because the controls may have been damaged, so I rolled it on fairly slowly and stopped. That was the end of the first mission. The whole operation had taken half an hour.

Shortly after I landed, the three from Goose Green came back, so out of the twelve aircraft we recovered twelve, and only one had a hole in the tail. Everyone was totally elated! I'd personally expected to lose three or four aircraft on that trip.

Stanley was considered a successful raid. We'd damaged the runway with two 1,000 lb bombs and torn the hell out of everything that was in the area – set light to the fuel dumps, blown the tower away and taken out a hell of a lot of the Pucarás and light aircraft scattered around. Unfortunately, we didn't really have the weapons to put the airport out of action. The thousand pounder had to be put in from medium level to get the penetration and the angle, because at low level even if you toss them, they still only hit at about a thirty-degree angle and tend to skip before they explode. The Argentinians' morale must have reached rock bottom that day because they had thought Stanley was invulnerable from the air.

Day one over – jubilation. On the 4th we lost Nick Taylor at Goose Green and the *Sheffield* was hit. I was on deck when I saw this great ball of smoke: it was a ship turning, about ten miles away, with its side all glowing white. There was a hell of a lot of smoke. Then the casualties started coming back onto the *Hermes* and everyone was rather subdued and gritting their teeth and saying, 'Okay, this is it. Let's go and have those bastards.' I think that was when the guys suddenly realized that the Argentinians were going to fight back and we were going to lose a lot of people, so we'd really got to go for it. We'd gone into action, we'd heard of a death but we hadn't seen it; our first actual contact with war was the survivors from the *Sheffield*.

At that stage we were pulled up to sleep above the water level because of the submarine threat, which made life very uncomfortable. I was sleeping on the floor of the Captain's day cabin with five other people. Most of us had camp beds but some of us were just sleeping on the cushions. There were about forty people sleeping in the bar. We got some sleep and as the days progressed you got a bit more because you were a bit more tired, but there were nearly always two or three action stations to disturb you. It was irritating, but because you always knew that this might be the time you were going to get a torpedo through the side, you didn't actually get irritated. It was, however, debilitating because you never really got very much sleep. Over the first couple of weeks we all got very, very tired and people were asleep in the cockpit on the deck.

The next real action was on 9 May. During the previous four days we'd been flying patrols around the fleet and the odd harassing trip over the islands just to let them know we were still there – nothing major and no one was shot down for a couple of days. The weather was appalling. While I was flying on the 8th I broke cloud at ninety feet and all I could see were grey sea, grey ship and grey clouds, everything ill-defined, so I had to do a quick circuit at about sixty feet and plonk on deck. That was one of the worst days.

At this stage I went off with Gordie Batt, who was later killed, to drop high-level bombs on the airfield. We couldn't drop the bombs because there was total cloud cover and we'd been told not to drop if we couldn't see the airfield because we might put them into Stanley itself. So we turned out from there. I found a contact on the radar, went to investigate and found a big stern trawler called the *Narwal*, which the Argentinians had been using to gather information. We asked what to do and the Navy said, 'Engage it.' Gordie fired a few rounds across her bows to try and stop her, unsuccessfully. So we dropped our 1,000 lb bombs – we couldn't land back on board with them, so we had to drop them somewhere! The weather was pretty bad which meant we had to drop them at low level and since they were fused for an 18,000-foot drop we knew they probably weren't going to go off. Mine, in fact, missed and we thought Gordie's had too but it went into the fo'c'sle, down two decks, and stopped. It didn't actually go off so we didn't know we'd hit her at that stage. She still kept going so

117

we each emptied 200 rounds of 30mm into the side of the bridge and the engine room. On the last pass she stopped and hove to, so we radioed back and some Sea Kings went in to capture her. Unfortunately, she was blown to pieces. The engine room was completely knackered and there were holes below the water line from the 30mm, so we just let her sink.

Just before D-Day, on 20 May, we lost a hell of a lot of SAS men when their Sea King crashed. We'd become very, very friendly with them on the trip down. One of them was a flight lieutenant who was the only one working with the SAS. He was a particular friend of mine who I'd known for years and years. He had a special function which we were looking forward to using, but that went down with him, which was a bit of a blow. We could ill afford to lose a quarter of the SAS strength, give or take, in one crash. Their raid on Pebble Island was a classic case of how good they are. It was fantastic. We took some recce pictures the following morning, just after dawn, and it was a bloody mess: aircraft burning, bits all over the place – a classic SAS raid. They never really resolved what happened to that helicopter. There was an albatross found dead in the area, but no one will ever actually know, not even the guys who were flying it. It's bloody dark in the back of a helicopter at night in the water and if you're hit and get knocked unconscious, then that's it, you'll never get out. Even if you're conscious you can very easily get disorientated in the back of a helicopter – you'll never find the exit.

So far we'd shot down nine, the Special Forces had got a Pucará, and the ships had claimed a few more. But I personally hadn't shot anything down up until then. Unlike in the Second World War, we didn't put anything on the side of the aircraft. Instead, we covered up the glass tiles behind the bar with a bit of hardboard and one of the stewards put up a stencil for everything hit. People were coming down from sorties, rushing down to the bar and saying, 'Another A4 on there!' So morale was pretty high.

I next got involved two days after D-Day. I was doing a CAP (combat air patrol) with John Leeming who unfortunately was killed in an accident after the Falklands. By this stage we'd moved our CAP from round the fleet to around the landings, so we were actually capping at very long range – 200 miles plus – so we were pretty short of fuel. I was capping with John over the Mount Maria area and I happened to see a helicopter fly across a lake at Shag Cove. I saw it from 8,000 feet, called it to John and asked the ship in San Carlos controlling us if we'd got any helicopters on West Falkland. They didn't know and had to check. But because of fuel problems, I couldn't afford to wait so I just dived in and took him head on down the valley. He was flying at about fifty feet and I was slightly above him. It wasn't until I'd got within about 500 yards that I realized it was a Puma and we didn't have any Pumas down there. By then it was too late to get a missile off and I couldn't actually push the aircraft down low enough to get the guns on him. So I just flew very low over the top and banked away. Meanwhile, John Leeming, who was coming from the other end, had seen three more following him. As I banked away, I looked back over my shoulder to try and pick up the Puma again, to come back round and have him. All of a sudden I saw a great ball of flame shoot from the ground. Apparently, he'd been caught by my down-wash as I broke over him and this had swept him into the side of the hill. I went back later and found that he'd had 200 rounds of 120mm mortar on board which explains why he'd gone bang!

John, meanwhile, had picked up an Augusta 109 gunship and he had a go at that, then I had a go and hit it. There was another large explosion and bits were flying off it in all directions. Then, as we were pulling off, very short of fuel, John saw another Puma shut down on the ground with people running away from it, so I emptied my last few rounds into it and then went home. I handed over the position to some guys from the *Invincible*, and when they arrived they found three more lots of burning wreckage on the ground and a fourth Puma which they then wrote off. So it would appear possible that we got all four of them. It was apparently one of the major arms lifts from Fox Bay, where

119

they'd got a supply ship. It's still to be confirmed, but we certainly got three.

I've got in my diary for the day, 'Could've been a good day but this evening Gordie Batt actually flew off the front of the carrier on a night bombing raid, exploded and went into the water!' He was flying the aircraft in which I'd shot the helicopters down, which was also the one I'd been hit in over Stanley.

On the 25th, the *Conveyor* was hit literally hours after we'd got all fourteen Harriers off her – we were very, very lucky. The *Conveyor* was going in that night to unload the rest of the stuff when she was hit. If they'd managed to get the helicopters off it would've made such a difference. But had the Argentinians hit it twenty-four hours earlier, things would have been very difficult for us. The GR3s, the Air Force Harriers, had arrived a couple of days earlier, and they'd taken over the ground-attack role from us, which was a great relief.

Our daily pattern then was flying CAP and trying to keep the heat off the fleet while they were deploying. The GR3s did a lot of good work supporting 2 Para at Goose Green; in fact, Bob Iveson was shot down there. Then on 8 June came the disaster at Bluff Cove – it was actually at Port Pleasant which isn't the right name for a place to have a disaster. I was sitting on deck on alert when we were told there was an air raid ashore. We scrambled but got there too late to catch the first wave. I relieved the guys who'd been there for about half an hour. My CAP area was Lively Island. As I approached it I called up the previous lot and said, 'Okay, where's the action?' They said, 'Just to the north of your CAP station. We've got a problem.' I said, 'Okay. Well, I can't see you, I can't see any problem. Just tell me roughly where.' They told me to head north from Lively and I'd see it. As I came in I saw the two great columns of smoke coming from the *Galahad* and *Lancelot*. Dave Smith and myself spent thirty minutes on CAP there. The only reason we'd been sent on this particular sortie was because we needed one more night landing to make us night qualified. We were both fairly new guys on the machines and we'd

120

done our three night launches – dawn, pre-dawn and inky-poo (pitch dark) launch. We'd also completed a dusk landing, and a fairly dark landing. This was the last inky-poo landing before we actually became night qualified. Anyway, here we were on a dusk strike, we'd been out about thirty minutes and now had only very little fuel remaining. I could see below me *Fearless*'s little landing craft coming round the coast, so I thought I would give it a two-minute orbit and then we'd have to head for home.

As I turned round I saw an enemy aircraft running in to attack the landing craft. I'd briefed Dave Smith beforehand that if we saw anything at low level the guy who saw it would attack and the other chap would just try and hang on and clear his tail. I was at 10,000 feet and fairly slow. I stood the Harrier on its nose and accelerated down towards this aircraft which was about eight miles away. Unfortunately, I didn't get there in time to stop him, but I locked on to the guy with my eyes and saw him miss with his bomb and disappear off. Then I saw a second guy running in from a different direction and he hit the back of the ship, which made me very, very angry. The most angry I've been in my life, because I knew from this bloody great explosion that he'd killed people, and because I hadn't been able to intercept and because he'd had the audacity to actually kill somebody while I was there. So I decided that he was the guy who was going to get killed. As I was going for him, a third one appeared from underneath me and attacked the ship again, but missed. So I thought, 'Okay, you'll do.' As I went for him, a fourth one appeared on the lefthand side of me, so I just pulled my plane across, got him in my sights and hit him with a missile. There was a bloody great explosion and then a great fireball falling into the water – no chance of him getting out.

I was going very, very fast – probably around the speed of sound. Because I was flying so much faster than the machine was supposed to be flown at and so much faster than the missile was supposed to be fired at, it rolled dramatically to the right which really took me by surprise as I was only 100 feet away from the water then. That was fairly startling. I recovered and found that the roll had pointed me directly at their third guy, so I came in behind him and fired a missile. He saw it coming and tried to reverse away but it took his tail off completely and he went into the water. I thought, 'That's the end of him,' but about three seconds later a parachute opened right in front of me and just whistled over my port wing. I subsequently heard that his parachute was on fire and he didn't make it anyway. That left two aircraft still in front of me, flying fairly close together and beetling towards Goose Green, so I went in on those. Dave was behind me, but he couldn't see me because it was virtually dark. All he could see were the missiles going off. At this stage, my gun sight went u/s and I was just left with a blank head-up display with nothing there to aim with, which really pissed me off. Anyway, I closed in behind these two, still going fairly fast, and fired a quick long-range burst at them. One of them broke across in front of me, so I just followed him in to about 300 yards, pulling my nose right ahead of him and squeezing the trigger. Then I just relaxed the nose very, very gently back down, pulled it back and tried again. I did that twice, didn't see any hits and didn't know where the bloody bullets were going. I then ran out of bullets with this guy right in front of me, which was very frustrating. So I just rolled the wings level and pulled straight up because there was no point in hanging about there any more – I'd nothing left. Luckily Dave Smith, who was about a mile behind me, saw my bullets exploding in the water and this guy flying through them, and locked him up with his missile. He didn't know whether it was me or the other guy, but then he saw me go up through the sunset and said to himself, 'Okay, whoosh!' He fired his missile and destroyed the guy – he just became a great fireball, whumff, into the ground.

By now, of course, we were both very low on fuel. I went in first on *Hermes* and landed with about two minutes' fuel remaining and he had about one minute's when he got back, so that was fairly close. We discovered when we got back that another pair who had been coming in to help us out had seen a fourth explosion. So for quite some time we thought that my stray rounds might have hit him, but in the end we reckoned it was only three and the fourth guy got back.

That really was the last bit of excitement that I had out there, the last time I actually got engaged. But we did become night qualified! The Argentine Air Force and Navy never really came out after that. There were a couple of quick raids but that was all.

Everyone was absolutely over the moon when the Argies surrendered. We'd just launched a GR3 raid to put a guided bomb onto a target very close to Stanley. It was called off in mid-air. The guy came back and said, 'I want to see the Admiral because I think they've given in.' That was the first we knew. One of the Admiral's staff came down and said, 'Hey, don't say anything yet, boys, but we think we've seen white flags on the outskirts of Stanley and everyone's streaming back, so we'll scrub all the attack missions and we'll just go defensive – see what happens.' And sure enough, it happened. It was absolutely amazing. But we still didn't know if the Argentines were going to give in totally or whether we were going to have to fight the guys on West Falkland. We still had the Exocet threat and the air attack threat, so for a few days we hung around, really not doing anything.

When I think about the whole campaign the most frightening fraction of a second was on the very first raid when I saw people actually firing at me and obviously trying to kill me. I think that's what really brought it home, made me absolutely scared stiff that fraction of a second. Then the old brain said, 'Sod it. We've got to get in there and drop the bombs anyway, so go do it.' I think everyone felt that on the first mission. Apart from that, the most uncomfortable times were during air attacks on the *Hermes* when we were sitting down between decks with everything closed up around us, at almost perfect Exocet height, just waiting for a big rocket to appear through the wall. That was disturbing. When you're in the air, nothing matters, you're the master of your own destiny and you can do what you like, but sitting there in that ship not being able to do anything, that was most disturbing.

My saddest moment was on Ascension Island. There were about eight of us who stayed behind on the way back and we had a service the evening we were leaving. It was a lovely, still, tropical night and the old sun was setting and we had this very, very moving memorial service. They'd flown out a whole lot of the wreaths from the UK and one rose-grower had sent us a great box of roses, and we stood on the back end of the ship and said a few words, tossed the wreaths over the back, scattered the roses, and just sort of sat there with our own thoughts. When it was all over and it had all gone quiet and there was no shouting, hooting or roaring any more, we could just think about the guys who would not be going back. That was very, very sad.

I don't think I ever felt that sort of remorse and sadness during the confrontation. Obviously, when you're in the flying world, you get used to losing friends; it never gets any easier, but the effects don't last quite so long. I've lost forty or fifty people, I suppose, since I've been flying, not all close friends, but people I've been on the squadron with. I must've lost fifteen or twenty real, good, close friends and it hurts like hell, but after a day or so, it's over, you know, life goes on. It's something you live with.

When a guy was shot down or disappeared, you thought, 'Ah shit, not him. Why him?' Then you knew the answer before you'd actually said it: because that's the job we'd got to do. The sadness never lasted more than a few minutes, and certainly never put anybody off their stroke at all. If anything, it made them more determined. But when it was all over and it all went quiet, then that was the time for grief.

And when we came back home, that was the most amazing moment of my life! We were all standing, lining the deck, and everyone had tears streaming down their faces. At long last we could actually let it all go. That I think was the most amazing moment of my life, absolutely fantastic. TV reporter Brian Hanrahan, the bugger, had come on board the night before and said to us privately, 'Look, don't be disappointed if there aren't too many people there, because, you know, the *QE2*'s been back, a whole load of people have been back and it's not that we don't appreciate what you've done, it's just that people are getting on with their lives.' And then we saw Plymouth Hoe heaving with people – absolutely amazing.

8 June

The Sinking of *Sir Galahad*

Major Charles Bremner

Welsh Guards

When rumblings of the Falklands campaign started we had just come off a six-week period as Spearhead Battalion for the UK, which meant we had been on twenty-four-hour standby for anywhere we might be needed. My Commanding Officer, Colonel Johnny Rickett, sent for me and said, 'What are the chances of the Welsh Guards being picked?' I said, 'Well, we've just come off Spearhead, so that heightens our chances, but on the other hand we are just hitting the Public Duties season in London, with the Birthday Parade, so there will be tremendous opposition to deploying a Footguards battalion. There are also twenty-six other battalions in the UK. They must be able to pick one of them.' He said, 'Well, ring up your mates in UKLF and see what the chances are!' I rang up the chap I had handed over to recently and he said, 'You are the first battalion who've said that you would like to get involved. Get your Commanding Officer to ring up the Chief of Staff or the Brigadier and put the case to him.' So we did and we got it.

We didn't know what we were volunteering for; if we'd known we were going to be blown off the *Galahad* obviously no one would have volunteered. As far as everybody was concerned we were volunteering for a great adventure, which surely would end up in the UK's favour. Our feeling was, why not get involved, why sit back and watch everybody else? Let's get down there!

The adventure began at the beginning of April. We went to South Wales to start training in earnest. That

127

exercise had to be seen to be believed. We suddenly found we could have anything we wanted. We were given ranges that normally we would never have been able to get onto; ammunition we would never before have been able to get; it was no holds barred. It was a marvellous period of training, heightened tremendously by the knowledge that we were going off to positive dealings. It is normally very difficult to convince a chap that he is training for something that is really going to happen. Germany's a bit like that; it's very difficult to convince Guardsmen that the Russians are actually going to pile across the border tomorrow morning. But now one really could say when people were getting things wrong, 'You are God's gift to the Argies. If you go and approach an Argentine position like that you are going to bore me rigid, because I shall have to write to your mother and say what a silly boy you've been.' That sort of thing got home absolutely beautifully, and by the end of those three weeks the standard these young men had achieved was phenomenal. The exercise had sharpened their mental and physical agility, and their determination to do the job properly and do it well. I had a super lot of lads and an excellent Company Sergeant-Major. The more I saw how they reacted in training, the more confident I got in them. I never had any worries about them at all.

The order came and the order said the *QE2*, which was a very peculiar ship to go to war on. How on earth do you set about training for war on a luxury liner? We maintained fitness by running round the deck four times, which was about a mile. We kept up a level of expertise on technical skills, practising weapon-handling until we were blue in the face, zeroing weapons, keeping people at their peak, firing weapons just to keep people's hands in. We also did a lot of training on weapon-handling with great big, thick arctic gloves on, a strange thing to do in your bathing trunks or shorts! The weather got better and better and we were literally staggering around the deck in bathing trunks with arctic gloves on, carrying machine guns – it was an astonishing sight! But everything would stop at six o'clock in the evening when the men went off to have their tea and the officers went off to have a bath and change and go to dinner. You'd go to dinner and have smoked salmon and a fillet steak, all washed down with two or three bottles of wine, followed by a glass of port and a film, and then go to bed about midnight! Sometimes it was hard to believe that 5 Brigade was going to war.

When we got trans-shipped from the *QE2* to the *Canberra* it really came home: we were at war and it was obvious that 5 Brigade were going to get employed. The whole atmosphere became more sinister, more real, and the weather got worse, and worse still. The weather somehow picked up the mood.

We slipped into San Carlos harbour early on the morning of 2 June and were disgorged off the *Canberra* as quickly as possible into landing craft. We were carrying a most massive amount of kit and staggered up to our defence positions about five miles inland, where we dug ourselves in. We were ordered to Fitzroy and set out over the Sussex Mountains with those huge, great bergens. We'd heard stories of weather casualties from other battalions and decided we couldn't risk leaving the kit behind. We borrowed a couple of tractors and tried to tow the kit, but the tractors got stuck. The move was called off and we went back to our first defensive positions.

The plan was then to fly us round to Fitzroy but the weather clamped in; in any case, the priority was to use the available helicopters to move guns and ammunition forward. So a fresh plan was made: HMS *Fearless* would take us round the bottom of East Falkland, south of Lively Island, to Bluff Cove with her two landing craft, meeting two more at the drop-off point. So we all walked back down to San Carlos and stood in the pissing rain for two and a half hours waiting to embark. At Bluff Cove about 250 men went ashore in *Fearless*'s landing craft, but for some reason the two landing craft from the shore didn't appear, so the Prince of Wales Company and 3 Company, together with the mortar platoon and the rest of the echelon, had to go back to San Carlos with the object of trying again next night. Then *Fearless* reckoned that going round the same route two nights in a row was asking for trouble, so we disembarked in the afternoon and were put on the *Galahad*. It took rather longer to load the *Galahad* than was expected, because at the last moment it was decided to include 16 Field Ambulance.

We arrived at Fitzroy Creek in daylight, on the morning of 8 June. Once there we realized we weren't expected. The message to say we were coming was the one message which didn't get through, so the landing craft to get us off weren't there. We were expecting two to take us round to Bluff Cove, which was a three-hour trip; if we'd got off at Fitzroy, it would have meant about a twenty-six-mile walk, which, with our kit, would have taken much too long.

It was oddly quiet now that the engines of the *Galahad* had stopped; there was no wind, the sea was glassy and calm, the sun, with no heat, was beginning to show itself over the mountains. The men were ordered to muster on the tank deck and assemble their weapons and equipment. It would not be long before we started to unload our ammunition and begin the last leg of our journey to Bluff Cove. We waited, but received no orders. Eventually a landing craft returning to shore from *Sir Tristram* arrived at the stern ramp; it was full of ammunition. We were offered space for some twenty men but we turned this down. It had been bad enough being split from the battalion, let alone now splitting our companies. Sea King helicopters started to arrive to offload Rapier. Welsh Guardsmen stood down to await the arrival of the two landing craft and start the move to Bluff Cove. About one and a half hours later one did turn up, with the news that the second was otherwise employed and so we would have to move in two groups. The trip would now take six hours plus loading and unloading time. Then there was a change of policy: 16 Field Ambulance, who were loaded last at San Carlos, were to unload first. More delay; kit off again while we set to help with vehicles and stores; two or three trips to the shore, some 500 metres away.

130

At last it was our turn. The Prince of Wales Company were to go first with some mortarmen and some from the echelon, then it was to be 3 Company's turn. The landing craft approached, Prince of Wales Company loaded up, 3 Company prepared to load ammunition. Then, another problem: the front loading ramp of the landing craft failed to operate, which meant that it could no longer dock against the stern ramp of *Sir Galahad*. Running repairs failed; spare parts were unavailable. The only solution was to bring the landing craft alongside and disembark from *Sir Galahad* down scramble nets, whilst heavy equipment, including bergens, were loaded into nets and lowered over the side using the ship's crane. The Prince of Wales Company went up the port-side companionway to the deck and began to climb down the scramble net, and 3 Company loaded nets for the crane. The Prince of Wales Company's HQ went first into the landing craft and two net loads of equipment were despatched. Further equipment was being prepared.

I looked up through the open hatch of the tank deck just in time to see a cylindrical object fly through the air. There was a loud metallic clang. I had no idea what it was, but something made me shout, 'Take cover!' My CSM took up the cry. A split second later there was a deafening explosion towards the stern of the ship, and almost immediately a second. A blinding, intensely hot flash roared through the tank deck. I was incredibly lucky; the CSM and I were beside a great pile of bergens which were just about to be lifted off when the bomb fell. We dived over to one side whilst the CQMS went to the other. He was a burns victim; the CSM and I got away with it.

The lights went out and breathing became difficult. Miraculously, after what seemed like only a few seconds, they came back on. The thick, black, acrid smoke that now filled the tank deck dulled their effect but there was enough light to see with and I became aware of the full and sudden horror of what had happened. The sound was the first thing: the sound of horribly mutilated and frightened, disorientated men – a noise from a different world. Then

131

the sights – unbelievable. The first thing I saw was a man running through a wall of flame from the far stern of the ship. He was on fire from head to foot, in excruciating pain and was begging his fellow Guardsmen to shoot him and put him out of his misery. Somehow he was smothered and the fire extinguished; morphine was torn off a dog-tag string and applied to give blessed, if only temporary, relief. What he must have seen on the other side of the wall of flame, I shudder to think. Then I saw a group of men standing stock-still, all with dark, burnt, curling hair, heads swollen like footballs, piercing but faraway eyes, bright red scorched faces, and all holding their hands in the air as if in surrender. All had been burned in the initial flash. A man had his leg blown off at the knee and was writhing in agony, shouting, 'My leg, my leg, where's my fucking leg?' while one of his mates administered morphine.

Then the 81mm mortar bombs, 66mm rounds, small-arms ammunition and grenades in the tank deck started to cook off. Evacuation was now the priority. There was no panic. The CSM, Neck, bawled instructions and instinctively they were obeyed. He was doing everything as he did in barracks, making everything appear normal; he organized everything in a typical Footguards way. We found a way up and out of the tank deck; a queue was formed and men filed out. One man got half-way up a companionway when the CSM called him back, against the flow of traffic: 'Did you fill in your ADAT (Army Dependants' Association Trust)?' he cried. 'Yes, Sir!' 'Good. Now you see the bloody point of it. Go on, get a move on, you're holding everyone up.' It was a brilliant move that relieved the tension.

I went up on deck to see what we were evacuating men to. The sight was incredible: there seemed to be helicopters everywhere, picking men out of the sea, blowing life rafts away from the blazing ship, and lifting casualties from the deck. Those trained as medics and even those with the barest knowledge of first aid were tending the wounded. Some were just comforting others.

There was no panic; just men making sure that their friends were all right. Thank heavens we had spent time teaching people how to use field dressings and morphine, which were carried by all.

I saw Lance-Corporal Loveridge being very brave. His Platoon Commander was down at the stern of the ship, where most of the casualties were, and was very badly burned, his face and hands particularly. Loveridge made it his business to make sure that this young man got out safely. He carried him out. Loveridge could have just joined the queue, but he didn't. Once he had got this fellow on deck, he rushed around looking after other people, darting back to the Platoon Commander, organizing other young men, doing things way in excess of his rank or experience. There is nothing that the Army can give a man to make him behave like that; the guy has either got it or he hasn't. Loveridge had a sense of duty and loyalty, an idea of what is best in life and what had to be done under the circumstances; the best of human nature suddenly took over. There are some people who are able to be utterly expressive at the moment it counts; this boy Loveridge is one.

It is almost unfair to single out CSM Neck and Corporal Loveridge. They were all astonishing: how loyal they were, how good they were, how professional they were, how brave they were. Some of the things people saw were really unbelievable. Under normal circumstances on an exercise you can get good casualty make-up, but these injuries were for real and were absolutely disgusting. You would have thought that it might have turned people right off. Not at all. It turned people right on, to the extent that everybody dived in to see what they could do. It is no easy job at all to carry a burnt man because every move for him is agony.

The full price paid was only learnt later, when we reached land. Burns casualties queued, hands in the air, to be doused in cold, fresh water and then evacuated, and stretcher after stretcher was loaded into a never-ending stream of helicopters by the men of 16 Field Ambulance, who had been taken off the *Galahad* shortly before the strike. 2 Para were there, on the shore, and they helped and looked after us. We couldn't have landed in a better lap. I shouted for my CSM to gather the company together so we could assess the damage, but he had dislocated his shoulder on going down the scramble net and had himself been evacuated! So the senior sergeant took over and called the roll and everyone sprang to attention and answered 'Sir' exactly as they'd done in barracks; it brought order out of chaos.

We had lost two killed and twenty-one wounded. The final total for the Welsh Guards was thirty-nine killed and seventy-nine wounded. It took three and a half days to arrive at the final count. The casualty evacuation was not pre-planned and casualties were taken to some seven different agencies, on land and sea, for treatment. Tracing them was a real problem, and those three days were filled with such mixed emotions – loss, grief, and anger were all there. The horrors had been appalling, and the sights, the sounds and the smells will live with me for ever.

We carried on after the *Galahad*, taking over defensive tasks at San Carlos, with the minimum of equipment. We had a rifle and one magazine each, three blankets between two, twenty-two mess tins and sixteen spoons between eighty-eight men. We felt at times like Second World War refugees. We remained at San Carlos until the battle was won and on 17 June joined the rest of the battalion for the move to Port Stanley to start the clearing-up operation. Having lost more men than any other regiment we then suffered another tragedy at Port Stanley airfield. Some of our soldiers were terribly injured whilst on fatigues in an accident involving a Sidewinder missile.

As for the *Galahad*, they towed her out about twelve miles and sank her: it's now an official war grave. We weren't allowed to go and see the sinking. The Padre conducted the service. He was the only Welsh Guard witness, which I think was probably right and proper. The Welsh have a peculiar trait: given the opportunity they will wallow in grief because they are a very, very emotional people. We'd said our bit, had our church service at Fitzroy and built a memorial on the shore where it all happened. We decided life was for living, not for looking back. It would have been a harrowing event, watching the *Galahad* die.

When we'd cleared up all the mess in Port Stanley a North Sea ferry took us up to Ascension Island, and on 29 July we flew back to Brize Norton. I was to lead my company out, and when I got to the top of the steps of the VC10, all I could see was a mass of people waiting to welcome us. At the foot of the steps the Prince of Wales headed a group that included the Chief of the General Staff, the Commander-in-Chief of the United Kingdom Land Forces, and senior officers from the Royal Navy and Royal Air Force. It took about ten minutes before I got to meet my wife, who was the only person in the world I wanted to see. Six thousand people turned up. An entire village, all 287 of them, had hired a fleet of coaches to greet one boy. When we got to Pirbright every man from the Guards depot turned out and lined the route to the barracks, all presenting arms, and the whole place was bedecked with flags and bunting. It was a remarkable homecoming.

I think that now it's all over there will always be slight disappointment that the Falklands didn't go better for the Welsh Guards. By that I mean how much better it would have been to have taken casualties in some glorious action capturing an enemy position rather than being blown off a ship. But if you go and fight a war, people are going to get hurt, get killed, get bombed, get maimed, because that's war and war is hell.

Captain Hilarian Roberts

Welsh Guards

After the disappointment of not being put off at Bluff
Cove with the rest of the battalion we sailed back for San
Carlos on the *Fearless*. There, the fleet went on Air Raid
Red Alert. We were sitting in the wardroom which is right
up on top of the boat. Everything around us was very
efficient and everyone immediately went to action stations,
rushing round with their white hoods and gloves. We were
just sitting in there. So I asked one of their crew, 'What do
you want us to do?' and he said, 'There's absolutely
nothing you can do. You can't even go downstairs to the
men because all the doors are automatically locked and
you'd be no use anyway. If you hear "Get down, get
down", lie on the floor, because then we are being
attacked.'

We listened to an amazing commentary on a sort of
tannoy. The chap was saying, 'We've just picked up two
dago aeroplanes – they're closing in – thirty-eight miles.'
They then fired two missiles at the planes. The first one
went berserk and just exploded, but one of them hit – a
'confirmed hit' at thirty-eight miles! The other plane
high-tailed it back. This gave us a staggering sense of
security, and a sense of invulnerability because they had
on hand weapons that could actually knock out planes at
that distance.

Fearless was not going to risk a second journey and so
they sent us on the *Galahad*, which is a bit like a ferry with
a tank deck. We'd been told it would be a slow, bumpy
ride but we were going to get round there. She was
supposed to have all the sort of amenities which they

136

didn't have on the *Fearless*. On *Fearless*, apart from the officers and the sergeants who were taken up to the wardrooms, people were just dumped in the bellies of the ship as there was nowhere else for them to go. We were told that on the *Galahad* there were going to be some rooms for us all. But she had been hit some time before. The ship was pretty well out of action on the lefthand side and so again everybody was just basically in the tank deck. However, there was a sort of recreation room half-way up the stairs, where the Guardsmen could eat, and there was an internal television system with endless films, and this staggering Chinese crew. I just couldn't believe it; I had no idea there were Chinese crew down in the Falklands. The *Galahad* didn't have any guns or anything like that, she was just a baggage ship.

We loaded up and got on board and ended up with an amazing sort of motley collection. There was one group who came onto this thing thinking we were going up to Teal Inlet to unload them, and a medical team came who were furious as they'd only had a few hours to sort their equipment out. Anyway, eventually we all got on board and I spoke to Charles Bremner. I said to him, 'What's the form? What are we actually doing?' He said, 'I don't know what we're doing at the moment, but don't worry, we're not getting off the boat again until we're at the right place.' Which, in retrospect, was rather a sad remark.

We had a perfectly peaceful night but with the extraordinary timescale you still woke up at about 6 or 7 a.m. but it wasn't daylight until 11. So we had about four hours of everybody being up in darkness, all making sure their weapons were properly cleaned and that sort of thing. We were all ready to get off the bloody thing. At dawn some of us went up on deck and there was a really superb view up over the hills to Mount Kent. They looked to me a bit like the isles off Scotland.

The first thing they started moving was the Rapier off the deck. It turned out that that was the protection for the Brigade area. So we were bringing in our own defences on our own boat, which was completely back to front.

We'd been taken to Fitzroy and not Bluff Cove and so we were told by the company commanders to stay put and wait until they could lay on a landing craft. The only means of getting off was one wretched boat which, of course, first took people like the medical troops who were considered top priority and wanted to be at Fitzroy anyway.

I think part of that particular problem was that Brigade Headquarters had heard that the Welsh Guards had gone round on the night of the 6th in *Fearless* and so they had put a little flag on their map to indicate the Welsh Guards had landed and were up at Bluff Cove. What they didn't note was that over half of our battalion was still at sea, and by that stage we had taken on a low, low priority. But to be perfectly honest, I had no real fear that we were completely vulnerable, partly because it had never entered my head that there wasn't some form of defence on the ground to protect the boats at Fitzroy and partly because we'd got from the night before this incredible reassurance that we'd got missiles that could knock planes out at any distance.

We were given a time for the disembarkation, which was delayed as the rear ramp jammed and everything went wrong. All the kit had then to be taken out through the hatches. So I walked down to explain to my Platoon Sergeant that without any doubt our company wouldn't get off until dark, at about eight o'clock at least. I talked to a few people and watched how my platoon was helping get all the heavy kit ready for unloading. After that I turned to make my way towards the bottom of the flight of stairs to go back up to the wardroom.

It's an extraordinary thing but there was just an instant of complete unease, which is a bit uncanny really, because everything was still going on as before. Then my Platoon Sergeant, Roberts 32, just shouted, 'Get down, get down!' I hadn't heard any planes or anything like that, but I went straight to the ground. There was this rather dull, all-embracing crack, a terrifically enveloping thud, and a huge flame ahead where all these people had been sitting.

It just billowed straight over me and I experienced an extraordinary slow-motion feeling of being burnt and watched my hands become the colour of those rather sickly white-grey washing-up gloves. Under the intense heat my hands enlarged and the skin peeled off like talons of wax. It was amazing, it couldn't have taken long, it must have been so quick, but I saw it like a slow-motion film. Then I found my hair on fire and with these useless hands I was trying to put my hair out!

All sorts of extraordinary things were happening so quickly and I felt complete resignation. I thought, 'Well, that's it, it's finished, it's all over.' I was just enveloped in smoke and the smell of burnt flesh, but there was no sort of anger, just the feeling that it's over, finished. Then I suppose some sort of instinct to survive took over because suddenly I thought, 'I'm not dead and I'm damn well not going to die now.' By now the blast had gone over and there was black smoke beginning to billow up terrifically at our end. It was, of course, a dead end. Well, there were one or two people in the smoke and the flames, but there was no way you could get to them. I saw a man burning in the most extraordinary way – he was like a human torch.

I'd be dead if I hadn't been flat on the ground. The blast went right over the top of me; otherwise I would still be down there. The blast could have thrown anything at you. In fact, I was completely and utterly covered in feathers from an exploding sleeping bag. If it had been anything heavy I would have gone. The combat trousers saved my legs because they don't burn much; if I'd been wearing plastic or lightweight trousers, I would have burnt. Fortunately, I just sort of had burn holes from things that had fallen on me; they had gone through to the skin and I remember the extraordinary sight of just a frizz of wool – the rest of my jumper had vanished.

I got up and could see very little, really. I knew there was one way out, the one upstairs way, and I moved towards it, thinking, 'What can I do?' I couldn't touch anything. My hands, my God they hurt, they really hurt. I felt, 'What on earth can I do?' because this was where you, as an officer, had to do something. I heard CQMS Morgan shouting, 'Keep calm, one at a time, keep calm,' in complete darkness. It was strange but tremendously reassuring. So I just repeated what he was saying, over and over again.

All the while and in front of me they were putting out people still on fire; there must have been about ten or fifteen of them. For us in the smoke, in that bottleneck, the only way out was up the stairs and there was that awful feeling that if they didn't keep completely calm, someone would stumble or get caught and there would be chaos. A lot of people were in my state, rather shocked and hands sort of dripping and faces beginning to blacken all over. By now the skin of my hands had just vanished and was lying in terrible grey straggles. We were going up the stairs very slowly and we got stuck in a sort of dead end and had to back out to get up again but no one panicked – they behaved really beautifully, of that there is no question. There was a lot of shouting but it wasn't panic-struck shouting, because if anybody had got really panicky, we just wouldn't have got out at all. Eventually, we did get out. It couldn't have taken very long, a couple of minutes, I think, but it felt a lot longer. We came staggering out onto the deck, and then I suppose the adrenalin, the immediate instinct to get out, began to wear off. My God, you felt as sick as a dog. But there was this marvellous thing as well, seeing people whom you knew you had to encourage – it's such a great advantage to have something to do instead of just sitting there. I didn't see anybody on the deck who performed badly. Everybody got on with it, basically. I think our CQMS did bloody well.

My orderly, Badham, who was unhurt, came rushing up and immediately took off my watch because my hands were swelling terrifically. Where the watch had been it had protected the skin. He took it off and kept it. Months later I got it back from the Padre, who said that about two days after the *Galahad*, when everybody had other things to think about, a Guardsman had come up to him and said, 'Mr Roberts gave me this watch, and there's only one

140

person I can trust and he's the Padre.' He was really an excellent man; he had something, he knew his job, he knew what to do and looked after me beautifully and stopped people trying to fuss me when all I wanted was to be left alone until I was steady enough to get off the boat. I suppose it's natural for you to think that the person next to you is worse. So whenever they came up with these wretched bandages, you'd say, 'No, no, for God's sake, give it to him, give him the morphine,' which is again a convenient thing to take your mind off your own pain.

The problem then arose of getting off the boat because we had to go down the rope ladder. One of my corporals, Loveridge, went below and my orderly went above and they literally supported me, which was excellent of them, because at any moment I could have lost my grip. They offered to carry me down. I said, 'No, I've got to go down this ladder and I'll grip it.' It was hell, but everything hurt so much that I don't think it made any difference. I thought I'd feel safer clawing my way down. I managed to make the bottom and the two of them lifted me, one above and one below, and they got me into a little dinghy.

Inside the tent-like dinghy it was airless and hot, burning hot to the burns. Then my wounds began to get very painful indeed. It was going in sort of waves. I suppose it's basic shock, there were waves of feeling pain and then complete numb cold, nothing; and it took an eternity to get to shore. We had great difficulty getting away from the ship; we bounced along, explosions and things coming through the portholes! It was getting very dodgy, we were being blown straight into the smoke and mess and I just thought, 'Oh, come on, we've had enough now. If we go in there that's it.' I began to get very miserable, very low, but two of the boys kept on turning round, even in this tight little dinghy, and making that marvellous gesture, you know, thumbs up, 'All right, Sir?'

Everybody did really well and we eventually got helped out by one of the brave helicopters who drove us away from the smoke. The draught from the blades also gave blessed relief. We struggled up to the shore, and almost

141

immediately got the next attack. Someone said, 'Air raid, air raid,' or something like that. I think people were panicking. I don't know exactly what happened but I remember being thrown onto the ground and just saying to myself, 'Look, leave us alone, honestly, we've had enough.' Then when the panic was over, they got me into a helicopter and took me to Fitzroy where they eventually gave me morphine.

I'd seen about two of my men up till then and they finally came in dribs and drabs with terribly blackened faces and bright red eyes, limping about. The greatest pleasure of all was seeing Roberts 32, burnt black like a sweep but alive. They all got ashore except two who'd been killed immediately. I think most of the people who were killed must have died in the first blast. With all the pain, the desire to burst into tears was enormous; it was all so sad. Charles Bremner was very badly shaken by the whole thing. The first thing he said to me at Fitzroy, before I was taken on to Ajax Bay, was, 'I'm sorry, I'm just terribly sorry.' He felt it all very deeply.

After Ajax Bay and *Fearless* we were flown to *Uganda* and into the hands of the Red Cross. It was on the hospital ship, *Hydra*, that we heard the World Service News of white flags over Stanley. With my hands in Flamozine bags I couldn't hold anything but I toasted victory with a pint of lime juice through a straw.

They flew us back to England. There weren't thousands to greet us, not even parents, and no one took photographs – they weren't allowed to unless we wished, but there was no press at all. At Woolwich Hospital I kept on asking what had happened and who else was hurt. I spoke to an officer from London District, who told me of the Scots Guards casualties from Tumbledown. He said that Robert Lawrence was seriously ill. He'd been shot in the head. I thought, 'This makes me look a bit pathetic.' Then, to my absolute amazement, I saw him in the hospital, admittedly in a wheelchair, but he turned round and recognized me, and I thought, 'Bloody hell!' He'd had such awful injuries yet there he was, cheerful and able to remember me.

The other man that impressed me at Woolwich was Grimshaw. Everyone must have seen the TV film of us being brought off the *Galahad* and seen where he'd had his leg taken off – it's in everyone's memory. He'd been fitted with a leg and he came in walking. I just could not believe it. I mean, if men like him and Robert are going to recover, what are we moaning about? What they both had were guts and humour – humour plays such a great part in recovery.

I remember when I was lying ill in hospital I was told that as long as someone took me I could go with my family to Italy and also that it would be very good for me. I was very anxious because I still had a very red face. Fortunately, it wasn't scarred but I certainly had rather gungy hands, which I had to keep covered while abroad. So this absurd sight arrives at Gatwick with large gloves and a great big hat to keep the heat off my face. Going through the check-in my hands were really irritating. I got these terrible twinges where I just couldn't make the bloody things move at all, so I couldn't handle anything. My sister, who was flying out with me, handed in the tickets and this woman handed them back to me and said something like, 'Oh dear, what have you done to your hands?' I said, 'It wasn't me, it was an Argentinian!' She said, 'Oh, go on, what happened? Did you spill paint on them or scald them or something?' So I said, 'No, it was an Argentinian bomber.' And she said, 'Oh dear, I'm sorry. Well done!' She was very sweet – you know, 'Go on, tell us another.' I could only smile – you see, I was still relieved to be alive, and it hasn't worn off yet.

I'm very proud of how we performed on the *Galahad* and I think it's sad that people don't talk about it, as that implies something is wrong, which it isn't. You see, although we were not injured in battle, we were injured in war, because the *Galahad* was part of the war – and these things happen in war. So the scars of the Welsh Guards are honourable scars, the scars of war, and like my chicken-skin hands they will be with us for ever.

Sergeant Peter Naya

Royal Army Medical Corps

Military Medal

On 8 June 1982, whilst at anchor in Fitzroy Sound, East Falkland, RFA Sir Galahad *was bombed and set on fire by enemy aircraft. Embarked troops included two companies of infantry and the main body of 16 Field Ambulance, men and equipment. At the time of the attack, most of the troops were positioned in the tank deck where substantial quantities of ammunition soon began to explode as the fire worked through the ship.*

Sergeant Naya Royal Army Medical Corps was standing in the tank deck when he was thrown against a bulkhead by an explosion and partially stunned. The lights went out and the tank deck began to fill with dense black smoke. A second explosion set his large pack alight and scorched the back of his head. Shrugging off the burning material he managed to lead a soldier up two flights of stairs to daylight on the upper deck. He then helped to carry a man who had lost a leg up to the forecastle, having first administered first aid. He treated many more casualties, including another amputee, and set up several infusions until, with all the casualties evacuated, he left the ship on the last helicopter, later to be evacuated from Fitzroy as a casualty himself. After only three days he returned to duty in the Advance Surgical Centre of the field ambulance where he worked steadfastly through the most intense period of military activity and the passage of many battle casualties.

Sergeant Naya, being a casualty himself, was well aware of the dangers he faced by remaining in the stricken vessel and yet, with no thought for his own safety, devoted himself to the care of his injured comrades until such care was no longer required.

Sergeant Naya's conduct throughout showed immense personal courage. He acted in the highest tradition of the Royal Army Medical Corps.

The first inkling I had of us being attacked was this loud roaring, whooshing noise and I looked up just in time to see an aircraft zooming past; it was flying so low you could tell it was going to rocket or shell us. I instantly registered the colour was wrong. It was a dingy, browny, chocolate colour. I shouted 'It's not ours' and simultaneously someone else shouted 'Hit the deck', then bang, it struck and all hell broke loose!

This massive orange fireball started the devastation. It burnt blokes, it killed blokes, everywhere there was the screaming of men in agony, pain, shock, fear, panic – it had all happened in seconds. I was very bewildered and struggling around totally dazed. It was pitch black and I could feel this intense heat burning the back of my head – then I realized my backpack was on fire, so I pulled it off and beat out the flames. Everywhere around me was in chaos. My first thought was that we'd been wiped out. I couldn't see a thing; all I could smell was the burning metal and flesh and this acrid smoke. It was stifling and the heat was scorching my lungs – all I wanted to do was get out from the tank deck. I knew there was a hatch behind me so I made a beeline for that. Needless to say, there must have been about 100 other people with the same idea, some of whom were in a terrible mess.

I managed to haul myself and pull others and push others up two flights of stairs towards daylight. On the way up to the top deck I grabbed hold of this injured Guardsman – he was in agony but I knew I had to get him up on deck. He kept screaming, 'Mind my leg, mind my leg,' but he'd lost his leg – it was a phantom pain. I tried to pull him up the stairs by his belt but he was too heavy for me and we both fell backwards but I somehow struggled up those stairs with him. How I got him out of there I don't know, it must have been pure adrenalin. I'd got my arm round this poor sod and took him to the bow of the

145

ship to evade the smoke. All the time I was carrying him his bone was hitting the deck and leaving a trail of blood.

It was chaos everywhere on deck. Smoke and flames were billowing up from below, ammunition was going off, and there were blokes running around screaming because their plastic all-weather gear had caught fire and was sticking to them, burning their skin away – it was pitiful to watch them trying to tear it off. That was an awful sight – such pain, such terrible pain. I'd never seen anything like it, they were just rolling about on the decks.

This was the fastest my mind had ever worked; I was trying to decipher what was going on and to sort out priorities. I wanted to find the others, my mates, but I couldn't. It felt as if I had been caught up in a big machine that was going round and round. Helicopters were suddenly appearing and men were jumping off the ship onto lifeboats, into the flaming seas; and some were being winched off by helicopter. People were shouting orders, and all the time there were explosions after explosions and flames everywhere.

I didn't have time to think. If they'd attacked us again I wouldn't have known it because there was so much smoke and confusion – it was horrendous. I couldn't see any doctors working (I found out later they'd been taken off before the bomb struck) and I couldn't see any medics working; I thought I was probably the last medic alive. So I thought, 'Come on, Pierre, you're the only medic, get to it.' So I got stuck in with what medical kit I had – a pair of scissors! The rest had been blown to pieces, wiped out.

So I got on my knees and started to cut away at some of the badly burnt clothes to expose the wounds. I became a focus for people – they knew at least someone was there to help. The NCOs were marvellous, keeping everyone calm and bringing the injured men up to me and talking to them while they waited. I began smashing up crates of wood to make splints because there was nothing else. The Welsh Guards who'd survived came by and dropped their field dressings for me; others gave me their intravenous drips or held someone while I got at his injuries. Everyone rallied

146

round – they'd got over the initial shock and were doing all they could to help me.

I didn't have time to look up, I couldn't answer anyone, I'd just say to one of them, 'You grab that, just hold it there and I'll start putting up a drip.' I managed to get a few drips into the very worst, those who'd had legs and ankles blown off. I'd never seen injuries like these – I'd never seen action in all the twenty years I'd been in the Army!

I don't know how I kept a sober head on me at the time. All I remember was fixing guys, trying to put a figure-of-eight bandage round some poor bugger's legs that were smashed, then kicking a pallet to pieces trying to get splints from it – it was all so primitive. I was putting the field dressings over this fellow's stumps, I then grabbed someone's webbing straps to use as a tourniquet on what was left of his leg and used a guy's bayonet to tighten it. Then I looked up at the poor devil and saw his face was swollen to twice its size, like a pumpkin, and was completely black with the flash burn. All the time Warrant Officer Mike McHale, the other medic and RSM, was organizing everything – I was glad he'd survived. He was getting the casualties off the ship; he'd come alongside and say, 'Which one, Pierre, which one?' I'd point them out in order of priority. Then I'd be back on the next. It was decisions, decisions: could I leave him, should I go on to save one who was dying? How much time have I got? Will this bloody ship blow up? Who's next for the chopper? All this was rushing through my mind. I just carried on, totally absorbed, for what seemed an eternity.

A three-ringer Naval officer came up and said, 'Can I help?' So I said, 'Yes, Sir, that one there, shunt him off quick.' The lad had lost a leg and had the other broken, as well as one of his arms. I stuck in a drip but of course we couldn't strap him in a harness as there was this stump. So this Naval officer suggested we used a pallet. We laid the lad out and tried to hook the harness round with rope, but as the chopper pulled it up he rolled off in agony. So we called for the harness again and somehow wrapped it round him and got him up there. He was the last of the severe casualties, so then I started on the burns victims.

All I could do was start cutting the plastic clothing, because it had impregnated their skin and was still smouldering. Where the lads had grabbed hold of red-hot handrailings they had 'de-gloved' the palms of their hands and their skin had bunched up all their fingers, so I had to cut down between the webs to separate the fingers – all this without morphine. Some of the lads were still burning because they couldn't use their hands – there was no water on the ship. If I could have peed on them, I would have; they just needed to be put out, to be cooled down. All that bloody sea and we didn't have any water. It was the exposed areas of the body which really suffered – the face, the neck, the ears, the hair, the hands, whatever was exposed at the time of the flash got scorched. Many of those lads will carry the scars all their life. Some were completely burnt from the neck up, no hair, no eyebrows, all black and swollen. I wouldn't recognize them now.

While I was waiting to get the last of the burns cases off, I could see one particular lad who was in pain. There wasn't a thing I could do for him except loosen his collar where the plastic had burnt into his neck. He was holding his fingers apart where I'd just cut them and he was standing there bewildered and exhausted. I had a packet of cigarettes so I lit one and put it in his mouth and the pleasure of his grin was wonderful – he just stood there holding his blackened and bleeding hands in the air, puffing merrily away.

Later I met blokes who, the moment they hit the beach, started smoking for the first time in their lives – it was the heat of the moment! The adrenalin was flowing something shocking. It was like being very high, but it wasn't a good high, it was a fearful thing – I'd never seen such horror in all my life.

Slowly we got them all off. Those chopper pilots performed miracles. They were unbelievably brave – time and time again they came back.

I realized I'd been on my knees for probably over an

hour, tending the wounded, with the heat of the deck burning into my own skin. But we'd done it, we'd got everyone off. Then I thought, 'Okay, you can get off now,' but all the lifeboats had gone. Then for the first time I looked over the side of the ship to see where we were – I'd never done this, we'd been down in the tank deck when it had happened, so I never did see the land. Now I could see it and it looked a long swim. I stood on the side of that ship on this beautifully clear day and realized that I'd survived and now, after all that, I was probably going to drown in the icy water. I knew the survival time in the water was about five minutes. I knew I'd had it. Then there were more explosions, bullets started whizzing about – and I'd lost my helmet in the initial blast. I thought, 'I can't just stand here. I've got to get off or I'll get it in the head,' so I started to take my boots off. Suddenly a Naval officer came out of the smoke and shouted, 'A chopper's coming.' I was almost the last man off that ship but I have never been more grateful to a pilot in my life – I was so grateful I put the sign of the cross on his visor. He just smiled – he was so young – but they saved our lives that day, they saved over 300 lives. As we veered away from the ship I began to tremble and shake like a leaf. I'd survived, I'd got my hands, my legs, and I was in one piece.

Out of our advance party we'd lost our major, a lance-corporal and a private. When I got ashore, the first voice I could just about make out was our RSM. He was shouting at me but I hadn't realized that I'd gone deaf. I was so pleased to see him and the rest of my mates that I gave them a hug and a kiss. As we were taken to some huts I saw all the doctors busy working. I was delighted, because I thought they'd all been wiped out. I immediately set about helping to tend the wounded, putting up drips and getting the lads ready for casevacing.

The first person I spoke to was my CO. I said, 'I'm sorry, Sir, I've lost my pistol on the *Galahad*. There is the magazine.' I felt really guilty that I had lost it.

Later the RSM gathered all 16 Field Ambulance and some other medics and did a head count to see who was alive, who was dead, who was missing and who'd been casevac'd, and it was then that I realized I was really stone deaf. This officer came up and he was saying something like, 'Thank you for the good job you did on the ship for the men.' I can lip-read a little bit, because some of my wife's relatives are a little hard of hearing, and I'm used to talking to some of their friends who are deaf and often when you mix and talk to deaf people you tend to lip-read like them. The next thing I knew, the RSM had detailed two lads to look after me, 'just in case we have an air raid'.

The RSM via the Estate Manager at Fitzroy had discovered there was a house empty and they would allow us, as survivors, to use it. When we got there everybody said, 'Keep the house clean. Don't smoke. If you're going to smoke put your ash in the trays. Take your boots off, don't put them on the floor. When you leave, clean up behind you.' It was like coming from hell to suburbia! So we all huddled on the floor on the carpet and just slid down and slept there, almost upright, half crouching, half sitting. I had my head under the sideboard for a bit of protection in case somebody came over at night.

It was a fitful sleep because all my thoughts were racing. What had happened? What had gone wrong? Did I do enough? How were my mates? Because even then there were some of my friends I hadn't seen. I didn't see my Warrant Officer, Mr Viner, for ages after I got on to the shore. With all this turmoil that had been going on, the feeling was incredible, first of all of being alive, and second, how fortunate that I was, and third, what a blooming disaster it had been. And, of course, I thought of my wife and four children. I thought of how I could contact her, because this news was bound to break some way. It had to get back some time and she'd hear it through the grapevine. I had nothing to write on, no paper, so eventually when I did write a letter it got to her about three weeks after this incident! It was only when I got to Stanley, when things were quieter, that I could sneak off to the Cable and Wireless place and send her a telegram. Just a few words, 'I'm safe and well – Love, Pete.' It cost me every penny I had, but it was worth it.

I was woken by someone saying, 'You're going back. A helicopter's coming to take you away. Leave your boots for the lads who are left behind as survivors, they've got no boots.' So I took off my boots and left them. They took us to this helicopter in just what we stood up in. The next thing I knew, we were back on a ship, I presume near Ajax Bay, which we'd sailed out of thirty-six hours ago. It was very dark as it was night-time, and darkened ship routine was in force. It was almost as though it hadn't happened: you'd gone and thirty-six hours later you were back. But you were back as a different person.

While we were on there, they had a Red Alert. So we were all bundled below decks into a bunk area. Of course the hatch was closed down again on top of us and I thought, 'Oh God, not again.' But nothing happened. Then I went to see the ship's doctor who told me that my hearing would come back and that it was nature's way of shutting down without damaging the ears. He then asked me if I wanted to do something – so he set me to work in the sick bay where there were three badly burnt patients from the *Galahad*. I think one of them was the cook, his face was twice its normal size. I ended up trying to look after these three lads in order to give the ship's medic a break. It took my mind off things until we were lifted back to Ajax Bay, where at least we were able to relax for a day. The Paras and Marines knew what had happened and they were very good and made us hot meals!

After resupply we were then flown to Fitzroy again. When we got there some of us were accommodated in a house occupied by a very kind family who already had an assortment of troops lodging there. One evening the lady of the house produced some rice pudding and from somewhere bottles of whisky appeared. Then – what a joy – she gave us a guitar which I enjoy playing and we had a sing-song. I ended up being spoon-fed rice pudding by an artillery major, who kept saying, 'Play it again, Sam.' He really got drunk that night. He was trying to get death out of his system as well; I could understand how he felt.

We all had a job to do and I would have felt guilty if I

hadn't done it. I could certainly have gone off the *Galahad* straight away, but I didn't – it never crossed my mind. I don't know, perhaps it was my upbringing, my family life; to me those men were my family. There were all my mates, my comrades – they were looking to me as a medic. I just did it without thinking about it. Those lads were hurting, hurting bad. I just had to do something. I felt great afterwards, I felt I had achieved something, contributed some small part in this horrific mess. I felt satisfied, felt proud, but also sad.

Later I stood for hours on the cliff and looked at the *Galahad*. The tears were just rolling down my face. I couldn't believe that this was the ship that had brought us so far, and there it was, burning in the water. It was just an eerie red glow in the dusk. It burnt for days. I stood on the shoreline just looking at it. It was pitiful. The whole bridge caved in and there was just the occasional bang, and a bout of smoke, then it would go all quiet. About half the back end of the ship had patches of rust and brown, the top was black and charred, but where the paint had freshly peeled it was shining in the fading light. We all expected it to go with one almighty explosion and collapse in half and sink, but somehow, for some reason, it never did.

I have overriding impressions of the war. First is pain, there was a lot of pain. No matter where you went, there was pain. Because that's what I came into contact with, not so much fear, but pain. Pain and death. The ones who were coming back to us were the ones who were alive. The dead weren't coming back to us – and that is another kind of pain.

The second thing that really hit me was the desolation of the Falklands. There was nothing there. It was a Godforsaken place. It was empty, cold, naked and without a single tree. It was almost as if there was no life. You wondered what you were doing there. As for the thousands of sheep, I didn't see any, apart from two or three running on a hillside. The people kept within their houses; you saw two or three locals, that's all. There really was nothing there – it was desolate, cold and bleak, a very inhospitable place.

The final impression would be humility. It has to be. I was awed by what happened. I was absolutely gripped by the throat. The humility of it all, how pitiful a person can be in a situation amongst such horror, such terror against all those incredibly powerful weapons. You just feel so insignificant.

I went through an experience that I'll never, ever forget, which has brought me closer to God, because it certainly was Him that carried me through. I used to say my prayers every night I was out there, even in the trenches and sangars. I used to pray I wouldn't get injured or killed. I didn't want to come home in a bag.

I feel humble, and lucky, that I survived. But it still comes back, it plays on your mind, especially at night. You see, the experience was so traumatic that it hurt to talk about it, so I just clammed up – I couldn't talk about it to anyone. A thousand emotions still rage through me when I think of it. Of course we put on a brave face – we can't collapse in a heap. I hope over the years it will fade. People ask, 'Why did you get a medal?' But how can you give them an answer in one sentence? You can't – it was all too real.

The one thing I'm trying to do is shed the *Galahad* but sometimes it catches me when I'm unware, and images flash back. So I bottle it up. I'm not alone, many of us have done that. We can't really tell our wives what we went through. There are certain things I will never tell. But there are also experiences that I shared that, unless you were there, would probably seem sentimental and incomprehensible to an outsider: sharing the same plate, the same fork, the same sleeping bag, the last fag, surviving, making a joke out of the misery – lads with black, burnt faces and you'd say, 'Cor, you look rough, what hole have you come from?' – anything, anything to break the tension and ease the pain. They were brave men.

Sometimes we got the impression from the media that we were losing and that gripped us. We thought, 'If we lose here, we've had it. We must not lose.' It gave us more incentive to go on. You just worked, no matter what you were doing, whether you were the cook, or digging a sandbank, you did it with zeal, you got stuck in. I shudder to think what would have happened if we'd lost. I don't know what would have happened. I really don't. We couldn't get off and there was no way they could take all of us off. I can't imagine being marshalled into Buenos Aires as a British prisoner.

When people talk of heroism I think of the Paras and the Marines and the other people who had to fight the enemy, tooth and nail and eye to eye. It takes real guts to do that, it really does. As far as I'm concerned, heroism is a bit like madness. You have to be mad to face an enemy like they did. You have to be completely detached from the situation as it presents itself at the time. You have to jump in with both feet but be completely switched off. You know it's a deliberate act, and you know you might get killed. But you do it. You're either very brave or mad – there is no logic. I certainly don't consider myself a hero. I just did my job.

Lieutenant John Boughton

Royal Navy

Queen's Gallantry Medal

On 8 June 1982, RFA Sir Galahad and RFA Sir Tristram, carrying large numbers of troops, were attacked by aircraft of the Argentine air force. RFA Sir Galahad was left damaged and burning with a considerable number of casualties. Aircraft of 825 Naval Air Squadron were on the scene within minutes and were joined for a time by a Sea King IV and Wessex V.

The helicopters, captained by Lieutenant Boughton and Lieutenant Sheldon, conducted pick-ups of troops and crew mustered in the extremely confined area of the LSL foredeck. Many were injured or in shock. The rescues were conducted close to masts and rigging, with little clearance for the aircraft, and with no regard to personal safety. Ammunition and pyrotechnics were exploding and there was a threat of a further attack by enemy aircraft. Evacuation and rescue continued until darkness and were, in fact, interrupted by a further air attack.

The professionalism and bravery demonstrated in these operations by Lieutenant Boughton and Lieutenant Sheldon are representative of the crews and their squadron.

I always wanted to fly – my father had been in the Navy and his uniform and flying log book were in a trunk at home which I used to look through.

The Falklands blew up on the day we were finishing for Easter break and everyone had gone except the instructors. On 1 May 1982 I got married which was as planned, and about 9:30 that night there was a phone call from Culdrose telling me to return tomorrow. I wasn't surprised; everyone was very much aware that the possibility was there. They were running out of helicopters down south and basically decided they needed another Commando Squadron, so they looked at their resources and chose the Sea Kings because of their lifting capacity.

We went back on the Sunday to Cornwall and waited at home for the phone call and on the Monday afternoon I got a message that they were forming a squadron that afternoon. It turned out that they'd taken all the pilots they needed, nine pilots from the training squad, and had decided who could go. Bearing in mind my family commitments, they thought I should be left out. I was left out! I was desperately disappointed, but Sally said I ought to volunteer, which I did – I really wanted to go. A phone call came on the Wednesday to ask me to help with some night flying, they were a man short; and then they told me to pitch up the next day as well. I was in! I was over the moon.

We left a few days later after re-equipping the planes, changing their colours and weapons. Some of us were on the *Atlantic Causeway*, but two crews and my boss were on the *QE2*. I was with Phil Sheldon on *Causeway* to begin with, but then he went onto the *QE2*. On the way down we had lectures from two Commando pilots on the *Causeway*, to teach us all the basic skills that we didn't already know.

At first we went into San Carlos Water and were told to assist in unloading ships. We each had our own aircraft: eight guys, myself, a second pilot, an experienced crewman and five maintainers. We arrived at the end of the day through a snowstorm and landed right next to the Marine HQ which was at the San Carlos settlement. We shut the aircraft down and were promptly told to shift them because we'd landed on one of the landing sites that was going to be used at night! We moved the aircraft, got our tents up, and a sergeant in charge of the perimeter fence told us to keep our heads down because there were possible snipers in the area. We were outside the perimeter fence so if the Argentinian patrols came down, we were in their path, which of course made our day! My first night in the Falklands was spent sharing sentry duty with my team. We each had our own weapons which we had spent two weeks solidly re-learning how to use on the *Causeway* on the way down.

In the morning we received some tasking but that was only to move POWs from San Carlos. They stank after being out in the fields, soaking wet and just generally unclean. That really surprised us, actually; we all talked about it that evening. The smell was quite unbelievable.

There was tremendous friendly rivalry between the Commando helicopter squadrons and our own anti-submarine warfare squadron. As soon as the Commandos knew that some of the 'pingers', as they call us (because of the noise of the sonar), were coming ashore, we felt they were all looking for one of us to make a mistake. We were very conscious of that, especially as we were operating in an unfamiliar environment. We felt, at the time, that the taskers basically gave us the shitty jobs to see how well we did and, luckily, because we were all experienced instructors, our aircraft flying and general skills in the Sea King were possibly better than some of the 'junglies' because they were fairly new to the aircraft.

We'd come to understand the Sea King – it's a challenge.

Unlike the Gazelle, which is like a racing machine, the Sea King is stable, solid and more like an aeroplane than a light aircraft. You need to spend a lot of time understanding it – it won't be hurried. Our appreciation of landing sites and map work wasn't up to speed, however; some of it was totally new and navigation over the sea is a very different skill. When you're talking about 30–50 feet altitude at 100 miles an hour, trying to evade rather than go in a straight line, we had to progress very quickly! Also, we weren't equipped in the best way. Our second pilots hadn't completely finished training, so they could end up turning the map round in circles, which was a bit of a problem. Considering their inexperience, they did a good job.

On the third day we started being given different tasks to do, such as moving gun batteries from A to B. We were all very excited, although a bit frustrated as we knew we were getting the less complicated jobs, but we were still very conscious of the fact that we didn't want to make any mistakes. We were able to run our own show, with our maintainers, which included one or two petty officers and three juniors, and the actual *esprit de corps* was very strong when the rest of the squadron appeared. They'd been shifting the Guards and Gurkhas from the *QE2* to the *Canberra* and a couple of other ships. So all of a sudden, from four aircraft of ours, we had ten Sea Kings.

On our first day we were told firmly not to go beyond a certain line. Then we were given the task of moving a whole gun battery ten or twelve miles beyond that line, which I thought was a bit strange! I was the lead aircraft of eight and took a 105 gun, which weighs approximately 3,500 lbs. I also had an Army officer in the back. We set off, having been told to go via certain points. It was an unusual task, so I decided the best idea would be to get my co-pilot to navigate, and put the gun officer in the back. We got up towards Mount Kent, and it was all going very well at this stage. We hadn't seen anybody we didn't want to see. All of a sudden, I looked at my co-pilot to see he was having trouble with the navigation. I thought, 'Oh-oh, here we go!' I had to give him control of the aeroplane while I tried to sort exactly where we were. I found a small valley we had missed and as we got to the top I said, 'It's here.' We slowed down but couldn't see anything at all. We found out later that this was because the troops were hiding in the rocks.

Anyway, the Army chap who was in the back looked at his map, which had a chinagraph circle on it, and kept saying, 'No, no, it's over there! It's over there!' He sounded pretty confident, so I kept moving and all of a sudden, as we got to the rise of the hill, Port Stanley appeared! 'Oh shit,' I thought. We whipped round in a circle, back down the hill. He'd been following on the map but he obviously wasn't used to doing it from the air! Then the third aircraft in the line all of a sudden came on the radio and said, 'Smoke.' We didn't use the radios at all unless there was a problem. They thought, but weren't sure, that we'd been fired on from down the hill, but it turned out that the guys on Mount Kent, as the advance guard, had thrown up the smoke to warn us that we'd overshot. Evidently a patrol of Special Forces were up on the mountains and were watching all this.

So that was my first bad experience and I certainly learned from it. I was almost the first man into Stanley! The moral of the story is never trust an Army chap with a map in a chopper!

It took almost the rest of the afternoon to move the gun battery to Mount Kent, where it stayed for a week; then we got the job of moving it further forward. In doing that, we were shelled for the first time, which was rather frightening. I was flying down the hill with a gun and Phil Sheldon, who was in front of me, had two mortars land either side of him and came screaming back up the valley. We were going down Mount Kent into a valley, then just up a small ridge, but as we came down this hill hoping to disappear out of sight, using the terrain, the Argies were lobbing shells in roughly what they thought was the right area and they weren't far wrong. Phil had two mortars lobbed close to him and came back up the mountain with a high-pitched voice on his radio!

As we arrived to put the gun down, all the gunners had

taken cover in trenches but somebody leapt out of the hole and directed us to the position they wanted. It was certainly exciting. We received a bit of criticism from one or two of the Commando pilots about the way we were handling the aeroplanes. We were flying them to the limit but that was one thing we could do well. By that stage we were very much more up to speed, our navigation was better and we were learning what tasks to turn down. We'd had a very crash course and come through.

We were under a lot of pressure because the constant message coming through was very much to go – go hard. We'd had to be ready by a certain date but at the same time conserve our assets. It was planned, as far as we know, to end on the day it did. We knew that Stanley was being reinforced every day, and we knew that the longer the Argentinians had to think about it, the more likely they were to try a counter-offensive. (Why they didn't do that, God only knows.) There were rumours, on a number of occasions, that there were troops being landed on the north point from San Carlos by Argentinian Hercules and they were going to carry out a counter-attack from San Carlos. In fact, there was a very, very strong rumour about that. There was a feeling that they were being dropped all over the place to come and have a go at us. I think in some ways there would have been more lives lost had we dallied.

Two days before the *Galahad*, we'd taken the first troops up to Bluff Cove. 2 Para had made a phone call to Fitzroy and the residents there said the Argentinians had gone, so it was decided to snatch an advantage. Three Gazelles went in with a few troops, each armed for immediate attack with rockets. They landed at the settlement, found there weren't any Argentinians around and decided to reinforce the area very quickly. The next thing we heard was that the Brigadier jumped into our senior pilot's aircraft and said, 'Get three of your aircraft together. I've got a special job for you.' So three of us were sent to Goose Green to take some troops somewhere. We didn't know what was going on at that stage, all we knew was that we had to take some troops to a grid reference which the senior pilot had and we didn't, so we just followed him. We arrived to find 2 Para completely rigged out and ready to go to battle – completely camouflaged, ammunition wrapped round as far as it would go and all quite psyched up, so we thought, 'What's going on here?' We thought we were just moving personnel. We got them in and then were given the grid reference, which was Bluff Cove. We were most surprised because up till that morning the brief before dawn was, 'No go past Goose Green.' We flew in cloud all the way, flying at twenty feet and very slowly because we couldn't see very well. We dropped 2 Para off on a ridge which was in fact being overlooked by Argentinian look-outs. As soon as they'd all cleared the aircraft, we disappeared off again, and we did that for the rest of the day and the next day.

On 8 June we were sent to move some equipment from the *Galahad* and *Tristram* in the morning, but when we got there the task was being carried out by other aircraft so we were sent back to Goose Green, where we started moving the rest of the Guards forward. I had one of their Land-Rovers under the aircraft and was flying at about fifty feet below one of the ridge lines. It was a beautiful clear day. All of a sudden I saw four Skyhawks flying at very low level, all following each other, so I came up on the radio with a contact report, saying that there were four Skyhawks inbound towards Fitzroy. While I was doing that I descended to put the Land-Rover down. Firstly I went into a quick hide, because I thought there might be some more fighters coming behind. I went into a small gorge, where I hovered for about two minutes, still with this bloody Land-Rover underneath. Eventually, I came out of there and put it down in the middle of a field, next to a fence, so I'd know where to find it later.

As soon as I'd gone into the hide, I'd heard on the HF radio that there was an attack at Fitzroy, so I called Phil, who I thought was about ten miles behind me, and asked him if he'd accepted my radio transmission. He had, and I suggested he joined me as soon as he could, to see what was going on. I got about a mile or two closer and could see the smoke coming out of the *Galahad*. I didn't realize it was a ship at that time, but I got back to Phil and told him to get there as fast as he could.

As my aircraft arrived, there were survivors in dinghies and smoke was pouring out the back of only one ship – the other ship looked intact, I couldn't see any damage on it at all. We went straight onto the fo'c'sle with the hold open and smoke coming out. The blokes in the dinghies looked okay so we went to pick up the soldiers who were still on the ship. As soon as we came within about fifty yards we could see that the men at the front were pretty badly off: some of their clothes were still smouldering, others were jumping up and down to try and keep their circulation going, many had badly burnt hands and a few were just lying on the deck. There seemed to be a few able-bodied men who definitely knew what they were doing medically and they were trying to sort out the soldiers who were injured. There was also the Captain of the *Galahad*, who was excellent. He'd organized people to search the ship as best they could and was controlling everything.

All we did was winch up casualties as they got put onto the rescue strop. Normally we'd sit them down and strap them in as soon as they were in the aircraft, but in this case there wasn't any time so we just got them moving down the bus. I said to my crewman, 'As soon as someone comes in who looks badly injured, we'll take him directly ashore,' because it was only twenty seconds' flying time to a patch of fairly flat grass, which had been used as a landing point for ammunition. We knew about this because we'd taken a number of loads there. As soon as we picked up a badly injured man we went straight to the shore as fast as the aeroplane would go. We'd land them next to anybody we saw and call them in to help carry the casualties out. By that stage 2 Para were already organized and a few stretchers had appeared. They would take the injured out of the aircraft, and that set the pattern. From then on, it was just straight off from the beach back onto the fo'c'sle. Radio-wise, it was very quiet amongst the aeroplanes and the only thing you'd hear was someone saying, 'Next,' which was to tell anyone waiting that they were getting the last bloke in. Everyone had decided individually that as soon as they got a badly injured guy on board they'd go and then call 'Free space up here' or something similar. It was a bit chaotic, but calm.

After the first run, when my aircrewman had his hands full, I sent my second pilot down the back to become another 'dragger-in'. I just flew it on my own up front, which is no problem as long as you don't have an emergency. After we'd made four or five runs ashore, one of the other aircraft discovered they'd opened up a first aid post in the middle of the settlement. From then on, we started taking the casualties there.

By that stage, the fire was very well set in and occasionally there were a few large explosions, which was a bit hairy. We were sitting there in the hover, winching up these poor blokes. Hovering is all an art of watching for changes in your depth of field, or your perspective movement, and as soon as you see a change, you automatically correct to stop it. This is fairly easy if you're sitting over a nice big area where you can see all around you, but all we could see was three or four square feet of deck, because we were right over the fo'c'sle. The door of the Sea King, which is quite a long way back in the aeroplane, was the focal point. The door was over the bows while the cockpit was over the sea, out in front, which made it slightly difficult because I had to crane round to see. But I had a very, very good crewman in Leading Aircrewman Roy Eggleston, a young bloke, but probably one of the best to have there at the time. He kept the whole operation going very well, telling me what was going on, with the occasional 'Ugh' because obviously the sights were pretty gruesome. He was also trying to keep me in the correct position, so very much of the success of the task was due to him, which was sad because when it came to the awards, of course the captain of the aeroplane gets the medal. But Roy Eggleston was excellent.

As the fire set in more and more, it just got worse, and you could see right down into the hold. The pillars that were supporting the deck down in the hold were completely wrecked. The whole thing was just like looking into a furnace. The ammunition started to cook off and that was, I think, probably the worst bit of the lot, because Leading Eggleston was leaning out of the aeroplane, and he'd been shaken by these blasts – but he kept going. I had my window open and the first explosion was quite a smack against my face so goodness knows what it was like to be on the deck, because a lot of hot debris was flying out of the hold.

I could see a few blokes in my field of vision who were just sheltering, waiting to be lifted off, and the Captain who was walking up and down, obviously very concerned at this stage, trying to get everything sorted out. It must have been a very tough time for him. He used to come into my line of vision, which was a very small area of deck, and indicate the distance between the bottom of the aeroplane and the deck. I'll never forget him doing that – he really looked concerned. But of course Leading Eggleston was indicating our height all the time. 'You're four feet above the deck. You're in a good position,' or, 'You're fifteen feet over the deck – good position, hold that there.' I would ask him if we could move in a certain direction and he would 'talk' us into the best position. Certainly, working as a team was all-important. At our feet the men were being passed up from the deck. I'd told Leading Eggleston that we'd go as low as we could so the men wouldn't have to spend a long time being winched up, so we were definitely quite low at times. It was the quickest way to get these poor devils into the aircraft.

At one point we had to pick up a severely injured guy who'd lost his leg just below the knee. He was brought out on a stretcher in trauma. They got the bottom of a pallet and wrapped some ropes round it, put the ropes on the winch and he was lifted up and then dragged in by the aircrewmen. The smell of burning flesh was awful. Normally, you have to shout to be heard without the intercom, yet I could actually hear quite a few of the casualties shouting out in pain. This was no bad thing, because if they could shout they must be in a reasonable condition, so you didn't worry quite so much. It was the guys who were really quiet that worried me.

I don't have a clue how long it took. We picked up the second from last man from the ship, Sergeant Naya of the

RAMC. I'll never forget him; he was incredible. Eggleston said, 'Okay, the last guy before the Captain is just coming up now.' I must have had about six or seven on board and I remember that when we landed in the middle of the settlement to offload them, the Captain and two or three others came up and shook my hand and gave the thumbs up. But Naya came up and gave me a smacker of a kiss on my cheek. I was a bit surprised. He was the one guy I remember vividly. There was nothing I could say – he said it all. He'd done all he could and more, and I think he was overwhelmed with the thought that he had survived – not only that, but that others had survived because of our teamwork.

Lieutenant Philip Sheldon

Royal Navy

Queen's Gallantry Medal

On 8 June 1982, RFA Sir Galahad *and RFA* Sir Tristram, *carrying large numbers of troops, were attacked by aircraft of the Argentine air force. RFA* Sir Galahad *was left damaged and burning with a considerable number of casualties. Aircraft of 825 Naval Air Squadron were on the scene within minutes and were joined for a time by a Sea King IV and Wessex V.*

The helicopters, captained by Lieutenant Boughton and Lieutenant Sheldon, conducted pick-ups of troops and crew mustered in the extremely confined area of the LSL foredeck. Many were injured or in shock. The rescues were conducted close to masts and rigging, with little clearance for the aircraft, and with no regard for personal safety. Ammunition and pyrotechnics were exploding and there was a threat of further attack by enemy aircraft. Evacuation and rescue continued until darkness and were, in fact, interrupted by a further air attack.

The professionalism and bravery demonstrated in these operations by Lieutenant Boughton and Lieutenant Sheldon are representative of the crews and their squadron.

I never expected to go into action. I don't think many people ever have. When the whole thing suddenly exploded, and this great Task Force was sailing south, it seemed almost unreal, particularly for us in the training squadron, where we were a bit divorced in any case from the real Navy. We had become very much entrenched in our own routine. Then suddenly all these ships were going away, but I never thought it would come to anything.

At John Boughton's wedding it was almost like a fairy tale. The whole squadron was there, in all this sunshine, with flowers and champagne, yet that evening we got the formal news that we were off next Friday; that same night a Vulcan dropped its bombs on Stanley airfield. Even at the end of John's wedding and driving home the next day, it was all sort of, 'Well, all right, we'll form this squadron and it'll all be jolly, but are we going to get involved?'

That first week we had the novelty of preparing our aircraft and taking out the markings and wearing jungly gear. Later that same week, a large lorry arrived full of our personal kit. A supply officer and his team hastily set up makeshift benches in an empty hangar to issue the cold-weather garments and we all filed quietly past, only to discover that everything came in one size only – large! The reason, we were to learn, was that everything had gone south. 'Don't worry,' the supply officer assured us, 'you'll be able to draw it from the Army when you land ashore.' With men of many shapes and sizes drawing kit that day, the end result resembled something not far off 'Dad's Army'. By the end of this first busy week we further learnt that the majority of the aeroplanes would embark in the requisitioned Cunard Line *Atlantic Causeway*, but that a small detachment would also embark on the *QE2*. The residue of personnel would embark on the RFA *Engadine*. The squadron also had a name by then too, 825, and with it came the original motto, *Nihil Obstat* (Nothing Stops Us)!

Then things began to happen. The *Belgrano* got hit, which was a confirmation to me that we appeared to be controlling what was going on, and it made me think that we'd got such a tight grip on things we wouldn't get there in time. Then suddenly, on that Tuesday, *Sheffield* got hit. I felt immediate anger to start with, but because we hadn't been involved, I felt the same outrage the general public felt. Then, in no time, we were on the merry-go-round and we were ready to go. We took off from Culdrose and it was a lovely, sunny afternoon, it was maybe four o'clock or four-thirty on a Sunday and we were flying out to war, and again it was like a fairy story. We flew in formation towards Plymouth to the *Atlantic Causeway*; it still wasn't real, it was still Culdrose – a nice warm cocoon. I flew over my house on the way and I looked down and I thought many thoughts. I learnt later that my wife had watched the aeroplanes fly away until they were just tiny dots in the sky. Then abruptly, we were in Plymouth, on *Causeway*, and the *esprit de corps* was there, and we were bumping into friends; the professional thing had started. Thereafter there wasn't a great deal of time to reflect.

During the early days of the voyage nobody really knew how 825 Squadron were going to be employed by the battalions ashore. Our aeroplanes had been converted from ASW (anti-submarine warfare) helicopters into heavy-lift utility aircraft, all of which amounted to taking the dipping sonar and associated electronic equipment out of the rear cabin, leaving nothing more than a basic airframe. We were capable of lifting 6,000 lbs or carrying sixteen men and their kit. We did, however, retain our radar sets which proved invaluable to us on occasion since we neither had nor were trained to use pilot night goggles. A helicopter cannot generally fly low level in mountainous areas if the pilot can't see the underlying terrain, certainly not when approaching night-landing zones. In the broadest sense, therefore, we were capable of heavy lift and troop movements, but it was the ground environment and the tactical employment that we were likely to encounter once ashore in the Falklands that remained a mystery. We were not to discover these specifics until we got there.

Nevertheless, we prepared for any eventuality and generally speaking this fell into two distinct categories. We would operate from *Atlantic Causeway* either while she was under way or at anchor, or we would disembark and become an independent unit based ashore. To prepare for the former possibility meant that we had to practise day and night deck landings, helicopter moves around an already cluttered deck and, probably most important of all, we had to educate the merchant officers aboard how to operate a ship with helicopters embarked. As ASW aircrew we were unfamiliar with land operations so we also had to attend a number of briefings given by amphibious support pilots. A second squadron, 848, had been formed by the pilots to assist in the shore effort and a large number of older Wessex V helicopters were also on board.

It was a busy period and the time passed quickly. The only news that was available came to us via the World Service and it certainly conveyed that events in the South Atlantic were hotting up! Diplomatic discussions had begun to break down and it looked as if there would be a landing any day. At Ascension the second chapter of an amazing voyage to the Falklands began – I was transferred to the *QE2*.

I remember vividly landing on the aft flight deck of that great ship and being watched by hundreds of soldiers viewing from the sun decks and promenades that make up the aft section of the ship. There was intense military activity on her upper decks, but this didn't detract from the sumptuous, luxurious lines and fittings on the Cunard flagship. As I made my way below decks in an attempt to locate my friends who had been with the ship since Southampton, I could see the stark contrast to the rather cramped conditions of the *Atlantic Causeway*.

In the *QE2*, with her vast ballrooms and luxurious restaurants, it was initially difficult to comprehend that the 3,500 men aboard were not on a luxury cruise but were in fact on their way to fight a war! I remember entering the officers' restaurant for the first time and although I had been warned of what was to come it still came as quite a shock because there were dozens of Guards officers apparently quite at home taking lunch surrounded by Cunard luxury. It was a make-believe world of pristine tablecloths, silver cutlery and smoked salmon served by immaculately clad waiters. In the evenings the best wines from the *QE2* cellars were always available. The restaurant hadn't changed its exclusive standard, it had merely extended its services to a different clientele. Whether or not that was the right environment in which to prepare men for war is not for me to say, but certainly it was in distinct contrast to some of the hardships that were to follow for many of the men who sailed with her.

Whereas lack of information as to our future employment had caused minor irritations on the *Causeway*, on the *QE2* that same doubt and ignorance amongst so many officers and men (certainly of my rank) seemed far more marked. 5 Brigade had left England with many of the men believing that they would be employed as a garrison force. Some welcomed this, others were spoiling for a fight and were terrified to think that the fighting might be over when we arrived. In the officers' bar in the evening I was reminded on more than one occasion that the honour of the regiment was at stake: battle honours were there for the taking!

It started to become clear as we steamed south that 825 Squadron would be operating in support of 5 Brigade and we began to take more than a passing interest in their training activities. What also began to become clear was that many of the young Army officers had not worked with heavy-lift helicopters before and in particular with Sea Kings. We were told that the Scots and Welsh Guards were infantry and that 'the only way to move a regiment was to march'. Not being an Army officer I had little reason to doubt this principle, but what little knowledge of the Falklands terrain I did have meant it was clear that helicopters and the use of them in battle was going to be of immense importance. We were beginning to feel uneasy about the Army's attitude to helicopters.

Time, too, was running out and the *QE2* was of such immense proportions and capacity that communications between all the various units was not that easy. Many of us from time to time felt the whole environment had a distinct flavour of unreality.

This for me was illustrated one day when many of us were sitting in the ship's theatre which was situated in an enormous and quite un-shiplike auditorium in the heart of the *QE2*. The Master had agreed, in an effort to add light relief to the troops' daily training programme, to give a presentation on the rise and fall of the great ocean-going liners of the century. It was quite a long lecture, normally given to fee-paying passengers, and very well presented and illustrated with slides. As a Naval officer, obviously I was very interested, but I found my attention began to wander from time to time. While we looked and listened about great disasters that had struck luxury liners from the *Titanic* onwards I couldn't help wondering what would happen to the *QE2* should she be hit by an Exocet or torpedo. The danger of our own situation seemed of little consequence to the mainly Army audience who were listening with casual interest to the Master and his slides. The panic, confusion and loss of life portrayed in his lecture could have quite suddenly become a reality for all of us had things been different for the Cunard flagship.

I was rather glad when that was over and could go up on deck. There, however, was another sight, an awesome sight: icebergs! There we were, travelling at twenty-five knots in fog, and they were only speaking on the radio about once every five minutes because they didn't want to give our position away. I stood on the upper deck to watch these bloody great icebergs going by and I thought, 'Well, this is just totally unreal.'

One morning just before we arrived in South Georgia we conducted a helicopter transfer to the destroyer HMS *Antrim*. General Moore and his staff were going on ahead to set up their HQ while the officers and men would be transferred to the *Canberra* and *Norland*. Out of the mist in the eerie Antarctic silence came the sullen grey shape of *Antrim*. Down her port side was a line of charred cannon holes, damage inflicted on her from her adventures in the conflict. Her sailors on the upper deck looked drawn, pale and tired as we landed on her flight deck, but they were nevertheless in good spirits. As I looked at the *Antrim* at that moment I thought, 'Is this really happening in 1982?' Suddenly two things seemed very straightforward: we were at war and we had to win. The sooner we did, the sooner we could all go home.

After a major transfer of personnel and machinery, much of which was lifted by our squadron detachment aircraft, we embarked on *Canberra* for the voyage to the Falklands. The mood of her officers and ship's company was very warlike indeed. She had seen action during the early landings at San Carlos and had, no doubt, benefited operationally from this experience. Soon after sailing from South Georgia, however, I learnt that I was to change ships yet again and this time it was back to the *Atlantic Causeway* on which I had first started out from Plymouth. A warm welcome awaited us as we transferred by one of our own helicopters, but the officers and crew were a bit apprehensive since, by this time, her sister ship, *Atlantic Conveyor*, had been hit by an Exocet missile fired from a Super Etendard. On our arrival we also learnt that some of our aeroplanes had already disembarked from the ship and had flown over 200 miles or so ahead of the ship because heavy-lift helicopters were urgently needed ashore. They stopped to refuel on HMS *Hermes* en route to the islands.

Having made the voyage to the sea areas around the Falklands via South Georgia the sight of the British Fleet came as quite a surprise and it certainly looked impressive. The sky seemed full of Harriers and helicopters, many of the latter crewed by friends. The vulnerability of our situation in *Causeway*, however, was unnerving and I personally looked forward to getting ashore which I believed would be less exposed and afford greater cover. As the next few days passed this proved not to be entirely the case.

At last, under cover of the dawn, the *Causeway* quietly slipped into San Carlos Water and as she did so we sat ready to start our aeroplanes and disembark as soon as possible since there was still a risk of further air raids. We landed at

Port San Carlos where there was an established support helicopter operating base. I distinctly remember looking round the area where the camp existed and finding it hard to believe we were so far from home since the terrain and vegetation looked so like Scotland.

I was trying to dig a trench when John (Boughton) came over and said, 'Come with me, grab your co-pilot, we're going flying. We're moving guns from here up to Mount Kent.' So there I was, within an hour of landing, flying a helicopter at very, very low level, with a gun underneath, following John and three other guys all on this magical fairy tale up to Mount Kent. The fairy tale ended abruptly, because John blew the navigation and overshot the landing zone and suddenly we all were looking down on Stanley having flown over twenty miles of area that hadn't been cleared! We'd seen the intelligence pictures, we'd read about it in the newspapers, and suddenly there it was – Stanley! A hurried turnabout was called for! A great introduction to the Falklands.

After that initial scare we got into a routine. At the end of each day's flying we'd hide our Sea Kings. Our hides were quite widely dispersed so we would all get into one aeroplane in the morning, which would ferry us to our aircraft. I remember sitting there thinking, 'Today's the day. It's going to happen today. They are bound to get out today and disrupt the supply line.' But they never did. When we were flying our own Sea Kings we got to know the routes very well, and you could fly the aircraft without having to work very hard with the navigation. I just used to sit there in silence taking a load fifty miles, then fly back fifty miles without anything much going on. When there wasn't a load underneath the aircraft everyone could relax completely, although at the back of your mind was, 'Where are they? They must come soon. They've got to come soon, just one Pucará and some rockets.' If the Argentinians had just knocked down one major utility helicopter that would have probably stopped the day routes at least for a couple of days, and we would have had to start flying at night, and perhaps the whole thing would have just ground to a halt.

Bizarre really, their whole aero-strategy was bizarre. They showed such courage in some areas, such naivety in others; appalling professional naivety.

We'd been doing daily tasks until 8 June, which was the day of the *Galahad* disaster. We'd seen both of the ships there that morning because we'd been down in Bluff Cove putting artillery battery in. We didn't really pay much attention to what was going on; we presumed they were landing something. We'd seen activity throughout the morning, but in the afternoon my tasking was changed to go to Darwin to move elements of the Guards forward to Fitzroy. Whilst flying back towards Fitzroy we heard on the radio, 'Air Raid Warning Red'. So we went into a hide. When I considered it was all right, I began to move out. Then John came up on the radio that one of the ships had been hit and we were to get there quickly. When I arrived, the *Galahad* was on fire and surrounded by quite a few helicopters. John was clearly there and also my boss, and there was a Wessex helping to rescue people. So there was this honeypot of activity going on but I was desperately in need of fuel so I landed on *Tristram*. The Chinese crew on her flight deck when we landed seemed in a state of panic and it was only after we had refuelled and cleared from the ship that we saw that she had been hit too and was on fire. We had, in fact, refuelled the aeroplane above a burning deck!

I went straight across to the *Galahad* and began bringing the injured off the fo'c'sle and flying them straight into shore, boring round the corner into the wind and putting them straight down on the grass or into some buildings where they were stretchered off. No one was controlling this operation, we were working at our own discretion. Occasionally there'd be a shout on the radio saying, 'Come over here, I could do with some help.' John and I were there throughout the entire event, and the boss was doing his own thing working at the other end of the ship amongst all the smoke. Isaac, one of my squadron, was there doing the same as us, but regrettably he was overlooked when it came to the medals.

The rescue of survivors was not a difficult flying exercise – it was very straightforward and we'd been thoroughly trained to do it – but I'd never been so close to flames before. As we worked away, every now and again there would be an explosion within the hold and you'd find yourself looking down at these balls of fire and the shock waves would physically move the aircraft. Tug Wilson, my crewman, in the back, was unbelievable. He was incredibly calm, and suppressed his anxiety at what he was both seeing and touching. In a reassuring voice he'd say, 'That's a good hover, boss, nice hover, got one coming up now who's got no arms, badly burned, face has disintegrated, I'm going to push him down in front.' I felt him verbalizing his emotional reactions to what he was seeing. There was the standard pukka Naval chat, necessary to position the aircraft, interspersed with, 'Oh, fuck me, this guy's got no face.' I couldn't see because I was sitting ahead trying to keep the aircraft steady. Suddenly this injured person got pushed up the front and I felt quite ashamed of myself, because I had to bring myself to actually look down at him and I thought, 'Christ – what a mess.' I felt cowardly that I was having to try and pluck up the courage to actually look at this poor chap and yet here was this guy, suffering agonies.

At one point we got a big blast – ammunition in the hold went off – which was frightening. It sounds corny, but I prayed. I think a lot of people who'd never prayed before said them that day. I just said, 'If you're on my side, just hang in for the next hour or so.' Bits were flying everywhere and I was very aware of the fact that any second the *Galahad* could blow itself to pieces and after one big blast I closed my little window thinking, 'That will protect me!' Perhaps ships don't blow themselves to pieces like the movies would have us believe, but we knew there was ammunition in it, so all the time I was thinking, 'Well, if this thing goes bang now, they'd go down and we'd go with it.' That fear was always in the back of our minds.

The setting for this grotesque event was so bizarre because here on this lovely afternoon, among this glorious countryside, were all these poor lads lying all over the fields with their skin burnt off. I remember there was a negro, though maybe he was just black with burns, and some young lad who had no clothes on at all, who'd obviously been told to strip off and get the air to his skin to cool it down – it was all very moving. I was just sitting there watching him run around. It was unbelievable.

The next job was to get them from there up to Red Beach, where the hospital was, and that was absolutely remarkable because it was just like something out of *MASH*. It took about twenty minutes to get to San Carlos and I remember going over the top of the hill and hearing 'Air Raid Warning Red'. They told all the helicopters to 'Scram' but I just carried on and came round this headland and straight into the landing site next to the refrigerator ship. Everybody was running about getting these people out of the back of the helicopters which were swooping down one after another and landing all over the place. We'd been at it now for about two hours and it was just starting to get dark. I was carrying one particular bloke who was very, very badly burnt. They got him out of the back of the aircraft, onto a stretcher, and as they ran across the wet ground they dropped him and the bloke went straight into the mud. I just sat there and thought, 'God Almighty, hasn't he had enough?' It was nobody's fault, the medics were doing everything they could. There were these big double doors and they'd just disappear into them and run out again.

By late in the afternoon of that unforgettable day we had got everyone off. All that was left in the aircraft was the dreadful stench of burnt flesh.

We had no idea that back in the UK the British public were seeing it and saying, 'Look at those heroes in those helicopters.' I can understand why it was proclaimed such a big deal but, really, at the end of the day it was just another job, and there were more guys doing equally difficult things that were not recorded on videos.

After *Galahad*, in the final push, I got into another difficult situation. We'd been told to move a battery from one position up to another. I said to the guy who controlled helicopters at Teal Inlet, 'Is it safe to take these guns where the Army want them to go?' He said, 'Oh, yes, yes, you can go all points up to so and so,' which was a line of longitude on the map. I came out and I saw a friend of mine and I said to him, 'This guy says I can go up to there,' and he said, 'Yes, sure, it's okay, no sweat, you'll be all right, trust me, trust me.'

I got in the aircraft, loaded these guns and got going with a lot of other blue Sea Kings. It was a great yo-ho thing, the blue boys are here again! But I couldn't see a single green Sea King anywhere.

We were sitting in a hover, lowering the gun, when all of a sudden there was a bloody great big bang and earth went everywhere. The bloke in the back said, 'Christ, we've been mortared!' I dropped the gun, went to turn the aircraft to the left to run away, when suddenly, 'Bang!' there was another blast! The adrenalin was absolutely unbelievable! I came careering out of the valley screaming on the radio for everybody not to carry on with the job, and we then went back to the base. I landed the aircraft and there were one or two holes in it, but fortunately nothing very serious. Old 'Trust me, trust me' happened to be there. I went over and said, 'I just got mortared.' So he said, 'Well, lucky old you,' and suddenly my feelings of fear were totally dissolved by this guy saying, 'So what?' I'm sure there was a bit of gamesmanship – but it worked.

There were one or two little highlights. After the surrender I remember I went into Stanley on the second day for a day off and was walking along the front looking at all the filth and squalor. I was standing outside a little tin shack at the eastern end of Stanley when the door opened and a lady's head came out and said 'Can we come out now?' and I said, 'Yes, I think so.' She said, 'Well, there some Argentinians down at the garage, you know.' The Military Police picked them up later. She then asked me in for a cup of tea. They were the first Falklanders I'd really spoken to in Stanley. Just before I left she asked me if I'd been over to one of the islands on the west. I told her that we couldn't go there because they hadn't officially surrendered over there.

She said, 'Oh, my kids are there staying with my sister-in-law. If you're over that way could you just give them my love?' So I asked her when they were going to come home. She said, 'Well, I don't know, they went off in a Land-Rover halfway through the war and we haven't seen them since.' So I asked her if she would like me to bring them back. And she just fell to pieces with the thought.

Several days later they did surrender over there and I was back in Stanley again, flying. I spoke to my boss and he agreed that I could go and pick the kids up. We had a spare aircraft so we went to Keppel Island, which is a beautiful island, privately owned by this bloke with a lovely house. We landed and he came out. I introduced myself and said, 'I've come for the kids. She's ready to have them back.' The kids were looking over the hedge and within five minutes, swallows and amazons, they'd got into the back of the aircraft. Twenty-five minutes later we landed right next to their mother's house in Stanley. The kids got out, and even though they'd been away from their family for a couple of months, I got them hiding round the corner. I knocked and said, 'I've got a surprise for you', and she said, 'Oh, what?' and the kids jumped into her arms! Which was very moving.

After several weeks of flying we were recalled to the UK. All the lads I'd flown out with flew back from Ascension on a VC10 and we actually came home about the same time as we'd flown out together on that beautiful spring morning. Now of course it was summer, the most fabulous summer's evening, absolutely gin clear. We were probably at 35,000 feet in this VC10 but we spotted the navigational beacon at Land's End, so we knew we were home. Everyone was looking out of the window and there, right down below, was Culdrose, clear as a bell, and we could also see where we all lived, and I thought, 'As you begin, so shall you end.' It was remarkable that our unit should stay intact, right from birth to death really, and thank God suffered no casualties.

I feel incredibly grateful still to be about, and although I'm not a religious person at all, I value my life and my family much more than I did. The average soldier possibly

Major the Rev. David Cooper. 'His contribution was immense. He's not just a very practical Christian, he's also a very fine soldier so he knows what he's talking about' – Major Crosland

Major Mike Norman – 'As a military man, I couldn't have come to that decision; I'd have fought. It is not our job to surrender'

Able Seaman John Dillon –
'I was just going to say
forget it and wait there to
die. It was then the images
of my heroes Bruce Lee
and Silver Surfer started
flashing through my
mind ... that seemed to change
things. They wouldn't give up'

MEA (M) 1
Kenneth Enticknap –
'The bomb had gone off in
the galley and blasted
everywhere ... I most
certainly thought I'd had it'

Petty Officer John Leake – 'Just before we came under attack I brought up stacks of Mars Bars and Nutty and a crate of Gotters, because I thought we might need them'

Flight Lieutenant David Morgan – 'When you're in the air, nothing matters, you're the master of your own destiny and you can do what you like' (*HMS* Hermes *photo, courtesy Ministry of Defence*)

Captain John Coward –
'Then the second squadron
came at us, more spread
out. The Sea Wolf looked
at this lot, said,"That is
not a missile," and went
back to park' (*Photo by
Yarrow Shipbuilders Ltd*)

Flight Lieutenant
Alan Swan – 'It's always
better to work on a big
bomb, because, if you've
got to go, the best way to
go is with a really big one –
then it's clean'

Major Peter Cameron – 'Everyone else vamoosed, and some bastard took my old steel helmet which was outside my command tent. I was very glad that somebody had taken a photograph of me in it'

Major Charles Bremner – 'I looked up through the open hatch of the tank deck just in time to see a cylindrical object fly through the air. There was a loud metallic clang. A split second later there was a deafening explosion towards the stern of the ship'

Captain Hilarian Roberts – 'There was a huge flame ahead where all these people had been sitting. It just billowed straight over me and I experienced an extraordinary slow-motion feeling of being burnt'

Nurse Jackie Hayward – 'Everything was fairly easy and really there was a bit of a lull – but the *Galahad* changed all that ... That day the *Uganda* took 159 casualties'

Sergeant Pierre Naya – 'Smoke and flames were billowing up from below, ammunition was going off, and there were blokes running around screaming because their plastic all-weather gear had caught fire and was sticking to them, burning their skin away'

Lieutenants John Boughton (left) and Phil Sheldon – 'By late in the afternoon of that unforgettable day we had got everyone off the *Galahad*. All that was left in the aircraft was the dreadful stench of burnt flesh'

Major Chris Keeble – 'I remember my heart leapt when I heard Sergeant Blackburn's voice frantically saying, "Sunray is down" '

may have been so highly trained that it didn't mean anything to him, but maybe the odd Army officer might think the same as I do; he certainly has more cause to. I was suddenly thrust from a Cornish spring in my own little isolated world into a real live war where people were actually getting killed.

From a professional point of view, I had the fortune to have done the good bit. I didn't get the South Atlantic gales, I didn't get the bombings at San Carlos, I didn't get the days and days of intense boredom that other helicopter pilots were getting at sea, sitting in a hover looking for submarines. No, I went straight to the Falklands, got right in amongst what was a soldier's war, tasted it, but also tasted the smell of victory, which was euphoric when it came that afternoon. For me the war had a beginning, a middle, and an end.

Nurse Jackie Hayward

Queen Alexandra's
Royal Naval Nursing Service

I was on nights in an intensive care unit at Haslar Royal Naval Hospital when they told me I was going to the Falklands on Sunday – this was Friday night! But I got my things together because I'd volunteered and I wanted to go. My husband, who was in 42 Commando, was already down there. He later got a message from the Matron to say that I'd arrived on the *Uganda*.

We were flown in an uncomfortable Hercules from Brize Norton out to Uruguay and were met at the airport by armed guards and searched on the plane. It was then that it hit us that we were going to war. We had a police escort through the town and everyone stopped and stared at us.

We joined a small hospital ship but the Captain didn't know anything about us. He thought he was getting thirteen males, which is what he'd asked for on the signal; instead he got three females! We were soon transferred by helicopter to the *Uganda*, which was very exciting, and became the first Naval female nurses to be on a ship since the last world war.

We met up with the *Uganda* at the Red Cross box, which was an agreed safe area, somewhere in the middle of the ocean. During the day we went into Falkland Sound and took out casualties but at night we had to go back and rendevous in this Red Cross box with the other ships. We got onto *Uganda* after Goose Green and before the other major battles. When I arrived I was told that I was going to work on the intensive care unit. I'd worked on intensive care at Haslar but only for three weeks, during which time I hadn't actually got any patients! But at least I had become familiar with the machinery, which was a big help. The first day on board we were told to find our way about the ship. I'd never been on a big ship before and I was seasick, but not bad enough to keep me in bed all the time. I kept thinking about my puppy which I had left with a neighbour.

We were told to report to the ward. It was set in different watches and we started working four hours on and four hours off. Then, when we got lots of patients, things became too hectic and we got called back – casualties were coming in too quick for a normal routine. They tried six hours off and four hours on, but in the end we did four hours on and eight hours off, because we were getting so tired. When I actually started in intensive care there was only one patient, who was a Marine; the rest were on other wards.

Everything was fairly easy and really there was a bit of a lull – but the *Galahad* changed all that. I'd only seen one burns case before and that was an old lady who'd fallen into a fire, which was quite nasty. At eight that morning, I'd just come off duty when I heard the call, 'All Hands to Flying Stations'. I sensed immediately something was very wrong. I went straight back away to my ward to see these horrifying sights – so many burnt and disfigured men, you couldn't recognize any of them. They looked like teddy bears, their faces were all terribly swollen, and they were in such pain.

There were Chinese men as well as ordinary men and you couldn't tell the difference, they were all black and swollen. Their burnt flesh left a smell that I'll never forget. The fire had singed all their hair. The clothing they wore protected them, but their hands and faces really got it. One was burnt all over, the only thing that was perfect was his feet – they were immaculate. I think he was going up the ladder when the blast hit the whole of his back. He came straight to us in intensive care. It was a horrible sight.

I remember Simon Weston, who was really badly burnt, coming through with another Welsh Guard. I was amazed because they were talking to each other, they were really so cheerful, it was unbelievable. I just stood there and looked at them, and thought how can you be so cheerful when you really hurt so much. He was asked how everybody was, and had they seen so and so. This was because his face had swollen up so much his eyes had closed and he couldn't see. He really was so brave, he didn't often show he was in pain.

That day the *Uganda* took 159 casualties. The helicopters would land every five minutes and so many people would be brought off. The chaps that came were just so glad to be in bed, with clean sheets and feeling safe. There wasn't any noise of firing or people getting hurt – they were just there. Some of them looked so young.

Because they were so fit, they healed quickly. We had one that was really ill, but he never once blamed anybody, he didn't blame the Argentinians. He was more worried about getting home to his fiancée, but he died. Then we had another one who was three beds away from an Argentinian and he would call him all the names under the sun. He said he was going to kill him but in the end they were all talking to each other. One minute they had been

179

trying to kill each other on the battlefield and the next minute they're stuck in the same room together talking or trying to speak English or Spanish to each other. But the true Argentinian soldiers didn't really want to know. Yet some of the conscripts were only sixteen and they were petrified. They'd been told that once they got on board they would be tortured immediately, and the food would be poisoned. Because we were females, they thought it was a new tactic. But one who had been shot in the mouth on his eighteenth birthday underwent a tracheotomy – he was fantastic. In the end, when the Argentinians took him back, he cried because he didn't want to go home. He gave one of the sisters his rosary. It was ironic because another Argentinian had been shot on his eighteenth birthday and the same day one of ours who was twenty-one that day was also shot. They were both together; they cursed each other but then they apologized afterwards.

After the *Galahad* we took them from everywhere; wherever they were, we took them. The helicopters on the island used to fly them over to us. There were so many of the men that stand out, especially in intensive care. They each had their own particular way of showing how they were overcoming their pain. My friend Karen told me about this patient, a young Scots Guard, who was fantastic – Bob Lawrence. He was paralysed down one side and he used to sit there and joke about it. But I think he, like the rest, did it to keep his own spirits up. He also knew that he was going to meet the Queen so he was determined he was going to walk up and get his medal. But all of them had such really high spirits. In their own way they were determined that they were going to do something and get better.

There was one who had been hit in the leg and it was so badly damaged that the doctors said they may have to amputate. They gave him the choice and they let him phone his mum and dad and fiancée. He spoke with them and told them that to keep his leg he would have to go through years and years of operations. In the end he decided he wasn't going to have it amputated, he was going to keep his leg. He went home on leave on one of the hospital ships with a Portsmouth Bar on his leg, which pins and keeps his leg in plaster and holds the leg in traction. I didn't see anything more of him for a long time and then I came back off leave to his ward and it was lovely to see that his leg was healing. He was so determined that his leg wasn't going to come off and even more determined to walk up the aisle with a leg, with or without plaster, and he did. That leg fixed lovely. Then ironically she hurt her leg on honeymoon and finished up in plaster! He was fantastic, he was; he was a tall bloke with dark hair.

There was another called Paul, who was only nineteen, who'd been hit everywhere but badly in the back. He'd gone to theatre so many times but his only thought was to get home to his fiancée and their six-month-old baby. They were going to get married in the August but somehow before his last op he knew he wasn't going to get through and that was it, he just died. It cracked us all up because of the length of time we'd looked after him – he had six nurses looking after him. We did all we could for him. That night I went out and sat on my own on the flight deck. I think it was just to get away from everybody, from everything. It was a big ship but it wasn't that big. Of course I used to let out a lot of feeling in my letters home. Letters are very important. The soldiers used to get upset if they didn't get a letter from their girlfriends on the ward. But in the end, those who got letters would share out their news – they were like a family really, all helping each other.

We did our best but we couldn't take away completely the pain they had. At night a lot of their memories would come flooding back. We had one young lad who'd had to have his leg amputated. In his dreams he would re-live the moment when he'd been hit and he used to wake up in agony because, even though his foot wasn't there, he would still feel the pain. He used to shout and wake himself up and we'd have to calm him down and talk to him. The others would be shouting out, 'Take cover, take cover', really re-living the whole thing.

181

When everything was over, my husband managed to get on board to see some people in his company who had been injured. He looked so drawn and as if he needed a good meal. We went down to my cabin to get him some washing gear. I'd got some things on a cupboard when the ship rolled and they fell and bashed on the floor. I turned round to say something to my husband and he was laying on the floor! He got up and told me it was force of habit and laughed it off. But it worried me, seeing that sort of thing. I don't know how I would have responded if he'd been badly hurt and I'd had to nurse him. Three of us had husbands down there and other nurses had their boyfriends.

A lot of people who lost an arm or a leg really needed to be convinced that their wife or girlfriend would still need them. They used to say, 'She won't want me any more now.' They were all right while they were together on the ward – all in the same boat. So we really had to try and convince them that they'd be all right, because they knew there would be a different world for them once they left the ship and had to face reality.

One lad on the ward had been on a ship that sank. I was with him when two enemy planes went over very close and he could hear them. You could see the fear in his eyes. I couldn't convince him that he was safe. How can you convince someone that has just been blown out on a ship by aircraft that he's all right? It took a lot of doing but we got him to realize that at least he was part safe, but it took a lot of doing. We could deal with the physical things but the mental scars were something else.

I think it dawned on us when we all got back what we'd actually done. We had so much to do that we didn't have time to get frightened – but we used to get frightened for everyone else. It seemed ages before we got back to Southampton and that marvellous reception. There in the crowd I saw my husband who had arrived six weeks before me. It seemed funny, really, because all the wives were waiting for their husbands! I don't think I'd have missed it. I learnt a hell of a lot down there and met a lot of very brave people.

28/29 May

The Battle for Darwin and Goose Green

13/14 June

Attack on Wireless Ridge

Major Christopher Keeble

The Parachute Regiment

Distinguished Service Order

In the early hours of 28 May 1982, the 2nd Battalion the Parachute Regiment, of which Major Keeble was Second-in-Command, launched an attack on enemy positions in the area of the Darwin and Goose Green settlements on the Island of East Falkland. The enemy were thought to be entrenched in battalion strength. In the event they proved to be in far greater numbers, sited in depth with mutually supporting positions. At one stage the attack was held up by a number of well-sited enemy machine-gun positions and almost foundered. It was retrieved by the personal action of the Commanding Officer, who was killed at that time.

The loss of a Commanding Officer at such a crucial stage of the battle, when the outcome was uncertain, could have had a devastating effect upon the battalion. However, the speed and decisiveness with which Major Keeble assumed command and pressed forward with the attack was such that the battalion gained renewed vigour and determination and drove the enemy from their positions. It was a display of leadership, tactical skill and determination of the highest order.

On several other occasions in the battle, which lasted some thirty-six hours, the outcome hung in the balance. Supporting fire from the two 81mm mortars and three 105mm guns, which was all that was available, was insufficient to neutralize enemy positions. Inspired by Major Keeble, the fighting spirit of the battalion carried the day and by nightfall the enemy had been fought to a standstill and were confined to a small salient.

During the night and following morning Major Keeble, never loosening his grip on the battlefield, skilfully conducted *negotiations for the release of the local inhabitants who were confined within the enemy position, and for the surrender of the entire enemy force, which numbered in excess of twice that of his own battalion.*

This remarkable victory, the first major encounter of the campaign on land, established a moral superiority over the enemy which was to affect all subsequent actions in the Falklands campaign.

Credit for this must fall to 2nd Battalion the Parachute Regiment and to the outstanding leadership displayed by Major Keeble at a moment of particular danger.

Lieutenant-Colonel H. Jones was the originator and the source of everything that happened to 2 Para. The way the unit was constructed, the training, the emphasis and speed, and the offence all stemmed from him. I first met him three years earlier, when we were both instructors at the School of Infantry. Since we worked in separate wings of the school, I only met him infrequently, and we merely knew each other professionally. It wasn't until February 1982 when I joined the battalion as the Second-in-Command that I got to know him well. He was one of the few men I have met in my Army career with whom I felt immediately in harmony. I would like to think that he felt the same way about me. The relationship between the CO and Second-in-Command should ideally be a close one. The Second-in-Command actually does not command anything; the CO is the commander. The Second-in-Command's role, apart from his peacetime function of training the unit for its operational role, is to assume command in his absence. He should also serve as somebody for the Commanding Officer to bounce his ideas off, test the water, without upsetting the crucial position of the boss or rupturing the command structure. I found this relationship extremely straightforward with H. and, of course, because of the nature of the man, very demanding – as indeed did all the company commanders.

When the Falklands blew up he was actually in France, and I went up to Aldershot from Wiltshire to represent the

CO at a meeting with Brigadier Wilson, the Commander of 5 Infantry Brigade. I met up with H., breathless from France, and we spent the afternoon with Sarah, his wife, in their house, and talked about how we would reconstruct the battalion for war, should we be required to support the Royal Marines – 3 Commando Brigade. We had not at this point been earmarked for the Falklands.

We were actually on leave prior to departure for the jungle in Belize, in Central America, as the crisis blew up. Our sister battalion, 3 Para, had been selected to embark with the Royal Marines and it was felt that 2 Para should remain to fill the gap created by their departure. H., of course, was very impatient as we watched the Task Force depart, and more so when our overseas tour to Belize was cancelled. Despite these developments, we did not stop planning for the possibility of going, and as things developed, it was providential we had put so much effort into getting 2 Para geared for the offence.

The British Army has a strong tradition which is still evident, particularly in BAOR, for concentrating on the defence, unlike, say, the German Army. This is perhaps less so in the Parachute Regiment or the Royal Marines in terms of its philosophy towards conflict. It was clear the Falklands could only be recaptured by the attack. We therefore made it our business in the few days we had to plan to acquire what additional weapons and equipment we needed to increase our potential for the offence. We also spent much time studying the topography, the Argentinian armed forces and even working out how we could launch an airframe assault directly into Stanley; such was our enthusiasm to go! It was, of course, all rewarded when we heard we had been tasked to join 3 Commando Brigade at Ascension Island and had been allocated the North Sea ferry *Norland* to get there! We were to be the best jungle-trained battalion in the South Atlantic!

As soon as the battalion had been selected, H. left for Ascension Island to link up with the 3 Commando Brigade staff, leaving me to command. He said, 'Chris, train up the battalion and bring it down to me. I'll be in Ascension.' We then spent a week training in Aldershot, getting all the equipment we had planned to acquire, embarked the battalion on *Norland* and worked out a training programme for the remaining three weeks afloat. So I spent actually four weeks commanding 2 Para. It's not that important, but it's a measure of the trust that existed between H. and me that I was given the task, and I felt very privileged to work up 2 Para for war. And it was the first opportunity I think I've ever had in my military career when I actually had the chance to do what I wanted to do, and I knew that it would be in tune with what H. would want, 6,000 miles away.

There were innumerable things we did on the *Norland* to prepare ourselves for the offence. There were about 1,000 personnel on board; 2 Para made up the majority, but we also had merchant seamen, civilians and even two women cooks. We all lived in remarkable harmony and the relentless pursuit to work up the battalion for war was made to blend in with the workings of a commercial ferry. It took not a little time for the crew to come to terms with the possibility of war. I was desperately anxious to get to Ascension Island as fast as possible, and grew daily more impatient with the zig-zag pattern of the ship's course, obviously devised to comply with navigational and international rules of the sea!

We had a meeting, as we departed, to plan the training priorities and programme and to devise the seamanship skills required to turn the *Norland* – a commercial ferry – into an amphibious platform. There were several weaknesses in 2 Para, which I had seen on Salisbury Plain and at a major field exercise in Norfolk in January. These had to be got right.

The first was our approach to casualties. The current principle was based on patching up the injured and withdrawing them to expert help well behind the battle. We quickly appreciated that movement, other than by helicopter, would be too slow for casualty survival and so we decided to concentrate on battlefield resuscitation, rather than simple first aid. In other words, to sustain the injured for as long as possible at or near the site of wounding. This was put into operation by our brilliant Medical Officer, Captain Steve Hughes, RAMC, who had researched the medical experiences of various campaigns, particularly those of the Israelis. I well remember discussing with him in Aldershot, before we left, how we would achieve this objective and what additional medical resources we would need. As a result he acquired 1,000 drips for intravenous infusion to cope with blood loss and even purchased a dummy forearm, veins and all, to practise setting up these drips. The idea was that we would distribute these IVs to each man, along with the more usual morphine, and shell dressings. A soldier would then have his own 'repair kit' which either he or a combat medic could administer. During the journey south, we taught everyone how to set up a drip either intravenously or through the rectum should the former method not be possible. As a result of these measures, we were able dramatically to reduce the loss of life, and sustain the casualties until evacuation could occur, according to the needs of the battlefield rather than to the needs of the injured.

Very much tied in with these measures was the battalion's attitude to the mission. Throughout the training of a parachute soldier, the mission is regarded as paramount. Much of the testing, and selection, is based on assessing the ability of an individual's will to achieve a particular objective. If the mission is paramount, casualties are a secondary consideration, hence the emphasis on producing a method of sustaining the casualty without affecting the morale of the soldier. A fine balance was struck between the mission and the casualty.

Thirdly, one should consider the efforts made to prepare the men's minds for conflict. I remember speaking to the Padre, David Cooper, and said, 'Look, one of the problems we're going to have to face is how do you cope with the trauma of war? How do you cope with the effect on the mind of seeing your buddy's legs blown off? How do you cope with the stress of conflict, spiritually and mentally?' If you look at real conflict, it's not your weapons that win the war, it's not your equipment, it's your mental ability to sustain yourself under stress. The man who wins is the man who can hang on the longest and sustain the will to win. The whole point of war, really, is to apply violence to break the enemy's will, not destroy his weapons or his cities, but undermine his will to fight for what he believes in. Now, how do you reinforce that in a body of people who've never been to war? This is where David Cooper was so marvellous. He took each section (nine men), the smallest fighting unit in the battalion, and he sat down in front of them and said, 'Look, when we go on this battlefield, it's going to be bloody awful. Now, I don't know about you, but I'll tell you how I'm going to feel.'

He attempted to penetrate that macho facade that soldiers build around themselves to reinforce their own resistance to fear. By voicing their own fears for them he got them to talk about how they would actually cope with the trauma of war. Being a Padre, out of the military system, with no sergeants or platoon commanders there, the freedom to talk was provided. This sharing of emotions between one human being and another demands a giving to each other, and developed a spiritual bond within the sections, which is so essential if people are going to fight and be prepared to die for each other. It was a tremendous contribution. I suspect this preparation may have prevented some of the post-Falklands psychiatric cases that have subsequently developed. He was marvellous.

In that week after Goose Green you would have found this wonderful closeness of everybody – they were fused by fire. Very difficult to describe, but there was this tremendous brotherhood. The word 'brotherhood' conjures it up. It's a word used frequently by people who fought in the Second World War – Brotherhood of Arnhem – and it is a brotherhood, too. War is a very emotional business – more than people realize. Much more

190

than I'd ever anticipated and appreciated. I was enormously attracted to the Parachute Regiment because of this wonderful feeling of comradeship. We all have to go through a traumatic selection process, which weeds out a great number of people. We are united in our hardship, by what we have done. It is a very good way of preparing for the actual trauma of war. Soldiers do not fight for Queen and country, or even for Maggie – they fight for each other. But they need to know that their comrades would do the same. Selection produces that mutual trust.

I remember parachuting onto the Arnhem drop zone with our sister battalion, 10 Para, on their annual pilgrimage to the battlefields and the war cemetery. After the jump, we visited the Oosterbeck Crossroads, the scene of fierce fighting on the outskirts of Arnhem, and we listened to one of the very few survivors of that battalion describing the battle for the Crossroads. Someone in the audience said to the speaker, 'What made you go on fighting when the battalion had been largely destroyed, the cause lost and defeat inevitable?' He paused, looked across to the suburban junction and with tears brimming up in his eyes he said quietly and simply, 'They were my friends.' That's how it was for 2 Para. We had spent our practice-training fusing the individuals together. The fire of war merely tempered that process. We would never have given up. We would have fought to the last man rather than not achieve the mission.

When H. died what faced me was really very simple. Since I had been running the unit for most of the journey south, I knew exactly what could be done. I remember my heart leapt when I heard Sergeant Blackburn's voice frantically saying, 'Sunray is down,' and it took some seconds to appreciate what he was saying in veiled speech. My greatest problem was that I was 1,500 metres back from H. with our Main HQ and it took me some time to get the correct information back from the forward two companies, A and B, in order to decide what to do with the reserves.

A Company's battle around Darwin sounded a shambles and the ground favoured the defence there. There was little point in reinforcing failure. B Company with Johnny Crosland, on the other hand, were in a reasonable position, despite being pinned down, and so I told him to assume command until I could get forward with Major Hector Gullan, the ubiquitous and invaluable Brigade Liaison Officer, who had a direct line to Brigadier Julian Thompson. I also took with me my orderly-room clerk, Corporal Kelly, who had been at my side throughout, to man the battalion radio link. As we left, the RSM, Mr Simpson, called me back, much to my irritation. 'What is it?' I asked sharply. He looked me in the eye and said, 'You are going to do fucking well, Sir!' I felt a million dollars! A wonderful touch. He did terribly well in the battle, dealing with the whole procedure of accounting for the casualties, normally the Adjutant's job. Very sadly, David Wood had also been killed on Darwin Hill with his Commanding Officer.

The outcome of the battle was really achieved by the skill of Phil Neame's and Johnny Crosland's companies, D and B, reinforced by the Recce Platoon commanded by brave Roger Jenner. Subsequently, the devastating violence created by the Harriers who attacked the outskirts of the settlement at last light clinched it. It was at that moment it seemed to me that the will of the defence began to break. We, on the other hand, were very short of ammunition and so overnight I prepared two plans. I remember sitting in a gorse bush behind Darwin Hill that night and saying to Dair Farrar-Hockley, commanding A Company, and others that the way to crack the problem was to walk down the hill the next day and tell the bloody Argies the game was up and defeat inevitable. Dair looked at me wearily as if I had lost my marbles! If that failed, well, we would launch a massive assault with aircraft, artillery and infantry, and destroy the settlement. There was really no other option, since, not only had we little ammunition, we were all exhausted having been on the go for some forty hours without sleep. In addition, and perhaps the most profound factor of all, there were 112 civilians locked up in the Community Hall in Goose

Green! This fact was discovered overnight and re-emphasized the need to use more subtle means than the bayonet! After all, we had not journeyed 8,000 miles merely to destroy the very people we had come to save.

And so, standing in a small tin shed on the airfield next day, with Tony Rice, the Battery Commander, and our two bewildered journalists, Robert Fox and David Norris, we confronted the Argies with Plan A.

It was clear that the three Argentinian commanders we spoke to, navy, army and air force, had had enough. It became apparent later that one of the principal causes of the collapse of will was the breakdown in the relationship between officer and conscripted soldiers, which in itself reinforces the strength of a volunteer, albeit smaller, force.

The surrender was arranged on a sports field outside Goose Green, close to the hidden position of D Company who had closed up on the settlement. It was a straightforward affair requiring the defenders to lay down their arms, which I allowed them to do with a degree of honour, to avoid rubbing their noses in defeat. There was nothing to gain from such a humiliation. About 150 of them assembled in a hollow square and after singing their national anthem, the commander, an airman, saluted me and handed over his pistol. We were very concerned that we could not see any Argentine army personnel in the mass of defeated airmen. Some minutes later everything became clear as we watched about 1,000 soldiers marching up in files to surrender in the same way. It was an incredible sight. We held our breath hoping they wouldn't change their minds. It was a very significant situation. Here, the Argentines had all the resources to defend the settlement for a long time, but they lacked the bottle. This lack of will, evident throughout the whole Argentine ground defence, lost them the Malvinas. If their islands were such a precious Argentine possession, why were they not prepared to die to hold onto them? Clearly, the islands did not have that significance in the Argentinians' minds and the war was merely a device to distract the population from the desperate state of the government's fortunes on the mainland. I like to think that the evil that stalked the Argentine, in the shape of the right-wing dictatorship, was felled through the action on the Falklands and opened the way to a more liberal regime. That process started at Goose Green.

The victory, however, was H.'s. The inspiration of 2 Para came from him, and my role was merely to act on his behalf in his absence. For that I am the caretaker of an enamelled bit of metal, which I carry on behalf of every man in 2 Para, especially the junior non-commissioned officers and the soldiers. I miss the brotherhood of that gang of folk who were called 2 Para who are now dispersed to the four winds, but especially I miss H.

Major John Crosland

The Parachute Regiment

Military Cross

Major Crosland was in command of B Company 2nd Battalion the Parachute Regiment during operations in the Falklands. In the battle for Port Darwin and Goose Green on 28/29 May 1982 his company was ordered to attack a number of subsidiary positions, and then to capture the high ground overlooking Goose Green. Throughout all the engagements against a vastly numerically stronger enemy he demonstrated remarkable control and steadiness of command, despite the constant artillery, anti-aircraft and small-arms fire directed against his men. At every phase of the battalion's attack he was able to maintain the momentum by his determined leadership and his infectious bravado, which was an inspiration to his soldiers, enabling them to exploit every tactical advantage. Through his clever use of the ground, and by the novel use of anti-tank weapons against enemy bunkers, he was able to secure the critical high ground with the minimum of casualties. The final attack was crucial, enabling an assault to be launched to turn the enemy's flank, which resulted in the collapse of the entire enemy's defence.

Again on the night of 13/14 June 1982 in the attack on Wireless Ridge his unique style of leadership was an inspiration to his soldiers as they attacked through enemy artillery fire.

Throughout the campaign Major Crosland has displayed qualities of gallantry and tactical understanding in the very highest tradition of the Parachute Regiment.

After we had been on the *Norland* for four or five days I got the toms together and told them what my thoughts were, that we were going to war! The reason I felt this was that Margaret, who is a very determined lady, had set the ground rules very early on. She had said she wouldn't negotiate until the Argentinians had left, and having been involved in the Iranian Embassy siege in London in 1980 I knew her thinking because she'd set the ground rules there. When you look at the Argentinians and their psychological build-up, their macho was that they mustn't lose face and there's no way that Galtieri could pull out without doing something. So, at least we would have to land and fight some kind of battle, or maybe just land, and they may jack then; but I thought it was unlikely.

We had about three weeks before landing in which we could concentrate on one solid objective – training for war. We'd never had a period like this since Borneo, which was fourteen years ago. So, I could really concentrate the toms' minds because there were no outside imbuggerancies like duties and guards and everything else.

Fortunately, I'd given a lot of thought to the psychological preparation for battlefield stress, based around Lord Moran's book, *The Anatomy of Courage*. I'd also had previous experience in Northern Ireland and with the SAS in Oman.

Northern Ireland has its very violent periods and some prolonged operations but none with the full orchestration of war. There were shooting engagements but you can't compare those to a full-scale battle. The toms in my company hadn't heard the noise of a sustained battle or felt the intense loneliness and fear that results from such an experience. I was fortunate to have had that experience, so spent a lot of time talking to my company, to the officers and NCOs, taking them through a scenario which was to prove to be close to the actual reality of the battles that were to come.

On the *Norland* we were lucky because we embarked as a battalion group on our own, with supporting arms. We were moving as a unit, minus only a small party that had gone ahead, which we caught up with at Ascension. We also had on board two Field Surgical Teams (FSTs), some of whom I'd come across in the Middle East where they'd carried out a lot of field surgery. Partly because of the situation in Northern Ireland, where expert medical help is at hand, medical training prior to the Falklands was woefully weak. In Northern Ireland, if a bloke's hurt he's lifted straight into Musgrove, or wherever, and he's quickly under expert knifemen. Therefore the one thing I had to impress on my soldiers was that the Northern Ireland image of a casualty halting an operation wasn't going to happen in the Falklands. We had an objective to take, so whoever got bowled over had to administer their own first aid and look after themselves. Then, once we'd secured our objective, we'd come back and sort out the casualties. So, for ten days the highly professional medical people in the FSTs put the toms through an intensive medical cadre on life-saving, first aid, gunshot wounds, tears, rips, and all the rest of it. At the end of it, they could take blood, put in drips and repair all manner of wounds very efficiently. Because I'd instilled in them that we were going to war, they didn't play at it – they were totally committed.

The other way I chose to focus my toms' thoughts was by using the medium of the Resistance to Interrogation, which I got from training with the SAS. This is an area which normally gets swept under the carpet because it's pretty unpleasant. But we were going 8,000 miles to take on a numerically superior army, and therefore there was a distinct possibility of toms getting captured. I had to prepare them for that; I had to prepare them for every eventuality that could happen. This was going to be the most frightening thing they had ever come across in their lives but they'd have to get over that and get on and do their job. In their training, I'd tried to instil in them the need to be aggressive, because I don't think people understand the amount of violence that's got to be generated to impress your point of view on somebody who's equally keen to impress his view on you. Generally we were going to be the regiment at the end of a long line of supply, so we had to be able to fight with whatever we had and carry what we wanted.

The opposition would be a regular army with conscripts, so if we made our presence felt initially, they might just crack. This proved correct, because at Goose Green we not only beat them physically but psychologically. So from then on (although there were severe battles in the mountains), they never counter-attacked, yet they had the troops, ammunition and logistics. In the first encounter at Goose Green, we'd given them what's called a classic Parachute Regiment punch-up – a gutter fight – but then our blokes are bloody good at that, probably the best in the world. Some of the rumours about the Argentinians being ill-equipped, underfed and lacking ammunition were just not true. I mean, our blokes were amazed at what we found around the place. With our calibre of blokes in those positions, it would have been a Crete all over again and we would have wiped anyone out.

David Cooper, the Padre of 2 Para, was extremely good with the toms while we were on the *Norland*. His contribution was immense. His sermon at Stanley has been reported on, but his sermons on the boat on the way down had a tremendous amount to do with uniting an already very close battalion, because he wouldn't avoid issues. He has an inbuilt ability to talk to soldiers and gain their trust, which is not as easy as one might think. Because he's got a tremendous depth of wisdom, he doesn't talk down to a soldier – he talks at his level. He is very realistic but he can be very abrupt and down to earth. He said in one of his sermons, 'Okay, on the way down you're going to book in for some credits by coming to church, but I can't guarantee that's going to give you any luck; because some of you will not be coming back. All I will guarantee is that you will be looked after whether you come back or whether you don't.' There is nothing false about the man, so the toms can talk to David. He's not just a very practical Christian, he's also a very fine soldier so he knows what he's talking about. The blokes have a tremendous respect for him.

David encouraged them to find a quiet place to go and think about things. The great quality about our toms is that they do think. A lot of people don't give them credit for that – they think they're just dozy, hairy-arsed parachute soldiers, all blood and thunder, but they think as well. There's no doubt about it, one's extremely fortunate to command that calibre of men. With that quality of soldier and a bit of luck, you can take on the world.

We landed on 21 May, and had five or six days of bad weather until we moved off from Sussex Mountains towards Goose Green. Our first scheduled attack on Goose Green was cancelled. We moved off again on the 26/27th towards Camilla Creek House. On that march down, which was a four- or five-hour trog, we were carrying a lot of weight on our backs, but at least the toms were on the move. There were various shell holes on the way and I remember some of the younger ones asking what they were. I said, 'Well, they're not moles!' I then asked them what they thought they were; artillery or what? What I was trying to get them to do was to look for signs. I'd seen shell holes before and pointed out that these were fresh and had obviously been fired that night because there was ice on the others. The blokes then started to become attuned to what to look for and what the signs meant. I also told them to listen carefully so they would tune their ears to the incoming artillery fire. They could hear the guns firing and the whistle and they were all going down a bit bloody quick. So I explained that the shots that they'd just heard were well over to our east, to the left, but it was the first time they'd heard it and as it was coming vaguely towards them, they were obviously very wary. So I really had to orchestrate their ears.

The one thing I stressed was, 'You will get artillery and mortar fire against you but you've got to maintain your momentum – I may not be there, you may lose your section commanders or senior soldiers but someone's got to keep it going, that's what it's all about. Artillery falls in areas and at times you can judge this and at other times perhaps not. But if you see it coming into an area, then you want to keep well clear.' The thing I was trying to get across to them is that you have to think about your job; like any other, whether you're a journalist or a sportsman, you have got to think about the tactics of the game.

We stayed at Camilla Creek House for a period of time. While we were there a breach of security happened when, for some inexplicable reason, the World Service told the world and his wife where we were. That involved 400 of the enemy being flown in and positions being turned round to meet our likely advance. A fairly stressful time especially as H. had already told us that we were going into action against odds of two to one; these were sporting odds so we didn't need them increased!

We were fairly well forward of our own defensive position and well in range of enemy artillery and their air recce, facing a garrison which was fairly well equipped. H. gave an O Group and I got back to give my orders just after last light. I sat facing my company O Group, three young Platoon Commanders – the eldest could only have been in the army for a year and a bit, and the youngest had only been with me since January of that year, so for them it was a big occasion. My three Platoon Sergeants were not that experienced either, so it was not the best time to start giving out orders or talking about hundreds of the enemy. But one had to be fairly blunt about things, and enforce one's own personality on the orders performance as you have to do with any Orders Group. I told them that the training we had done before was all part of the great maxim that in peace we were training for war. We had trained aggressively and realistically and now we were at war.

I went through our battle plan of what I wanted them to do: how we were going to get on with it; how they would do their job in controlling their platoons and sections; how I would keep the direction with the Forward Observation Officer. I then talked about keeping the supporting fire moving ahead, casualty procedure and prisoners of war. I also told them that they were not to accept a white flag without telling me. We'd been put on the west side to blockbust down towards Boca House. H.'s plan was for a six-phase day/night or night/day silent/noisy attack. H. knew well that B Company was a fairly aggressive company because that's the way I had trained them and they had confidence in their own ability. I knew that we'd been put on a side that had a fair amount of problems. So we knew we were in for a hard slog and that time was precious. I told them that we must get on, that we were not interested in capturing hundreds of gringos, someone else could do that. What I wanted to do was go through position after position after position and keep battering away at them. Finally, I said to them, 'These people have nicked our islands – we're going to make them wish they had never heard of the Falkland Islands.' In other words, 'Let's get stuck in!'

Later we moved to the forming-up point at the neck of the isthmus leading down to Goose Green. A Company had to swing round to the east in order to take out Burntside House before the whole battalion could move straight down. If we hadn't done that we would have been hitting one another with crossfire. So we moved into position and just lay down in our assault formations. It was raining, very cold and windy. The blokes lit cigarettes and we listened to the night noises of HMS *Arrow* which was firing away, but unfortunately a mechanical problem negated her very impressive fire support which later we were to rue.

A Company started to make their attack and although there were shells coming over, they caused little problem.

Slowly my lads started to get attuned. But there was a tension around because we knew from our own patrols that facing us, about four or five hundred yards away, there was an enemy company defensive position with a machine gun.

In support for the attack we had three light guns based at Camilla Creek House which were firing ahead of us. We only had very limited helicopter lift to come forward with the small amount of ammunition that we had. The support boys carried forward two mortars with ammunition. A normal battalion would have six or eight, but we only had two. However, we did have six detachments of Milan, which is an anti-tank gun with a guided missile, and we also had six heavy machine guns. We had, of course, expected HMS *Arrow* to be the main thrust of our artillery attack.

It was such an awful night in terms of the weather that one of our problems was actually being able to see what we were coming into. Although it was dark, raining and even snowing at times, the toms got accustomed to it. At least they'd had some experience of night fighting during the previous November whilst carrying out exercises in Kenya. I've always felt strongly that night operations have got to become second nature.

The one thing I'd learnt in the Middle East was to keep the momentum going – if you stopped on a position, you got hammered. So all through the night we kept crashing on. Their artillery, which was generally well orchestrated, had a job to find us. When we did stop, because we got disorganized or we came across a position we didn't know about, the enemy rearranged their artillery to fire back on us and we took shells. What saved us in these situations was that the ground was very soft and a lot of shells ploughed in or blew up in the peat. If it had been a very hard surface, I think the casualties on both sides would have been far worse.

The company killed its first Argentinian about three minutes after the start. It was some of Corporal Margerison's men that took him out. This thing actually arose from a trench, in a helmet and poncho; there was no face, just a helmet and poncho. We challenged him twice and nothing happened. The third time, his hands moved and two of my machine gunners and two riflemen opened up and, rather naturally, this bloke fell over. So that was a release of tension; we knew our weapons worked. As they say in the vernacular, 'Target scream when hit.' Like the first punch from a boxer or the first run for a batsman, we'd played it and hit home.

That night, in the aggressive trench-to-trench action, we had them all over the place, there's no doubt about that, and we didn't sustain any casualties in my company. D Company, however, had two killed because they hit a machine-gun post behind us which we hadn't seen. We had to fight at really close quarters for four or five hours which showed our soldiers' durability and stamina; certainly their aggressive, hard training paid off. I think we had, without blowing one's own trumpet, the most problems to overcome but we kept moving in a classic formation of two platoons up and one platoon back. A Company was on our left and we couldn't link in with them, so it wasn't a classic two-company move which we achieved later at Wireless Ridge. Many of the actions were led by young NCOs, senior soldiers and young soldiers, a lot of whom were unsung and unseen, but that's a fact of life, and a tribute to their self-discipline.

Come the dawn we had lost control of the driving seat. We'd come up against the main defence position which was the ridge of Darwin Hill in the east and we were still about 800 metres short of Boca House which we'd expected to take in one run that night. We'd lost two hours of darkness due to D Company having a punch-up behind us, and we'd also hit another position which had taken forty-five minutes to clear. These things happen in battle. The great 'Chinagraph Line', as I call it, that starts here and finishes there, just doesn't work out that way. People must understand that the bloke over there doesn't want to be killed any more than you or I, so he's going to make life bloody awkward for you. It's like a game of chess. As I said to the soldiers, 'You must keep thinking. If one course of action is producing casualties, then you've got to start something else. You may be on your own, isolated and feeling afraid, but you must keep thinking, because if you don't, you'll get killed.'

Having said that and shaken them up a bit, I said, 'Let's face it, to get killed by artillery fire, by mortar, or to be shot is unlucky. An awful lot of shrapnel is going to come down without causing casualties. It will be frightening – I'm not disputing that – but not every bullet is aimed at you. You've got to listen, hear the shells coming and if you think they're coming close, then obviously you get down. But as soon as you think it's quiet, keep moving.' I think the little black woollen hat that I wore throughout the campaign helped the toms to identify me and I'm sure they thought, 'If that stupid bugger's still running around with that hat on, it can't be that bad.'

At first light, as we approached our objective, we were caught in a difficult position as we were subjected to over-fire from Darwin Hill. The only thing to do was to move forward, so I ordered the two leading platoons, 4 and 6, to move ahead with Company HQ into the gully in front of Boca House. We then started to fight our way down this gully into the bottom and up the other side towards a sort of gorse line which gave some cover from the enemy's fairly dominant position at Boca House. As the light increased, so did the accuracy of their fire. I had two options, either withdraw completely or get forward. I certainly wasn't going to withdraw so I ordered my two forward platoons ahead with my own HQ. I left my reserve, 5 Platoon, on the crest line to protect the whole of the high ground in case we had to beat a hasty retreat; it was that platoon that took a battering. We also got fairly well larded with artillery and mortars but 5 Platoon were taking a lot of long-range fire from machine guns and snipers and were beginning to take casualties. I said to them over the net, 'Right, once we get down into the gully you withdraw onto the hill line and just hold the ridge-line position.' It was during this action we lost young Stephen

Illingsworth. He had rescued Private Hall, who had been shot, and then, because we were short of ammunition, had gone back for Hall's kit and while doing this was killed. It was a very brave act, no doubt about it; a classic young soldier's act, extremely brave, totally unselfish, and one can only give the highest praise for him. Street (or 'Strasse' as he was known in the company) was also wounded. He is very much the old company soldier but I heard him scream when he got two shots in the left leg. Later, when seeing his wounds, I was not surprised he yelled.

A little later there was a pause in the action as each side tried to sum up its own situation. During this period the toms were able to see the devastation we'd created through the night because we were now standing in the positions we'd taken out. We could see the effects of artillery fire, mortars, grenades and our own handiwork. In this lull, a mortar bomb came through the air, spinning rather badly, hit the crest line and very seriously wounded my Second-in-Command, Captain John Young. Fortunately, Captain Rory Wagon, who had been our RMO (Regimental Medical Officer) before Stephen Hughes, was on hand. He did what he could but it was essential that Young be urgently casevac'd out. The helicopter pilot, Captain John Greenhalgh, heard that we were in a spot of bother and needed to get a casualty out. So after last light, in the most atrocious weather and guided only by the lights of torches, he brought his helicopter down to the outskirts of Goose Green. His extremely brave flying undoubtedly saved the lives of Captain Young and other casualties. Captain Greenhalgh had flown with us the previous November in Kenya so he knew the battalion; he knew all the officers and people intimately, so when he heard that our unit was in trouble it meant much more to him.

We were under increasing pressure because we'd been in action for four hours during the night without resupply. About four or five hundred yards in front of us, across a totally open field, was a very strong enemy position. They were in the driving seat and could put down artillery, air attack or mortar fire whenever they wanted. I had a sixth sense that they'd mined their approaches so I couldn't just say, 'Right, fellows, up the hill after me,' because we'd have been wiped out.

Although we were putting down fire onto their positions and hitting their bunkers, we weren't actually killing the blokes inside. So I said, 'Cool the fire.' I just kept one machine gun going because in the back of my mind was the thought that they could counter-attack. We were in a fairly tenuous position because toms were trying to hide behind gorse bushes which, needless to say, hardly provided adequate cover. Even in these circumstances, there was still a lot of humorous banter between the lads, which kept our spirits up. One of the radio operators who was forward with one of the platoons was on the net saying, 'For God's sake, beam me up, Scotty.' 'I haven't got the right channel,' I replied.

At this point all we had to influence the battle were the three light guns and two mortars, and these were running out of ammunition. And we were still getting hammered.

The situation changed when Corporal Margerison managed to clear a bunker and Corporal Robinson's lot flattened another. Robinson had a lucky escape when a bullet just missed his balls. All I could hear him saying was, 'If you hit me in the balls, the wife'll kill me.' But once he'd ascertained he'd still got a pair, he was all right. One of his other mates got his rifle butt smashed and a couple of people had misses in the backs of their helmets.

With these two positions cleared I was able to get the company reorganized. I wanted to withdraw one of the leading platoons to a slightly better position. We managed to land a smoke bomb close by which, whilst giving cover for the withdrawal, also ignited the gorse. While we were withdrawing, Corporal Margerison was hit by a bullet which went through the back of his left shoulder, out through his jaw and took all his teeth out. A couple of toms dragged him back to cover and he was brought back to Company HQ. Having looked at his back I thought he'd possibly punctured his lung because he was wheezing a bit and obviously the shock was starting to come on. So I said to Smith, the medic, 'There is no way that we can get him back up the hill we've just come down because we'd all get shot in the back. You're going to have to work on him and sort him out. Whatever kit you want from anyone, you get it, because he's a priority. Get a drip into him. I don't know how long we're going to be here but that's your problem at the moment. Don't use everything up because there are other blokes who might need it.' To his great credit, Smith got on with it and kept Corporal Margerison alive.

I then took command of directing our guns and mortars onto the positions that were giving us problems. To my simple brain, what's hurting you at the moment has got to be eradicated. You worry about positions at Goose Green once you get to Goose Green. It was during this period that I heard that H. was killed performing a very brave act. I think there have been criticisms raised as to why he was so far forward. I honestly believe that if you are trying to get blokes to do something you've got to be at the front. It's all very well to say you have to sit back and take an overall position, but I don't think people understand just how desperate the position was. We'd been at it for four or five hours, including a couple of hours of daylight, we were short of ammunition and we didn't have resources. If we'd had the Scorpions and the artillery support we had at Wireless Ridge it would've been a different ball game. This was a classic Parachute Regiment punch-up. When the news came over the net that H. had been killed, I said to Corporal Russell, my signalman, 'That doesn't go any further. We've got enough problems without letting that out.' I was very close to H. – we thought along the same sort of lines. His death certainly stiffened my resolve. I mean, I was always determined that we were going to win, but his death just added a bit more oomph.

Shortly after the news of H.'s death I heard that the Argentinians had landed another 200 people to our south; we were in for trouble. I thought of John Frost's *A Bridge Too Far* and I said to myself, 'We've gone an island too far.' We needed to strike again. Boca House was our major objective but with the weapons that we had, we couldn't get effective fire onto it, so I called up the Milan team. A Milan is an anti-tank weapon which fires a guided missile with a very substantial warhead over a range of 2,000 metres. I thought, if we can bust them with the Milans, we can probably get round their flank, get down to Darwin, knock that off and then worry about Goose Green. The Milan was an unorthodox choice, but it was the only powerful weapon we had. Much to our relief, the first round fired was a perfect bull's-eye. It went straight through the bunker window and blew it out completely, and the second one did the same. Four more rounds and that was Boca House cleared out. Everyone stood on their feet and cheered!

A Company achieved a breakthrough in their own right and cleared Darwin Hill. Chris Keeble had taken over command by then and sent D Company off to start attacking Goose Green. We then started to come under fairly intense fire from Goose Green and the airfield. Their anti-aircraft guns had very good optics so they could see us at about a mile and a half's distance. Chris Keeble had been calling for an air strike all day but weather conditions were bad. However, at last light, the Harriers came and I would say their effect was critical. They came in on a low pass and dropped cluster bombs, inflicting a lot of casualties. I think the psychological effect on the Argies of this attack was out of all proportion because it was a surgical strike, very precise, and I think this undermined their will to keep fighting.

Prior to the aerial attack we had continued towards Goose Green with D and C Companies. A Company remained on Darwin Hill. We'd heard that there were 112 civilians being held in Goose Green so our idea of going in and flattening the area was out of the question. I said to Chris Keeble that I would swing down the isthmus itself and come in from the south. I'd been looking at the map and seen there were a couple of streams and realized if we could get round and come in from the south, they would feel they were encircled. So psychologically the whole thing really shifted to our advantage; we'd broken the crust, they had no escape. However, their anti-aircraft guns were still extremely intense. I remember telling the two leading Platoon Commanders that I wanted to get to where we could see the tracers in the sky. I'm sure one or two of them thought J.C.'s deaf or daft, or both. I told them that we were going to go underneath the trajectory and, although there was a lot of fire, we had a fairly reasonable passage and got through only to realize later that we had been walking through a minefield!

We had to try and neutralize their anti-aircraft guns; some were forward and some were on the promontory of Goose Green. They had their guns in amongst the buildings and were going to be difficult to shift. When we arrived within three or four hundred yards to the south of Goose Green, we engaged them with machine guns and they returned very fierce fire. We then heard that six helicopters had landed to my south with reinforcements but we managed to get a few rounds of ammunition off which landed right on top of them and dispersed them. There was still the thought in the back of my mind that there were one or two hundred blokes who had been landed fresh and could catch us with a possible counter-attack. So, after the Harrier attack, I gathered everyone together and told them to go and scrounge all the ammunition they could find. They went off and plundered everything and carried back about seven or eight thousand Argentinian rounds, which fortunately were the same calibre as ours.

I told the lads to go firm, to get into fours, dig in, and then we'd have to wait and see. I don't think anyone knew quite how far round we were so we withdrew that night and dug in to a tight defensive position around a hill. It was a very long, cold night – it snowed and froze very hard. But the toms were very good indeed considering they'd been on their feet fighting for twenty-four hours. Morale-wise there were no problems; they were terrific. They'd had a bit of a baptism and they'd come through very well. The news had filtered through during the day that we'd lost H. I gave them a sort of Winston Churchill pull up. I said, 'Look, we've done bloody well today. Okay, we've lost some lads; we've lost the CO. Now we've really got to show our mettle. It's not over yet, we haven't got the place. We're about 1,000 metres from D Company; we're on our own and an enemy has landed to our south and there's a considerable force at Goose Green, so we could be in a fairly sticky position.'

While we lay there two guys in a hole received virtually a direct hit but fortunately it had gone into the peat. It hadn't wounded them, but it had blasted them, and they were shaken. I shouted to them to come back to the Company HQ and have a cup of tea. It was just what they needed; to get back into the main body and have a cup of tea and a cigarette. You could see the relief on their faces.

We were really set to go in for the last push but that wasn't necessary because the following morning the surrender negotiations had started – 2 Para had captured two senior Argentine NCOs. Chris Keeble explained his terms of surrender and sent them off to talk to their garrison commander. Eventually they accepted Chris's terms of agreement. Initially a couple of hundred air force men appeared. Then, to our amazement, a massive column of about 1,000 blokes marched out.

After the surrender we were told to stay firm and dig in where we were on the high ground. Later, I went into Goose Green and was pleased to meet some of the very relieved civilians, who had been released. I was also interested to see the state of the Argentinian forces and just how many officers they had, because as far as I knew, we had only killed one or two of them. The most senior bloke I'd come across during the battle was a sergeant, which I think was indicative of their hierarchy. As I had expected, there were very many fairly fresh-faced-looking officers in Goose Green who had obviously run off, leaving their conscripts to fight it out – which was an appalling mark on their performance. From a soldier's point of view, if their officers had no respect for their men, how could they ever expect to win? I was appalled at this macho characteristic, which was extremely shallow. They seemed pretty tough so long as we didn't get too close. Once we closed, they wanted to surrender. Well, I'm afraid that doesn't work in real life and at night it's impossible. So I think a lot of people were hurt, possibly unnecessarily. If you start an attack and then decide to surrender I think that suggests someone's got their ground rules wrong.

The casualty-clearing process then started. We swept the battlefield trying to get all the Argentinian casualties in and their bodies tidied up. Their officers appeared to have little interest and an extremely frail knowledge of how many men they had. We just lined the enemy bodies up against a hedge; there was nothing else we could do. David Cooper had the task of attempting to organize some kind of burial for them, with little help from the Argentinians.

We then flew to Ajax Bay for what we'd assumed was a memorial service for H. and the others. When we arrived, there was a hole dug ready to receive eighteen burial bags and a lot of people gathered round, saying their last farewells. We'd understood that the bodies of those killed would be repatriated. Yet here we were burying them. We didn't know what the hell was going on and a lot of people were, naturally, very upset. The company commanders acted as bearers for H., and for the Adjutant David Wood, Chris Dent and Jim Barry. The toms under Regimental Sergeant-Major Simpson, who had flown down with us, were the bearers for the other toms.

When we returned to Goose Green, David Cooper and Steve Hughes continued to work non-stop as we were still finding the enemy dead or wounded three or four days after the battle. Some of the wounded were suffering from fairly advanced gangrene and were in a bad state. We took over a large agricultural shed with enough room for the whole company. Colour-Sergeant Steve Gerrard organized the sleeping arrangements and got a brazier fire going.

The first time I had a moment of quietness, I sat down and wrote to the parents of Stephen Illingsworth and told them of his great gallantry. I also wrote to Sarah Jones about H. I hoped these letters would bring them some comfort. I felt responsible for Illingsworth. I don't mean that in a trite sort of way. I was his boss and basically he'd been killed working for me. I also wrote to Cathy Dent, whose husband Chris had been killed at A Company's action on Darwin Hill. I then asked the NCOs and officers to put down on paper the names of those they thought deserved some kind of award. I had no idea what the award system was going to be, but I thought we ought to get some notes down while our memories were still fresh.

Things were good within our own little group but I was very keen that now we had finished at Goose Green, the company got some rest.

The boys who had been wounded were recovering well. We had many instances of young lads being badly hurt but they'd heeded the lessons the medics had taught them on the *Norland* and looked after their own wounds and were able to hang on (in some cases for a number of hours) until we could get them out. They'd then arrive at Ajax Bay in a fit enough state for the doctors not to have to resuscitate or revive them. Even during their convalescence they showed great determination to get over their wounds. I think that's a tremendous tribute to their courage and to the courage of our medics, because without a doubt, if you're going into a punch-up it's encouraging to know that, not far behind you, are the medics who'll take care of you if you do get hurt. The medics at the hospital, nicknamed the Red and Green Life Machine, at Ajax Bay worked flat out and performed miracles. One can't give them enough credit, especially as not one single casualty who arrived alive had died.

The other blokes who did a great job of work were the logisticians. Logistics is not a glamour area; it's a mundane job of getting kit from A to B. Generally there was not too much finesse about it, just humping and dumping, and those boys did it. I think the whole logistic chain was amazing; it covered everything, from refuelling in the air to actually getting the kit to the right place.

Having called a nearby farm from a local telephone to

211

ascertain if it was clear of Argentinians, we moved on to Fitzroy. We got into Fitzroy by 3 or 4 June and dug in. We remained there until 10 or 11 June. These six days were interesting because there was a slight feeling of 'You've done your bit, 2 Para – you can stand back now', which was very dangerous. My message to my toms was quite simple: 'You can stand down when you get to Ascension Island on the way back because that's when it's finished. Drop your guard now and you will get one straight on the chin.' So we set about improving our positions and making ourselves comfortable; got ourselves dried out and maintained normal company position. The toms could now rest but with the understanding that there was still a war on.

Naturally, they were tired. After all, we'd been in a fairly major fracas for thirty-six hours and we'd lost eighteen men and had thirty-eight wounded. In *The Anatomy of Courage* Lord Moran talks about the 'bank of courage'. Our reserve had been pretty drained; it needed to be replenished, banked up. The next seven days were going to be a useful recuperation phase. After twenty-four hours we began preparing for other tasks. This kept the element of tension up sufficiently and didn't allow the toms to think too much about their experiences. Out there, there was no R & R (rest and recuperation) as there is in Northern Ireland. I was only too aware of the fact that the Argentinians could well have adopted the attitude of 'Okay, we've taken one on the nose, now we'll sling one back at you.' Their air force showed in the *Sir Galahad* attack that they had the capability of doing just that.

We were then told we would be the reserve battalion for the final push on Stanley. My great cry was, 'Follow the loot.' I told them to get themselves ready because, 'If there's a nut to be cracked, they'll ask 2 Para to crack it, not because anyone else can't, but we are the reserve force. In any plan the commander is going to have a reserve, and he will commit his reserve if he needs it.' What I tried to impress upon my toms was that the enemy wasn't finished until it decides to throw the towel in.

While 3 Para and the Marines took their objectives, we moved off from behind Mount Kent and began our next move towards Mount Longdon. It was a long, cold march of about sixteen kilometres over difficult terrain, carrying a load of over 50 lbs each. It was done as a classic airborne snake. Fortunately we were still pretty fit, yet despite the overboots we'd scrounged from the Welsh Guards to keep the frost off our feet, some of the unlikeliest blokes, the ones who were physically very fit, went down with trench foot. The only thing to do when that happens is to casevac them or keep them in their sleeping bags for a few days, until the whole body has thawed out. You have to de-thaw the whole body because once the feet have gone past a certain stage, the body temperature drops. Stephen Hughes did a tremendous job at Fitzroy because he managed to get the trench foot casualties into the Regimental Aid Post where they soon recovered enough to return to their companies. This was very important as we had more trench foot casualties than actual battle casualties. Foot care is vital, and that means when you stop at night, you undo your frozen boots, check your feet, massage them, put on dry socks and then put your wet socks under your armpits. In the morning, you've then got a spare pair of dry socks. Of course we were cold but the body temperature regulates itself. When we got to Stanley and were in warm houses, a lot of us couldn't sleep – it was too hot. It had been so cold on that particular night behind Longdon I think the whole battalion had marched round in circles, trying to keep warm. In the daylight we could see this great ring of footprints in the frost.

Towards Longdon we were the leading company, and I was trying to find a safe route through the Argentinian artillery that was ahead of us. It was only when I went round some peat bog for nature's call that I spotted a gap between two beaten zones of artillery fire. As I was finishing, to my surprise our new CO, David Chaundler, came round the corner. I told him that with the fire coming in from the left and right, we'd have to go through the middle and hope that they didn't shift their aim. This idea worked and the battalion moved up to its assembly position behind Mount Longdon.

Before the final push for Wireless Ridge there was a lot more tension – which was natural. The blokes were apprehensive because they'd seen the violence of battle; they'd seen their friends hurt and killed. But when the whistle went and the momentum started, that was it. It's rather like making a parachute jump – doesn't matter how many times you've done it, unless you're apprehensive, you're not switched on.

We were always going to be up against it down there but I maintained on the way there that we weren't going to lose. Someone else was going to take an early bath, and that's what they did.

As we lay behind Mount Longdon and contemplated our next attack there was a greater feeling of apprehension. The battle for Goose Green had shown us what could happen and now we were about to roll into the attack again. There were many differences between these two attacks, the main ones being that at Wireless Ridge we had tremendous dedicated fire support and I, as a Company Commander, had had a chance to recce from Mount Longdon over the ground that I was about to attack. The Goose Green attack could be classed as a 'come as you are party'. In many ways this was to be a classic battalion night attack consisting of a preliminary operation by D Company followed by the main attack put in by A and B Companies. C Company were also tasked to look after a further objective.

This was not to say that there were no problems. Although the attack was put back some twenty-four hours, our preparation for battle was held up by enemy activity. Due to heavy enemy fire on Mount Longdon no targets had been previously registered. Due to late intelligence, orders and their dissemination down the line was very hurried. Permission to make the attack was granted just two hours before last light – I then received my orders, 'Command and control'. Those throw-away words took on a new significance.

From the start line to the objective was about 1,500 metres over open rolling country with a wide stream about 400 metres from the objective. Paratroopers resent getting wet, especially when it is freezing cold! Our frontage was four platoons wide, held together by two lance-corporals in the middle. Control was going to be by shouting, so the more our artillery fire deafened the enemy the better – 3 Para said we sounded like a football crowd going into the attack! To help direction I had the direct fire from Scorpions and Scimitars, and this was excellent. The troop leader kept firing until I told him to switch, but otherwise he used the AFV (armoured fighting vehicle) optics to search for targets and engaged them immediately. I would suggest it is impossible to command an attack as well as totally control all your supporting fire – especially if you are my height and trying to see over the next tuft of grass!

Just to add spice to this situation, I was given the news of a possible minefield in front of our objective some five minutes before the attack was due to start. I decided to keep this good news to myself! My TAC HQ found themselves some five metres behind the leading soldiers instead of about the usual fifteen! I had discussed minefield tactics with the company and also with our four Royal Engineers. If close to an objective and under fire, the policy was to go straight through. In this case we had no option and in any case to breach a minefield is a long job.

The objective was a long oblong hill with no obvious landmarks. Enemy defences were going to be a problem. Once the enemy had lost this objective, we had no option but to dig in on his old positions, as the ground beyond fell away, leading us onto a long forward slope. Therefore it was vital to fight through quickly and, once secure, dig in as soon as possible. Although opposition was light in terms of small-arms fire, the enemy artillery responded as we had anticipated and the company needed no greater encouragement to dig in.

As I have said, there was a fair amount of tension before

the battle began. Added to that was the fact that the lights of Port Stanley were in sight. Our thoughts were shaken by enemy artillery hitting our positions on the start line. I had no need to give any orders – the toms were already in cover. When I tried to crouch down I found a signaller under each knee! I laughed and the tension eased.

Once on the move, into the attack, all signs of nerves vanished. Our attack started at about 0100 and we had consolidated by 0230. Whereas at Goose Green we had had to win the fire fight by using company weapons, this time our fire support had done the job. To win the fire fight is not as easy as it sounds but, once won, it is vital to press home the attack – i.e. keep the initiative.

The enemy now kept up a steady harassing fire barrage on and around us until dawn, some nine hours away.

It was a great responsibility and also a great privilege to lead such high-calibre blokes. If you have the privilege of commanding such men, then the battle is half won before you start. So I think it behoves you to try and think things out before, because there's no doubt that they are looking to you. I say this humbly, without meaning to sound pompous, but I think that within the battalion, I was the barometer. People knew that I'd had a lot of experience and therefore they were looking at me to see if there was any shake. If there was, then things could have been serious. We had a very good team led by H., and I think the toms knew that such a team thought conscientiously about problems and wouldn't commit them to something that they had no control over. People have said, 'Well, why the hell did you go to Goose Green?' And the answer to that is that the toms were keen to get at the enemy and attack them. It's a great privilege to have people of that nature ready to follow you.

Captain Steven Hughes

Regimental Medical Officer

The Parachute Regiment

Mention In Despatches

In a strange way I feel I was destined to be part of the magnificent 2 Para, and all the events that took place just fulfilled that destiny. I first developed the ambition to one day join the battalion in 1976, when I saw the painting by David Shepherd, *Arnhem Bridge, 5 p.m., The Second Day*. I felt a strong attraction to be part of that organization and started working towards that goal. As a student I joined the Territorial Army Parachute Field Ambulance to win my wings, so that when I took up my commission full time I would be already trained. With the TA I learnt the basics of soldiering which were to give me the background understanding which would later give me the basis on which to plan for war.

In the latter part of 1981 it was to be a major delight and challenge to find that I had secured the doctor's slot with 2 Para, which had come up for grabs. It was not without some trepidation, though, that I approached the job, and wondered if I would be up to it. I even had an odd sense of foreboding that something was about to happen, perhaps to do with Belize where we were due to spend six months of 1982.

I went into the job at the deep end. Three weeks after joining the battalion, I did my first parachute jump for two years. I should have done a retraining course after that time lag, especially as there had been a number of procedural changes in the interim. But there wasn't time, so on the advice of the Adjutant, David Wood, I kept quiet and went and jumped anyway. I think I was as frightened as at my very first jump.

The jump went without a hitch for me. But my vehicle and its trailer of medical supplies failed to materialize as its Hercules transport went u/s on the pan at Lyneham. It was this that prompted me to re-inaugurate the scales for carrying all our medical kit with us, in our bergens, when we jumped, and that was to set us up pre-prepared for a manpack war.

Subsequently, after a long discussion (and several beers) with David Wood, I devised a new mnemonic for immediate first aid. The standard response to a casualty lying on the drop zone or anywhere else is to yell 'Medic' and wait for help. We wanted to engender some reaction in either the casualty or his buddy. To this end we introduced the idea of the character of ABE, the Airborne Medic. By association of ideas, ABE's name would arise. The letters of his name stood for: Airway Bleeding Evacuation. It was a variant of peacetime civilian first-aid mnemonics which introduced a sense of urgency for evacuation of the casualty out of the area of danger.

With a proposed six-month tour of Belize, we started to run courses in advanced first aid to train 'patrol medics'. These were all part of the preparation for the tour that wasn't to be (not in 1982 anyway) but that left us in a high state of preparedness for what subsequently did happen. I was highly aware of the battalion's recent losses at Warren Point in Northern Ireland, and I wanted our preparedness for any similar incident to be as high as possible.

Six days before I was due to leave for Belize, the Argentinians invaded the Falkland Islands. I was moonlighting in the NHS, as a locum surgical Senior House Officer at the time. During the course of the Friday, as I went about a clinic, and theatre in the afternoon, I kept in touch by the radio news.

As I travelled back to my girlfriend Naomi's flat that night, I had a double take at a sign in Ealing Broadway tube station: 'All members of the 3rd Battalion the

218

Parachute Regiment return to barracks immediately.' But the only message I received that day from the Army was to check that I had had my Belize briefing. I had.

I spent the weekend saying goodbye to friends and was in the bar at the medical school on Sunday night when Naomi caught up with me. My mother had contacted her at work and she had been trying to find me for hours. 'The Army wants you,' she said, and burst into tears.

I rang Aldershot and spoke to John Holborn, the Rear Party Officer. H. wanted me back for an O Group the next day – Belize was on hold. I finished off my boozing session with my mates with a different destination in mind. I felt a mixture of elation and apprehension.

The O Group the following day served to brief us on the status of the impending departure of 3 Para with 3 Commando Brigade, and the uncertainty of 2 Para's position. It looked like Belize was off but rather than redeploy south, we would be required to remain in the UK as Parachute Contingency Force. Morale started to nose-dive. But H. wouldn't have us left out.

Initially, we started to consider the problems of an airborne assault on the Falklands. The logistics and casualty estimates were terrifying and in retrospect not a real option – but we planned anyway. It served to prepare us for a 'worst-case' option.

I had to re-equip. All my medical supplies were in mid-Atlantic, container-bound for Belize. This was the situation with most of the battalion's heavy equipment. I started comparing casualty statistics for previous wars with our projected estimates and ordered certain special items of equipment. The figures again were frightening. But they prompted me to consider the Israeli technique of issuing intravenous fluids to the individual soldier. Initially, the idea was purely to distribute the load for transport to the battlefield, but if the soldier was going to have fluid at the sharp end, wouldn't it make sense to train him to administer it?

To this end I spoke to Chris Keeble about funds and we purchased an artificial plastic arm-infusion trainer to teach setting up drips. But siting drips, even under ideal conditions, takes skill and aptitude; not everyone can pick it up. We were able to train some of the medics to site drips, but in the time available to us we couldn't achieve much more.

In the bar (where, in the evenings, so much of the multi-discipline discussion and planning was done) David Wood, Malcolm Jowitt (one of our Para anaesthetists), and I addressed the problem. Why not go back in the history of fluid replacement to rectal infusion – the administration of fluids by an enema technique? We didn't know how effective this technique would be, we couldn't find any really scientific evidence. But it was a technique that could be taught to everybody, and it would at least motivate the soldiers to carry the 1 lb bags of fluid. (If they didn't think it was of personal use they might 'bin' the bags.)

Subsequently, the weight of military medical opinion came down against rectal infusion as being ineffective. But we needed to motivate the soldier to believe that this fluid was for him and he wasn't just carrying the medics' load for them. It is funny now, but that attitude did pervade at the time. One 2 Para officer had a long argument with Malcolm Jowitt as to why I was making the soldiers carry my fluid for me. The same officer learnt the hard way, after nearly losing his life to a shrapnel fragment in his liver. After Goose Green, everyone wanted his bag of fluid and I and my medics were no longer 'idle knackers'.

Eventually H. resolved the problem of our not being on the order of battle for Operation Corporate (the code-name for the Falklands campaign), so the next problem was 25,000 seasick pills. The departure was delayed for nearly a week, prolonging the goodbyes, and the goodbye celebrations, to the extent of cirrhosis. By the time we actually sailed, on 26 April, we didn't really need the twice daily seasick pills to sedate the battalion whilst the ship settled into its routine, but the sergeant-major ensured compliance anyway.

During those initial days I liaised with the officers and seniors of the Parachute Clearing Troop (PCT) who were subsequently to form the 'red' half of the Red and Green Life Machine at Ajax Bay (the Marines formed the 'green' half). We set up a training cadre for patrol (subsequently to be renamed 'combat') medics. We were to run three such courses, each an intensive week of training.

The idea was to establish a system of 'double hatted' medics throughout the battalion infrastructure. We didn't believe that much 'buddy-buddy' care would be performed on the battlefield. So we had to provide a back-up between front line and company medic – thus the combat medic – one in every ten men. Their training included elements of anatomy and physiology, but mainly we explained the reasons for, and therefore the important points of, the various procedures to enable them to work more efficiently and more effectively.

Apart from my role as ship's doctor, in which I was helped by the other doctors in the PCT, I was busy planning, briefing my brother officers and lecturing to soldiers. Now I had a demanding audience: 'Why do we do this?' 'Why can't we do it that way?' and I, in turn, challenged them, 'How are you going to react? How are you going to carry your casualties? Go away and think about it. I don't have the answer – if you come up with one, let me know.' We made everyone aware of the potential problems and they tried to come up with solutions.

We didn't really solve the problem. We started to make up lightweight casualty-carrying sheets. To do this we had to despatch someone to HMS *Fearless* with material and nylon strapping. But we only managed to make up four in time. On the day, it was all improvised, using, where we could, teams from the Defence Platoon to carry forward resupply and bring back the wounded.

As war grew more certain, the preparations became more earnest and anxiety levels higher. We started breaking out the issues of supplies and ammunition. From my point of view this included three field dressings, one half-litre of intravenous fluid, and a syrette of morphine per man. We overcame the problem of fragility of the morphine syrettes by taping them to the insides of our helmets.

The cock-up of our late notification of 'D-Day' is now well known. As a result, that night was so rushed that, in retrospect, it was a good thing. There was too much else to think about to let fear get too strong a grip. Before we boarded our landing craft the *Norland* crew prepared a feast of egg banjos – fried egg sandwiches – for us. There were two reactions to the fear – some ate none, others ate a large number. I was in the latter group. My stomach will always rule my heart.

My first patient that night was the BBC's Robert Fox. He was hit in the mouth by a rucksack, splitting his lip. It would have been a fine thing for our radio journalist to be *hors de combat* before we even started. I repaired his lip with some steristrip adhesive tapes from my pocket.

I expected to have customers a short time later. About 200 metres offshore in the landing craft someone had a negligent discharge. We were so tightly packed in, I couldn't believe the shot hadn't hit someone. But we could only wait for the craft to empty. When it did empty, miraculously there were no bodies in it.

We didn't actually hit the beach that night but, rather, the sloping foreshore about 20–30 feet out. The wade in through the icy water of the South Atlantic was to precipitate a lot of problems with feet. Boots, which had been effectively waterproofed, now served only to keep the water in.

Relatively silent pandemonium existed on the beach, where the landing craft had beached out of pattern. The battalion tried to recognize its constituent parts in the dark, and snake out in its projected order of march. I married up with the second half of my team and we eventually moved off at the tail end of the column, where we could 'minesweep' any casualties.

The first land-based casualty was a lad named Hemphill who fell, injuring his back and knocking himself out with the Blowpipe missile he was carrying. A good number of the column walked straight past him until someone tripped over him and realized he was a casualty.

In doubling forward to the casualty we had to negotiate a ford in a thigh-deep brook. As luck would have it, one of the medics, Cleggie, tripped and went right under. He was soaked through. We now had two casualties to cope with, or would have two if we didn't keep Cleggie moving. Luckily I had filled my stainless steel thermos with hot, sweet drinking chocolate for just such an eventuality and this revived Cleggie somewhat.

At this stage, I didn't want to leave any bodies behind on the route so we pressed on, carrying the still unconscious Hemphill in one of the carrying sheets we had had made up on *Fearless*. We all took turns at the carry, the Padre, David Cooper, probably more than most, and as we went we picked up stragglers – the gunners carrying the Blowpipe missiles. The crippling weights everybody was carrying were telling and we were way behind schedule. H. was to admit to me later that he had made a mistake with regard to personal loads.

We kept Cleggie moving to help keep him warm; there was little we could do at this stage about his wet clothes. By this time it was getting to the point of finishing a carry on the stretcher; walking with just your load for a bit, then taking over a carry on the Blowpipe missile. Knackered barely does justice to the way we felt. David Cooper must have made three or four trips back and forth picking up ditched Blowpipe missiles.

Eventually, as daylight dawned and we neared the base of Sussex Mountains (the top of which was our destination), I found a suitable spot to leave Hemphill and Cleggie. We put them in a gully, both in the same sleeping bag, leaving the thermos and some signal flares. At lifting of radio silence, we would signal a chopper to pick them up – which is what subsequently happened, Surgeon Commander Rick Jolly their rescuer.

We meanwhile made our way on to the base of Sussex Mountains, having to cross a frost-covered wooden bridge. By this time I had lost count of the number of times I had fallen crossing the peat, but it had all been in the dark. Crossing the wooden bridge it was now daylight, and I provided some entertainment when both feet went out from under me and I went down on my back with an explosive 'Fuck!' This was to prove most people's favourite word for the campaign, and we meant it every time we said it.

The initial plan was for the medics to dig in at the base of Sussex Mountains. We were thankful at this because the task of climbing to the top was just about beyond us. As we dug in we processed two or three ankle and other minor injuries for evacuation to *Norland*. At some stage Cleggie was restored to us, complete with dry clothing and his testicles back in their normal place.

The first Mirage and Skyhawk jets to overfly us lent a certain sense of urgency to our digging, as had the first helicopter earlier until we recognized the sound as friendly. We had barely got down to our knees in the peat when it was decided to ferry us to the top of the mountain to join the rest of the battalion. This task was performed relatively effortlessly for us by means of a hover taxi, a helicopter, in about four stages.

By now the surreal impressions of the voyage through the South Atlantic had exchanged themselves for the surreal patterns of life ashore.

Once established on the ridge line opposite Battalion HQ, we set to digging in. I picked a large vertical rock, about 8–10 feet high, against which to construct a shelter for treating casualties. I placed three stretchers against this rock to form a lean-to shelter; then, covering the stretchers with waterproof nylon camouflage sheets, I used peat blocks to build up a protective and camouflage layer on top. Inside this small area, when we did not have an in-patient, I would sleep. The rest of the lads, including my radio operator, dug in amongst the rocks around. (I had the capability to split the RAP – Regimental Aid Post – into two teams, each with a radio and capable of independent movement in leapfrog fashion. This would later prove a godsend.) From the entrance to my RAP – my stand-to position – I was to have a magnificent view of the ensuing air battles over Bomb Alley.

We had barely settled in before casualties started arriving, proving the age-old lesson of military medicine – 'battle sick outnumber battle wounded'. Predominantly, we had trench foot problems, although we did have one case of heat exhaustion, from a lad in Patrol Company, who had marched too fast with too much arctic clothing on!

We also had minor cuts, burns, dental sick, as well as one case of suspected appendicitis. With the first dental extraction I performed I don't know who was more surprised, the patient or myself, when all went smoothly. Considering I was relying on memory of a half-hour dentistry film, and guidance from the Padre, I was delighted. The second did not go so well. After my local anaesthetic infiltration failed, I had to resort to a general anaesthetic called Ketamine. This drug gives general anaesthesia with retention of normal breathing and airway reflexes; however, it gives rise to what are euphemistically called 'emergence phenomena'. In this case, the tooth came out okay but the patient was euphoric. He decided that he was so grateful he wanted to give me a present, and duly presented me with a live grenade. After we had disarmed him and set him aside to sober up, I largely refrained from dentistry.

Not all the time on the mountains was spent on treatment. We also performed a fair amount of preventative medicine, mainly in terms of visiting the various locations and inspecting feet. We developed 'Feet R&R Centres' where problem feet convalesced before they got too far.

It was a frustrating time of relative inactivity for the battalion but, nevertheless, a busy time for David Cooper and myself. The Padre and the Doctor moved nearly everywhere as one, we became almost Tweedledum and Tweedledee, a pattern that was to remain for the rest of the campaign. I was to find David a tower of strength and whilst not being a religious man myself, I respected David's strong faith. As Christ said of Peter, 'Upon this rock I will build my church'; David Cooper was the rock upon which I built my Regimental Aid Post.

What follows are extracts taken from my diary, with subsequent amendments.

Tuesday, 25 May

Last night David Cooper and I made our way across to Battalion HQ after the evening stand-to. Not least of the dangers was that we had to cross the valley, from the top of which was aimed one of D Company's machine guns. (D Company had already shot up the RAP once during over-enthusiastic anti-aircraft fire). We had to warn everyone before we left that we were coming, so we weren't shot by mistake. There had been reports of Argentinian 'special forces' patrols in the area and as we crossed the valley we heard noises and movement. We went to ground briefly and then made a beeline for Battalion HQ. Shortly after, all hell broke loose down in the valley with D Company's machine gun opening up and flares and automatic fire further down the valley, nearer A Company's position. A lot of rounds were expended but, in the light of day, there were no Argie bodies – had they been there, or had it been a friendly patrol? Today a flight of Argentinian A4s (Skyhawks) came in, and the *Sir Galahad* came in for quite a pounding and, maybe, a close miss with a bomb. One A4 at least was hit. A pilot ejected and was captured. The Rapier again failed to work. B Company had eight cases of trench foot for evacuation.

Wednesday, 26 May

This morning we tabbed down to the mortar line, so that I could manipulate a frozen shoulder. When we tabbed back up the hill, at 17:00, we were told we were off for Darwin tonight. Two days before, when a similar foray was cancelled at the last minute, I had had to make a difficult decision about which men to leave behind. Not so this time, as the whole battalion would be involved. Frantic repacking again, stripping down our bergens to the minimum (about 60 lbs), we tabbed off at an horrific pace, which eventually settled down when one of A Company collapsed. I left Cleggie with him, and the rest of us tabbed on to Camilla Creek House. Six hours and fourteen kilometres. During that tab, in the darkness, across a largely peat terrain, many people fell. Some of us repetitively. Those with heavier weight fared worse. At one stage, whilst negotiating a rut in a track, I turned my ankle quite severely and felt something go. The air turned blue, and my ankle would have been the same colour, I am sure, if I had taken my boot off. But I knew that if I did, it would swell up and I would be unable to put the boot back on again. So I did the opposite, I tightened my lace to give me as much extra support as possible, and limped on, favouring my bad ankle, with the inevitable result that I fell regularly on the other leg, although luckily without such severe consequence. After a fall what sapped one's strength was the painful process of rolling onto one's front, climbing to one's knees, then planting one foot, then the other on the ground in order to rise slowly with the weight of the bergen.

Finally, we reached Camilla Creek House, in darkness, and moved into an outhouse and spent a cold night. There was not enough space for us all to stretch our legs so we piled them on top of one another in the centre of the floor like 'pat-a-cake'. Then, like 'pat-a-cake', every half hour one would wake with one's feet at the bottom of the pile, extract them, put them on the top, only to wake again half an hour later with crushed legs.

Thursday, 27 May

We awoke at 9:30 Zulu time, and brewed up. It was still dark. The rest of the battalion did not stir for some time. One case of frostbite casevac'd. Chris Keeble's ingrowing toenail sorted out. We moved out into the surrounding terrain during the afternoon to prepare for the night, not least because John Nott announced over the World Service where we were. We expected to be shelled any minute, but weren't. During the O Group, after our first Harrier strike, call-sign 97, Peter Ketley's party, took four prisoners including one casualty. In fact, there were two Argy casualties Peter brought in, both with gunshot wounds to their thighs. The first, a sergeant, had a through and through SLR (self-loading rifle) wound with a fractured femur – he required IV fluid and IV morphine. The second had a submachine-gun wound in each leg with a possible fracture of the right femur. Both patients were treated dispassionately, with firm wound dressings applied to stop bleeding, intravenous lines set up to replace fluid loss, and both antibiotics and painkillers were given by injection.

None of us had dealt with real gunshot wounds before. I was glad to be able to 'blood' my medics with casualties whom they did not know or identify with. They would find it a damn sight harder to cope with such injuries in their mates. I was proud of the professional manner in which they handled their job, without prejudice to the nationality of our patients.

The O Group was put back until 17:50 Zulu time to allow for the incorporation of information gleaned from the prisoners, and the CO outlined a six-phase battalion plan to take the Goose Green/Darwin isthmus, with the initial fire support of HMS *Arrow*. We all retired away from Camilla Creek House until start time to make our individual preparations. The medical plan I formulated was for two medical sections forward, each with a Medical Officer: Rory Wagon and myself. I would leave Sergeant Bradshaw, Private Buchanan and two PCT guys at Camilla Creek to deal with any casualties we managed to evacuate by the captured Land-Rover. We retired to the cud to eat and kip down until 02:00. As it was, I spent until midnight trying to tie up casevac details with the helicopter-handling teams.

Friday, 28 May

I got the lads up at 01:20 after spending a freezing night in the cud. We brewed up, packed up and moved close into Camilla House, moving off behind Battalion Main Headquarters just after 02:00. Moving with the medical kit divided amongst us, in our bergens, the order of march was myself, Hall, Clegg, Polky, Gibson, Bentley, Rory Wagon, Taff Jones, Hamer, Davis, Hood, Corporal Thornborough and the Padre.

We harboured for about two hours, just off the isthmus, whilst Phase One went in – apparently without casualties on our side. There was a light drizzle, I slept a little. We then moved, in darkness, onto the isthmus about 06:00, moving down a farm track on which I repeatedly fell, to the amusement of the RSM. My ankle was becoming increasingly unstable. Around the area of Burntside House we came under mortar and artillery fire, quite close, for about ninety minutes. The peat, as throughout the campaign, damped down most of the blast. At one stage, when mortar bombs started to land near our position, it didn't ease the soul at all to be told by Hamer, my second radio operator, 'It's all right, Sir, they're ours.'

We were also under fire from a sniper/snipers on the right of the track and at one stage a round whistled inches above my head. It was at this stage that D Company took casualties and we were asked to move forward. I was petrified, especially of the sniper, as I was wearing a waterproof, the lining of which glowed white from its snow-camouflage reverse. The sniper fire had been quite accurate previously although no one had been hit. We moved forward about 400 metres, under fire still, taking cover once or twice, and found two casualties from D Company, one (Parr) with a round lodged in his umbilicus, the other lad (Grey) with a suspected fractured pelvis where a round had bounced off his webbing. Subsequently we found this to be only bruising – no fracture.

We were again shelled in this location and came across TAC 1 with the CO and David Wood, the Adjutant, who had a shell land between them, without injury. As David said, 'These Argies have got some shit ammunition.' It was the last time I was to see either of them alive – two men I respected immensely. We then found out about the first dead, Lance-Corporal Bingley, who had been put by the side of the track. We stayed where we were for several hours and treated Mort, who had a gunshot wound to the arm. We couldn't evacuate him until first light. We dressed his wound to stop the bleeding, set up an intravenous infusion and started antibiotics. He did not need any morphine, as the shock of the wound had numbed his arm. Main Headquarters moved in and we brought the bodies of Private Fletcher and Lance-Corporal Cork, both dead. Fletcher had been about to apply a shell dressing to Lance-Corporal Cork when he was shot dead.

About 11:00

We again came under heavy shelling especially as Main moved in. Shells landed either side of us. The companies ahead of us, A and B, were pinned down. By this stage HMS *Arrow* had left, our artillery had stopped and the mortars were out of rounds. Things looked sticky and the fighter ground attack was fogged out by weather. At least the Scout and Gazelle helicopters were bringing ammunition forward, dumping it with us, then, in turn, taking out our casualties. It was about 13:30 Zulu when I heard call-sign Golf 69 on the net – the CO had been hit and was trapped in a re-entrant. A and B Companies had both taken casualties and were also calling for help. I ventured to Chris Keeble that the RAP go forward, Team A to A Company, Team B to B Company. Chris was busy, I didn't get a reply but took it as a tacit agreement. We took with us members of the Defence Platoon and ammunition for the companies, who were running low. We advanced ahead of Main, with Mike Ford, Colour-Sergeant Caldwell and others. As we came forward, two Pucará came over. They buzzed us and then attacked two Scout helicopters which appeared on the horizon. They swooped like birds of prey, and one Scout went down. I saw it blow up – I'm not sure of the other, it seemed to escape up the valley whence it came.

At this stage we came across Golf 69, alias Major Tony Rice, and he told us how to get to A Company. The captured Land-Rover appeared – it had previously bogged down in the rain and mud and had been unable to evacuate casualties – so we put the ammo on it. We skirted Darwin Bay and met up with A Company at the base of the smoking gorse-lined gully known as the Bower. There were a number of casualties, Argies and ours. We first treated Shorrock, A Company's medic, who was shot in the back, then Worrall who was shot in the belly, Lance-Corporal Adams, shot in the back, and Kirkwood, who had a leg gunshot wound. Tuffin had a serious head wound but was conscious and had been for several hours. We almost missed him because he had been placed under a corrugated iron sheet for protection. We learnt Shorrock had been lying in a ditch for five hours! All wounds dressed, intravenous fluid, pain relief and antibiotics given. I instructed one of the medics to keep Tuffin talking so he wouldn't lapse into a coma.

Speaking to Company Sergeant-Major Price I learnt of the deaths of the CO, the Adjutant Dave Wood, and Chris Dent, Second-in-Command of A Company – his wife was a Royal Army Medical Corps doctor. I was devastated. I wanted to cry, with anger, fear and frustration, but there was more work to do. I had to set an example for the others who were also feeling personal losses, perhaps more so than myself. After all, I was, supposedly, more accustomed to bodily violence.

We treated the casualties, and just as we were finishing, a magnificent sight occurred. Four helos, casevac equipped, led by John Greenhalgh, came over the horizon. We had just got Worrall away in a Gazelle but they are not really designed for casevac. We got all our casualties away in due course, and some Argentinians.

Shortly after, Main moved forward to the hillside to our right. Soon after, we came under heavy bombardment in the gully, with shells whistling not twenty feet overhead. The rear slope position saved our bacon. There seemed to be one hell of a battle over the hill and we could not move forward. There were a few casualties occurring from shrapnel wounds and after cries of 'Medic' we dealt with a couple of wounds on the brow of the hill above Main, until continuous artillery barrage forced us back round to the gully where I decided to go firm.

Shrapnel casualties drifted in, the smoke and cordite streamed through our position doing its damnedest to fog us out at times. We were under fairly constant artillery fire, with rain a lot of the time. However, we were getting stretcher parties forward, and helicopters in, to evacuate our casualties.

One lad came in almost in tears. He was okay but his mucker, Private 'Chopsey' Gray, was pinned down, dying on the forward slope with his leg blown half off. I knew I had to send a medic forward. It was difficult to ask, I felt almost as if I ought to do it myself, but knew that was out of the question. Bill (Lance-Corporal Bentley) accepted the task without qualm. Together with a stretcher party he precariously made his way into the forward slope to Gray. He completed the partial amputation with his clasp knife and was able to stem the blood loss with a tourniquet. They were then able to bring him into the RAP. Gray was the colour of his surname. He had no veins visible anywhere, he had lost so much blood. I had no option but to try and cut down, with a scalpel, onto one of his veins. He was so far gone he couldn't feel anything. I don't think I quite got the vein but I left the cannula in the soft tissues – probably not in the vein, but at least infusing fluid. The tourniquet had stemmed the blood loss. He went out on the next chopper. Apparently when they started to transfuse Gray at Ajax, as his colour returned he miraculously came back to life.

We kept on dealing with the casualties as and when they arrived until light faded and the casualties stopped. Just as well because the helicopters weren't equipped to fly at night. We were left with three minor injuries – a back injury, a knee sprain, and an ankle sprain. All in all, we dealt with thirty-four of our own casualties and I'm not sure how many enemy.

We worked long into the dark, by which time the battle had lulled. A Company overlooked Darwin and B

Company, Goose Green. The battle halted and, as darkness closed in, the dribs and drabs flowed in. We heard our first of Rory Wagon's team who were still holding casualties. They were expecting a lift out for them but the chopper got lost and their lift never came. Later, when John Greenhalgh heard this, he flew back in and took out their seriously wounded. Prior to this, at dusk, he had, remarkably, taken his Scout onto the forward slope to drop off Lance-Corporal Bentley and to pick up casualties. He had flown, guided by lads on the ground, by a radio version of the 'Golden Shot' – 'left a bit, right a bit' and 'here'.

We had brought in our dead, including H., to the side of a gorse bush at the bottom of the gully: a grim reminder of the cost. David Cooper, the RSM, Roger Miller (the Operations Officer) and myself sat down to try and work out our losses of dead and wounded so that next of kin could be notified. We had to be very careful and delay notification until we had definite proof of death or injury. We knew some cock-ups had been made after the *Sheffield* went up.

Eventually, when I settled down to sleep on top of a gorse bush, I lay exhausted and frozen, aware that my mind was behaving abnormally. It was as if it had reached sensory overload. Although the fighting had stopped, I was interpreting the rustle of my space blanket (my sole covering) as machine-gun fire, the crackling of burning gorse as artillery. Yet one part of my mind was functioning and was able to recognize this. I wondered if I was cracking up. But nature can be very kind, and very quickly I fell into an exhausted sleep, not to stir until dawn. When I awoke, I was cold. I couldn't feel my feet at first. But then early physiotherapy for ankle injuries is ice treatment, so I suppose nature had spontaneously treated my injury. I still refrained from removing my boot.

Saturday, 29 May

Dawn broke at 11:00 Zulu time and as there were no further casualties at that stage I stayed in my space blanket in my bush. Chris Keeble, now commanding, came round and explained his plan. Two Argentine warrant officers had been returned – one to Darwin, one to Goose Green – having been told that there were two possible courses of action: 1) they surrender; 2) military action to level both settlements. Chris had laid on a mortar, gunnery and fighter ground attack demonstration. It was not needed. They chose the former option.

During the negotiations, we dealt with the remaining Argentine wounded and prisoners who lay at the bottom of the gully, next to the burning gorse. Many different wounds but little noise. One spoke a little English. As I put up a drip, he said, 'Why you treat me?' God knows what they'd been told of us.

They were such a pathetic group that even though we had not eaten properly ourselves for twenty-four hours many of us (not just medics) dug into our pockets and found whatever glucose sweets or biscuits we had to hand to hungry fingers. We moved their wounded out and shortly afterwards Team B were choppered into our position, only to move on to Goose Green. Because we had been on the central axis, most of the casualties had come to us. Team B had dealt with about seven casualties from B Company, two of which were near fatal. They had had problems with communications and had not been able to get a helicopter for nearly fourteen hours. But all the wounded survived.

A television news crew choppered in and tried to film the tragic spectacle of our dead. I sent Bill to see them off. We soon processed the remaining Argentinians and then packed ourselves to move on to Goose Green, pausing briefly for an historic photograph. We'd thought during the night that another officer, Peter Kennedy, was dead – he was missing. But he wandered through the RAP having lain up all night after procuring the Argentinian flag from Goose Green.

However, Jim Barry was dead, we passed his body as we moved down the track to Goose Green. Jim shouldn't have been with us. He had been picked for the America's Cup sailing team and should have been in the States. However, when the Belize tour was called off he had hung around and had volunteered to come with us when we mobilized. He was machine-gunned in the chest by an adjacent trench when he moved forward to accept the surrender from the trench in front of his. His corporal was killed in the same incident.

As we moved into Goose Green, the population were out to greet us with cheering, food, and drink. A seven-year-old offered me a bottle of vodka. I deferred, but took a sip of Fanta instead from her friend. Hank, one of my medics (a Scotsman), was not so reticent with a bottle of Scotch! We set up the RAP in the eating house for the sheep-shearing station. We moved into the warmth of civilized habitation for the first time since coming ashore. It was almost uncomfortable after so long outdoors. The lads settled in and we cleaned up. One or two minor injuries appeared for treatment. We all had a beer and brooded amongst ourselves. The boss's death was announced on the World News. We worried what our families would make of it.

Sunday, 30 May

We all got up, late-ish for us, at midday. After cleaning up ourselves and the building we started to process our lads – mainly feet problems. I made myself temporarily unpopular by insisting that everyone who reported sick must first wash and shave, utilizing captured Argentinian razors and soap.

We had an Argy with gangrene on the foot, still alive after thirty-six hours on the battlefield. He was duly treated and despatched by helicopter to Ajax Bay. I sorted out one or two minor shrapnel wounds by excising dead tissue under local anaesthetic. The wounds were then dressed for closure in two or three days.

Fifteen of us travelled to Ajax Bay in a Wessex, to what we thought was a memorial service for Lt-Col. H. It turned out to be the funeral of all our dead. At least David Cooper presided. At present the policy is that this is the final burial but we are determined that this will not be so. As H. said, 'We will take all our dead home with us.'

Monday, 31 May

Having spent last night in the house across the way and frozen, I decided to move back into the RAP for warmth. Just as well because the civvies wanted to move back into one room of their house.

It now seems definite we go back under command of 5 Brigade. Although they say at present that we won't be garrison force. Time will tell.

Apparently there is mail on the island but Brigade have lost it. At least we are now able to contact Brigade on the radio. Two more Argies were found alive on the battlefield, one I treated at the RAP, the other I treated at the site of his wounds. I flew out there by Scout. The gully was still smoking – it was eerie to fly over the land where there'd been so much violence. The Argentine had been found in a trench under a body. He had a gunshot wound through the left eye and a gunshot wound through the leg. Both wounds showed signs of gangrene. He had a raging fever. His wounds and the cold had produced a strange symbiosis. The cold had stopped his gangrene from spreading and the fever had kept him alive.

I set up a drip and gave him an injection of morphine, followed by the intravenous equivalent of Domestos, in antibiotic terms. It was miraculous that he had survived so long, but if he'd come this far. . . . Then, having splinted his wounded leg to the other, I despatched him to Ajax Bay. (He lost his leg and his eye, but he survived.)

That morning we had our own service of memorial for our dead, and Major Keeble gave us a briefing on what lies ahead. The other forces seem to have encountered little resistance so far. There is a strange atmosphere – I can't quite place the oddity. It's all due to the reactions of people to the last few days. Even I have been acting oddly and very possessive about my soldiers. We're now losing a lot to trench foot and other foot problems; I am trying to bed them down locally. The time has come for a move towards normality. The holiday is over. We had a tom with a fever today. I hope it's an isolated case and that it's not malarial. How many of them have taken their Paludrine since Freetown (Ascension Island)?

Tuesday, 1 June

I've woken up this morning with a clearer mind and a will to re-assert my authority, and get things back to a semblance of order. The operation is by no means over, who knows what is ahead, but we have to get a grip again now.

Mal Worsley-Tonks is the new Adjutant. Although when we went to Ajax we heard that all our casualties were alive on the *Uganda*, we have had no further news. He is going to push for a copy of the signal, difficult when we're out of communications with Brigade again. I travelled into Darwin to visit A Company and Lance-Corporal Bentley. He is having second thoughts about leaving the Army. It would seem a shame now to lose all the ground we've made in terms of experience – we must consolidate. I must try and keep him. Bill's performance has been nothing short of outstanding. He is both a soldier and a very brave man. From the first time we came under fire he stayed cool and set an example to those around him, including me. He has a calming influence, projected not least by his immense practical sense. If there was nothing else to do whilst we were under shellfire in the gully, Bill was brewing up! Understandably, just his presence instils confidence in all those around him and the others have come on immeasurably.

When I got back to Goose Green the mail had arrived and silence reigned. But there was a sudden reminder of the perpetual danger of violent death. There was a huge bang and nine POWs were blown up while clearing a pile of ammo which had been booby-trapped. We rushed to the scene, to find several severely injured and two killed outright. Bullets were exploding in the fire and shooting off in all directions, a potential hazard to those who came too close. Sergeant Fowler of the PCT had pulled two of the injured from the fire itself. Occasionally a charge bag would explode with a crump. I took the most serious case – he had both legs blown off, one above the knee, the other below the knee. He was in agony with both lower limbs gyrating in a grotesque manner. With Sergeant Fowler assisting, I found a vein, we gave him intravenous morphine and managed to set up an intravenous line – unfortunately his thrashings pulled it out. We moved him and the others back to the RAP where Rory Wagon and I tried desperately to resite a line. We tried every trick in the book including attempts at central venous lines, but we just couldn't find a vein. After ten minutes we gave up and crashed him back to Ajax Bay. He arrived alive, but died shortly after. He was probably a dead man from the moment he lost his legs. Later on, after we had moved out the casualties, I was finally able to read my mail. The smell of burning flesh still pervaded the RAP.

Wednesday, 2 June

Finally we prepared to move on. The next move is to Bluff Cove and Fitzroy and we're told we stop there (I've heard that before). I continued to deal with large numbers of foot problems and started to sort out the delayed primary suturing from a couple of days ago. With typical precision, no one knew exactly what would happen until last thing, when I was told to take two medics with A Company. Then, when I was about to board the Chinook, I was told I was not to go. Still, 'flexibility' – we go tomorrow.

Thursday, 3 June

After countless delays, not least showing round the CO of 16 Field Ambulance and two Gurkha Rifles doctors, Martin Entwhistle and Paul Edmondson-Jones, we flew out by Sea King, alighting at Bluff Cove. We had to travel light and leave most of our supplies as well as a few casualties behind. They should follow us by sea, once we are established. We settled ourselves into the garage with a treatment area in the kitchen. Diane, the housewife, is a nurse, trained in London, who is incredibly helpful. We were given tea and scones – delicious! Having established ourselves, we really just sorted ourselves out. I met, for the first time, the new CO, Lt-Col. David Chaundler, who parachuted into the sea from a Hercules. I reserve judgement on him for the moment. I have too vivid memories of H. We had a briefing on what the folks back home think of 2 Para. They obviously reckon we're pretty shit hot.

Friday, 4 June

Having set up the RAP in the kitchen, I moved off with the CO, RSM Simpson, Tony Rice and Colour-Sergeant Caldwell to Fitzroy. We were driven to the downed Fitzroy bridge by tractor, as the helos weren't flying. We ended up doing a shuffle-bar stint across the struts of the bridge. (Shades of 'P' Company.) In Fitzroy I examined all of B Company's feet – still large numbers of u/s feet, approximately six per platoon. We will have to arrange for rest and foot care. Most of these feet will respond to rest, elevation, warmth and simple hygiene measures, supplemented, where necessary, by painkillers. However, all will be more susceptible in future to a recurrence of trench foot.

The civilians again treated us to the tea treatment. It's so nice to be nearly civilized at times. We ended up tabbing back – quite a refreshing hike. I've lost count of the number of miles we must have tabbed in total. When we arrived back I did a bit of minor surgery on Col-Sgt, Caldwell's foot. He had a low-velocity missile wound to the outer side of his big toe, just missing the bone. We couldn't evacuate him because the helicopters were still not playing. We therefore cleared the kitchen table and I borrowed a knitting needle from Di, to use as a probe. I infiltrated the wound with local and gave Caldwell a shot of Valium and pethidine intravenously (he obviously enjoyed the experience). He didn't enjoy what followed. I donned a pair of gloves and cleaned the entry and exit wounds. Then I passed the now sterilized knitting needle through the wound track, so that it demonstrated the wound track and projected from entry and exit wounds. Using a scalpel I incised down onto the needle, so opening the wound track. It was then a fairly simple, although somewhat painful (for Colour Caldwell), procedure to incise the dead tissue and dress the wound open. I will close the wound (if that is possible) in three or four days.

Diane was super – giving us steaks this afternoon. A beautiful mutton steak, the best I've had and the first fresh rations for ages.

The O Group didn't offer much information – although the CO and I did decide to move Team B to Fitzroy to man an R & R Centre for recuperation of foot problems. Tonight, as we were bedding ourselves down in the garage, we could hear the Argentinian big guns, the 155s, probing the areas around Stanley. We weren't sure whether we were in range and were all a bit apprehensive. Just as we were about to switch off the light, I noticed there were an awful lot of flies buzzing around it and remarked, 'Someone better go shit in the corner or the flies will have nowhere to go.' Polky either liked my joke or was just plain nervous, he chuckled on for about fifteen minutes.

Saturday, 5 June

I did the rounds again this morning with the CO, this time with a bit more style, by Gazelle helicopter. After despatching Team B to Fitzroy, I proceeded to visit D Company and still beat B to Fitzroy. I was even back by lunchtime, although there was no lunch. No rations had come in as yet. There wasn't even any water because the Blues and Royals came through in their Scorpions last night and drove over the water pipes. But Di cooked us some chops so we ate well on meat again. Then the rations came in, but there was still no water to cook them (the only problem with dried rations).

Sunday, 6 June

Not D-Day, but the Scots Guards landed at Bluff Cove. It poured down and the Fitzroy bridge was treacherous. We moved via the bridge to Fitzroy. Later the whole of Battalion Main moved back to make room for the Guards. Thirty bodies were bedded down in the RAP, mostly trench foot cases. They all lay, in bundles of kit, with their feet exposed and elevated. We were using the Fitzroy Community Hall, which was heated, and allowed us to treat the casualties properly. A lot of the feet were very severely swollen and painful.

Monday, 7 June

Now established in Fitzroy Community Hall after the move yesterday. The trench foot problems have started to improve. The medical supplies we left behind have arrived but some of our kit was taken by 7 Gurkha Rifles. I had a very exhilarating ride back to Goose Green in a fast, low-flying Gazelle (it had to be fast and low flying – a Gazelle had been shot down on this route the previous day) to sort out the problem. I had a stand-up row with their RMO because he hadn't taken me at my word about sending for the foot casualties I had to leave in Goose Green. He evacuated them before I sent for them. As a result, they are lost to us. As soon as they reach the Red Cross ship *Uganda*, they must, under the Geneva Convention, be repatriated to the UK. Their medics had taken some of our medical supplies because they had made the mistake of being separated from their kit – most of theirs was still on the ship. I suppose the same principle was the reason why I was now having to make such a trip back. But I nearly blew a fuse when they started a 'Now, we know you've been through a hard time but it's all over now' routine. Instead, I calmed down, and took the RMO aside to defuse the confrontation, if only to prove that I was rational. I don't think there was any ill intent. We had been ashore longer and were better aware of the problems of resupply. They handed over the missing supplies and John Greenhalgh arranged to get me back in a Scout. The Scout did well – 100 knots with an underslung load. When I got back I found that the advance party of 16 Field Ambulance had arrived at Fitzroy.

Tuesday, 8 June/Wednesday, 9 June

The foot problem is much improved. However, I had a stand-up row with the CO of 16 Field Ambulance. He wanted the casualties evacuated, over my head, so he could move his kit into the only centrally-heated building in Fitzroy. I refused. We were at stalemate and it was as David and I were on our way to the CO to explain the situation that the Argentine air attack came in. We were walking towards Battalion HQ when we realized everyone had taken cover. We joined a machine gunner in the nearest trench. *Galahad* and *Tristram* both went up with a bang. I made my way back to clear the decks for action; David carried on to Battalion HQ to see what he could do.

A flash of Cooperism hit me, and I told the foot casualties, 'Pick up your beds and walk. Fuck off back to your companies and we'll catch up with you later.' These casualties made something of a pathetic sight as they trooped out, but they all knew that more serious casualties were likely to be appearing any minute. As an RAP we are trained to work out at front line so it seemed logical for us to deploy out to the shoreline and leave the Community Hall free for the Field Ambulance to set up. To this end, we grabbed our crash bags and ran down to the shore. I didn't have my radio operator at that stage, and chaos was all around me. Helicopters were starting to fly in casualties and I noticed a landing craft heading for the jetty. Taking Taff Jones with me I made for the jetty, leaving Bill and the rest of the medics, aided by ordinary members of the battalion, to deploy along the headland.

The RSM was there and I was able to allocate priorities on evacuees from the craft and the RSM allocated manpower from the numerous helping hands. One young lad was burnt and had a fracture so I set up a drip and gave him some morphine in the landing craft before manhandling him. Most of the rest of the survivors in this craft just had minor flash burns. One of the other officers helping out was Captain Peter Coombes, the training officer from the Field Ambulance. He told me that most of the surgical teams' kit was still on the *Galahad*. When we had emptied the landing craft he and I decided to take it out to the *Galahad*, he to try and salvage the kit, myself to salvage the injured. Although we would both help each other where necessary.

Taff came with me, and a number of lads from the Field Ambulance went with Peter. The Boatswain of the landing craft navigated the craft in towards the now incendiary *Galahad*. I was somewhat nervous about sailing towards a potential time bomb, so I lit up my remaining King Edward cigar. After all, one more flame wouldn't make any difference. We sailed in alongside *Galahad* and it became apparent that, by now, most of the casualties had been lifted off. Peter managed to get over the guard rail onto one of the seadecks but was beaten back by the flames. We therefore decided to make a tactful withdrawal. Having pulled clear of the *Galahad* we rounded up the remaining life rafts floating in the bay, one or two of which had casualties amongst their survivors. Those we ferried back to the shore.

Thus, by the time I got back to the Community Hall, the more serious casualties had been evacuated. There were still large numbers of Guardsmen, though, with flash burns on the face and head. As I was dispensing penicillin to a line of Welsh rumps, one hapless Guardsman asked me, 'Is it all right, Sir, if I smoke?' I'm afraid it was all too much for me. I replied, 'You've only just stopped, haven't you?' He didn't quite know how to take it at first but then he saw the funny side of it and I lit the cigarette he held between his blistered fingers.

It then became apparent, after the casualties had gone, that most of 16 Field Ambulance's kit had gone up in the *Galahad*. With the aim of setting up a Brigade Aid Post, I gathered all my lads and all our medical kit back in the Community Hall. This upset 16 Field Ambulance so the next day I moved the lads and all our kit down to the greenhouse of Ron Binney's house, and here we reclaimed and bedded down our foot casualties in a slightly less favourable environment but at least we were autonomous. We then spent most of the day digging in for an air attack that didn't materialize. In the evening David and I were invited to a select O Group and we had rather an excellent compo meal supplemented with gin, Martini and pilchards. We finished off with Ovaltine! What ordinarily would have been a revolting mixture was to us a banquet.

Thursday, 10 June

Again no Argy raid and things seemed set for Friday night. It transpires that we revert to 3 Brigade from 5. We actually had some mail arrive at last after David Cooper chased it up from *Fearless*. David said to this bloke, 'Who the hell are you?' He replied, 'I'm Admiral Woodward. Who the hell are you?' David answered, 'I'm 2 Para's Padre, and where's our bloody mail?' It was traced and turned up at Bluff Cove. I had two letters and a card from Podge and Den and a letter from Dad. Dave and I visited a couple of the locals for a cup of tea and cake. It's quite handy visiting with the Vicar!

Friday, 11 June

The old tension is building up now as we prepare to move at 16:00. Tonight 3 Brigade goes for the high ground around Stanley and 2 Para is reserve. I have this awful sensation that I won't survive tomorrow, my twenty-fifth birthday. I can't seem to shake it. Even logic says the more times you expose yourself to danger, the smaller your chances. We were choppered by Sea King up to Bluff Cove peak where we lay up on the hillside overlooking Teal Inlet. I listened to Lance-Corporal Bentley and Private Gibson discuss the satellites pinging overhead, and the conundrum of infinity: 'There must be another planet out there the same as ours – with two identical armies about to pitch into battle. . . .'

Finally, at 23:30, we moved off, laden down like beasts of burden once more, tripping and falling and cursing in the rough ground. Every fifty metres a man stopped to drop his trousers – Galtieri's Revenge.

Saturday, 12 June

As we moved up onto the track round the north of Mount Kent, we could see the sky ahead lit up by Naval star shells and tracer ammunition. The pace was hard and the cooks and the stretcher-bearers started to fall by the wayside. Despite them having lighter loads than us, we found ourselves picking them up, booting them up the arse, and forcing them on. Pushing them made things seem easier for us. By 02:00, however, we had reached the forming-up point and dug in temporarily. By this time one of the cooks had twisted his ankle and another had jacked, fallen into the mud and was going into exposure. There was no means of casevacing them so I bundled them together in a sleeping bag.

With brew lights lit up everywhere, the hillside looked like a fairy grotto. David Cooper, my signaller Hall and I bundled into a shallow trench to keep warm. At 03:00, when I was up inspecting the 'sickies', Mark Coe and Sergeant Bradshaw chimed up with 'Happy Birthday To You', after first singing to the Padre by mistake. My first birthday greeting.

Eventually, about 04:00, we got the order to move into a position of support for 3 Para who were having difficulties on Mount Longdon. We were told the Marines were doing well and were on Mount Harriet and Two Sisters. We again pushed forward at a forced pace to try and cover the seven or eight kilometres to the far side of the valley before daylight. The bergen loads once more began to tell.

The airburst shells over Longdon loomed nearer as we

approached and the odd shell they'd overshot came even closer. The battalion snaked on. As daylight fell we were stretched round the foothills of Mount Longdon and as the light got up things quietened down enough for us to have a brew. I dug out the last of my Weetabix and had a birthday feast with hot powdered milk. The World News at 2:00 p.m. Zulu had no mention of the Stanley conflict – it was all Beirut.

Towards the evening, OC Headquarter Company, David and myself were called to Zero for an O Group, only to find Zero was about four kilometres ahead. We arrived as the CO was putting the finishing touches to his orders for an attack on Wireless Ridge – just in time for a message to come from Brigade cancelling the op.

Mike Ryan and I tabbed back to bring forward the lads of Echelon Platoon and the RAP to a nearer site. Towards last light, together with some attached Marine engineers, we moved in next to a waterfall. After a hot meal, I was about to fall into a deep sleep when Lance-Corporal Bentley presented me with the RAP torch as a birthday present on behalf of the lads. I survived my birthday and slept deeply – I didn't hear much shelling, little else happened that night. My birthday had passed; I felt a great weight off my mind. Stupid of course, but although more dangerous times were ahead, I was never as frightened as I had been on 12 June.

Sunday, 13 June

We moved out of our location before first light to move nearer to Zero's location, north of Longdon. There had been reports of enemy helicopter activity near us the night before, so we needed to move closer in. We moved in, but not right in, and lay up during the daylight in a gully. Basically, we tried to get as much rest as we could, and a hot meal. We partially dug in, which was well worthwhile because quite a few overs came our way, exploding in the valley and on the far ridge. We were also treated to a flight of Mirages and Skyhawks which swooped over the ridge to the north and made for Teal Inlet and Brigade Headquarters. Only one came back that way. I really took my life in my hands and went over the top of the ridge to have a shit.

During the course of the afternoon we finally had the go-ahead for our previously planned attack on Wireless Ridge. The company commanders departed for a recce from 3 Para's location. All suddenly changed as we closed in last light for the move off. A hill we thought was occupied by C Company, 3 Para, was in fact an enemy position and so the whole attack plan had to be modified. This changed the RAP to a much more satisfactory position (and stopped us getting wiped out, as it happened).

We were rubber dicked on rations though – not enough came for a forty-eight-hour supply per man and one pack for each of us was withdrawn from A Company. But they'd had them for nearly three hours and, needless to say, the goodies had gone. Two letters even turned up for me before we moved off. One from Leslie and one from Nay, but it was too dark to read much more than the signatures.

As light faded the familiar battalion snake appeared. The bergens were crippling now – the overall mileage was showing. After about two hours of sweat and slog we reached the new Zero location and dropped off between the mortar line and Zero, digging in next to a rocky outcrop as our own gunners shelled the enemy position. Already two mortar men had broken their ankles supporting the mortar base plates on the soft ground – two more subsequently did the same. One could make the diagnosis in the dark from twenty metres: bang, crack, '*Fuck!*' The snow began to fall as we watched for D Company's attack to go in.

Diary Ends

Whereas at Goose Green we had been short on firepower support, Chris Keeble and the new CO had made sure that this wouldn't be the case for Wireless Ridge. Not only did

247

we have dedicated Naval and artillery support, we also had two light tanks from the Blues and Royals.

In fact, one of the subalterns from the Blues and Royals was my first casualty with a case of 'hatch rash' – his hatch had come loose and knocked him out.

The Argentines also had pretty good firepower support, including three 155mm guns, but they had other targets as well as us, which was just as well because they could make a pretty big bang.

It was one such shell landing near the A Company Aid Post that killed the company Colour-Sergeant and took several fingers and the shoulder joint out of Private Davies, the medic who had replaced Shorrock.

Davies was brought in to us on the back of a Scorpion and after treating him we got him out on a Scout. He caused quite a stir when they cut his clothes off – they didn't expect a medic to be wearing a shoulder holster and pistol. After Goose Green we'd all got a bit dubious, even I had a pistol and a submachine gun.

One spin-off from Davies's injury was that the lads knew that I would need to replace him. Two A Company medics in two battles – the post wasn't popular. They all became solicitous of my comfort suddenly: 'Want a brew, boss?' 'Want some chocolate?' As it was, A Company had its combat medics so I made no immediate decisions.

The companies on the ridges between us and Stanley were finding the enemy artillery their only real obstacle. It created problems for us as well. One of the stretcher-bearers who was resting in his sleeping bag near the RAP was injured by a piece of shrapnel in his bag. We had dug trenches in which we huddled in the steadily increasing snowstorm.

From my point of view there were fewer casualties to deal with than at Goose Green, which was as well because the distances involved were much greater this time. I spent much of my time co-ordinating casualty retrieval by radio from my trench.

There were two nets to listen to, the Command net to 'read' the battle, and the Admin net to control the casevac procedure. By now the cold and fatigue were numbing my brain. David Cooper and I were huddled together in the same sleeping bag, shivering. At times I wasn't sure whether I was hearing real or imagined messages over the net.

At least we kept our casualties moving as the battle started going our way. But the weather steadily worsened. The cold seemed to concentrate in my left ankle, which whilst now less unstable was consistently larger than the other.

In between episodes of activity we half dozed, only to be woken by our next turn for the attentions of the Argentinian artillery.

As daylight approached the weather improved; at least, it stopped snowing. The fight was now several kilometres ahead of us. Even Battalion Headquarters was moving forward. We in turn packed our bergens and moved off, by now several kilometres behind the lead companies. It was obvious that things were breaking in our favour.

We were all suffering now from the extra burden of the medical equipment and, at David Cooper's insistence, I flew forward in a flagged-down helicopter to try and secure some transport for the rest. As I walked up to Main Headquarters on the ridge overlooking Stanley and saw the unimpressive capital for the first time, the message came over the radio that the surrender had been made.

I heard the message and as the others rejoiced I wandered off to be on my own. As I looked over onto Stanley the tears and sobs welled up. The relief uncapped all the pent-up frustration and suppressed grief; it was finally the time for self-indulgence.

As I regained my composure, I gained a new lease of energy, as did the lads when they arrived shortly afterwards. It was with a tremendous sense of elation and absence of fatigue that we finally made our way down the last ridge and down the road into Stanley.

Now there would be the paperwork to do.

Major Philip Neame

The Parachute Regiment

Mention In Despatches

There were a few tears on the dockside as we set off, rather more cheers than tears with the band playing and so on – all real lump-in-the-throat stuff. There were toms on board yelling to their wives, 'I'll be back soon,' and shedding the odd crocodile tear. It all fell into perspective when 300 yards down the Sound we passed a group of WRENS and those same toms who'd been shedding the crocodile tears three minutes earlier were wolf-whistling and catcalling, so everyone was rather high in morale.

From then on we were preparing ourselves for what might be. There was a lot of training and sorting out of stores and so on. But no one really took the exercise seriously, it all looked likely that we would go for a nice South Atlantic cruise, a big show of arms and maybe even go ashore, but no one really thought that we were going to shed blood at that stage – they were all hoping we would, but didn't really believe it was going to happen.

I suppose it all started to change when the *Belgrano* was sunk. That of course got everyone chauvinistic and excited; then a couple of days later the *Sheffield* was sunk. It was at that point that the ship became rather more quiet than it had been, everyone wrapped up in their own thoughts, but probably not until then had it dawned really that this could be rather a bloody business and that we might not all be coming back. But this slight feeling of uncertainty didn't last; within about three hours there were some fairly ripe old jokes on the matter going round on the toms' deck – a sort of defence mechanism, I suppose.

250

From the more serious preparation point of view we were trying to assess if there were any shortfalls in our training and to anticipate areas where we needed to improve before we went ashore. I know I was concerned, amongst other things, about the medical training because at platoon level when it came down to keeping people alive we were short of well-trained medics. So my emphasis was to get at least two well-trained medics per platoon and with Steve Hughes's medical supervision we by and large achieved that. By the end of the trip everyone was running around the deck shoving anal drips up any bare backsides that happened to be around – personally I always went round with my back to the bulkhead so no one could have a crack at me. Steve Hughes, who was only twenty-four, was a quite remarkable character and showed the foresight and organizational ability that one might be lucky to find in a half-colonel medic. He also had the spunk to register his views with H. and Chris Keeble, both strong characters. In my view his greatest contribution was before we landed; that work counted an enormous amount in subsequent life-saving and, of course, people's morale, because they had confidence in him and the medical system he'd trained.

The other aspect which concerned me quite a lot was the mental preparation of blokes going into combat for the first time. A lot of us looked to John Crosland who was by far the most experienced man on the trip. People looked to him to some extent for reactions, not so much for guidance, because at the end of the day each had to find his own way of doing things. I got my company to prepare in the finest detail so that everyone was minutely ready for every contingency. I think the biggest loss of confidence occurs when you are caught on the hop. The object therefore was to try to reach the stage where at least we had the reassurance that we'd talked through every situation, which could only help morale. I couldn't very well tell them what it was like because I didn't know myself. All I could do was to try and anticipate the difficult areas beyond the military textbook and to try and

251

get across to platoon commanders and, through them, the whole way down, what I was expecting of them and what I was likely to do in certain situations. Then at least my behaviour and actions would be predictable and expected and we'd all be working along the same lines.

I was also concerned about how much kit we should take ashore. I spent days trying to pare it down to essentials. H. even decreed that to reduce weight we wouldn't take bayonets as we were going to win the battle with firepower. I thought, 'That's all right until things go wrong.' So I managed to persuade him that we should take them as tin openers. He didn't normally brook agruments but that rather appealed to him.

The other thing I found myself lumbered with was Sports Day. I must admit it was quite a good day really, the sun was beginning to shine and the blokes were out in their swimming suits and so on. The real trouble was that on a small boat with a lot of people on board, the object being to involve as many people as possible, one had to be fairly ingenious about the games one dreamed up. We were a bit limited for space but I set up a tug-of-war which got everyone on the top deck cheering away. In the orienteering competition we sent men from the bowels of the ship to the very top which upset the crew a bit as some of them were trying to sleep. But it was all good stuff, and gave everyone a laugh. As we went further south I had to organize a second Sports Day and by then the weather was getting rather rougher and H. took one look at the steeple-chase and the slippery decks and the force 5 winds and decided that we were more likely to lose more men on a repeat performance of that than going up against the Argentinians!

We finally disembarked on 21 May. Everyone seemed more concerned at not getting their feet wet than the fact that there might be enemy on the beach-head. Soon after we got ashore we secured our little area and nothing happened. As we moved off we ended up at the rear of the battalion snake going up to Sussex Mountain. I suppose everyone was carrying about 80 lbs but the guys with the mortars must have been carrying around 120 lbs and of course were holding us up at the back. With Argentinian air strikes expected at daybreak this was a little trying. Knowing our rear was by then secure, I overtook them, but we were still left struggling up Sussex Mountain when the first strike came in. Fortunately, the pilot seemed to have rather poor eyesight and his load of stuff went well wide of us. We'd been worrying about their air attacks till then, but thereafter became quite blasé, as long as we were well dispersed. This was an important lesson for later at Goose Green.

Then the real frustrating bit started when we were warned on two separate occasions that we were going to go down for a raid on Goose Green. On each occasion my company was the one which was picked to lead the way down to the start point at Camilla Creek. On one occasion, having psyched ourselves up, we actually got half-way there when the order was given that the whole thing had been shelved and we were to make our way back. We trudged back late into the night to be told Brigade had changed their minds and helicopters were being laid on at first light and that we were going to give it another go. We turned up at first light, after a very short night's rest, to be told that the helicopters couldn't fly and that the whole thing had been shelved once more! One began to form comparisons between this particular affair and the Crimean War! It was cold, wet, miserable and no one seemed to know what they were supposed to be doing or what was going to happen. I think it was due more to H.'s persistence than anything else that eventually someone did get off their arse and decide to give us a positive mission rather than have us sit there holding this ground against no one.

Eventually, with my company – D Company – leading the way, we went south to Goose Green. Our objective was Camilla Creek House. We wandered off down there in the dark, without much to navigate by. We weren't sure whether it was occupied or not, so when we got about 1,500 yards away, I thought the sensible thing to do was to send down a few rounds on the house. Even if it wasn't occupied at least they would show us where the house was! The rounds came whistling over and landed about 1,000 metres behind us, rather than 1,000 metres ahead of us as I had expected. We hadn't overshot the objective, the artillery were just living up to their reputation of dropping short! So we eventually went in on blind speculation. I sent in one patrol, just to see what things looked like, and we found the whole place completely deserted so we made ourselves at home. It was a sort of two up, two down with a little loo downstairs and a few outbuildings, so I moved the whole company into this house. I kept two patrols north and south of us just to keep an eye on things. Then we sat and waited for the rest of the battalion to come in, which was really the worst news of the night because as soon as they arrived they also wanted to come in out of the bad weather. It had been quite a tight squeeze getting my ninety blokes into this house, so trying to get almost 500 blokes in was really very tight! We would have stayed in the house a while but our move south had been announced in Parliament and so it became quite clear that if we were going to be anywhere, we were going to be in the area of that particular house. H. very sensibly dispersed us all as far and wide as possible.

In the evening the O Group was called and we were told that Goose Green was held by four or five hundred men who weren't up to much and that their defences were facing seawards and southwards rather than in our direction and all one had to do was to knock hard at the front door, or the back door in our case, and we'd just sort of walk in. I had spent that day looking at the map and there was a very narrow strip of land we had to advance down. I was concerned, to say the least, as this meant there would be little room for manoeuvre and therefore little scope for bold and imaginative tactics – just a straight slog. Also, as they knew we were coming they would have obviously deployed north. I remember saying to Nobby Clark, my Sergeant-Major, that this was either going to be a cakewalk because they would just give up as everyone predicted, or a very bloody do. Not much in between. I came back to my HQ after the O Group with red blots representing enemy positions smeared all over my map. I tossed it down in front of Nobby and said that I thought it was going to be the second of the two options.

There was nothing very startling or original about the battalion plan – A and B forward and D in reserve (it's totally against the training of the military mind to do anything other than follow the alphabet). So we started off down there, following the rest of the battalion, and it really should have been very easy because all we really had to do was follow everyone else. The only trouble was Battalion HQ stopped off half-way down to the start line and we moved through them expecting guides from the recce patrol to be on the track to show us exactly where to go. But there were no guides and there was a complete mass of tracks leading off in every direction. With so many tracks around we got hopelessly lost and overshot the track in question. The last thing I wanted to do was to end up ahead of A and B Companies and get caught up in their crossfire. So we trod a very careful path back to a known start point, found the track and sat down to wait for the battle to start.

Fortunately A and B Companies were still ahead of us, but what I hadn't taken into account was that we had got ahead of H.'s Tactical HQ. He came stomping down the track, found us there, and took this as a most immense personal affront that his reserve company was actually closer to the battle than he was. Suitably chastened we just sat where we were and watched him go stomping further down the track only to find himself caught in crossfire further down. By this time both A and B Companies had put in an attack of sorts. H. came stomping back and, having been shot at, identified one position where he thought the fire came from and directed me to go and destroy it. My only difficulty was that I couldn't really see where this position was and he didn't really know exactly where it was on the map. So we called up a fire mission from the ship that was offshore, hoping it was one of the pre-targeted objectives. They gave us about two rounds and then the gun jammed on the ship, so that was a great start! We were already underway, so it just became an advance to contact and hope for the best.

By then we were ahead of the other two companies. We dimly saw a position on the skyline ahead of us which offered no opposition at all. So we just went straight into a frontal assault which was the first time I'd been in action in my life. It all seemed to be going well, when suddenly two machine guns opened up on us from the right. Up until then I had thought, if this is war, it's all dead easy. But now we were suddenly really caught flat-footed. There was already one platoon clearing the position in front of us, the platoon on my right was completely pinned down by two machine guns, and the difficulty was getting any troops available to manoeuvre around and actually assault this position. My only other force available was my third platoon on my left, and any direction they were likely to attack from would mean assaulting straight in towards the direction that I thought B Company was. After a certain amount of flat-footedness, sucking of teeth and wondering what the hell to do, I saw that Chris Waddington had already started bringing his platoon across so that they could assault. I was still concerned that they'd be shooting up B Company in the process, but there was no option.

By this time H. was yelling to find out what the hell was holding us up. So I told Chris to go in and assault and in he went. I got a few expletives from John Crosland about the number of rounds that were coming his way and I answered with expletives about the number of rounds that were coming my way and we just got on with it. This assault led to four casualties. One of those killed was Corporal Bingley who was very brave. He'd gone to ground not really knowing quite where these machine guns were and found himself virtually overlooking the position. He and Grayling just went in and did an immediate assault, and the two of them took the five-strong position out between them. But Bingley was killed in the process and Grayling slightly injured. It was that sort of immediate get up and go and flair that really got us out of a very sticky situation.

The real problems started because we found ourselves scattered to the four winds. We'd taken out these two machine-gun positions and another platoon position on top of the hill in a single company assault. But in the process people had been going everywhere and it was very featureless ground. Trying to regroup everyone was almost impossible. Much as the School of Infantry would have decried it, I felt the only way to get them together was to put up some light myself to tell everyone where I was. It was also telling the enemy where we were, but I had to take the chance on that. It worked and we got everyone together, less two unaccounted for. There was a long delay while we tried to find out where they were; they weren't found until daylight. Corporal Cork had been shot and Fletcher had been bending over applying a field dressing when he was shot himself and so they had both been killed.

To reorganize took us about an hour and a half and it was quite clear that this was a problem besetting the other companies, which was really why H. had fed us, the reserve, in so soon. The whole encounter had been a little chaotic but of course at this stage we had no perspective of the normal. We just accepted this as the norm – feeling it was not totally different from the average exercise! Life became reasonably simple for us for the next hour or so, we just trogged down behind everyone else. At about daylight we ended up on this little knoll about 1,000 metres short of what became known as the Gorse Line, with A Company at this time fairly heavily engaged around Darwin Hill and B Company brought to a stop on the Gorse Line itself, overlooking Boca House. Then everything began to bog down and I started to move my company up closer to the other two lead companies to get under the lee of the hill and out of sight of the enemy. I was told in very certain terms by H. that he didn't want me getting any closer. So we amused ourselves by taking the odd pot shot at some stray Argentinians who we could see about 1,000 yards away. I had to put a stop to that otherwise we wouldn't have had the ammunition when we needed it.

Life then began to get a bit uncomfortable. There was a minefield either side of the track ahead of us and we were on a very exposed knoll. The enemy artillery started sending in fire periodically. The first rounds were some way away but the next came closer. It suddenly dawned on me that whatever else was going on, they still had an observation post that could see this far back up the peninsula. That observation post was busy getting the enemy artillery zeroed in on us. 'Orders notwithstanding', as they say, I decided to push on into the lee of the hill as soon as possible rather than stay around and cop the whole lot – just in time, because as we moved off the hill a fire mission landed smack on it right where we'd been sitting!

We suffered our first daylight casualty, Mechan. At night in the confusion one couldn't see immediately what had happened but with Mechan everyone saw it happen and it obviously had some effect on people's confidence.

We moved round into the lee of this hill and then closer towards the west coast. From there it became obvious to me that there was scope for exploiting the position that we were in. A Company were well bogged in and fighting a fairly fierce battle stage by stage. B Company were apparently in a position where they really couldn't move forward at all. I felt I could move down to the right of everyone else along the shoreline and possibly turn the enemy's position; it seemed worth having a look, at least. I put this idea to H. and he was clearly of the frame of mind where he didn't want his reserve committed at this stage and I suspected he felt that things were very much on a tightrope where he was, so he gave me pretty short shrift.

By then we'd been on the go for eight hours and it seemed obvious to me that we weren't going anywhere for at least half an hour so I decided the most sensible thing to do was to get a brew on because it looked like it was going to be a very long day. Stopping in mid-battle and having a brew was met with complete amazement by my blokes. It is not in the book of rules but there seemed nothing better to do. My porridge had just come to the boil when the news came over that H. had been shot. News travelled fast and it wasn't something that could be kept quiet for long, especially as soon after that the battalion Second-in-Command, Chris Keeble, came along giving orders. He gave me orders straight away to move up and join John Crosland to see what we could do to help him. John was at this stage temporarily in charge of the battalion. Well, I was buggered if I was going to waste my porridge so this vagabond army got on the move with everyone trying to take the odd sip of their brew as they went and I was trying to get down the odd spoonful of hot porridge.

We got up to the Gorse Line where John was, crested the hill, and could see the enemy 1,200 metres away. I was convinced that we were out of small-arms range and was bowling along quite confidently when I suddenly felt this 'thing' whip past my leg and looked at my signaller who'd just had his ammunition pouch shot away! We gingerly reversed a few crucial yards behind this slope, back to relatively safe ground. I couldn't see where John was exactly and by the appearance of things he was fairly far forward himself, and I figured that if I was going to go off and find him, all that was going to happen was that I was going to get shot, which didn't seem an attractive idea. So I had another look at the shoreline which did seem to offer quite a lot of promise for an approach to Boca House. At Boca House the enemy had their own heavy machine guns which were simply out-ranging our stuff. I thought that even if we couldn't get to a position where we could assault Boca House, at least we might be able to get our machine guns in range and start causing some damage.

I got on the radio to let Chris know what I was doing. I went down with a section along the shoreline, and got within about 500 yards of the position before it became clear that we were going to be fairly exposed. So I got all the company down, less one platoon and Pete Adams who I left up on the hilltop to liaise between myself and John

Crosland and Chris Keeble. At that stage half my radios had packed up and really it could only be done by me relaying to Pete and him passing on the message. Our six machine guns were in range so I lined them up on this spur just down by the beach.

Then it all happened. John Crosland started blasting away at Boca House with his Milan and with our machine guns in position we set up a rather good duo, with John blasting the sangars and us chopping off the rather stunned survivors who were staggering to other sangars. This seemed to have a very salutary effect on the Argentinians. They gathered very quickly that they didn't have much of a future going for them and after John had got three or four Milans off, all of a sudden white flags started appearing all over the place. Sitting where I was, looking at the position through field glasses, it was quite clear that these buggers were absolutely knackered and they just wanted no more of it. I had all my six machine guns and half the company ready to move on to their position. The Milans and the guns were also set up to cover us. Then nothing seemed to happen for twenty minutes or so and I was getting more and more impatient, feeling the longer I stayed down on this beach, sooner or later someone was going to spot us and start to direct some shit our way. So I got this wheeze to Chris on the radio that if he didn't give us permission to advance straight away we would get cut off by the tide, which was coming in. I don't think that it would have cut us off but it seemed a useful excuse! We got permission to move.

I decided that it was a moment of commitment when someone had to expose himself first and it looked like this time officers would earn their pay. I was about to start forward when Corporal Hanley went dashing ahead of me, saying, 'This isn't your job, Sir, you're too valuable. This is toms' work.' So he was really the first guy to take the chance about the surrender. I always had rather a soft spot for him after that, especially having such faith in my judgement! But it was quite clear that it was a completely genuine surrender and they had totally lost interest. We

260

advanced up to the position and one of the platoons, in their eagerness to be first into the position, blundered straight into a minefield rather than follow my directive to stay on the beach. One of them tripped a mine which turned him head over heels. I think Argentinian mines were much like the rest of the Argentinians – not too effective – so he picked himself up, shrugged and carried on going! When we got to Boca House we found a considerable scene of carnage – I suppose thirty or forty casualties and probably eighteen to twenty dead. In the distance one could see the fitter ones who had hightailed at the last moment and were literally fleeing across the airfield.

After ten minutes Chris Keeble came up on the radio and congratulated us on securing Boca House and told me to head straight for Goose Green. With some smugness I told him that we were already on our way. As we were about half the way there we saw what looked like a deserted HQ so I sent one of the platoons off that way and headed with the remaining two down towards Goose Green. At this stage a combination of ack-ack fire overhead and some mines diverted us into a shallow valley which led to the schoolhouse. So we went down towards it and got to the stage where we were almost surrounded by minefields. They were not well laid and were partially visible but the lead platoon at this stage was getting just a little bit nervous. We eventually got into a little hollow ground just short of the schoolhouse where we could actually start forming up ready for an assault. The way to Goose Green lay up the track and there was no way we could move without being exposed to the schoolhouse. In addition there was another position on the skyline with a flag flying a bit further up the track. This became known as the Flagpole Position. It was quite clear what had to be done: first the schoolhouse with fire support from our present position and then the Flagpole Position with support from the school.

I suppose the real difficulty at this stage was that we were really a little bit off balance as the platoon which I had detached to check the enemy HQ had by this time come under fire from the Flagpole Position and was unable to join us. The nature of the game from Boca House had been attack and exploitation and almost hot pursuit. Now suddenly we were not exactly in the face of fierce opposition but were clearly in a potentially very dangerous situation. I left one platoon to try and neutralize the Flagpole Position and with the remaining platoon I got ready to assault the schoolhouse. Then things really began to happen in a fierce way. We got small-arms fire down on us from the Flagpole Position and also from the schoolhouse. More alarming still was that we began to get extremely accurate and heavy artillery fire down on us. I suppose the only saving grace was that the ground was so soft the rounds were landing relatively close to you but not having any really serious effect. However, life began to get rather unpleasant. We were also at this stage very much on our own, the rest of the battalion separated by a forward slope behind us which was being raked with ack-ack fire.

We were then joined by one of C Company's platoons which gave us the added momentum we needed for the school. Just as we were about to assault the school, I got the news that Jim Barry, the other Platoon Commander, had been shot when he had gone to take a surrender under a white flag. He and half his section had been shot down. It was such a tragic waste of life. After a little deliberation as to where my priorities were, I left Pete Adams to command the assault on the school and I went back to join 12 Platoon to find that Sergeant Meredith by this stage had got the situation firmly under control. His platoon was busily knocking shit out of the Flagpole Position with 66 rocket launchers and machine guns. We didn't know who had been killed or injured with Jim Barry, but certainly some of the injured were trying to get back. There were one or two very brave people there – Shevill who was very badly shot managed to pull himself back about 200 yards, finding his own cover, refusing help from others who would have had to expose themselves, and a couple of others who performed extraordinarily well for just private soldiers in organizing themselves and getting their injured companions back under covering fire from Meredith and his crew. Meredith, of course, held it all together, and made sure the platoon continued to work together – a real solid number, hard as nails and with the ability to think. He never appeared fussed which is what I think really helped at this time, at least for his blokes. Private Carter was the other guy who really came through. He'd been one of the blokes up with Jim Barry and was perhaps the first to recover from the shock and get the four of them still alive to start reacting. He'd only just joined the company and for a young inexperienced soldier he showed incredible resilience and presence of mind and initiative. Carter and Meredith, between them, probably saved the lives of the other three involved in the incident.

The assault went in on the school with no problems and we made many schoolchildren happy by burning down the schoolhouse. It was all they could talk about when we finally entered the village. However, we couldn't stay in the area as we were coming under very heavy direct fire from Goose Green itself, and we had no way of neutralizing it because there were civilians in the village. For the same reason, we couldn't actually occupy the Flagpole Position, although Meredith's crew had knocked seven kinds of shit out of it, having set off an ammunition dump. This continued to give an excellent firework display for the rest of the day.

Chris Waddington and his platoon had joined us by this stage. We were all tightly grouped on the track leading to Goose Green. We couldn't move off to the left without coming under fire from Goose Green nor to the right because of the minefield. So we were sitting there, having been told that there was going to be a Harrier strike onto the enemy gun position. Over came this aircraft which wasn't a Harrier at all but an enemy Skyhawk. I saw this cannon-fire zipping towards us and felt utterly helpless and angry that I'd fucked up everything because I'd tightly grouped the whole company. It was the only time that day that I was really scared. Thank God we didn't get any casualties. When a Pucará decided to do the same we shot him down. The track itself and the exploding bomb dump were, I guessed, the obvious indicators for the aircraft. Rather than remain as a target for aircraft I decided to take our chances in the minefield, so we moved off into a nice reverse-slope position.

By this stage it was just coming up to last light and we heard from Chris Keeble that we weren't to exploit further because he had other moves afoot. John Crosland had by then gone round to the south-west and so we had the village encircled. This was one of John's canny moves, because they tried to land reinforcements for Goose Green down there but old John had pre-empted them and got himself between them and the village. Probably no one else had sussed out that possibility.

We began to unwind slightly. We were very low on food; more important, we had very little ammunition left; most people had run out of water and we had no warm clothing. We spent the night in this position and were very cold. Under cover of darkness we were able to bring down the bodies of Jim Barry, Lance-Corporal Smith and Corporal Sullivan. Jim, of course, shouldn't have been with us at all. He'd been picked for the America's Cup trials in Newport and I'd given him the choice of a cruise there or a cruise in the South Atlantic. Being the sort of bloke he was, he returned from the America's Cup team to join us without a second thought. A snowcat came forward with some ammunition and took their bodies and our other casualties back at last. It was not until then that we had any direct link with the rest of the battalion.

We entered the village the next day and my company went up with Chris Keeble to organize the surrender. It was something of an eye-opener to see over 900 Argentinians still fully armed come out to meet our three small platoons. It seemed a little incongruous to say the least. In Goose Green the welcome was fairly rapturous – we went into the village house where everyone had been cooped up and we were given cups of tea. It was quite nice to be treated like the conquering hero for a bit. My

Company HQ ended up in the farm manager's house and we were looked after very well.

We realized we had fought a major battle against fairly remarkable odds. I think that we had stuck our necks out and it had not been a controlled or typical situation at all. In saner moments we probably realized that it wasn't the sort of thing to commit a single battalion to at all but we had been committed and done it. So everyone was pleased with themselves. I think that what we had achieved as a battalion was very much a reflection of H. A more phlegmatic person probably would not have committed us to such uncertainty. But he was a real warrior and was determined to get stuck in. Not only that, but he had imbued such a faith in the battalion, in our abilities, that I don't think the idea of failure entered anyone's mind. We just assumed we would win and this did a lot for everyone's approach when things got rough – 'Just a minor hiccup – soon sort it out.' Anyway, the Argentinians were a lot less frightening than he could be! I think that was his major contribution; that, and not expecting anything more than he was prepared to do himself and making that clear to everyone. That's why he got killed, but what he'd set in motion of course didn't die with him. The act just kept rolling. We all knew what was expected of us and it would have taken a deliberate act at that stage to stop what he'd started. I sometimes disagreed with his military judgement, but I had no doubts about him as a man – an extraordinary personality. I just don't think that the Battle of Goose Green as we know it could have ever happened without him.

Without a doubt there was also a reaction setting in, that we all rather felt that we had done our bit, now let the rest of the Army do theirs. No one imagined we were going to have anything like this to do again. There was a definite awareness that we had scored, not only a very important tactical victory, but probably a very significant psychological victory. One or two of the younger toms I think were a little overawed by what they'd been through and the number going sick with trench foot increased perceptibly – a sort of subconscious way of getting a break. Really all they needed was a little reassurance so I made sure all going sick were seen by the Sergeant-Major, and I went round the positions talking to people and getting them ready to commit themselves once more. I told them how well they'd done but warned them that there was more to come. We debriefed in great detail. I told them we'd learned a lot from Goose Green and that we had to put those lessons into effect and that the next battle was bound to be a more sure-fire thing.

We began our move to Wireless Ridge with Lieutenant-Colonel David Chaundler as our new CO. The move there involved a long night march in the snow. Just before, I had had a dose of the cook's special brew as had most of the company. Every time we stopped I had to step out of the line and drop my trousers in the freezing cold for a quick one, much to the amusement of everyone else. The only consolation was that the rest of the battalion were caught in the same way. It was terribly demoralizing being faced with these personal inconveniences – and not at all cool!

We went up into position just north of Longdon and waited for the order to assault Wireless Ridge. Our new CO had been up and promised that next time we weren't going anywhere without our full ration of artillery, so we began to feel a little more confident. But there was still that lingering feeling that we had already been through the mangle – my company had picked up eight dead, over half the battalion's total at Goose Green. So there was a definite feeling that we had done our share once and would just rather not go through the whole thing again, but that if we had to, we had to.

Come the night, things weren't helped by the fact that the plan had changed at least three times. But then we had the reassurance that we'd never known an airborne exercise go off as planned. So when we went ashore at Sussex Mountain and again that night before Wireless Ridge, the toms took the very phlegmatic approach that it was like any other exercise they had ever been on – one big fuck-up! I didn't beat around the bush on this, reckoning it was better to admit things weren't going as planned, but at least keeping them in the picture. That made them feel involved in what was happening, not just pawns, and they were more ready to accept last-minute changes as a result. This helped morale which I think was the difference between us and the Argentinians. They weren't used to all this fucking around, and when it happened, as it always does in war, it got to them. In the case of our toms, it was almost a source of strength.

The main thing about Wireless Ridge was that we were the only company in the whole of the battle that actually had to assault in the face of organized opposition. We actually carried out three separate company attacks in that one night. While waiting to attack our first position, the inevitable bit of farce came right on cue. We could barely identify the objective, and one or two people had doubts if we were facing the right way. Then we heard other people moving about in the dark at our start line. We were just about to have a go at them when we realized they were the mortars and some stretcher-bearers retracing their steps!

In the event, the attack went in with little opposition. We had really leathered it up with artillery before we actually got onto the position. We had also had light tanks from the Blues and Royals, and machine guns supporting us, so by the time we started moving through it, whatever enemy had been there – anything between a platoon and a company – had already thinned out and all we found was isolated resistance and a few casualties which were quickly despatched. So we got onto the position quite pleased with ourselves. The thing about the Argentinians really was that you'd attack positions, and you'd find a large proportion of them completely unready. With all this battle going on around them they would be lying in the bottom of the trenches, or even asleep in their sleeping bags – a sleep of fear really. They would be right down inside their sleeping bags, or have their hoods pulled up. It's what I call the ostrich factor: they had buried their heads, thinking, 'It's not happening, it won't happen to me, I'm not here . . .'

At Goose Green we never met co-ordinated resistance but here for the first time we did. We were still clearing the first position when we began to get extremely heavy artillery down on us such as 155 mm and 105 mm rounds. I had been told to reorganize on the position but there was just no way I was going to do that so we pushed straight through and reorganized about 300 yards further on.

After A and B Companies had taken their objectives we set off for our next target – the first part of the main ridge line. Again with artillery support and the Blues and Royals providing spot-on response, we met very little opposition. We should have gone straight into an attack on our third and final objective which was known to be very strongly held. I told our FOO (Forward Observation Officer) to fire the final target but for one reason or another the wrong target number was called up and the next five rounds landed straight on us, which completely broke our momentum. It wounded one Section Commander and killed another. This lad had already been injured and casevac'd; he'd recovered, returned to us and now, of all things, he'd been killed by our own artillery. It seemed a complete waste. These things do happen in war, far worse has happened in the past and far worse will probably happen in the future, but it made me really mad.

We tried again, but the rounds were now landing rather closer to B Company than the enemy. I was getting all ready to assault and then had to call a halt while the artillery went through this long system of adjusting the fire onto the target. We were actually overlooking the enemy position at this time and thank God we had the tanks in support, because they were able, from the flank, to keep firing at the enemy positions and keep them occupied. Fortunately, the enemy were totally unaware that we were sitting on a bald, open slope just a few hundred yards to their left and above them. If they had turned and looked at us we would have been really in the shit.

The artillery finally got some rounds on target. 'At last,' I thought. We were literally about to assault when once again the artillery had to stop firing because some rounds had again been landing on B Company. It clearly wasn't B Company's night! I could not advance without fire support and my feelings were, especially having already had thirty-odd rounds of our own artillery on my position, that B Company could live with one gun sending the odd round their way while we got on with the war and out of a very nasty situation. But there was no way I could persuade anyone to change their minds. So we then had to go through the rigmarole of firing each gun in turn to try and find out which one needed re-aligning, which was approaching the farcical. There we were, literally within spitting distance of the enemy, while this sort of peacetime safety procedure went on – and I got a bollocking for not assaulting earlier! I began to think that it really wasn't my night either, and began to get extremely short-tempered with a large number of people. The only bright point in the whole night so far was that from where we sat we could see the lights of Stanley burning as if it were a peaceful winter's evening. All very different to what was going on around us. We had rather expected a black-out.

Eventually we had four out of six guns lined up. I said, 'Sod it, I've had enough. We won't bother with the other two, we'll just go in with what we've got.' I gave the order to attack. The trouble was we'd completely lost our momentum. The toms had almost grown roots waiting in the cold and by this time were very sceptical of our artillery support. I yelled, 'Advance!' and stood up myself, and nothing happened! I thought, 'Shit,' and yelled 'Advance!' again and the cry was taken up and slowly everyone began to move forward unopposed. We got within about 100 yards of the enemy position when one of the toms put up an illuminating round earlier than he should have done, which just attracted the enemy who suddenly realized that the assault was coming not from the front but from their flank. So of course everything that they'd got was turned on us. There we were, in the middle of a very exposed, totally bald, little valley with no cover at all, suddenly confronted with this withering hail of small-arms fire, accompanied all the time by incoming enemy artillery! Everyone hit the deck. Direct fire at night always is rather more frightening than in daylight. You can see it coming and you just hope they can't see you.

I thought, 'Fucking hell, what do I do next?' I was almost at a loss, knowing that it was my job to get the assault going but not at all keen on moving myself! I learned a great truth from that moment – if in doubt, start shouting. I'm not normally a great shouter, but I started shouting for all I was worth! Then I heard other people start to shout. I got up and ran a few yards and I could see other people moving and suddenly it all got into its stride again. The blokes started working as they had been trained to do: fire and manoeuvre, moving in pairs, and so on. It suddenly began to happen once more. I lost my signaller in the middle of it all. I thought he had been shot. I needed communications and looked round for him, but as he is as black as the ace of spades there was little chance of finding him that night, so I moved off without him.

The assault went in and everyone started to work very well together from that moment on. Fortunately I had my own personal radio so I was able to talk to the Platoon Commanders, but there was no way that I could talk back to the Battalion HQ. I had also by that stage lost touch with our artillery observation officer. So the only fire I had in support were the tanks which were on the company net. I was able to keep talking to them and they did a great job in chasing the enemy off the ridge in front of us. As we hit the enemy they began to cut and run. If I had gone by the School of Infantry handbook we'd have cleared each position systematically step by step, at a relatively slow and controlled pace, one position at a time. But I remember this distinct feeling that all we had to do was to keep moving very fast and keep the enemy on the run ahead of us. If we went slowly they'd leave one set of positions and reorganize in a further set of positions and we'd have to fight all the way along. So I started to keep the pace moving as briskly as I could, but the platoons on either side of me were trying to conduct things as they'd been trained, in a slightly more measured and controlled way. At one stage, Sergeant Meredith or Sergeant O'Rawe was yelling at some of his guys because the Company Commander was ahead of them. He thought that this was absolute heresy. But I was sure that if I kept the pace moving then the opposition we'd encounter would be very light.

We kept on the move so quickly that the enemy didn't have the chance to go firm anywhere until we got to this area called the Telegraph Wires. This was the limit of our exploitation as the SAS were operating further east of that. The ridge line carried on ahead of us, so it was an absurd place to stop, just no obvious feature, but we stopped there as ordered. I was quite sure that the Argentinians who were running along ahead of us must have thought we had run out of steam. We had been going non-stop for over 800 yards.

Then from the east we got this counter-attack. Jon Page, whose platoon I had left up that end, did a really bloody good job. He managed to get hold of our artillery by flicking his radio onto their net, as we were still without our FOO. That broke up their attack. I made my way back to Meredith and Page. In the last thirty or forty yards I had to get across the top of the hillside itself. I became vaguely aware of a lot of shit coming my way. This was confirmed by Meredith who told me to 'Fuck off' as I was attracting a lot of shit his way! His platoon was having a very, very rough time indeed. They couldn't move without attracting extremely accurate small-arms fire.

There was sporadic artillery fire going on the whole time which one began to live with, but this was really most uncomfortable and the whole platoon was virtually pinned down and couldn't move. A lot of this fire was coming from Tumbledown as 5 Brigade's attack had started late and the Argentinian positions there dominated Wireless Ridge. But I think a lot was coming from snipers on the slope above Moody Brook that we hadn't cleared. It was something we had to live with, but something Jon Page nearly didn't live with. He was moving round his position and got hit by a round which knocked him off his feet and split the difference between his magazine pouch and a grenade on his belt. It didn't actually pierce him; he got up and got on with the job! There was a lot of shit flying around and it was very hairy for anyone to move about. All this had rather delayed my sorting out exactly what ground I wanted 10 and 11 Platoons to cover. I'd sent my runner, Hanley, back to try and locate the rest of my Company HQ, but he'd not found them as they were further back, still dealing with casualties. So he'd got the two Platoon Commanders together and started tying up details with them on his own initiative. When I did get to them, I found he'd actually done a rather good job and there was little else in that respect for me to do.

Then as daylight began to come up we got another counter-attack, this time from the Moody Brook side onto Sean Webster's platoon. I thought, 'Bloody hell, what's going on around here?' I wondered what we had got into and thought that this was most unlike the Argentinians. For a while they were quite persistent. They got close enough to throw grenades but they didn't drive home their attack – a 'Latin' gesture, and we won.

I then met up with Corporal Osborne, my signaller, who I'd lost at the start of the attack. I thought he'd been hit but he'd actually fallen into an Argentinian shit hole. As I could now get on the battalion net again I called up a fire mission onto the Moody Brook area which quickly discouraged any other counter-attack.

Those three hours between starting our final attack and daylight were for me the most harrowing period of the whole war, especially with the cock-ups from the artillery breaking our momentum and losing contact with the CO, and then the counter-attacks. But about half an hour after daylight we saw the Argentinians pulling off Tumbledown. It was an amazing sight. They virtually marched off in single file.

I had been trying to get fire missions down on the retreating closely-packed formation of troops but was told that there was no artillery available. I was going quite spare, because I was supposed to have two batteries at my

Major John Crosland – 'I think the little black woollen hat that I wore throughout the campaign helped the toms to identify me and I'm sure they thought, "If that stupid bugger's still running around with that hat on, it can't be all that bad"'

Captain Steve Hughes – 'It was with a tremendous sense of elation that we finally made our way down the last ridge and down the road into Stanley' (*Photo courtesy Ministry of Defence*)

Major Phil Neame –
'I decided the most
sensible thing to do was to
get a brew on because it
looked like it was going to
be a very long day.
Stopping in mid-battle and
having a brew was met
with complete amazement
by my blokes'

Sergeant John Meredith –
'Then there was the shock
of seeing all those
hundreds of Argentinians
at the surrender. I couldn't
believe it. We'd attacked
with a battalion, which
was about 400 to 500 men,
and they'd had 1,200'

Colour-Sergeant
Brian Faulkner –
'We fought the battle for
eleven hours – eleven long
hours – and then we stayed
on that bleak, bloody
mountain for another
two days ... I think that
Mount Longdon will stay with
me for ever'

Warrant Officer 2
John Weeks –
'We waited five
days before we got
our orders for the attack
on Mount Longdon ...
I got the company
together and told them
that some of them would
not come off this hill'

Captain Willie McCracken – 'With all our modern-day sophistication it was interesting just how quickly we reverted to the well-tried and tested techniques. KISS, Keep It Simple Stupid, seemed to stand the best chance of success when situations became confused'

Captain Peter Babbington – 'Mount Harriet was a silent night attack and it was uphill. We were defying one of the principles of war, which is that the odds should be three of us to one of them in the attack; in fact the reverse was true. But I must say morale wasn't a problem'

Corporal Steve Newland –
'I was worried about the
blokes in my section. I
didn't care about anything
else – I didn't care if it
meant my legs were
coming off after, I wanted
to get back into action'

Sergeant George Matthews –
'I was very proud of what
we did down there and
particularly proud of the
young lads in my company'

Captain Ian Gardiner –
'We moved off, all 150 of
us, about one hour after
last light. The Chaplain,
Wynne-Jones, came with
us. I was sufficiently
apprehensive to say to
him quietly, "Pray for our
souls, Vicar." "I won't
need to," he said, "I won't
need to" '

Major John Kiszely –
'Fear is infectious; but
what I never realized until
Tumbledown is the fact
that, in exactly the same
way, courage is also
infectious' (*Photo Crown
copyright/COI*)

Lieutenant Bob Lawrence – 'I got behind the rock and I threw the grenade and then I was screaming for my platoon to come on. This was probably the most fantastic thing I have ever seen in my life because they all did: every single man got up and went in – we just ran over that machine-gun post'

Captain Sam Drennan – 'Although it was freezing cold, Jay, my co-pilot, took off his gloves and held this poor lad's hand really tight, as if willing his strength to go from him into the other guy – and this lad did survive'

Rear-Admiral Sandy Woodward – 'Despite your cares, you have to calculate the odds, the gains and the losses'

priority call. Here was a golden opportunity being missed. I assumed the enemy were withdrawing to regroup on Sapper Hill and the last thing I wanted was another major battle. Eventually we got the artillery and started blasting away with everything else we had as well. But as soon as we opened up we got very accurate artillery fire back at our own position. I guessed that they were adjusting onto our muzzle flashes so I told all the company to stop firing with their small arms. I decided that the only thing was to keep fighting this battle with artillery, otherwise we were just going to have a lot of shit knocked out of ourselves.

The CO then came up and couldn't understand this – he felt we should have been firing with everything we had and I tried to explain what my reservations were but he told me to keep firing with everything I had. Very gingerly I got just two machine guns to open up to avoid exposing our own position. The machine guns opened up and nothing came back at us so I felt an absolute idiot! What had of course happened was that during my conversation with the CO the Argentinians had thrown in the towel. We were now able to do anything we liked, so the whole thing turned into a turkey shoot. We were firing away with machine guns and it was just a slaughter. I think for different reasons David Chaundler told us to stop firing. The change was just so abrupt, within the space of a few minutes, from well-organized opposition to the surrender. After that it was plain sailing into Stanley. We were still on the hilltop when the news of the ceasefire came over. The toms saw it as an end to an exercise. Everywhere you could hear 'Endex.'

Everyone stood up and took their helmets off and put their red berets on for the first time in months, just to let everyone know that it was the Parachute Regiment who had won the war. And in much the same way as on the end of an exercise, everyone who had spare ammunition fired it off – smoke grenades, the lot. It was childish really but it was very amusing and rewarding to watch, and great fun. It even got to the stage where my Sergeant-Major started to get people to make their weapons safe – probably a prudent move, it would have been terrible to have had an own goal at this stage. But it struck me as too ironic that he'd used the same words as he would have done at the end of an exercise. It really was a quite farcical end to a really incredible night where we had been on the go for eight hours. We'd been more or less the only company in any serious contact that night and had been very much out on a limb for most of it.

Looking back, I wouldn't have missed it for anything. There was almost a feeling of disappointment after Wireless Ridge. In a perverse sense I would've liked it to have gone on. After Goose Green I felt, well, if nothing else happens, I've fought my battle. I've trained for it for fifteen years and it was a bloody good battle, a unique battle, and I wouldn't be at all sorry if I never had anything else like that again in my life. I'd had my moment of excitement.

With Goose Green we had the feeling of approaching the unknown and complete uncertainty. At Wireless Ridge we knew what to expect but there was more apprehension. There was the feeling that we had been lucky and how much did we want to push our luck? I know the toms felt it and took positive measures to make sure that sort of feeling didn't get out of hand.

After Wireless Ridge I suppose I began to feel kind of immortal! I thought, well, I've come through this, come through Goose Green, I'm not bad at this job, I quite enjoy it and it's a pity there's no more of it. Whether I felt that because in the bottom of my heart I knew there was no more I don't know. If you feel that you are doing your job well and you have a group of blokes around you who respect you and who you respect, you feel you can take on the bloody world. I got very emotional immediately after the ceasefire. I told the blokes how well they had done and what a great bunch I thought they all were. Of course, you shouldn't tell them that too often – they'd get complacent! But without any doubt what really won the day was the quality of the blokes we had, probably the best trained soldiers in the world and they performed as that. We had come through the cauldron and had lost some very brave blokes indeed. Now this fantastic little force one had built up and worked with had done its bit and no longer had anything to do with it. It was a moment of sadness. We marched into Stanley knowing in the back of our minds that we were never going to do anything like that again. It was difficult to come to terms with.

A week later, on the boat going back home, it was almost as if the war had never happened. It was, 'Ah, Phil, you're the guy who organizes sports. We'd like you to organize the sports for Airborne Forces Day.'

I think we all came back more mature people. The toms didn't have a great requirement to beat up Aldershot any more because they had already shown the world what they could do, and what was Aldershot?

I suppose the other thing one remembers was the humour and light-heartedness of it all. People had got uptight at times and very frustrated before Goose Green, wondering what the hell we were going to do, but all the time there were funny little events which broke the gloom. At O Group I tried not to get too gripped about things. I didn't think it would help if people saw me as very intense and serious. Soldiering is a tough, cruel world and we all had our problems, but it is counter-productive to take everything too seriously. It was a happy company, a jovial company. The NCOs used to take the piss out of me and I used to do the same back, and in this way we all knew each other very well. We knew where to touch the right chords. Chris Waddington, for instance, was renowned for coming up at the end of every O Group with a 'question', irrelevant, complicated, difficult to answer, it didn't matter, he had to have a 'question'. It could have become irritating but it didn't. It actually became a source of amusement: instead of 'Oh fucking hell, Chris, shut up,' I'd say, 'Right, any questions?' There would be a lull and the Sergeant-Major would pipe up with, 'Mr Waddington has still got *his* question, Sir.' And everyone would fall about laughing and Chris would blush. It was all great fun, all this great drama around us but we were still laughing and ribbing each other as if we were down at the boozer. I suppose it was a bit out of place, but it kept things going very well.

Of course what it really did was to weld a close team built on trust and on knowing each other's strengths and weaknesses. And that's what really scored for us – team effort. I think I was lucky, I had some excellent subordinates and it didn't need too much from me to produce results. It was all very effortless and rewarding, very rarely lonely or frightening. As much as I led them they carried me. And though not all of us got back, and I'm sad for the families, I never really mourned them, because for me they're still there, part of the team.

Sergeant John Meredith

The Parachute Regiment

Distinguished Conduct Medal

Sergeant Meredith was a Platoon Sergeant in D Company 2nd Battalion the Parachute Regiment during the twenty-four days of the Falkland Islands campaign. He was a dedicated and devoted leader, encouraging and steadying the younger soldiers under fire and inspiring the platoon by his personal example. In the battle for Port Darwin and Goose Green on 28/29 May 1982, during the later stages of a long and demanding day, his Platoon Commander was killed while advancing on an enemy position which it was assumed had surrendered. Five men, including one wounded, survived in the Platoon Commander's party but were in a perilous and exposed position. With conspicuous gallantry and presence of mind, Sergeant Meredith rapidly assumed command of the platoon, organized covering fire for the trapped men and stabilized the situation. He then personally took a machine gun and moved forward under heavy enemy fire to where he could neutralize the remainder of the enemy and give directions to extricate the trapped men. Subsequently, the platoon under his direction captured the enemy position.

Later in the campaign, with a new and inexperienced Platoon Commander, he again showed conspicuous bravery, professionalism and leadership at the battle for Wireless Ridge on the night of 13/14 June 1982. At a critical moment, when the platoon's assault on this 1,000-metre-long ridge looked as if it might flounder, he moved forward in the face of heavy machine-gun fire.

These two incidents typify Sergeant Meredith's outstanding skill and gallantry throughout the campaign which were in the very highest tradition of the Parachute Regiment.

We moved down from Sussex Mountain into Camilla Creek. The artillery had fired on the area around the house and there had been no response from the Argies. So 10 and 11 Platoons went in and searched the house and found it empty. As it was the only house around, every company decided that they wanted to get their men in, which caused a bit of chaos. The next day, the World Service told its listeners exactly where we were which obviously upset Colonel Jones and really pissed us off. We were then briefed by our Company Commander, Major Phil Neame, as to what the plan of attack was on Goose Green. As we began to prepare ourselves for that, from out of nowhere a blue and white Land-Rover carrying four Argentinians came on the horizon. A patrol of C Company opened fire, wounded two of them and brought the rest in. These were the first Argies we'd seen. They were interrogated by Captain Bell of the Marines who spoke Spanish and he got some information from them. We'd been given a piece of paper on the ship with Spanish phrases suitable for Benidorm on it – like 'hands up' – but it was all double-Dutch to me. We worked it out that if we pointed a rifle at them or stabbed them with a bayonet they'd stick their hands up anyway.

We moved off that night, but a lot of people weren't

happy with the artillery support we were going to get. We could only use two of the battalion's mortars because we didn't have enough ammunition to keep the six of them going. We'd taken a whole artillery battery down there with us but they'd taken them away and given us three guns from another battery as support. So, we had three guns and two mortars instead of a full mortar platoon and a battery of guns.

As we moved off down across the creek, A Company was to go over Burntside House and B Company was to swing forward to the right, and we were in reserve at the rear. There was a navigational error on the way down, so we ended somewhere in front of Colonel Jones which didn't please him. Major Neame realized the mistake and told everybody to come back on to line. When we were in position, ready to go, A Company then went up to Burntside House. They opened up on it; luckily they didn't hit any of the three civilians in there. Then B Company went and did their attack on the right and had trouble from fire coming from their lefthand side as they were advancing. Colonel Jones realized that A Company were having to reorganize so he pushed us through and we cleared a position in the centre. We took out about a dozen trenches in front of us and then went firm. Unfortunately, in this move 10 Platoon ended up with two killed, and 11 Platoon, who should have been on our left, crossed over behind us and went in on the right as well and had one killed and one injured.

One of my sections became split up from us and I had to go back and try and find them but I couldn't. As I was moving back in, coming up a fence line to my right I could see four helmets moving. I asked the Second-in-Command if we had anybody forward on my right and he said, 'No.' We put a mini-flare up and these four Argentinians stood up so we wallied them. I used my M79 and we killed two of them and wounded one; the other tried to get through my forward section but he was soon captured, and we went firm around the trenches that we'd cleared. Then 11 Platoon came back behind us and cleared some trenches

278

on the left which we had already done, but they went and cleared them again – what for, I don't know. Then we all went firm on the top of the hill, checked casualties, ammunition states and all the rest of the stuff.

To the left there was a small hill so we waited there. B Company had sorted out their problems so the CO decided to revert to the original plan, which meant that A and B would go forward to carry on the attack, and we had to sit it out. By then it had become daylight. A Company then got caught up at Darwin, and B Company was starting to get caught up at Boca House, so Major Neame decided to move forward. Behind us we could see Argentinians coming out of trenches and moving along the beach, which was a bit worrying, so we just opened up on them with the GPMGs and wiped out quite a few. Again due to sniper and artillery fire, Major Neame moved up forward behind the ridge that B Company was on which sheltered us from the shelling. While we were waiting there we had another lad killed, named Mechan.

We sat there and the OC passed the word to brew up. It was then we were told that the Colonel was injured. Major Crosland and Major Neame got together and had a confab, because B Company had one of their platoons in a very exposed position. They brought the Milan up and attacked Boca House. Before we started our next move to the beach the Argentinians began to surrender. There were white flags so we started to go in, but were stopped. I think Major Keeble, who'd taken over, had decided that B Company needed a supply of ammunition before we could move.

After waiting a bit we went forward through a shallow valley going towards the Argentinian position that appeared to have surrendered. Ahead of us was a minefield with anti-tank mines below the surface; they had orange cord tied between each mine to act as trip-wires. I told the lads to watch the orange cord while we were moving through. Then suddenly there was a great bloody bang and the next minute we were lying on the ground with our ears ringing. As I got myself together and looked round there was one of my lads, Spencer, with this orange cord on his foot saying, 'It wasn't me, it wasn't me!' Somebody came running over and said, 'Get him out of the minefield.' I said, 'Leave him in the bloody minefield, he tripped it.' He was all right, just bowled over. I wasn't very happy with him at all, and so we left him there. I'd have kicked him, but I wasn't going to walk over there and do it! There was another little Irish lad attached to us, who'd also been knocked over and was groaning a bit. One of the other blokes said, 'There's nothing wrong with you,' and he got a boot for his pains! We then moved up towards the Argentinians who had surrendered. We gave first aid to their injured, some of whom were badly hurt. We got them out of the trenches and laid them there but they were obviously going to die. We then dealt with our own casualties and left a section to look after the prisoners with Sergeant-Major Nobby Clark.

Major Neame then pushed us straight on towards the schoolhouse at Goose Green. 11 Platoon opened fire on the little house first. The trouble was, they used 66s (anti-tank rockets) and phosphorus grenades which caused a fire, which didn't give them very much cover. Then our C Company came down, ready to go in. My platoon were tasked to go up the track and give covering fire on the schoolhouse and also cover behind it to get anybody that tried to withdraw. The plan was to bottle them in there.

One of the rear sections saw some white flags waving near the airfield and he reported this to our Platoon Commander, Mr Barry, who said to me, 'I'll go forward and take the surrender, you look after these two sections.' So I moved where I could control both sections and see what was going on. I told the radio operator so that he could get into contact with the Company Commander about what was happening, and the runner as protection.

Mr Barry went over the rise with his men and I watched them move towards the two Argentinians who had come forward with their hands in the air. The others were sitting behind them on the floor with their hands up. Because I had to watch my own section I had to keep my eyes in both directions as I was a bit concerned about Mr Barry going forward. I saw him talking to two Argentinians, who seemed to be worried about the firing still going on at the schoolhouse. Then, for some reason, Mr Barry put a rifle against a fence. Suddenly, a burst of fire, probably from someone who wasn't aware that a surrender was taking place, came whistling over the top. The Argentinians who'd been sitting there reacted immediately by picking up their weapons and firing. Mr Barry was killed instantly. Knight, the radio operator, killed two with his SMG but Lance-Corporal Smith, who was trying to give covering fire with a 66, and CPC Sullivan were also killed. Shevill was wounded in the shoulder and the hip. There was now an awful lot of firing going on.

As the senior person there I was doing the chasing about. I saw some of my lads hit the deck because of the volume of fire that was coming our way, but I got a grip on them, got them up and firing. I was covering a lot of ground, but that's my job, that's what I'm paid for. I got across another section and picked up a machine gun and knocked off three Argies with a couple of bursts each. Then, as I moved again, I took out two more. We moved forward and took their position and dealt with Shevill who was badly hurt. He crawled back into cover and so did Roach, who shouted that he thought that he'd been hit. I shouted back that he would know if he had been hit! However, he had had the arse shot out of his trousers. Roach, with the help of Wilson, then gave first aid to Shevill while still under heavy fire. Unfortunately we couldn't get him out for five hours.

There were so many sensations at that time that I had to think fast and hard because everything was changing from second to second – there were rounds going everywhere. I didn't have time to be frightened. When Mr Barry was killed there was a lot of anger; the thing was, to kill them. So for each one I knocked down, I thought, 'Well, that's another.' The thing was to kill them as fast as we could, it was just whack, whack, and the more I knocked down the easier it became, the easier the feeling was – I was paying them back. The feeling was anger, a mixture of both anger and sadness – sadness because three good blokes should die that way.

Then as we reorganized we were told that there would be a Harrier strike coming in, three friendly aircraft from the north. But the next minute we got strafed by enemy aircraft coming in from the south! Before we could reorganize we had to get Shevill back, as he had taken off across a fence as soon as the strafing came to a close, with his trousers down around his knees and a saline drip hanging out of his backside. We then reorganized and obviously wanted to go forward to collect our dead, but we weren't allowed to. So we dug in, and stayed there all night. While we were digging in, Lance-Corporal Burridge was hit by a round that had come over the hill. It cut through his equipment, on his back. If it had gone a bit deeper it would have caused him problems, but we kept him with us. I couldn't afford to lose any more men.

They then attacked us with a Pucará that dropped napalm. It just missed the Sergeant-Major's party with the prisoners and wounded. It also missed a big ammunition dump – so we were lucky. However, this napalm attack did the CSM some good as he had his first crap that night – his first since the *Norland*. He nearly had another the next morning when he realized he had dug his cat hole next to a mine! We shot the Pucará down and captured the pilot. (He was one of the ones they sent in for the surrender, which they did the next day.)

We moved into Goose Green the next morning and dug in. I kept the lads working – most of them were all right but one or two were a bit shaken. I had one who was very shaken; it took us about three days to get him really back round. He was usually a cheerful lad, but he'd lost a couple of NCOs who'd looked after him and he'd taken it badly. So I kept him working. After Goose Green I felt that I had to look after those who were alive, rather than worry about people that had been killed. I wanted to get those that were alive performing properly, because we were out on a limb at Goose Green. But I was very pleased with the way the lads had behaved. I had mixed feelings about the battle but it felt good to have won. Then there was the shock of seeing all those hundreds of Argentinians at the surrender. I couldn't believe it. We'd attacked with a battalion, which was about 400 to 500 men, and they'd had 1,200. In the end we sent one platoon of twenty-four men in to guard them. I felt we'd won a strategic battle – if we'd by-passed Goose Green we'd have left 1,200 men there with a usable airfield, and that could have later been a big thorn in our side. They could have caused a lot of damage from there.

As we reorganized ourselves, three lads who were casevac'd in San Carlos came back and they weren't very happy; they'd missed the battle and felt a little put out. Two of them were very put out, because they were two of the longest serving members of 12 Platoon and they knew the two NCOs who had been killed very well, so they were quiet and really didn't know whether to mix in or not. I gave them their jobs to do, sorting everything out, and got them working. There was sentry duty to do and one of my NCOs managed to exchange some Argie weapons with the civvies for one and a half bottles of whisky and a crate of beer. I also managed to scrounge three bottles of rum. I gave the lads a tot before they went out on sentry – it warmed them up, lifted their morale and kept their chins up.

Then we were moved by Chinook and Sea Kings to Fitzroy. The Chinook was only meant to hold a maximum of forty men but I think there were between sixty and eighty squeezed in there. We got dumped at Bluff Cove and dug in again. That's when the new CO, Lieutenant-Colonel Chaundler, came round. He was straight in and spoke to every platoon and reassured us that if we attacked again, we'd have full artillery support.

Then the advance to Stanley started. They were going to chopper us up over Bluff Mountain to join up with 3 Brigade. Everybody was given a meal before we moved and most suffered from that – there was a bit of a smell on the aircraft as one of my lads shit himself. We had a few hours before we had to start the advance, so we got our heads down; the bergens were left there, as we were going in light order. We moved off in the old battalion snake. People were suffering from this deadly attack by the cooks: it was a sort of germ warfare! All you could see in the light was a body disappear, then a white bum, followed by a horrible smell; they'd run back again, then disappear again, and this went on for ages – some of them really suffering badly.

After the CO and Company Commanders had flown on to Longdon to check Wireless Ridge, the plan of attack was amended. They'd really planned it well, because we had pre-recorded artillery targets, two mortar platoons and machine guns to support us. We were the lead company and were to advance as long as the OC reckoned we could do it. As we started, the pre-recorded artillery fire was going down on certain points. We kept the advance going and as we got close in for 10 and 11 Platoons to do their bit, a lot of shells started coming and my runner, Godfrey, took evasive action and dived straight into an Argentinian latrine; he came up smelling of roses! I sent him off to get some more ammunition, hoping the smell would go away.

We were talking all the way up, encouraging each other, getting the odd joke in. Some platoons had fixed bayonets. You really need a bayonet at night, when people just pop out of trenches, but most of the time the blokes didn't bother. They just shot them – it's much quicker that way. A bayonet is also an encumbrance, because it extends the length of your rifle and makes the barrel end heavier, which tends to make you shoot low.

As we were going in, Godfrey came back a bit upset because the Sergeant-Major had obviously smelt him coming and starting throwing mortar bombs at him telling him to piss off. He told us about this, which had us in stitches; he kept saying, 'He wouldn't let me close, he kept throwing the bombs at me.' Still, he brought them back with him.

There was no opposition from the position 10 and 11

Platoons had to assault; we moved on and the OC put 12 Platoon forward. We had no problems over the first craggy ridge until another fire mission was called. This dropped short and landed amongst the platoons. My platoon was lucky; we had no casualties. However, 11 Platoon had one man killed and one seriously injured by our own fire. It took some time for the gunners to sort themselves out; we just picked ourselves up and started off again on the OC's orders. We started to come round to two little ponds, and as we did so the mortars put up white light. The enemy saw us, so we came under fire. Everybody hit the ground but they didn't do what they should have done, i.e. move straight to ground and then return the fire. So I had to chase round to get people firing which meant kicking the rears of the nearest and throwing rocks at the furthest and doing a lot of shouting, 'Fire, you fuckers, fire.' It was a dangerous pause because with the enemy firing at us, if we didn't return it they'd get the upper hand. But once the odd one or two had been kick-started into action, the rest clicked on and began their drills properly. A roll of fire went down, whack, whack, into the cover of the rocks. Lieutenant Page and the NCOs got the lads moving forward; we would fire illuminating rounds to expose the enemy and then lay down fire onto any we could see. Then, when the illum died, we would move and the sections would leapfrog each other.

As the Platoon Sergeant, it was my job to control the amount of ammunition going forward and back, and the movement of the two sections; I had to keep them spaced out ready to move forward when needed. Major Neame was everywhere; he knew his job very well and was controlling everything. I had to come back and start kicking people's backsides in another platoon that were falling back, leaving our flank exposed. Then I had to get back to my own platoon who had moved up and were up to 200 metres in front of everybody. We had reached the limit of exploitation and weren't to go any further because, supposedly, the SAS were coming up from the other way, and that was the meeting point. But the SAS never came.

We moved forward, and as we did we could hear the Argentinians talking to each other so we cleared them very quickly and didn't take any casualties. This was surprising because there was an awful lot of fierce fire from both sides, as the other two companies were hard at it and our Scimitars and Scorpions were firing as well.

At one point we went firm with what cover we could find and while we waited we heard the Argentinians down at Moody Brook. I shouted to the section on that side, 'What's going on?' The reply came back, 'I don't know – I can't see.' So I said, 'Use the IWS (individual weapon sight).' They had a look and said, 'There's bloody hundreds of them!' We opened up, but this wall of fire came back at us so everybody took cover again, but the enemy kept firing because they were making a counter-attack, and they meant it. There were an awful lot of them and plenty of fire was coming up. So Lieutenant Page called in artillery to try and stop them since some of them had got close enough to start using grenades on us. The artillery fire was not hitting them, so we got Corporal Dick Barton to get onto the Forward Observation Officer and told him to drop 100 metres. He came over the radio and said, 'Do you realize if we do that, they'll come closer to you?' So with a few choice words he was told to get on with it and they dropped their shells in close to us which stopped the Argies in their tracks. But it was a bit worrying for us!

We sat there all night while sniper rounds were going off everywhere. Major Neame, cool as a cucumber, walked up past where I was and I said, 'Sod off, Sir, you're attracting the bullets wherever you go.' So he went off and had a chat to the Platoon Commander and then walked back to the rest of the company, but all the time he was doing this there were rounds going all round him. He was all on his own; he was amazing, great guts. It really helped the lads' morale, they were saying, 'Look at that crazy sod up there.' But he kept going, he knew what he was doing. He was very brave. He was there all the time, whenever he knew there was a lot of firing coming down and it was a bit sticky and there was trouble, he was there, the same as at Goose Green. He did an excellent job, and because of his guts and his attitude the company worked very well and they thought the world of him, in the same way as B Company thought of John Crosland.

At first light we reorganized our positions and moved into better ones. Then 11 Platoon took out the snipers and 10 Platoon had an attack come in at them, about 200 metres back from us. They weren't sure if it was a party trying to get back into Stanley or if it was an actual attack, but they fought them off. We then started shooting at all the Argentinians that were coming off Tumbledown – we could see them clearly as they came down. What was strange was that they came down there in good order, marching down in three ranks, until we all fired on them. We took out about fifty, then we were told to stop firing because they reckoned it wasn't right: it was a turkey shoot. We could then sniff surrender in the air, especially when the anti-aircraft guns at Moody Brook which had just been firing on us turned round in the air and blasted straight off into the sky. There were no aircraft about, so something was afoot.

It had been a short battle, an intense battle, but compared with Goose Green it was definitely briefer and it seemed we were moving quicker. The adrenalin was pumping very fast and although we'd had the long advance marches to Wireless Ridge, once we'd started we weren't so tired. You just got into it; you got into a frame of mind where you could fight. We'd been for days and days with only a couple of hours' sleep but that was all you needed to perform on. The same with food. We had food, we carried one day's rations on our belts and worked a buddy-buddy system. We'd eat one day's food between three of us and we could go quite a while on that; we only went to the toilet about once every four days.

That morning we'd seen an Argentinian company come out of Stanley towards Sapper Hill to reinforce it. Major Neame asked for the artillery and was told, 'You can't have the guns for an hour.' But he insisted, so they brought fire down on them. Then another Argie company started up, and this time the guns were ready – about six batteries of them! While they were firing away we were sitting in their bunkers making a scoff and having a brew, which was more important to us at that time than killing more Argentinians, which seemed pointless. We were also having a look round to see what had been left and trying boots on and things.

Then the helicopters came in with the SS-11s. One came in behind us, fired a missile off into Stanley and then went away, but he came back with five more. The first one popped up and fired his missile, and this started atracting anti-aircraft fire; of course, we were sitting on the ground below it! We didn't like that, so every time a chopper tried to pop up we just jumped in front of him waving our arms and making funny noises and he couldn't fire his missiles. They kept moving further along the ridge when we jumped up, until they were out of our area. It was like a game – we didn't want those buggers spoiling our peace and quiet!

We were then told that we had fifteen minutes to move. B Company moved through to Moody Brook and A Company moved to the other side of the valley to start advancing towards Stanley. B Company then started off down the road and we followed on. It was full steam ahead for Stanley. A and B Company 2 Para were the first into Stanley followed by the rest of us. We were just sort of slumping in because all the adrenalin had started to go down and we were feeling a bit tired. Everybody was walking in and saying, 'Is this what we've been fighting for?' We were stopped from going any further than the memorial but I know a couple of blokes did get into Government House, because there were bits and pieces hanging up in the mess. And a few got into the wine cellar! Then we found accommodation.

We settled down to a sort of routine, cleaning the place up and looking after the prisoners. Every day parties went out for a scott, a couple of blokes here and a couple of blokes there, to see what they could get. We found this empty house and got some peat for the Raeburn and got a fire going and a brew and some scoff on. That was satisfying, we didn't want anything else – that and a bit of time to think about things and about the lads who wouldn't be coming back. We found a good bloke in Mr Page, our Platoon Commander, because he and one of the blokes walked into Stanley, which they weren't supposed to do. They went to one of the shops and said, 'Any chance of credit, until the pay catches up with us?' To their amazement the shopkeeper said, 'Yes, what would you like?' He said, 'I'll have a couple of loaves and two crates of beer!' Now that was brilliant. He even started making some bread with bread mix he'd found – he'd worked as a baker in his holidays from university. Every bit of food that was found was shared out. Myself and the other NCOs did the cooking, while the lads did the cleaning up. There was a good 2 Para spirit about, but the general feeling was, 'Now we've done it, let's go home.' All we wanted to do was pick up a few souvenirs and go home. We all had pistols and things but they were eventually taken from us. One bloke, though, collected brass shell cases – he had so many he could hardly pick up his bergen!

Throughout the campaign we did quite a lot as a company because we were always the reserve company who got thrown in when things got a bit sticky. When you get told you're reserve you think, 'Well, that's not too bad.' But once things get sticky and somebody else gets bogged down, as the reserve company you're in there. That's what happened at Goose Green; when A or B Company got a bit of a problem, bang, we were in the centre of it to sort that out. But then Goose Green itself was rather sticky, a complicated and confusing pattern. It was a battle where a lot of people did well, did their jobs as they'd been taught, and only the odd one needed a kick up the backside. Really, at times it was fear which worked the most. People need to be treated in different ways. There were some you could shout at all day and they wouldn't move, and you'd give others the word and they'd work quite happily. But a dig in the head and a kick on the backside helps – for all of us. It's the friendly policeman really – a quick thump around the ear at the right time is all you need. We went down there with a job to do and we did it. I was very proud of what 2 Para did.

What I did is not important as far as I'm concerned. You see, I'm a professional soldier, I'm proud to say I'm a professional soldier, and as far as I'm concerned I did my job. I did what I'm paid to do, what I've been trained to do for the last fifteen years, and if somebody else thinks that I did maybe something a bit above what I consider to be my job, I can't do much about that. I was lucky. All I had was a few holes in my kit – nothing serious. My wife was worried about me but I reassured her that the bullet that's going to get me hasn't been made yet. You've got to be confident about those things.

11/12 June

Attack on Mount Longdon

Colour-Sergeant Brian Faulkner

The Parachute Regiment

Distinguished Conduct Medal

Colour-Sergeant Faulkner, as the Regimental Aid Post Colour-Sergeant during the attack by 3rd Battalion The Parachute Regiment on Mount Longdon on the night 11/12 June, performed throughout with the utmost dedication and bravery in extreme conditions of weather and under constant, accurate artillery and mortar bombardment. He never faltered, setting a magnificent personal example of courage and competence that was well beyond anything that could reasonably be expected. One burst of shellfire left him concussed, but he swiftly returned to his duties. One minute he could be seen consoling young soldiers severely distressed by the experience of losing their comrades, and by the sight of terrible wounds, and then yet again he would be busy with his prime duty of tending the casualties themselves. His personal coolness and bravery did much to calm those around him. Twice under alarm of counter-attack he forcefully rallied the Regimental Aid Post, stretcher-bearers, and those passing through the area to form a defensive perimeter, and these actions typified his constant alertness to the tactical situation which overlaid his special responsibilities. Once he himself led a counter-attack up the ridge to an area where he knew soldiers had been killed.

Colour-Sergeant Faulkner's gallantry and example on this night and in the subsequent two days of bombardment on Mount Longdon were in the highest tradition of the Army, and were typical of his consistently brave and outstanding performance throughout the operation.

We had a real slog up to the start line of Mount Longdon. To make matters worse, we had to cross the River Murrell, so my feet were freezing. I was part of the Fire Support Team at the time, so I was carrying 300 rounds of ammunition, missiles, an SLR plus a GPMG, and a lot of medical kit in my bergen to cover every type of injury. This was for when we reverted back to being medics.

We were carrying all the armaments because we were not certain if the armoured vehicles would be supporting our initial barrage on Longdon. I made up three teams of four men for each stretcher. When we got to about 150 metres from Longdon we set up a RAP and started to unpack. Within minutes all hell was let loose. We got it over the net that we'd taken casualties, so we immediately left the Fire Support Team and ran towards where we'd heard the casualties were. We actually ran straight through a minefield, where, later, a corporal and a cook were blown up. As we worked our way up we came under intense fire – it was just like being on a machine-gun firing range and everyone was using us as a target. We could see the lads going down. I thought, 'Oh my God, this is real.' I'd never seen anything like it before – blokes were being killed, losing limbs and having their intestines blown out. We were doing all we could but at the top we lost our first medic, Mark Dodsworth, who'd been looking after one of the wounded. That was a great blow.

In those first few hours the casualties were phenomenal, they were everywhere and we had no way of getting them out and, worse, we didn't have a lot of supplies. Then, just as I was about to put a saline drip into a severely wounded lad, I realized it was ice-cold and would go through his heart and kill him. So we couldn't give them any drips. Everything was happening all at once and we were getting calls over the net or being screamed at for medics. So all the time I was treating the wounded I was having to direct the lads. You know, 'Go left, go centre, go right, go as far forward as you can and start picking them up. Leave the dead, let's get the ones that we can get out.' Then I'd be back down the hill again assisting with the bandaging and evacuation and then back up again, gradually moving forward all the time behind B Company. I kept looking up and there was all this tracer and gunfire coming down and bodies being blown up by shells and I was having to say to these lads, 'Up you go – get them out,' and up they went without hesitation.

I could see the rifle companies going forward, taking positions, and as their mates went down, sticking their rifles in the ground and attending to them as best as they could and then moving on, fighting forward in teams of twos and threes – they were really getting in there.

Then a sniper began picking us off and it was bloody frightening because we had nowhere to hide, but thank God he was taken out. As we moved forward finding the men, we came across Private Grinham, who'd had his leg blown off stepping out of a sangar. All he could shout was, 'The bastards have blown my leg off. I'm only twenty-one and the bastards have blown my leg off!'

Then we pulled Lance-Corporal Connick out of a sangar. A shell had landed right inside and he was the only survivor. He'd lost a leg and severely damaged the other and was absolutely grey because he'd lost so much blood. Yet, in that state, all he could say was, 'Get the map and give it to Steve Knight, give it to him, it marks all the positions.'

When Lance-Corporal Dominic Gray got shot in the head as he was carrying a wounded man, he just wrapped his head with a field dressing and carried on. He actually got a bullet in his head but he kept going, him and two lads called Gough and Bennett – there they were, smiling, cheery and fighting through, picking up the wounded and the dead. I thought it was amazing that this lad could carry on with a bullet in his head. He kept working until everything slackened off, and only then did he agree to be casevac'd out. He stayed on that hill, that dirty, filthy, treacherous hill, where everyone was dying – he could have stopped at any time, but no, he carried on up and down, up and down. He got a Mention in Despatches for that.

Then there was Ian McKay. He got a VC. He was a Platoon Sergeant of 4 Platoon. He had leadership, and he had, I would say, charisma. People would look to him and when he made a decision they'd feel it was correct. They'd think he was worthwhile following. When he saw Lieutenant Bickerdike, the Platoon Commander, get shot, he could have stopped down behind the ridge they were trying to clear and stayed there. The Argentines had machine guns on the ridge and were causing a lot of casualties. There was nobody forcing him to go, but something inside him said, 'I've got to go across that ground and get them.' It was 'One, two, three, okay, lads, let's go!' And they did it. He had three men with him. Two were wounded and one killed in the charge, so he went on alone.

It was amazing really. I think he had to do it, and he knew he had to do it and the people that followed him knew it had to be done and were quite prepared to go with him; they were so confident in him. He had a natural ability to lead men. He was a born leader, the perfect man for action. I mean anybody can get made up to be a sergeant-major or captain, but can they lead, does anybody have any respect for them? Basically they're there because they want to be there, but having the respect of the men is a completely different thing, which was a quality he had.

He cleared out the enemy with grenades, and was killed doing it. His was a tremendous act of courage, because the action he carried out relieved the pressure on the remainder of the platoon who were under intense small-arms fire from that area and were getting heavy casualties. He was a very brave man. I will always remember him stood on the hill laughing and smiling. He'd always been a tubby lad, but he'd lost a lot of weight over the four weeks with all that marching and the conditions we'd been in. 'All right, Brian, are you?' he said as I staggered up the hill with all my kit and my GPMG. He was laughing away – lovely man. 'I'll see you in Stanley,' he said. He was still laughing as he moved off. Just four hours later he was killed.

Many of the wounded made their own way back to us – I

remember Corporal Ned Kelly, who'd been shot in the back and had his intestines hanging out, struggling down the hill towards us, and 3 Para, being what they are, were all taking the mickey out of him!

Then I saw a young private with a completely smashed arm coming down towards us. The shock of that to any normal person would have killed them, they'd just lie down and die, but not this lad, he got up and, obviously in great pain, walked down the hill with the battle raging all around him.

At one point, at first light, while the Argentinians were still hammering us, I could see out of the corner of my eye this young lad. He was sitting there with a dead Argentinian next to him. He looks at this Argentinian who's got these boots which we all wanted, except this dead soldier has only got one leg. The lad measures his foot up against the dead bloke's, sees that it fits, and takes his boot off – and at the same time he's making himself a brew! All this is while the battle's going on. He then puts the boot on, ties it up and I could see he was thinking it was a good fit. He then looks round and finds the Argentinian's other leg, takes the boot off, puts it on and then goes back to his brew! I thought, 'God, that lad's only eighteen and probably doesn't even shave yet!' Fantastic – cool, calm and collected. 'Can't get any further, have a brew; I've got wet boots, he's got dry ones.'

All the while the battle was on, lads were coming back wounded, or we were going forward picking them up. We had one Cook Sergeant, Peter Marshall, who was blown up three times with the same casualty! He finally got down the hill to us, brought himself round with a cup of tea and then looked at me. All I said was, 'Pete . . .' He smiled and said, 'Yes, I know, I've got to go back again.' And away he went. He got a Mention in Despatches.

As I was standing on a rock directing the lads towards the casualties, a shell fell about ten metres away and completely blew me away – I was out for about fifteen minutes. I came round with no one about and thought, 'Go and make yourself a cup of tea, Brian,' but the blast had destroyed my favourite black mug, so I went and got another one as I wasn't going to miss my tea.

We had the photographer, Tom Smith, with us. He didn't manage to take many photographs because all the real fighting was at night. But he earned our respect that day because although he's only got one lung he carried a couple of wounded guys down – that takes a lot of guts. It takes a lot of guts just to stay there, let alone carry down two blokes under fire. He deserved something for that.

As the injured arrived, I separated them from the dead because I didn't want the wounded to see the bodies. While I was doing this, the Padre shouted, 'Cover, cover, Argentinians.' That was it for me, I'd had enough – I'd seen enough and wasn't going to take any more. They weren't going to kill or maim any more of my blokes. I thought of Denzyl Connick, Graham Heaton and Ian Bailey all lying there shot to pieces. I was their Platoon Sergeant; we'd all gone through the same journey together and now it had come to this. I picked four blokes and got up on this high feature, and as I did so this troop of twenty or thirty Argentinians were coming towards us. We just opened fire on them. I don't know how many we killed, but they got what they deserved, because none of them were left standing when we'd finished. That was satisfying.

Then I went back and continued directing the casualty clearance. But we came under some fire from the high ground ahead so I engaged the gun flashes. There were about four riflemen in a trench who were holding up our lads bringing up the stretchers, so I fought them for about half an hour, but because the casualties were piling up, I had to let good sense prevail and withdraw to let someone else take them out.

We fought the battle for eleven hours – eleven long hours – and then we stayed on that bleak, bloody mountain for another two days and lost more men while we just lay there being shelled. But that's war. We'd lost 23 killed and 47 wounded, including 12 stretcher-bearers. Among those killed was a very good friend of mine, Chris

Lovett. He was a good lad. He was killed at first light towards the end of the battle. As he turned over one of the casualties, a shell landed next to him, killing him instantly. It was hard, very hard, when I saw him lying there. The Padre, who was also a good friend of his, broke down as well. I'd only seen Chris an hour before and there he was now, dead. When we were searching the bodies for personal documents, you didn't get involved, but it was very different when it was a close friend.

I think that Mount Longdon will stay with me for ever. I still see eyes, dead eyes, looking at me, but it never entered my mind that I could possibly die. I wouldn't let myself die. I put myself in a dangerous predicament three or four times, but I didn't think it would happen to me. I think God Almighty was looking after me that day.

It was a tough battle, but we won and I shall always feel proud of that. Our guys got in there with fist and bayonet, sometimes two lads taking on eight Argentinians; I was proud of them. But then my father was a proud man – a military man, a big, fine, stocky fellow, who always wore a shirt and tie, military moustache, sideboards, hair trimmed, trilby, a regimental badge on his jacket, highly polished shoes and always pressed his own kit. 'Cleanliness is next to Godliness,' he used to say. He was a sergeant. I've beaten him now, but he was an inspiration to me.

On the boat back to Ascension, General Bramall came on board and gave us a tremendous speech. Afterwards he was asked one question. 'Sir, why did you send the Parachute Regiment?' He looked at us and said, 'Gentlemen, because I wanted to win.'

Warrant Officer 2 John Weeks

The Parachute Regiment

British Empire Medal

We waited five days before we got our orders for the attack
on Mount Longdon. We were told that there were seventy
men on the hill and that ours would be a company silent
night attack. I was surprised because the lesson we'd
learnt from Goose Green was that no way should we ever
do a silent attack. I thought we should stomp everything,
but we didn't have artillery on call, because it was being
used in the other battles. I got the company together and
told them that some of them would not come off this hill.
I'd been their Company Sergeant-Major for two years. I'd
like to think all of them were pretty close to me and I knew
them well, but I knew some of them were going to die. I
knew because I had a feeling that there was more on that
bloody hill than seventy guys. I told them, 'It's going to be
hand-to-hand fighting from trench to trench and it will be
very, very slow and, believe you me, you can't visualize,
lads, what it's going to be like, because it's going to be so
slow and you're going to have things happen that you've
never had before when we've been practising. You're
going to have live things coming at you and exploding
around you and it's going to confuse you. But you will do
well. Now, if you have any thoughts, or if any of you
believe in Christ, here's the time to sit down and have a
little talk to Him. It's not stupid, because I'm certainly
going away now and have a little prayer.' I think a load of
them probably did pray. I'm not a religious person but
having spoken to the guys afterwards, they all said that at
some stage during that night they'd said a prayer. After

that battle I sincerely believe that there is Someone who listens to us, but if your number's up, your number's up.

Then I went to speak to personal friends like Doc Murdoch. It was new to him, so I said, 'Well, it's the same for me, Doc, because I haven't done anything like this. But all we can do is give of our best.' You don't know how anyone is going to react in battle. You couldn't line up many people you've known for years and say, 'Well, he's going to be all right in battle,' because guys you wouldn't dream of are those that come up and shine, and the guys you thought would be brave are not very brave at all.

The battalion did a sort of follow-the-leader up to the start line, where we split up to our fighting order. I was with B Company Commander, Major Argue, and we were deployed to the rear of 4 and 5 Platoons; 6 Platoon was taking the opposite way up. We crossed the start line on time. It was a very eerie, very quiet, cold night. We were going quite well towards the hill and were 500 metres short of the rock formation when Corporal Milne trod on a mine. That was the end of our silent night attack. It then became like Guy Fawkes night; I've never seen so many illuminations. I think most of the Argies must have been asleep. But what came at us was bad enough, so if they'd all been awake, they'd have wiped our two platoons off the face of the mountain. For the next eleven hours it was unbelievable non-stop action.

Initially there was confusion. We branched off right and ran into the cover. Myself, Sergeant Pettinger and Captain McCracken, the Gunnery Officer, all got down into this rock division. The Platoon Commanders, on the radio, were telling us what was going on up front. You didn't need the brain of an archbishop to realize that 4 Platoon were involved in some considerable fighting, but there were no decisions being made from Company HQ at the time, because we were in limbo. I was calling to Major Argue, 'What are we going to do now, Sir? Are we going to push forward and see what's going on?' He told me to push forward and clear the way. Myself and Sergeant Pettinger then went forward rock by rock and cleared the

301

position to make sure there was nobody there. Once we'd cleared it we'd shout back to Major Argue, 'Okay, Sir, it's clear.' I then started to clear another side with Captain McCracken, but we were stopped and held up by snipers. We couldn't move because we couldn't see them and we didn't have the nightscope with us. But later John Pettinger's sniper came up and with his rifle that has a nightsight took them both out.

We then eventually got up into the rock grooves where they had been. The first thing I heard was John Ross shouting up front and I realized that we were close to the enemy now. As we went forward, we cleared a bunker that someone obviously had gone through before us. There was a body lying with a blanket over it. I stopped the Company HQ moving towards it and said, 'Stay there. You don't find a body on a battlefield with a blanket over it. Something's wrong.' I said to this Engineer Corporal, 'Stand at the bottom with my SMG and when I pull this blanket, if his hands move, shoot him.' As I pulled the blanket his hand moved to release a phosphorus grenade. My lad just let loose the magazine.

We had to push forward and from then onwards I was on the net a lot. We'd taken casualties by this time and Sergeant Des Fuller was looking pretty grim about what was going on. So he was despatched forward to find exactly what had happened to 4 Platoon. He came back a half-hour later and said that 4 Platoon had been virtually wiped out, there were bodies all over the place, the casualties needed to be evacuated and the lads were out of ammunition. They were now using the enemy weapons and ammo. He said that Sergeant McKay had gone forward with a few guns to try and take out gun positions but the rest of the platoon were either injured or without leaders. Fuller was then given the order that he would take over 4 Platoon.

I went forward with Privates Lewis and Clarkson-Kearsley to see what the situation was. When I got down there, there was an officer lying injured and alongside him was Corporal Kelly. Further forward of them there was a number of dead, and to the left Sergeant McKay was in action, although I couldn't see him. I could hear Corporal McLaughlin shouting and a number of people doing their best to try and fight forward to take these gun positions out. I heard over the net that 6 Platoon had taken some heavy casualties. I then went back to HQ and told them that I needed guys to evacuate casualties. Something had to be done – they were lying there in the battle zone, and they had to be got away from there and have treatment. I didn't have enough guys and because there were so many casualties it meant a number of trips which took a couple of hours. These four or five guys and I were going backwards and forwards under fire, taking guys out. I remember carrying one young lad out, I'll never forget him, he was alive when I carried him out, but he died in my arms – it was terrible. It was his eighteenth birthday.

I only had one medic, so on the net to Major Patton I said that I needed more and I needed stretcher-bearers who could carry out my casualties to the RAP. He was trying to reassure me that they were coming, but they were a long time getting there. So I was still going backwards and forwards with the casualties – I didn't move the dead, there was nothing I could do for them. They could stay there and we could sort them out later. The priority was getting these casualties back. I got hold of Corporal Kelly, who was badly hurt, but he said, 'It's okay, John, I'll walk,' and he did. He was holding on to us, walking; it was unbelievable. The first man I carried out was Lieutenant Bickerdike, who was heavy. I was running with him on my back and he was screaming with pain. We got him out, but the problem was going back for the rest because all the time we were getting sniped at. We couldn't just run in and run out because it took so much time. By this stage I'd got Corporal Probets, my medic, who did some fantastic jobs. The lads started to cry for ammunition, i.e. grenades and 66mms, so I had to go forward and grab the ammunition off the casualties and the dead and then get back and give it to the guys who needed it. But I wasn't the only one doing this.

I then got back and briefed Major Argue about 4 Platoon's situation. There was only a few guys left with Sergeant Fuller out of twenty-odd. He'd taken command and just as I got back he'd also come back to brief Major Argue. He'd seen Sergeant McKay killed, and all the other men that had gone in with him were either injured or dead, so it meant we had to go down again to get the casualties out. While I was doing this Sergeant Ross and Mr Cox had lost contact with each other so 5 Platoon had got split. Mr Cox was running in one place and Sergeant Ross in another. It was chaos.

Something needed to be done to regroup and establish what we wanted to do. I got back from looking for the Second-in-Command to find a Platoon Commander crying. He'd seen death for the first time and it had shaken him. I gave him a good smack in the mouth because he was hysterical. I said, 'Pick your weapon up and get back and sort your platoon out. They need you.' I'll give him his due, he went back and sorted himself out, and did bloody well. It was sheer inexperience, because he'd never seen anything like it.

I then went back to see the casualties and although Corporal Probets was still doing a fantastic job, I was still getting no joy on the net trying to get somebody to help. I needed people to get the injured down to the RAP because they were losing blood. Corporal Kelly, who knew that if he lost much more blood he would die, also told them in fairly tough terms that he wanted somebody up there to get him out. The Second-in-Command had his problems, because he'd been ordered to bring ammunition up on the stretchers and the stretchers had got some distance away. So some of my injured guys were there seven to eleven hours, which is a long time. Eventually we got stretcher-bearers up and the guy who came up and down that hill the most times was Cook Sergeant Marshall. He was up and down that hill all bloody night long. He was excellent and got a Mention in Despatches.

Other guys throughout the night were bayonet fighting, taking out the enemy trench by trench. I saw Gray and another lad take ground: they threw a grenade into the trench and then as soon as it had gone off they'd go in with bayonets. I jumped in one trench which they had cleared and there was a bloke lying in the bottom. I got the shock of my life when he moved. I nearly shot my toe off with my SMG trying to unload it! The enemy had to be taken out and the only way they could be taken out was by actual bayonet fighting. Dominic Gray and Ben Geoff and another little guy were into it all night long, because they had to be – there was no other way of taking the ground.

We then got A Company coming up and the first person I saw from A Company was Sergeant-Major Docherty, who was the Sergeant-Major of B Company before I took over. I said to him, 'Sammy, they've done bloody well tonight, but we can't do any more, we're just out of numbers.' Then I saw Major Collet come up and go forward to where he could see what the problem was. It was an anti-aircraft gun and obviously A Company would have to take that out – but that was their problem.

Before A Company arrived some of our company had tried a left-flanking move and four had been killed when they opened up on us. Captain McCracken came forward and fired a 66 straight into where the enemy were which stopped them straight away. He was really switched on, that guy, he was everywhere – he had a big walrus moustache. We then went in and pulled the casualties out. By this time I'd got another medic, Lance-Corporal Lovett, who was helping to assist. Sadly, he was killed by shellfire.

The Argentinian artillery now realized we'd taken their positions so they were stomping us and we were starting to take casualties from this. We moved all platoons to the bottom of Mount Longdon. We stayed there about another twenty-four hours getting stomped. A Company moved forward and they called in Captain McCracken and asked him if he could bring in artillery fire. He said that he could bring it in within twenty-five metres. He brought it in brilliantly and without that we would have been bollocksed because we'd never have taken that ground. It was a natural feature for defence. There was everything you could want for a defence and the only thing they didn't have was the bottle, they didn't have the guts to go with it. By the time they had moved off, or surrendered, my lads had given everything, and I mean everything, and some had given their lives.

The next thing we had to do was to get the bodies. The following morning when it was light, in between artillery and mortar coming down, we had to go and sort out the bodies and do the documentation. Although it sounds stupid, in battle you still have to account for everything and everybody and you have to fill in the bloody paperwork. I went round to the lads who were left and I asked if any of them would come and help me remove the bodies. I didn't particularly want to do it. I found it terribly hard to ask the guys and they found it terribly hard to say no outright. They tried to make an excuse that they were too busy doing other things rather than say they didn't want to go down to their friends and bring their bodies up. Lewis and Clarkson-Kearsley were the only ones who said they'd come. Sammy Docherty also came because it needed four to carry a body on a poncho and get them all down to a central place.

Then Corporal Probets and myself had the task of doing the documentation, taking off wedding rings and any personal effects and leaving one dog tag on. I then had to fill in the form to say where they had got the wounds. There was still artillery fire going on all the time we were doing this. Sammy Docherty and me were in tears taking Ian McKay's body, we knew him so well. I've seen dead bodies, loads of dead bodies; bodies don't actually bother me, but when they're people you actually know and you've got to get them into a body bag, which is a flat polythene thing, it's terrible. Sergeant Brian Faulkner and his crew came up to remove the body bags. Then I went down to the RAP to the Padre with the personal effects of the dead.

One of those who died that black night was Corporal McLaughlin. He'd been a tower of strength throughout. Everywhere I looked, there he was: directing blokes, encouraging blokes forward to take these positions out, screaming and shouting, 'We're taking this one, I am now going right.' Telling the guys what to do, then moving back to brief the boss on what was going on. And again, when I went forward some hours later in a similar sort of area, there he was, screaming at blokes, 'We're taking them out – follow me!' He then came back after I got the casualties out and said, 'Is there anything else?' He was one of those guys that if there was anything going on, he wanted to be amongst it. He was an extremely brave man. He was with Ian McKay when he took out bunkers and came out of that unscathed. People like him and Dominic Gray were the lifestay; they were all over the place, assisting everybody. Gray got two rounds in his head and still carried on fighting until he actually collapsed through lack of blood. Yet he didn't want to be carried back out, he wanted to stay till the bitter end. He was doing things beyond his job as a private soldier.

When there was a lull in battle we had to check equipment. We'd carried 84s (anti-tank rockets) all the way across the Falklands to find that every one we fired, misfired. The lads had carried a weapon weighing 35lbs plus four shells, weighing 6lbs each, only to find the bloody things didn't work. When they needed it to fire, it wouldn't bloody fire. That made them really angry.

We then moved towards Stanley itself to take the racecourse, but on the way down the surrender went up. Then it was a race between 2 and 3 Para to get into Stanley. The helmets came off for the first time and the red berets went on.

The next two weeks in Stanley gave the lads time to think, and a lot of sad boys there were in my company. They had time to reflect on what had happened. They'd lost friends. One minute their mate had been standing there, and the next he'd been hit by a shell and was just a mass of flesh all over the place. That scars the mind. It took a while to reassure them that they'd not died for nothing. But like us all they understood that we couldn't allow the Argentinians to take over the Falklands. Thank Christ we had Maggie, because she proved that you can't hold this country to ransom.

Captain William McCracken

Royal Regiment of Artillery

Military Cross

Captain McCracken, 29 Commando Regiment Royal Artillery, was in command of an Artillery and Naval Gunfire Forward Observation Party grouped with B Company 3rd Battalion the Parachute Regiment during the period 13–14 June 1982. During the attack on Mount Longdon in the early hours of 12 June, Captain McCracken consistently brought down artillery and Naval gunfire safely in close proximity to his own troops, allowing them to manoeuvre whilst still maintaining contact with the enemy. Throughout this period he and his party were continually under heavy enemy small-arms, mortar and artillery fire. Much of the time the Company Headquarters with which Captain McCracken and his party were co-located were involved in the small-arms firefight and in this firefight Captain McCracken made a significant personal contribution, accounting for several enemy dead. Captain McCracken showed outstanding personal courage whilst carrying out his duties in a most professional, calm and competent manner. His contrast of artillery and Naval gunfire undoubtedly accounted for many enemy casualties and greatly assisted in minimizing our own. His determination, professionalism and courage were an example to all. Always in the thick of the fight, he made a significant personal contribution to the success of the mission and to the minimizing of casualties to the battalion.

During the night of 14 June, Captain McCracken and his party were regrouped with 2nd Battalion the Parachute Regiment for their attack on Wireless Ridge. Throughout this attack Captain McCracken was sited in an exposed OP

308

position on Mount Longdon. Under constant enemy mortar and artillery bombardment Captain McCracken continued to bring down accurate and effective Naval fire. This fire resulted in the successful neutralization of at least one company objective and the harassment of enemy gun positions. The application of indirect fire played a major part in the success of the battalion's attack, the minimizing of our own casualties and the eventual surrender of the enemy.

Captain McCracken's high courage and professional skill were in the highest tradition of the Royal Artillery.

I had been in New Zealand for about six weeks on an exercise when I received a signal telling me to return to Poole by the fastest possible means. I was back in the UK within thirty-six hours. Purely by chance, this was courtesy of the RAF in a VC10 as far as Hong Kong. From there I was brought down to earth, so to speak, and became a mere tourist-class passenger with B Cal to Gatwick. All in all, I was pretty annoyed, because for once in my life I had made a plan and had organized myself. This plan included a stop-off in Hong Kong at endex for ten days' leave on the way home. I had even managed to arrange for my wife to come out and join me. Furthermore, my great plan had kept me out of the January sales in England in the certain knowledge that I would be able to re-vamp my wardrobe 'tailor-made' in Hong Kong. Have you ever had the feeling that things are going too well? I should have known better as I'm old enough to know what they say about 'best laid plans of mice and men'.

This feeling of annoyance was enhanced by the certain knowledge that we would huff and puff, jump into ships, sail into the sunset and sit somewhere off Lands End while round after round of sabre-rattling went on and the UN would eventually sort it all out. It was all a question of priorities. It really is a bit serious when work interferes with your social life!

The next few days did absolutely nothing to dispel the certain knowledge. We were subjected to order, counter-order and well, yes, a fair amount of the other. The most painful part of this process was the effect it was having on the families. We, the soldiers, were totally wrapped up in tasks – preparation of equipment, briefings, adaptation to the latest plan, etc. – while the girls never quite knew when we left if they would ever see us again. This lasted for three or four days and every day I went through a fond farewell scene (and in one day as many as three!). The emotional strain on loved ones was enormous.

Eventually my team were deployed on the operation to recapture South Georgia – Operation Paraquat. I was the leader of a Naval Gunfire Support Forward Observation Team (NGSFO). Our primary task was to direct Naval gunfire support (NGS). The team was also trained and equipped to direct fighter ground-attack aircraft, and to direct artillery once a main force was ashore. Two teams from the battery were tasked on Op Paraquat and we flew to Ascension Island on 9 April where we zeroed our weapons and then married up with HMS *Antrim* and HMS *Plymouth*. We were in little doubt by the time we left Ascension that Op Paraquat would go ahead, almost by way of a declaration of intent. By this stage the talking had been going on for over a week and nothing had been achieved. I must say we hoped that the South Georgia op would serve as a blow which would hopefully bring people to their senses and precipitate an early Argentinian withdrawal from the Falklands and an intervention by the UN. Nobody wanted to attack and there was a feeling of what are they (the politicians) doing? However, the closer we got, the more steadfast our resolve became – we now had little choice, we were committed.

When the assault came it took us by surprise, as it did the enemy. On the evening of 24 April a submarine had been detected and as a result of this threat the Task Force had been split. RFA *Tidespring* with the majority of M Company on board had been ordered out of the immediate danger zone. This left the two warships to concentrate on anti-submarine operations. There was much activity, lots of action stations, which was all very exciting for us pongos (a Navy term of endearment for soldiers), who up until this time were firmly of the opinion that the grey funnel line (an Army term of endearment for the Royal Navy), with its quaint customs, strange jargon, heated mess decks, apparent lack of recent operational experience and the Amusement Arcade (the Ops Room filled with masses of radar screens which for all the world looked like Space Invader machines and commanded about the same attention) did not constitute a force in war.

At action stations everyone in the ship has a job to do and we 'brown jobs' (another Navy term of endearment for soldiers) were 'volunteered' to man the machine guns on the open outer decks. I still believe that this was a cunning way to keep us out of the way and out of the wardroom bar when its only guardian was the ship's doctor.

The next morning, as luck would have it, the submarine (the *Santa Fe*) was located during a routine helicopter patrol. The choppers attacked and caused enough damage to cause it to change course and limp back into Grytviken, South Georgia. It was then decided as we had seized the initiative and were keen to keep it we should press home the attack. The plan was simple – it had to be, because there were so few troops available that the deployment options were extremely limited. The force was made up of M Company, HQ elements, D Squadron SAS, 2SBS and our two NGSFO teams, about eighty men in total, who were cobbled together to make a composite company. It was decided that the assault was to be preceded by a fire plan (bombardment) which in effect was to become an NGS firepower demonstration. The shape of King Edward Cove was a natural amphitheatre which provided the enemy with a superb grandstand view of the persuasive nature of Naval firepower.

The other team leader, Captain Chris Brown, who I knew very well, had flown ashore earlier by helicopter and was spotting and directing the fire plan from an OP on Dartmouth Point which was on the other side of the bay directly opposite Grytviken. My team went ashore in the leading Lynx with the OC of D Squadron and his HQ group. The barrage continued while the troop build-up on the landing site was going on. It seemed to take one hell of a long time to get everyone ashore since our limited helicopter assets had to make several trips out to the ships and bring troops ashore in penny packets. We'd lost our main troop-carrying assets earlier when two Wessex helicopters had crashed during an SAS patrol exfiltration.

As soon as we were all ashore we started our advance towards Grytviken. All this time the barrage had been continuing. During the advance we neared the end of a piece of open ground in the lee of Brown Mountain. That morning we had had several reports of enemy on the ridge of Brown Mountain and as we approached its base we saw dark shapes moving through the tussock grass. Everyone was pretty well on edge, mindful of stories of Argentinian special forces being on the island. This movement certainly tied in with the earlier reports. These shapes, in what appeared to be black balaclavas, were engaged with small-arms fire and several M79 grenades. When we reached the position, these 'special forces' turned out to be no more than harmless seals going about their daily business. However, I must say that they looked remarkably like men crawling through the grass at the initial engagement distances. This 'battle' had the effect of putting people very much more at ease and in a strange way of building confidence. It was a bit like the effect you get during the tense settling-down period of an evenly balanced rugby game when suddenly you break the deadlock and score. It was that sort of morale boost.

All the time this 'battle' and the advance had been taking place, Chris Brown had been doing an excellent job with his firepower demonstration by creeping the barrage closer and closer to the enemy positions.

Unfortunately, because of the mass of Brown Mountain I was screened from the ships, that is to say my radio signals were being screened, so I had to relay through Chris Brown to get a response out of the ships. Our communications link worked well and as I updated him on our advance he in turn moved the fire along in front of us. Once or twice the odd salvos came a little bit close for comfort. I would have to explain to the accompanying infanteers that of course gunfire is an area weapon!

The advance to Grytviken was a fairly straightforward affair, with the exception of a slight miscalculation or, rather, misappreciation about the size of Brown Mountain. This was largely as a result of our map recces. Normally we work off 1 in 50,000-scale maps which have contour intervals of 15 metres whereas our maps of Georgia had intervals of 500 feet, so that when looking at the map you would see two contour lines on the planned route and subconsciously register a 30-metre climb to the ridge of a feature, whereas in reality we were faced with a 1,000-foot climb. I personally believe that this was a contributory factor in the series of disasters that befell the SAS mountain troop a few days earlier – but that's another story.

We got onto the ridge of Brown Mountain and established a fire base. From our position we had a clear view straight down into Grytviken and to the enemy locations.

While we had been grunting and puffing our way up the side of the mountain, reports were coming across on the radio that white flags were being flown from one or two of the buildings in the village. I was able to confirm this when I got to the ridge. With a fire base of Milan missiles, GPMGs and mortars consolidated on the ridge, we again moved forward, with the point platoon, towards the village to take the surrender. Fortunately the 250-plus Argentinians at Grytviken offered no resistance. As we approached they formed up in three ranks outside Discovery House, sang their national anthem and just waited for us to arrive to take the surrender.

There were more Argentinians still on Georgia, the notorious Captain Astiz, who led the Argentinian detachment on the island, was still at large, and reports indicated that both Stromness and Leith whaling stations were defended and that the enemy there intended to fight.

At first light the next morning my signaller and I went with the OCD Squadron to Stromness to work with HMS *Plymouth* which was on station ready to support if required. We were to call on support in an attempt to persuade the enemy that there was not much point in losing their lives in defence of this particular plot. *Plymouth* cleared her guns out to sea with an ear-shattering noise which echoed around the bay and must have made Astiz's troops wonder if it was their turn next. This gentle persuasion had the desired effect and the enemy surrendered. They had wired their defensive positions very professionally. I was very glad we did not have to fight; if we had, it would have been very bloody indeed and I seriously doubt if we would have done it with the resources we had ashore at the time. Like so many of the positions throughout the campaign, they were defenders' paradises and we'd come to realize that had we been defending them, we'd still be there.

During the recapture of Georgia the two ships had fired about 180 or so salvos guided in by the OPs ashore. My NGS team consisted of four men: myself; my Second-in-Command, a bombardier, (Jacko) Jackson; a gunner signaller, Tich Barfoot; and a matelot radio operator, Stan Hardy. The team members were all experienced and highly motivated hands, all had undergone a hefty selection procedure and a minimum of one year's specialized training before joining a team. This training included the commando course, P Company which is the Parachute Regiment's selection course for airborne forces, artillery and Naval gunfire technical courses, and signal courses. My team was allocated as advance force support, so consequently all were divers and boat handlers, and since we are co-located with SBS in England we exercised with them regularly and so were familiar with advance force procedures and techniques. We carried four radios and had the capability to talk to ships, aircraft, the artillery and to the infantry or supported troops. As mentioned earlier, the primary task was to pass target information to the ships. We would pass

314

the following basic information: where the target was, what it was, what you wanted doing with it and for how long. This, of course, was all sent in a standard pattern encompassed in artillery-Naval mumbo jumbo. Once the Gunnery Officer on board had this information he fed the target co-ordinates into his computer which also took into account such things as the ship's location, direction and speed of travel, direction and speed of the tide, plus several other related factors.

Unlike field artillery, which is static and relatively simple, Naval gunfire with its mobile platform is quite a complicated art. Problems in calculations tend to compound, which can be costly in terms of time penalties and effect should rounds start falling rogue. The NGS shell has much more destroying power than the field artillery in use with commando or airborne forces. It is not a point weapon, that is, you shouldn't use it to knock out a machine-gun post. It is an area weapon and should be used to neutralize area targets, for example a company or platoon position. However, having said that, if a Naval shell were to drop in beside you in your trench or vehicle it would certainly make your eyes water.

One other group in the system is worthy of mention – Naval Gunfire Liaison Officers (NGLOs). These are Army officers located in the ships' Ops Rooms. They are our answer to ACAS. When the situation requires, they translate Army speak into Navy speak and vice versa, and time after time they proved their worth.

After Georgia I think most people thought, 'Well, they must see sense now, this must be the end of the silliness, surely common sense has got to prevail.' The Task Force was hovering and we appeared to be demonstrating a degree of reserve. Yet we would hear on the World Service that the Argentinians were saying that our forces on Georgia had taken heavy casualties and that their forces were still putting up a brave defence. Knowing how easily they had given in, we were very surprised and not a little dismayed about what this augured for the future.

Both our teams and the special forces were withdrawn

from Georgia and re-established on HMS *Antrim* and HMS *Plymouth* for a voyage north to rendezvous with the main Task Force. We were surprised how far away it was. While we felt as if we'd spent ages in terrible weather conditions, the main force seemed to have spent endless weeks basking in the sun off Ascension Island. On joining with the Task Force we cross-decked to *Invincible* for interminable briefings and debriefings on Op Paraquat. Here we met the press for the first time and, boy, were they hungry for stories, but of course there was a pretty strict set of rules covering U and non-U subjects to be discussed. I was even offered £1,000 for photographs of the Georgia op. For once in my life it looked as if I was in the right place at the right time. Unfortunately, my camera and film were still on board *Antrim*.

From 1 May until my team went ashore on the 16th, I spent much time on the gun line directing NGS at various venues. Much of the spotting had to be done from helicopter. The bombardment onto the airfield on 1 May was done in broad daylight in mid-afternoon, but all the rest were at night. It didn't take the brains of an archbishop to work out that a helicopter was not the best place to be when people were firing at you. I must say that in my youth I'd often fancied myself as a steely-eyed helicopter pilot, able to give the girls all those good, over-rehearsed throw-away lines which never work. Now I'm firmly of the opinion that those overgrown hairdryers are no way to go to war. There are just no hiding places in a perspex bubble.

Morale among my team at this time was pretty good despite the fact that during this period we were on HMS *Arrow* when she went alongside *Sheffield* and took off many of the survivors. When I saw the effect on the sailors I was glad I was a soldier; at least we generally get the opportunity to get acclimatized to our environment. But these fellows, one moment they were warm and cosy, had all the home comforts, and the next they just had the clothes they stood up in. Total shock.

All the time I, like my team, was wondering what was

taking us so long to get on with it. From a military point of view it seemed so obvious what needed to be done, and the sooner the better. We listened daily to the World Service and were getting very frustrated with the inactivity. The politicians seemed to be getting nowhere.

On D–7 I got a call on secure radio from the CO of my regiment who must have done a summer sales job at some time. First he gave me the good news, which was about my promotion exam, then he gave me the other news. He wanted me to take my team ashore on D–6 with an SBS team and then to establish an advance force OP on the south-western side of Sussex Mountain on East Falkland. This signalled a hectic period of cross-deckings, maybe seven or eight, to gather up all my team and equipment. I also needed to liaise with quite a few agencies and attend several Order Groups and briefings, and to tie up last-minute fine details such as where will the ships be if the landing is off/postponed/brought forward, how will we pick up casualties, etc., etc.

My team and an SBS team went ashore in a pretty simple, straightforward operation. We were taken into Falkland Sound on HMS *Alacrity* to a point about four kilometres off Rookery Point on East Falkland, which was to be roughly our drop-off point. Here we launched our Geminis and headed off towards the shore. At about 200 metres from our landing point we cut engines and lifted the propeller shaft. The reasons for doing this were twofold. Firstly it cut noise and made a stealthy approach possible, and secondly it stopped the propeller becoming entangled in the kelp. From here on we relied on oars for propulsion. This was a terrible position to be in because if we did encounter enemy we'd have a hell of a job to bug out at speed. We would be unable to use the engines until we were clear of the kelp. The drill was fairly simple – it's best that way because it stands a better chance of working. One boat sat off, covering the other going in, so that if it got into trouble at least one would be able to manoeuvre and act as a firm base. When the first boat had dropped off its patrol it recovered to the stand-off position. The team on shore now offered extra protection as the second boat went in and dropped its team – my team.

It was as black as the ace of spades, we couldn't see a thing, even through our nightscopes. There was just no light at all. Once we were both firm the two teams parted company at the drop-off point. The SBS headed off on their task and we started on ours. Probably the most vulnerable time was moving from the sea to the land, but once we were off the boat we 'brown jobs' were in our own environment, and I must say it felt good to be on dry land again. We had arrived silently and according to plan and were stealthily creeping off the beach when the cox in our boat, who was supposed to wait with the machine gunner in the stand-off position until he was sure that we were well-established on shore, had cleared the beach and weren't in any trouble, suddenly started the engine and the whole world echoed with the noise it made. We just hit the deck and lay there absolutely motionless, not daring even to breathe. I swore to myself and made the young man in the boat a promise that would have given me the utmost pleasure to carry out there and then. Thankfully the enemy were not there so up we got and took our first unsteady steps off the beach. With the engine starting and its retreat into the night came the inescapable realization that here we were alone, the Task Force God only knew where. If anything went wrong the earliest that we could expect any help or escape would be twenty-four hours later and at a point some few kilometres away. But it wasn't any feelings of bravery that moved us. It was cold and we wanted to get going.

From our drop-off point to our proposed OP position was a distance of about eleven or twelve kilometres, and on my map appreciation I had hoped to make it in about four hours or so. However, the going was extremely difficult. I reckoned we were only making good about one kilometre per hour, and getting across the beach had been slower than we had hoped.

As we continued, the moon began to rise. Our hearts sank. Ahead of us we spotted a four-man patrol coming up on the skyline. At this stage we hadn't covered more than one kilometre from the drop-off. We immediately went to ground. Our brief had been to go ashore for up to fourteen days and establish an OP, so the last thing on earth one wanted to do was to get involved in a firefight and blow our cover in the first hours of the mission. We stayed to ground hoping they would pass and we could continue avoiding contact. As far as we could make out they weren't speaking English, so they had to be Argentinian. They were moving very slowly and deliberately towards our position. We released our safety catches. Stan whispered to me that the third guy was carrying a machine gun, and I was sure the second was the radio operator. Each of us took our target; another few metres and we would let them have it. In this situation the order to open fire and target acquisition to prevent us all firing on the same man were part of our SOPs (standard operating procedures). They were only metres away now. We lay totally motionless and as they closed we could just make out a white front; then we moved to surprise them. Recognition! Four waddling *penguins*! No sooner had we started to relax than the rest of the gang came to have a look and greet their liberators – about 200 of the buggers came waddling over the skyline, all chattering away. The sound was infinitely worse than the Gemini taking off. Not the greatest start we could have hoped for. It took about another hour for the penguins to settle down and get used to us. They were very inquisitive. They had come to see what was going on. I just hoped they were happy to be liberated and that they could keep a secret!

Our task was to move onto the back of Sussex Mountain and establish an OP with an arc of observation that would cover any possible attack from the area of Darwin or Goose Green or from Western Island on the main landings in San Carlos.

It was to take us four nights to get into position, stumbling over tussock grass in the dark with our huge great packs. We had to move at the dead of night because the ground over which we were travelling afforded no cover. The last couple of hours before daylight were spent preparing our hides for the next day of lying up. So the move to the OP was very slow and deliberate. When we arrived in the area the CO had designated I wasn't very happy with it and we moved off to search for a better position; this again took up valuable time. However, we eventually moved into a large rocky outcrop which gave a superb view over more than was in our sphere of interest.

Every day we had watched a Hercules and two escort Pucarás travelling very low south on the eastern side of the Sound towards Darwin. Then we observed the Hercules travelling north along the western side of the Sound before turning west and heading out towards the mainland. We also observed quite a bit of helo traffic between the islands, and this included helicopters carrying out grid searches. At one point a helicopter on one of these searches came dangerously close to our position and we thought that he had seen us. We were prepared and could have easily blown him out of the air, but we were still keen to remain undetected and avoid contact.

We had not been getting through to the Task Force on our scheduled radio calls so we really didn't know what the situation was as far as the landing was concerned. It transpired that on occasions our HQ on the ships had picked up our signals but we couldn't hear theirs. We went ahead hoping that D-Day would be on the 21st. On the night of 20 May we achieved good each-way communications, confirmed D-Day and passed our sitrep. The landing went ahead. For us it was fairly uneventful. We could see the ships in the Sound and the SAS diversionary raids to the south. We watched the Argentinian air raids coming in on the ships and saw a Pucará being shot down.

After the landings were secure and the battalions were moving out to occupy the high ground around San Carlos we had our next adventure. This time it nearly involved a blue on blue contact (an attack on your own side) with a patrol from 2 Para who were digging in on Sussex Mountain.

We saw a four-man patrol coming towards our location. We made frantic calls on the radio to try and get a positive ID on them, but nobody admitted to having anybody in that sector. This tallied with our expectations of where to expect friendlies. While this build-up was taking place we were getting reports of the action on Fanning Head through our radio net, which advised that Argentinians were withdrawing from their locations towards the south.

We were in a very strong position in good cover on the high ground. We set an ambush and watched them walk towards it. They stopped just below us. It was then and only then that we recognized that they were Paras. Next problem. How do we make ourselves known to them without somebody losing their life? Obviously they would be jumpy. Eventually we tied a Union Jack to a stick and waved it over a rock, accompanying it with a greeting to the effect – What kept you?

Shortly after we married up with 2 Para they took over my OP position and my team was withdrawn by helicopter to a debriefing and degunging session on board HMS *Fearless*. We were all pretty knackered; we'd expended a lot of energy over the last week.

Next on the horizon was the Goose Green battle. 2 Para needed a Forward Air Controller to go to their location and bring in an air attack mission onto a suspected target. I happened to be in the wrong place at the wrong time and was 'volunteered'. I was choppered to Goose Green on the morning after the battle. That was a very sobering experience. I met the Falkland Islanders who had been liberated and I talked with the boys from 2 Para. There was a most strange atmosphere. The Falklanders were obviously delighted but absolutely shattered. The Paras appeared as if they were in delayed shock; they had lost a lot of people the day before. They had a drawn, white look about them, their eyes were ringed and staring. I met Johnny Crosland who was being very professional and was intent on motivating his boys to get on with the job. I also met Tony Rice, the Battery Commander; he and Johnny pointed out the target area to me. Every now and again, when the conversation lulled, you could sense them falling back into a sort of zombie-like state. They were obviously reflecting on recent events.

For the next week or so I was tasked every night to work with various ships to continue the harassing NGS. This meant being back in helicopters again to do the spotting – and another shock of grey hair, not to mention a twitch whenever anybody mentions helicopters.

At the end of this period my team were tasked to go ashore again and join with 3 Para. The chopper pilot unfortunately dropped us off about two kilometres from where we needed to be. I jumped down off the aircraft and soon realized I was in the wrong place. I began waving and gesturing to the pilot, who just gave a thumbs up, a cheerful grin and flew off. Again I made a promise and noted the aircraft number for future reference!

Eventually, after a bit of a slog cross country, we met up with 3 Para and their Adjutant, Kevin McGimpsey, who I knew well. He told us to stick with Battalion HQ until we went firm, then we would be allocated to a particular company. At the time, the battalion was advancing and making good progress. The lead elements by this stage were not far away from the Murrell River Bridge. It was then that we got called back. I had only just joined them and this hacked me off. For the battalion it was a real sickener as they had to slog back over ground that they had covered in the previous day. This had the most terrible effect on morale. It was very interesting to experience first hand this fairly well-documented phenomenon. However, they recovered quickly and got on with it. Later I met Colonel Pike, the CO, and gave him my notion as to where I thought I'd be best employed – always a tricky ploy. But amazingly he agreed and I was allocated to B Company. Normally I would have stayed around the Battalion HQ and close to the CO, but the battalion only had two FOO (Forward Observation Officer) parties and the CO really needed three, one to each of his rifle companies. My team had the ability to direct both artillery and Naval gunfire, hence this grouping.

322

I met up with the Company Commander, Mike Argue, and co-located with his HQ group. During the next ten days before the attack on Mount Longdon I had a gunship on station virtually every night, firing onto Longdon. On a number of occasions I went forward with recce patrols to clear the route that we would use on the night and to make adjustments to my fire plan. Also, by bringing part of my team on these recces it meant that the patrol had direct access to fire support to extricate themselves should they have a contact. By the time I'd covered the route three or four times and crossed the river the same, I was pretty well motivated to get off that particular plot.

On the night of the attack I had registered all my targets and I had a ship coming on station. I had two gun batteries allocated to me and all target information had been circulated. So we were well prepared, all set up and ready to go. Everything was up and running, ticking over beautifully. As we moved off out of the battalion area all my radio nets were in. I had that twinge – you know, this is all too smooth, what's going to go wrong?

I didn't have long to wait to find out. Colonel Pike had decided to go for a silent attack. That's not how I personally would have liked to have played it, I'd seen the effect of firepower at Grytviken and had spoken to the boys at Goose Green who'd had only half a battery in support but had soon realized the value of good, timely fire support. I'm firmly of the view that the Argentinians were expecting us, anyway; in fact like most of us they were probably wondering what the hell was keeping us. Therefore I believe that in this situation it is much easier to put in a hefty bombardment and then go in and pick up the pieces, instead of trying to take everything with just the rifle and bayonet. Bombardment may not be quite so subtle but by God it's effective. But a fact of life was that Colonel Hew was a colonel and I was a captain so that night we would go silently. This created a problem for me. I had laid the guns on the main target and as we closed on it had to constantly update and readjust my targets so that if we had to open fire the rounds would fall plus of the target and not on it, as we had by now advanced onto the main target area. The effect of this was that I now couldn't be exactly sure where my first lot of rounds would land. As we continued up the feature all was going very well when one of our men stepped on a mine and that was the end of our silent attack; all hell broke loose. I immediately called in artillery fire. One battery was slap bang on target, but unfortunately the other one was firing in another parish. I didn't have time to readjust them so I thinned them out and used only one battery at this time.

It was at about this point that I came to suspect that Murphy of Murphy's Law fame was on the hill with us. His law is to the effect that if something can go wrong, it will.

As we started to move among the rocks our radios began to become screened and communications with the Command Posts became intermittent. This was about as welcome as a hole in the head. Luckily the BC of 8 Battery, Major Mike Goodfellow, who was listening on net, realized our plight and picked up my messages which he relayed to the Command Posts. This caused a slight delay, but it worked and got us going up the hill again.

No sooner were we underway than our group, which comprised my team and Company HQ, started to come under effective fire from some enemy in the rocks about fifty metres away. My team and a couple of riflemen from the HQ group formed a fire group and decided that the best form of defence would be attack. We began taking the enemy on. The arrangement worked very well as it left Mike Argue free to worry about fighting the main battle without the added distraction of the immediate problem of protecting himself. During this time the artillery continued to rain down, and it was still falling on target. This I was thankful for because the enemy snipers had us pinned down. We manoeuvred into fire positions and put down suppressive fire which allowed people to move out to a flank with 66s. We drew enemy fire and the boys with the 66s fired at the muzzle flashes. The snipers were killed and we continued up the hill. This simple tactic was to work time and time again. The 66, although designed as an anti-tank weapon, certainly proved its worth as a bunker buster.

We were not the only ones having difficulty making headway. The platoon on the back of the feature had been brought to a standstill and the platoon to our left was also making very slow headway under stiff opposition. Both platoons were now taking considerable casualties. The main problem was that the enemy were well concealed in the rocks, and on the ridge they had several machine-gun nests which were spewing out a deadly hail. The .50 gun positions at the eastern end of the feature were engaged by NGS. This was very accurate and allowed us to start manoeuvring again. I kept moving the NGS along the ridge; this was doing the trick and neutralizing the guns. It must have been pretty uncomfortable for the enemy.

Our little group was now making headway up the north side of the feature, but the battle as a whole was not going quite so well. Mike Argue was receiving confused reports, but what was becoming obvious was that his boys were not moving forward. It was about now that the decision was taken to withdraw a little bit and attempt to gain a closer picture of the situation and to consolidate.

The platoon on our left flank had now become totally bogged and were coming under very effective enemy fire. I started creeping the artillery fire in very close to our own forward troops in an effort to enable them to effect a withdrawal. This was a bit nerve-racking since the two sides were probably no more than forty or fifty metres apart and at night it is very difficult to determine exactly where the front element of your own troops is. I had a radio on the company net and was talking to the forward left platoon by a series of chats which resembled the Golden Shot Phone-in rather than Infantry Artillery Target Indication procedures. However, the main thing is that it worked. The platoon was able to withdraw under cover of a heavy barrage and get out of a sticky situation.

The consolidation was now going ahead. As a result of mounting casualties, Mike Argue had been forced to

325

reorganize his company, essentially by amalgamating the front two platoons into one unit. Shortly after this regrouping we attempted to move forward again; we didn't get too far before we became pinned down. Mr Cox's platoon was trying to go round the edge of the feature left-flanking. They didn't get too far either before they had a soldier killed by snipers. From their position the platoon could not locate the snipers. From my position I could. I moved into a fire position and armed a 66 rocket. Sighting on the target was difficult – at night it is not easy to pick out the foresight of the weapon. I fired and thought that it had gone low, but almost immediately there was a secondary explosion. I think the rocket must have hit the snipers' grenades or magazines because there was an almighty flash. This shot was followed quickly by very decisive action by the platoon who wasted no time at all in pressing home the advantage. The snipers were silenced and the advance began again.

We had now cleared the bottom and the back of the main position. The top of the mountain along the ridge was still very much a live issue. We in the HQ group made steady progress to the top and with adrenalin-powered momentum suddenly found ourselves over the top and on an exposed forward slope. There was a quick application of the brakes, speedy engagement of reverse, and we found ourselves in cover in some rocks. We couldn't see all we wanted to from here so my signaller Tich Barfoot and I moved forward again, a bit down the forward slope behind some more rocks to a position where we could see to control the fire.

Mark Cox's platoon was now very exposed and unable to move forwards or backwards. They were taking the full brunt of the enemy effort which was now centred on the eastern end of the ridge. The enemy still had several .50 machine guns in action as well as some very capable snipers in well-protected hides. Both artillery and NGS were now brought to bear on the main enemy locations. I ordered a heavy rate of fire to help neutralize the enemy and to allow our men to get into better positions. This barrage silenced a .50 calibre and much of the sniper fire.

Meantime Barfoot and myself were under a bit of pressure ourselves. In our OP we became the subject of attention for an enemy section. Shots were coming over our heads and ricocheting off the rocks behind us. This was a bit disconcerting, to say the least. We continued to control the NGS and artillery onto the enemy locations with revived vigour.

B Company had now been fighting all night and had taken the brunt of the battalion's casualties. Basically, they had fought themselves to a standstill. Just before first light the CO came forward to see the situation for himself and we pointed out the enemy locations.

At first light A Company, commanded by Major David Collett, was passed through B Company and on to the forward slopes. This movement was carried out under cover of a heavy barrage. B Company regrouped and reorganized on the feature and went firm. A Company quickly mopped up the remaining enemy resistance and reported that they were firm on their objective. Mount Longdon had been captured.

Just as we were beginning to relax slightly and allow ourselves for the first time to reflect on some of the events of the night we were subjected to a heavy enemy artillery and mortar bombardment. This bombardment caused us several casualties, some fatal. I was missed by the shells but on jumping for cover as the initial shells were incoming I scored a direct hit of my own. I dived for cover behind some rocks and landed slap bang in the middle of what had been the local sanitary system. I tried to convince myself it was lucky to do this sort of thing. What was good about it was that I was guaranteed a trench or hide all to myself.

The enemy bombardment continued to harass us all morning. It was decided that the company would withdraw off the top of the feature and regroup in a more sheltered area to the western end of Longdon. My OP was left on the exposed forward eastern edge of the feature. It seemed that the potency of my lucky charm was wearing off! We spent the next forty-eight hours or so forward in the OP and had some very near misses from both snipers and artillery. Much too close for comfort. I in turn continued to bring harassing fire on any enemy locations that I could see, particularly the heavy mortar positions.

It was extremely cold and miserable at night and because the ships came onto the gun line only after dark we were up all night directing NGS, and then by day we would direct field artillery.

During these couple of days there was plenty of time to reflect. One of the points that kept coming back to me was how the battle had been fought on the very basic, simple, almost section-level tactics that we'd been taught at Sandhurst. These tactics were, of course, based on the experiences of many through the First and Second World Wars. With all our modern-day sophistication it was interesting just how quickly we reverted to the well-tried and tested techniques. KISS, Keep It Simple Stupid, seemed to stand the best chance of success when situations became confused and plans needed rapid amendment. We had just spent several weeks re-inventing the wheel, so to speak.

My team was transferred from 3 Para to 2 Para for the move forward onto Wireless Ridge. Their new CO, Colonel Chaundler, came forward onto Longdon to see the ground from my OP. He looked to me as if he was from another world. I remember thinking that we'd been ten or so days on the side of the hill at the mercy of the elements and anything else that cared to come our way. We were all lean and drawn and pretty dirty (some dirtier than others!) and there he was, looking remarkably clean and chubby. He didn't look tired like the rest of us, but then he'd left his job behind a desk at the MoD only a few days before. I wonder what he thought of us.

Tony Rice, the Battery Commander with 2 Para, had also come forward and between us we worked out the fire plan for the attack. It was by now about ten o'clock in the morning and I was to adjust four targets before it got dark at about six o'clock. This would normally have been a fairly easy task; however, Murphy had reappeared. At midnight I still hadn't managed to adjust all the targets.

We had remained on the forward edge of Longdon as an anchor OP. We had a superb arc of observation over the complete area of interest, but every time I tried to get on with the adjustment we became the focus of attention for either artillery mortars or snipers. Once those had passed we then had communications problems. These were sorted out and then in came snow squalls which obscured the target areas. Then the guns were having trouble staying on their platforms, and so on it went. Miraculously it all went very well on the night. Obviously Murphy was tired and had gone off to get his head down. The bombardments went very well and the attack was a complete success. Later that morning we got the news that endex had been called.

We advanced to the outskirts of Stanley and went firm in a building near the racecourse. As we were firming up and becoming the victims of rumour and counter-rumour, British troops were pouring into Stanley. I remember one incident particularly well. We (Paras, although my team was from the Commando Brigade) had been in Stanley for a couple of hours when the first Commando unit came in past our position and some bright spark greeted the Commandos with, 'Well, we've got it back for you, now look after it this time!' I won't recount the Marines' reply.

My team was withdrawn to HMS *Fearless* the next morning. I found it impossible to slow down or rest. I'd been up and moving on such a high plane for quite some time. In fact, for the first three or four nights after endex I couldn't sleep, plus I had frostbite on one of my toes. As I settled down and began to thaw out I had an excruciating pain in my foot. The good aspect was that the doctor on *Canberra* when I got there advised me to drink plenty of alcohol because it dilutes the blood and assists it to circulate to the extremities!

Luckily we managed to return home on the *Canberra*. This was a superb way to recuperate and unwind for a few weeks. We were remarkably well looked after by the crew. The stewards even went as far as telling us how nice it was to have some real men aboard again.

One evening during the voyage I went down to the Crow's Nest Bar – my foot was giving me trouble – and at a fairly late stage in the treatment the Brigadier (Julian Thompson) came over to join a few of us 'invalids'. Well, it seemed only fitting that I should debrief the Brigadier on how I thought the campaign had gone. After lots of 'And another thing, Brigadier' and much finger-waving, the 'debrief' came to a somewhat noncommittal conclusion.

Rumours on ship have to be heard to be believed, so to speak. You can say something to somebody quite innocently and by the time it's done one circuit you're making promises to join a silent order. So it was with the 'debrief' and by the time it reached me in the morning I wasn't quite so sure any more about one or two of the finer points. Discretion being the better part of valour I decided to lie low for a few days.

On about the third night my foot was hurting again so off I went for treatment. After a liberal medication I decided it was time to make my way to the heads (Naval expression for loos). On arriving at the heads all the urinals were occupied by a row of large Marine officers obviously engrossed in some grand story of derring-do. They were all senior to me, I could tell by the way they were standing. I couldn't tell them to hurry up. I danced from leg to leg until I could wait no more. There was only one thing for it – I would have to ease springs in the sink. And who should walk in at that precise moment but the Brigadier. I hadn't seen him since the 'debrief'. He just smiled and made a comment to the effect that it was nice to see a gunner on target for once. I looked down at my 'area' weapon and decided it was time to spread fire. After all, we gunners have a reputation to maintain.

The entry back into Southampton was quite amazing, very, very moving indeed. We were absolutely astounded by the welcome. I don't think there were many people who didn't feel at least a lump in the throat.

11/12 June

Attack on Mount Harriet

Captain Peter Babbington

Royal Marines

Military Cross

On the night of 11/12 June 1982, on the island of East Falkland, 42 Commando Royal Marines began a silent night attack against strongly-held enemy positions on the Mount Harriet feature, five kilometres to the west of Port Stanley.

Initially, in getting onto and amongst the rocky crags of Mount Harriet, undetected by the enemy, they achieved brilliant surprise. The enemy, caught off balance, reacted fiercely. Captain Babbington was commanding the leading company as the fighting erupted.

In the midst of a ferocious firefight, Captain Babbington calmly directed his men and used his tactical and support weapons to maximum devastating effect. His personal courage and cool professionalism were an inspiring example and a crucial factor in defeating the enemy.

We had been on leave for about three days. I was on holiday in Scotland when I was phoned up and told, 'Come back. Something's gone wrong in the South Atlantic and we are going down there.' We were at my parents' house up in Kirkcudbright when I got this phone call—I thought it was an April fool that had gone wrong. So I broke the news to my wife and family, and we packed the car up. Then I thought, 'Well, I'll just check,' so I got back on the phone to the Adjutant and said, 'Are you sure this isn't a bite? I'm about to drive 400 miles with a family that are all crying and saying that I've ruined their holiday.' He said, 'No, you've got to get back.' So we all jumped in the car and raced back – one of those delightful trips when I was literally dying for the police to stop me as I roared down the motorway at eighty miles an hour, but I never saw a police car the whole way! First time I ever had a justifiable excuse! So we all sort of poured back here to Bickleigh and formed up our companies, kitted them out with all we reckoned we were going to need. Within forty-eight hours the unit was operational, which was surprising because we had people all over the world, in the United States, Morocco and Denmark. There was even one officer getting married in the USA and as he was going down the aisle he was grabbed and told to get back minus his honeymoon.

So we came back obviously to a certain amount of organized pandemonium, as people were trying to work out what we would need and what ships to put us on. The decision about *Canberra* hadn't been made at this stage. It was a big 'rush to wait' event. I think we hung around in Bickleigh for six days; we didn't board the ship until 8 April – my wedding anniversary, which went down well! The Argentinians captured the Falklands on 2 April, and the whole island was under their control by the time we left.

Initially I never thought we'd go into action but by the time we reached Ascension Island I thought it was inevitable. I think I knew the way Margaret Thatcher operated; she wasn't going to compromise on their takeover. We sat at Ascension for about two weeks. We got off the *Canberra* for a day here and there and an afternoon on the beach, but we basically sat on the *Canberra*. There was fairly intensive training going on. It's a big ship and it's surprising how much training you can do with 2,000-odd troops on board. There were ourselves, 40 Commando and 3 Para, plus odds and sods.

There was one collective wardroom for all the officers, so we got on well and mixed with all other units. We all knew each other very well by the time we arrived in Falkland Sound. There wasn't any particular regimental rivalry. The press were dying to create this great rivalry that is always supposed to happen between Marines and Paras and, in fact, there wasn't any. There wasn't one punch-up on the way south that involved a Marine and a Para.

334

After disembarking we were involved in the capture of Mount Kent and were then called to attack Mount Harriet as part of 3 Commando Brigade's attacks on the night of 11 June. I was extremely confident with K Company and knew that we'd do well. This was my first real battle situation after sixteen years in the Royal Marines. I found it amazingly exhilarating; one definitely goes on an adrenalin high. The battle lasted about six hours, and throughout that time I was on this high, and I think that must apply to all those that were in that action.

The moments of doubt occurred before the action started really. We were briefed by the Colonel on the morning of the action. It was a full O Group, and by the time the Intelligence Officer had finished telling us what was on Mount Harriet, I was beginning to feel a little bit twitched and a trifle concerned; there were an awful lot of enemy there, who didn't exactly want me to go and play with them! Then the Colonel's orders came out, and it became obvious that I was going to be in action for a good hour before the next company joined; and I'd be up against a very large number of enemy. It was a silent night attack and it was uphill. We were defying one of the principles of war, which is that the odds should be three of us to one of them in the attack; in fact the reverse was true. But I must say morale wasn't a problem. I mean, we knew we were going to win, so in that sense, I knew they were beatable. However, I did feel concerned that there were maybe a lot more than we really should have been taking on.

I then had to go back and tell my Troop Commanders and the support team, in a nice confident way, that there were all these enemy up there, but it'd be no problem, we were going to deal with them. All the lads were sitting there, going: 'Fucking hell, Sir! Who's kidding who?' I was saying, 'Now, there's no problem. This hour on our own, before anybody else joins in the battle, is going to be to our benefit, because we're going to have all the guns, we're going to have the ships – everybody's going to be there to support K Company.' That was the only way I could put it over convincingly.

That night we did the move round, which was obviously fairly nerve-racking. We went through a minefield, but because we didn't tread on any we thought it was clear! There was intermittent shellfire, from both sides. We didn't want to do anything unusual at this stage, because we had about five kilometres to move around across the open ground below the hill features of Mount Challenger, Wall Mountain and Mount Harriet. I felt then they were waiting for us. They put up two or three star shells, which was a bit unnerving, because we thought, 'Christ! They've seen us and they're just watching us!' So we all took cover, it was quite worrying. Eventually we got round to the start line, which was the track which runs between Goose Green and Stanley. We were supposed to have met up with the Welsh Guards' recce troop – but they were not where we expected them. So we said, 'Well, sod them,' but we had to wait around. Eventually they were found. We lined out ready. The moon was just starting to come up and with binoculars you could see the objective very clearly. I got my Troop Commanders to look through their binoculars, so that they could all see their specific objectives – each troop had their own – and I made sure they were all quite happy with what they had to do.

By this time I suppose the adrenalin was starting to pump. Ahead, looming up in the darkness, was this big hill. We had to walk about 800 metres in the open, all uphill until we got to the rocks at its base. There was to be no artillery bombardment – it was a silent attack. As I sat there I thought, 'Well, there's nothing else for it – we'd better start.' So I sent the message on our radio, 'Let's go!' We started walking up. Basically, there were two troops forward with my little party walking between them, but a little behind, and then I had a third troop behind us.

We just kept on walking. Nothing. Nothing. We couldn't believe we weren't being opposed. My Forward Observation Officer, a gunner captain, who was walking along with me, kept saying, 'We'll have to cancel that target.' We had put a lot of targets down in front of us for the artillery to track our move silently. HMS *Falmouth* was firing and she was hitting the side of the hill, further over to our flank. As this was going on we were just walking up this hill unopposed. We were wondering all the time how much longer the Argentinians would hold their fire.

We got to within about 100 yards of the boulder area when my left troop saw a couple of Argentinians move across on the skyline and I thought they'd seen us. So I ordered the troop to engage whilst surprise was still in our favour. Our guys opened fire and pinned them down and then went in and cleared them. Then the troops set about their various tasks. Sadly, I got the news over the radio, 'We've got one dead.' So I asked who it was and they told me and I thought, 'Why does it have to be him, a married man?' Still, that's how a war goes, I'm afraid. It's not particularly choosy of its victims.

At this point, the troop behind me passed through and moved up onto the ridge itself – the lefthand troop stayed on the low ground – and they started working their way along the rocks to the west. I couldn't see what was going on particularly well, so myself and the gunner officer stayed on the open hillside. We just sat on a rock, because from there we could control the supporting fire of mortars, guns and Naval gunfire and therefore the action better. I had two radio operators with me and I had the handsets to their radios. They were sitting underneath the rock. I was having difficulty getting the radio handsets to my mouth and whilst I was pulling at the cable I was shouting, 'For Christ's sake! Give me some more cable!' And they said, 'Fuck off, Sir. We're under fucking fire!' Which indeed we were – they'd sensibly got beneath some rocks. So more patiently I said, 'Oh, well, just give me some more cable.' I'd been sitting on the rock and I hadn't really noticed, but there was a lot of machine-gun fire coming down at us. I didn't think it was particularly aimed at us. I think they were just shooting. But there was a lot of .5 heavy machine-gun fire and assorted small arms flying around and the rocks were pinging a bit, but you don't actually notice this sort of thing when you're busy trying to control a battle.

This is where I think people end up getting awards,

because they don't actually realize they're doing anything particularly brave – they're just doing their job, and this means they get exposed to fire. This is how people win VCs – you know, they're strolling along with their walking stick or the umbrella, like the major in *A Bridge Too Far*; they're totally indifferent to what's going on around them because they're so busy worrying about other things.

So we stayed out on this rock whilst my Marines started working their way along the ridge; they were making steady progress, about twenty or thirty yards at a time, clearing a position and moving on. My righthand troop was now facing the east towards Stanley. I'd come up behind them and as we were expecting a counter-attack I wanted to get this troop established to protect our rear while we cleared the positions to our west.

I then went up, along the ridge line, to join up behind what had been my reserve troop. It was at this stage that we started coming under some very heavy incoming artillery fire. I turned round to one of the party with me and said, 'Well, toss up which side we go. Left or right?' They said, 'We'll go down the left, Sir, it looks quiet down there.' So we all ran down to the lefthand side into some rocks, and that was a disastrous mistake because we ran right into very concentrated Argentinian artillery fire. That really was quite, quite frightening, horrifically frightening, because it's totally impersonal, you've got no control over it, you feel particularly helpless – it's mindless. It's just coming in, 105mm shells landing four or five feet away from you, the whole ground lifting and bits of splintered rock going winging around. You're just lying curled up by the side of a rock and hoping you're not going to get hit. Then there was this almighty scream close to me. I thought, 'Oh, fuck. Somebody's got it.' So I shouted, 'Who is it? Who is it?' I stuck my head up and this Sergeant sniper near me yelled, 'I've got it in the backside, Sir,' which indeed he had – he'd also been blown about twenty feet and had dislocated his ankle. But everybody burst into laughter. That was the amazing thing, while all this artillery fire was smashing in, the most amazing jokes were coming out about this poor man having two arseholes! I got some of my party to casevac him back down to where my Sergeant-Major was, about 100 metres behind me; he was also collecting the prisoners.

I must admit to getting rather edgy about all this shrapnel flying about. Marine Titchmarsh said to me, 'C'mon, Sir, let's get the fuck outa here,' and I said, 'What are you talking about, Titchmarsh? I'm already ahead of you!' And we shot back up onto the top again and got ourselves into some rocks just behind one of the troops which by now had finished clearing their area. We then sort of steadied down for a while because we were now at the end of our part of the objective, and the other company was coming up to attack the other end.

The battle took six hours; time went very, very quickly. I remember that when the shelling was going on I turned round to the ever present Titchmarsh and said, 'For Christ's sake, light me a cigarette.' I must have said it in a loud voice, the whole company heard, and the next thing I saw was everybody lighting up – you know, 'The boss is smoking, therefore it must be okay.' You don't smoke at night, but it was almost daylight with all the illuminations, the flares and artillery rounds coming in. All I saw were the boys sitting behind rocks, puffing away like a giant Hamlet advert. Out of a company where only about 20 per cent smoked when we landed, we had about 98 per cent of us confirmed smokers by the end of that night! I normally smoke cigars but I had run out after about ten days ashore and as NAAFI weren't operating, there were no cigars. So I switched to cigarettes and by this time we'd captured a lot of Argentinian cigarettes, so there was no shortage. In fact, one of the prime things I told my Troop Commanders to check as they cleared the positions was to see if they could find any cigars. They never found any but they found marijuana. I told them to hang on to it as we might need it before this war was over!

The shellfire had caused us four casualties: my sniper Sergeant; my Company Second-in-Command; and two other guys with splinter wounds in Company Headquarters. I'd also lost the corporal who was shot dead, and Corporal Newland, who was shot and wounded whilst attacking an enemy position, so that was a total of six casualties. Happily, the wounded ones were all waiting for us when we got back to Bickleigh. They were all standing there, fit and ready to go; it was amazing.

After Harriet, we moved onto Goat Ridge which separated us from Two Sisters. We sat there, underneath the rocks, and watched the Scots Guards come up to get themselves prepared for their attack on Tumbledown. We were taking incoming rounds, but by then we were very used to this. You could tell whether they were 'overs' or 'unders' – or 'Oh, my Christs', as 'unders' were known! I think we were there resting for about twelve hours, then we pulled back up onto Harriet and went into the rocks again. I took another four casualties through shellfire over this period of time. The shelling was indiscriminate and spasmodic; there'd be a couple of hours of absolutely nothing and then, all of a sudden, two dozen rounds started landing in amongst you.

The morning before the surrender I got three presents through the mail. One was a letter from my wife with a packet full of wine gums – a treat, I do enjoy wine gums; one was a torch which didn't work, with a message from the Quartermaster which said, 'Here is a cigar . . . and a light!' I unscrewed the base of the torch and there inside was this huge Havana cigar. He'd also sent up in a big bag, well-wrapped, a litre bottle of whisky, which was most welcome. Then the surrender started and we all bolted into Stanley, so we didn't touch any of the goodies until we got into town. That night we all sat down and in about thirty minutes finished off the bottle of whisky.

Literally as the war finished, the Colonel said, 'I want you to write your citations, and get them to me tomorrow.' I was in Port Stanley, in this hole that my company was living in – a seaplane hangar that was about a foot deep in mud. The Argentinians had used it as a makeshift hospital for the severely wounded and dying, and the remains of human debris were everywhere, even on the roof. There was no light, so I was sitting there with a candle, unshaven, cammed out, soaking wet, very tired and drained. In a grubby notebook, with a stub of pencil, I scribbled out the citations.

Then there was the gradual wind-down. We cleared Stanley of the prisoners, then we disarmed them and looked after them on the airfield, which was quite good news, actually, it gave our unit something to do, and some time for thought. I realized that I'd carried a rifle all the way through, but I never had to pull the trigger. I don't believe it's the Commander's job to do that. If the Commander's having to fire his rifle, I think he's either in the wrong place or his plan has gone wrong or he's the sole survivor. The Commander is there to lead, by his presence, and if he has to fire his weapon something is wrong. People say you should only carry a pistol, because you only need something for self-defence. But a pistol is hopelessly inaccurate and, quite frankly, if I have to protect myself I have more faith in a rifle.

My thoughts now turned to home. We'd been out of touch; we'd had the odd newspaper but hadn't realized the euphoria that had built up back home. I sent a letter from Ascension Island to my wife, saying it would be nice to see her down at Southampton, but not to fuss if she couldn't make it. I'd see her back at Bickleigh. The day before, when we were just coming into the South-West Approaches, the press were flown on board. They were the same people that we'd gone down south with and who'd flown back from the Falklands. They all said, 'You guys just don't realize what's waiting for you up the Channel.' Then, as we started going up the Channel, the ship was ordered to steam within one mile of the coast all the way home. Everywhere you could see thousands of people on the cliff tops and hundreds of cars flashing their headlights! Boats were coming out from Falmouth and Dartmouth, loaded up with people all just coming out to cheer. At Southampton we estimated that probably 800 people would meet this unit, but there were 38,000 people waiting in the dockyard itself! They reckoned there were a quarter of a million people in Southampton that day. It was unbelievable – a lot of troops were very tearful over the whole show. We never realized just what an impact the war had made back here.

I suppose the most moving moment was when we were actually tied alongside, with the band playing on the jetty. The two songs that were sung by all the units on board the ship, both on the way down and on the way back, were 'Rule Britannia' and 'Jerusalem'. As the band broke into these, the whole ship burst into song. The people on the jetty sort of reeled back with the sheer volume of noise of these two songs being just roared out by 3,000-odd troops. It really was quite an amazing sight and sound.

All the families were there. We all had to file off, rather impatiently, in single file with our kit. It took about three hours, I suppose, to completely unload the ship. My wife and two eldest daughters were there to meet me.

Everybody was worried about the Customs – you know, 'Will they get excited about my extra bottle of whisky, or whatever?' And there were the Customs saying, 'We're not touching this lot. We'll have 38,000 relatives attacking us, as well as the Marines.' So they just stood to one side.

I really had no idea that I was to receive an MC; I don't actually believe I did anything brave or gallant to merit it. I feel that it was very much an award for the company's efforts. It was a particularly good company at that stage, all the way through, and they worked very well. People say, 'Well, they worked well, and they were good because you were leading them.' But I would have thought that the function of any Company Commander was to train up a good company – if he doesn't he's not doing his job. I was just doing my job. But people did more on Harriet. There was a remarkable act of courage when a Marine saved another Marine's life: the lad had virtually died from shell blast which had stopped his heart. Amidst a lot of incoming shellfire from the Argentinians, this Marine had the presence of mind, in the darkness, to realize what had happened and gave him mouth-to-mouth resuscitation, which I thought was amazing. Under shellfire he was jumping on this lad's heart and kept it up until he'd kick-started him back to life. He was the company clerk, the guy who did that, and he was also a very brave man.

Corporal Stephen Newland

Royal Marines

Military Medal

*On the night of 11/12 June 1982, on the Island of East
Falkland, 42 Commando Royal Marines began a silent night
attack against strongly defended enemy positions on the Mount
Harriet feature, five kilometres to the west of Port Stanley.*

*Initially, in getting onto and amongst the rocky crags of
Mount Harriet, they achieved brilliant surprise. Thereafter, a
fierce attack erupted and Corporal Newland's section were
pinned down by enemy machine-gun fire from a cliff above.*

*Ignoring the obvious dangers, Corporal Newland scaled the
cliff and, single-handed, attacked the enemy with bullet and
grenade. Although wounded in both legs he continued to engage
the enemy and direct his section onto their position.*

Before I joined the Marines at sixteen I had always hated
authority, but I realized that if I didn't get some discipline
I'd go off the rails. When I joined the corps I soon realized
what discipline was about because these people could really
hurt you if they wanted. You had no rights at all, you just
existed for them. They took you right down to basics, below
basics, so that you had absolutely nothing. Then they built
you how they wanted to. You really thought they didn't
care about whether you lived or died, but they did. Those
times were a bit grim, it was like a factory, like being a
robot. But I always knew there were two things they would
never do intentionally – one was kill me and the other was
make me pregnant. But it was a challenge, one against
something else – being tested to your limits. We all look for
that, although some people do not like to admit it. Anyone

343

can be a shopkeeper or dustman or whatever – if that's your bag, that's your bag. But I don't think anyone in the corps wants to do that; they join to do their job, to kill people. That's my job. They say 'Kill', I kill. They say 'Don't', I don't.

I was in Northern Ireland for my mate's wedding when I was recalled. As usual, I'd left an address in case anyone wanted to contact me. I didn't even think about it. We were watching the news in a hotel and getting blasted out of our minds. About twelve o'clock we got a phone message telling us to go back to his fiancée's house. The whole family was there, all the women were crying and they said, 'There's been a phone call. You've got to go back.' This meant that Mick couldn't get married because we were supposed to go straight away! So I phoned camp up and talked to our Movements Senior Sergeant, Paul Hayworth, who said, 'We're going south.' But as we weren't going until Tuesday, he said it'd be okay if we got back Monday morning. So Mick got married on the Saturday and we flew back to England on the Sunday. I think his wife understood really. I mean, all the blokes wanted to go. But you can't say in front of women, 'I wanna go away and kill people,' because they think there's something wrong with you.

Funnily enough, I'd been in the Falklands, I'd spent a year there in 1978/9. I swore then that I would never go back again. As we were leaving one of my mates said, 'If I gave you £10,000 now, would you stay for six months more?' I said, 'No way!' It's the middle of nowhere.

The only thing I remember about the boat journey south was being pissed off with politicians. I can't stomach the way they leap about trying to make decisions. As it was, we sat in Ascension while all the politicians squabbled about what was happening. All we were thinking was, 'Let's get on with it. Let's do it.' We wanted to go straight down and blast the Argies before they had time to do anything. I don't believe soldiers fight for political reasons; we do it because that's what we're paid for and that's what we wanna do – that's why I do it and because I get a kick out of it. It's the challenge. I don't like to be beaten. Second best just ain't good enough.

On the Falklands we had a bloody good Company

Commander, Captain Babbington. Mount Harriet was our target so we bumped it two days before with a recce/fighting patrol to find out what the Argies had put in. I was at the front with Lieutenant Mark Townsend RM leading. Terry Bellingham's section was rear, and Kev Dale was in the middle. Somehow we got within twenty-five metres of the Argentinian forward defences. Their sentries were just standing around, smoking. We were trying to go round them but just as our front lot got close, they saw us and opened up so we all went to ground and returned fire. Then the rest of the hill just opened up. The boss put himself in a little hole and asked for fire support from Captain Romburgh. I decided to take this young guy, Graham Flick, with me and go round the back to see if we could hit any of the nearest sentries. He had a 66, but what I didn't realize was as soon as the shit had come down, he'd cocked it, ready to go. We crawled round these rocks and as we were laying there he whispered, 'Steve, there's one, he's seen me.' So I said, 'Well, hit him then.' I thought he was just going to shoot him with his rifle but there was a tremendous whoosh sound and the next thing I saw was this spic disintegrate as a 66 hit him in the chest! There was nothing left of him from his kneecaps upwards. Because he was standing in front of a rock the ricocheting fragments killed at least two of his mates and bloody nearly killed us too. The 66 was then renamed the 66 Anti-Personnel Rocket.

The rest of the spic's section must've decided to bug out but they made one small error, because they ran straight into us. It was just like a duck shoot. When they broke cover there was nowhere for them to go but towards us. I waited until they were really close and gave each one a burst of five rounds. As the last one started to leg it, I kept firing in front of him, until he ran into the rounds.

I can't say if I was frightened or not because in a situation like that you don't feel – you just react. I mean, it's like a trigger. As soon as somebody presses your button, you react, you just switch into automatic and away you go. You don't think about it until it's all over. It was the first time I'd ever shot anyone at that range, that close, knowing I'd killed him. The young lad didn't say a lot, especially after I'd given him a roasting for firing a 66 that close to me. But now we had to get out fast because the spics had seen us shooting their mates and were now sending down grenades and mortar fire, so it was getting a bit hot. I called out to the boss for an artillery barrage which they got spot on.

We sprinted out shouting, 'We're coming,' and jumped into a hole where the boss was waiting. Our lot started firing back but I was practically out of bullets so I crawled behind this rock and with all this shit coming in I just lit up a fag and had a smoke – it was a real Condor moment! I was really enjoying it when someone screamed at me, 'You bastard!' It was my Second-in-Command, Chris Shepherd. 'You bastard. I thought you'd bought it. Why the fuck didn't you answer your radio?' He'd been trying to call me, but I'd switched off so that I could get on with what I had to do. But he was really angry. He really thought I'd been killed. We laugh about it now but he was really angry then. We were great mates, Chris and I.

Chris and I had this big thing in our section. My big thing was my watch. I kept saying, 'If I get wasted, you make sure my watch goes home.' If he'd been killed, I would have taken his watch home – that's how it works. It may seem small but it means a lot to us.

Then the boss told us to bug out across no-man's land. So doing a Sebastian Coe, we got to where we wanted to be, watched them put their defensive fire in the wrong place and then just bugged out back to base where we were debriefed by the CO. That was it, that was our first time in battle and we'd suffered no casualties.

Two days later we got our orders to go back and do it again! We all thought, 'For fuck's sake,' because we knew what was coming, we knew what they had. They told us the plan and we began to move to Harriet. We had a fair bit of a march which included crossing two minefields that had been recce'd by Sergeant Jumper Collins. Then we had to go across a track, and as we were moving down, the spics put two flares up and we thought we'd been seen. We all hit the deck but couldn't get off the track because we'd go straight into the minefield. So we're thinking, 'Oh God, where do I go? What do I do?' There was just nowhere to hide. We waited for the shit to come towards us. But, thank God, nothing happened so we got up and moved again, went through the minefields and snaked our way round until we got to the start line.

We laid up, adrenalin pumping, waiting for the go – this was it. The build-up is what starts the adrenalin pumping and once you start, it keeps pumping all the way through. Then at the finish, you've got nothing left – you're drained. But at that moment, I was full of adrenalin.

We could hear and see HMS *Glamorgan* giving the spics hell with her guns. Then just as she finished she was hit by an Exocet. We tried – we tried to shoot it down, but you can't hit an Exocet, not at the range we were at. It came straight towards us, this big, bright light, and as it got near, it just turned and started screaming out to sea. We all started shooting at it but we couldn't hit it, we didn't have anything to hit it with. We all felt so helpless. They told us over the net that the *Glamorgan* had caught it. But by then we were up to our necks in bullets again.

We wanted to get on but there was some talk about L Company who were adrift. Something had gone wrong because they hadn't made it to the start line. We just waited for what Colonel Vaux was going to say – whether we went by ourselves or waited for L Company. The word came to go, so we lined right out into attack formation and started going up. It was dark and quiet and I was thinking, 'I'll wake up in a minute.' Yet nothing happened. We must've got within 100 metres of them before they opened up. Then everybody's button got pressed and we all went into automatic and went in.

We had a split plan: we had a troop going to the righthand end of Harriet to sort out a bunch of spics who were there and another troop was going to leapfrog round them and clear round the back, then work along. We had to sweep along the front and then rendezvous at the top in a clear space. We'd rehearsed it the day before so everybody knew what they were doing. Terry Bellingham got in amongst the rocks first and you could hear him shouting at the top of his voice things like, 'Gun group left, stop firing. Rifle group right hand.' A guy we know as Little Thomo called out 'Fix bayonets', so they were right in among them. It all seemed to be going all right. There was stacks of lights going up and noise from the mortars and Milans that were shooting over our heads. It was really all going on.

There was about a fifty-metre space between Terry and us so we were still out and Terry and his lot were just in. We were also being stomped by the Argies' mortars but they weren't really keeping us at bay because we were in amongst the rocks and had plenty of cover. At the same time as Terry, Corporal Sharkie Ward and Corporal Mick Eccles were doing their thing round the back. I could hear the boss on the net saying, 'Go left, go right.' I heard somebody say, 'We've lost a Section Commander. We've lost a bloke – he's dead.' You just think, 'One's dead.' But we wanted to know who. We were under cover now, just waiting to see what was happening and who'd been killed.

L Company had now arrived at the start line and were shooting at targets higher up on Harriet. We couldn't see these targets because we were right underneath them and L Company couldn't see us so their rounds were missing us by about a foot, so we were getting shot at from both sides. We were screaming out over the net, 'For fuck's sake, stop firing at us.'

There we were in a gun battle with bullets coming in both ways when, all of a sudden, young George Pearson, our 84 gunner, just stood up, loaded his gun and fired it; he just stood there like John Wayne with all this shit coming at him. I couldn't believe it. I shouted at him, 'Get down, you daft bastard.' He screamed back, 'Fuck off, I can't see,' and continued firing until he'd run out of shells!

The message got through to L Company and they stopped shooting at us and came up on our left at about the half-way point. I can remember I got my section really well left and forward because that was where the best cover was. The troop officer was screaming, 'Stevie! Bring your men over here. . .' He was in clear ground so I shouted back, 'Leave it out, it's okay here.' I mean, in a situtation like that, there's no rank or anything as such! The other discipline that went for a ball of chalk was the radio procedure. We were just shouting down the net, 'Steve, Sharkie, Shiner. What's going on?' The adrenalin makes you do that.

In the middle of all this shit flying around, Tony Koleszar, my LMG (light machine gun) gunner, decided he needed a new pair of boots. As he was moving forward, he spotted this trench with this dead spic in it and because they looked the right size, Tony got in and started taking this bloke's boots off. All of a sudden, the geezer sat up! Tony had instant heart failure. Somebody put the spic away; I don't know whether Tony did, but he scrubbed round the boots – he didn't fancy them after that!

All the time we were lying there, rounds were ricocheting off the rocks at us and the cold was freezing our bollocks off. On the radio I heard Sharkie talking to his boss. He said, 'We're pinned down by a sniper and we can't move.' Which meant if he couldn't clear the back, then when we came over the top we'd be in all sorts of trouble. As I was listening to this, I was working it all out and realized we were underneath where this sniper was supposed to be. I thought, 'Right, someone's got to go for this bastard.' So I took off my 66 LAW, got on the radio to our boss and said, 'Wait there and I'll see what I can do.' Chris Shepherd said he'd back me up. He probably didn't want to lose me again! Just as we were moving off, someone shouted, 'Incoming!' so everybody hit the deck. I continued going up because I had huge boulders either side of me, but I didn't realize that Chris didn't have such good cover and had hit the deck with everybody else. I climbed up on my stomach, crawled over the top of this little crest and I went left with the purpose of linking up with L Company. I wanted to tell them I was going further up, because if anything happened up there, L Company would have shot me to shit. I ran over to Dougie Rowe and told him where I was going but he was up to his neck in what was happening, so I don't think he paid much attention to me.

I then crawled round this mega-sized boulder, climbed up a

little steep bit, went over the top on my stomach, rolled into cover, crawled a bit further and looked round the corner of this rock, thinking that the sniper had to be there somewhere. There was more than a sniper – there was half a troop! About ten of them were lying on a nice, flat, table-top rock overlooking Sharkie and Mick's positions. It was perfect for them. They had a machine gun on the left and the rest of them were lined out with rifles. Every time one of ours tried to move forward, one of them would shoot at him, so to us it looked as if there was only one sniper who was keeping on the move. They were waiting for us to break cover and try and clear this one sniper – then they would just waste us with their machine gun.

I sat back behind this rock and whispered down my throat mike to Sharkie about what I'd found. I told him to keep the lads there and I'd see what we could do. I looked round for Shep, who I expected to be right behind me, and he wasn't there. I thought, 'Shit, I'm on my own!' So I sat and had a quick think. Then having made up my mind I picked up my SLR, changed the magazine and put a fresh one on and slipped the safety catch. I then looped the pin of one grenade onto one finger of my left hand and did the same with another. I was ready. So I thought, 'Well, you've got to do something.' I pulled one grenade, *whack* – straight onto the machine gun. Pulled the other, *whack* – straight at the spics. I dodged back round the rock and heard the two bangs. As soon as they'd gone off I went in and anything that moved got three rounds. I don't know how many I shot, but they got a whole mag. I went back round the corner of the rock, changed the mag and I was about to go back and sort out anyone who was left, when Sharkie called on the net, 'Get out. We're putting two 66s in.' I screamed back, 'Wait out.' I was still in the general area and if he'd put 66s in, I'd have had it. So I ran back down the hill and dived into this little hollow I'd seen on the way up. Over the net I told him to 'Let it go!' The 66s exploded and the next thing I heard was Sharkie on the radio again. He said, 'It's clear. They've given up. Go back to where you were and make sure they don't get out the back.' I went up by a different route and as I rounded this rock, I saw one of the guys that I'd hit. I'd only got him in the shoulder but he'd gone down like the rest of them and in the dark I'd automatically thought he was dead. But he was far from that, because as I came back round the corner, he just squeezed off a burst from his automatic. He must've realized he was going to die unless he got me first. I felt the bullets go into both my legs. I thought, 'Shit, I'm hit.' I was so angry I fired fifteen rounds into his head.

The adrenalin took me back to my little rock where I'd been resting before, got on the radio and told Sharkie that I was hit. I took the field dressing out and looked at both of my legs to see which one was worse. I couldn't tell. Then I lost my temper and I just ditched the field dressing. I was so angry because I'd ballsed it up and let this bloke get to me. That really pissed me off.

I lay there waiting for Sharkie, all the time thinking I would bleed to death if someone didn't get to me soon; I tried to reassure myself that he was coming. Then it dawned on me that he didn't even know where I was! I would be somewhere up there to him. I decided that I would get back down to L Company, who at least knew I'd gone up ahead. But I realized if I went down carrying a weapon, they'd shoot me. So I put my rifle down and stood up. By this time my legs had stiffened up so I went staggering down this hill, walking like Frankenstein, with my arms out like Jesus so they wouldn't shoot me. I had about sixty metres to go downhill in the dark and I got within about twenty feet of L Company when somebody shouted 'Halt', so I stopped. He said, 'Who are you?' I said, 'Steve Newland, K Company. Can someone come and get me? I'm damaged.' 'Where are you hit?' I said, 'My legs.' They said, 'What?' I said, 'I'm fucking hit in both legs!' Two blokes ran out, grabbed hold of me and went, 'Fucking hell! You are!' They picked me up and ran me back down to where L Company were and threw me behind this rock. Just as they did this, an incoming stomp came down. Even with the shit coming down, Dougie Rowe ripped first field dressings off everybody who was near him and patched up my legs.

They sent for the doc and while I was waiting, I had a fag. As I sat there, all these blokes from L Company were looking at me. I could see their eyes lighting up, thinking he won't need his ammunition, his food, his. . . . So I handed them everything, the evil sods, but I would have done the same, 'cos to them I was finished. Then I got on the radio and told Captain Babbington that I'd been hit and would he send the rest of my section to me. Chris came up with them so I gave him the radio, reassured him I was all right and told him to take the section up to where I'd just been. A bit later I could hear shooting up there. Because the spics had had the audacity to shoot me I think the boys went for a bit of revenge and got a few of them.

K and L Company had to move out then and go on to secure Goat Ridge. They left me with a weapon and ammo and Corporal P. V. Linch who had been fragged. He was in a lot of pain and had had quite a lot of morphine – so he was at 25,000 feet. We looked after each other as best we could, and waited.

I sat there for six hours and froze. The medical team came up: one was Stevie Haywood who was a mate of mine. They had eight Argentinian POWs as a work party. They took P.V. down first. Steve checked my dressings and because I wanted my legs to be kept straight they finished up carrying me in a poncho. We were going through this clearing when someone shouted 'Incoming' and I thought, 'Fucking hell.' These spics who'd got hold of me were not stupid, they just dropped me and took cover. And I'm laying in the open with all this stuff coming in, screaming, 'Steve – for fuck's sake!' But there was nothing they could do – I couldn't even move. Luckily it all missed me.

Later I was left at the roadside because the medics had to rejoin the main column. Steve told me there would be someone coming along soon. As I was sitting in this half-light I suddenly saw a figure on top of Harriet stand up and slowly walk down. As he got nearer, I could see he was a spic who'd been laying there all the time. Nobody had seen him because he'd been dug in properly. Now he was walking down, weapon and everything, towards me! I'm laid there with these useless legs and he's walking down getting bigger and bigger every step. Then, to my relief, he suddenly threw down his weapon and surrendered.

I was soaking wet from the rain when the chopper arrived. They hauled me in next to a bloke under a blanket who didn't move a lot, which I thought a bit funny. 'Oh, he's dead,' they said. So I said, 'Well, who is it?' They told me to have a look and it was one of the blokes who'd been killed on Harriet, who I knew quite well. So me and him had ended up in the same chopper but he was more finished than I was.

That made me even more determined to get back into action. I wasn't bothered about my legs, I just wanted to get back. I thought, 'I'll get to the sick bay, they'll stitch me up, throw a bandage on and I'll be back in the field.' I was worried about the blokes in my section. I didn't care about anything else – I didn't care if it meant my legs were coming off after, I wanted to get back into action. But they flew me to the *Uganda* and told me it was a Red Cross ship so I wasn't allowed to go back and fight. I thought, 'Stuff that, the spics haven't surrendered yet.' We had little plans about how to get off. Incoming choppers were the word, you know, and as soon as they touched down, we'd run out and pretend to be a stretcher party and jump on a chopper when it lifted off – but they caught us. We really tried to make the chopper because our mates were out there dying. But we couldn't even run – just as we got near the chopper they spotted us and dragged us away.

The worst thing they could've done to me on the *Uganda* was put me into a nice clean bed, without giving me a shower. It was just alien to me. I mean, a month in the field, no washing or shaving – the only thing that was clean was my weapons. I said, 'Well, what about a shower like?' But they said, 'Oh no, we haven't got time.' The nurses were busy because all the battles had been going on, so they were getting an influx of casualties all in one go. They were running around like blue-arsed flies and I could see they didn't have time to give me a shower. But later, Frank O'Neill, who was one of our sergeants, filled up a bath, put a wooden chair in for me to sit on, and with my legs resting on the side of the bath he gave me a going over with a scrubbing brush because I was honking! That was good of him because if we'd been caught, we'd have been in the shit.

I had this little Gurkha next to me who didn't speak much English. The bloke on the other side of me was telling me how he was fragged. Round his neck he was wearing the piece of metal that had fragged him. This Gurkha obviously knew what we were talking about so he bent under his bed and pulled out this enormous piece of shrapnel, the size of a house brick, which had smashed into his ribs. So I said, 'How many did you get, John?' He showed me five fingers. So I said, 'You got five before they fragged you?' He shook his head and smiled. Then I realized he'd shot the five blokes after he'd been fragged. No wonder the Argies thought they were monsters.

The other brave bloke on our ward was Kevin Smith who was a matelot chef. He'd been in the galley when an Exocet hit it, so he was in a bad way. He had both legs in plaster, one arm missing and something wrong with his other arm because it didn't work properly. The Exocet had gone off in the bulkhead next to him and it had killed everybody in the galley except him. The missile had come past him and the fin of it had taken his arm straight off. But his brain didn't realize it. As he'd been fragged in both legs he collapsed, and as he went to put his arm down, it wasn't there and he fell and hit the deck. The whole galley was on fire and there was fat and shit going everywhere and everything's burning, including the bodies that had just been hit. To get to the door he had to drag himself with one arm because nothing else worked. He had to crawl over the bodies of his mates who were on fire on the floor and as he crawled over them, he got burnt himself. He got to the door and banged on it because matelots close everything down. Luckily there was someone running past who heard him banging and opened the door and dragged him out. He had a massive skin graft that they took off his back and put on his front. Every four hours the nurses had to lift him off his bed to change the dressing on his back to stop infection. We all used to lay there and dread this four-hour thing – you never heard a man scream like that in your life. I mean, every time they moved him, he screamed. He was a small, brave little shit – brave as hell. A real hero.

From the *Uganda* via HMS *Herald* I got put off at Montevideo and was then put on a plane and flown back to Brize Norton. I went on board *Uganda* with absolutely nothing except a blanket wrapped round me, so before we landed, the Navy wanted to dress me up in one of their survival kits. They have this dicky little box, a nice little box with a pair of plimsolls, some socks, blue trousers and a little blue shirt so you've actually got a uniform to wear. Now I'm a bootneck, I ain't a matelot. So I told them that I wasn't wearing no Naval stuff to get off the plane. I said, 'You either get me a green uniform or I'm going off in a blanket.' They said, 'You can't do that.' But I said, 'Get me a real uniform,' which they did in the end. For me, it was just personal pride – I'd gone out a Marine and I'd come back a Marine, and I walked down the stairs of the aircraft. I refused to be carried – no one was going to lift me off the plane.

11/12 June

Assault on Two Sisters

Sergeant George Matthews

Royal Marines

Our company was on adventure training when it all started, so had people scattered all over Scotland in various places. I had my troop down on the Roman Wall. I thought I'd take the lads there just for a change. It was all pretty relaxed and we would stop and have a couple of pints, so we were in a good mood on our way back, on the Thursday night, ready to go on leave on Friday. But, lo and behold, when we turned up the next day, everybody in civvies, ready to go on leave, we were told, 'Wait. Hold on. Pack yer kit boys, it's happened.'

We listened to it on the radio and to the eternal credit of the guys and the system, within two or three days we were fully air portable, ready to go. But we had to wait for the word, so we sat waiting for a few days before we actually left. We were all dressed up and nowhere to go.

Saying goodbye to my wife and two-year-old was difficult. We'd done it before – we'd gone to minor countries and nothing had happened. Usually when you go away you kiss your wife on the doorstep and say, 'I'll see you in a month, or whatever.' But this time it was different. We couldn't say when, or if, we were ever coming back. That was difficult, very difficult.

Captain Gardiner commanded X-Ray Company. What a man! We'd follow him to the ends of the earth. He was without doubt a superb, natural leader and tactician. Totally unflappable under fire, totally unflappable. He exudes confidence all the time, no matter what he's thinking, because naturally he must have doubts as well.

He has this remarkable way of putting things across to the guys. Being an ex-parade adjutant from Lympstone, his patter is fantastic, and he's so cool. He's destined for great things, hopefully, because he's got this tremendous way of communicating. He's a bit of an eccentric – he wears old baggy cords and things, deerstalker hats, and rides this battered old motorbike. On the Friday morning we all turned up and wondered what the hell was happening because there was nothing actually confirmed, only rumours flying left, right and centre. We were all standing around when up he drives on this motorbike in full fighting order, large pack and everything, steel helmet on, grin on his face. There he was, astride his bike, complete with his wellies on: 'I'm ready to go.' So we got off to a good start having him for Company Commander.

We left from Scotland and were very lucky because while everyone was suffering in the bloody Bay of Biscay, we flew from RAF Leuchars to Ascension Island by VC10. Not the whole of 45, just my company, X-Ray, and Yankee, and the Colonel with his Tactical Headquarters. When we got there we were really lucky, because we had time to build ranges and everything, and train. We used that time; we had something like ten days on the island, while the rest were bobbing around on boats. That was useful preparation. I'd been very lucky inasmuch as ever since the Northern Ireland tour a year before, my troop had changed very little. If there's one thing to be said for a Northern Ireland tour, it brings that closeness within a troop. I knew all my lads' weaknesses, all their pros and cons; they knew me, and we got on really well.

We left Ascension Island on board *Stromness*. She was a great ship, we got on really well with the skipper and crew. Once we left Ascension I think the realization began to dawn that something was going to happen, that this wasn't just another flash in the pan. When we actually did go in, it was a cock-up. We were supposed to land at first light and be met. Lo and behold, it was broad daylight when we actually set off and two landing craft collided so it wasn't a classic amphibious assault. We scrambled down the nets, loaded with ammunition and kit, off the *Stromness* into landing craft. HMS *Ardent* was shelling fire ahead as we were entering San Carlos. I think it was then that we really took it in, 'Oops, this is for real,' and we were wondering whether it would be an opposed landing. We were supposed to be met by SBS at night on the beach where they would flash us with torches. But that didn't happen because it was broad daylight!

We were all jammed in the landing craft with all our kit on. We had two companies, the mortar troop and the Colonel with his HQ all in one crate and we couldn't move. But somehow Captain Gardiner managed to find this mouth organ. It was ironic, really; there we were, all crunched together, waiting for an aircraft to come and blow us out of the water, and he's playing Scottish tunes and old reels. All the lads started singing and whistling, clapping their hands, and we actually went onto the beach laughing! He didn't take his mouth organ out again until we were in the Globe Hotel in Stanley. He was the man for the moment and at that moment we needed him.

We landed in Ajax Bay where our job was to clear the refrigeration settlement. It was broad daylight when we got there, so we went straight up into the hills surrounding San Carlos and dug in; the holes promptly proceeded to fill up with water. We were just in the process of setting up the machine guns when the first aircraft came over. We loosed off a few rounds but I don't think we hit it. On the day we landed at Ajax Bay there were two smokers in 2 Troop; when we reached Stanley there were fifteen. This may seem definite proof that smoking calms and relaxes you, but I'm more inclined to believe it was because they were free and *no* Marine is going to turn down something for nothing!

We settled down to six days of 'Air Raid Warning Red' and getting back into the trenches. The CO tried to brief us every day. We were told that talks were still going on but were faltering badly, so we just accepted the fact that we were going to have to fight for it. We started patrolling from San Carlos out towards Falkland Sound because we thought there might be enemy moving up the coast. We went on one epic patrol which lasted about fourteen hours over tussock grass and stubble and rocks. It was worse than the actual fight for Two Sisters. It was bloody dreadful. We covered minimal distances and it took a long time before we arrived. There was no one there.

As we were coming back off this mammoth patrol we really were knackered. Ahead of us we could see all the lads from the company sitting down and as we got nearer we could hear all these lads singing hymns. It was a marvellous sight and the singing really raised our spirits. It was really touching. George McMillan had gone to get the Padre, Wynne-Jones, and he was leading the lads in the hymn singing. But that was the sort of thing Wynne excelled at. He's a tremendous guy with a brilliant turn of phrase, broad Welsh. He was right up in the thick of the fighting later on Two Sisters, looking after casualties, but of course he'd refused to carry a rifle. In training he won the Commando Medal, which is for the guy with the most determination in the group – the one who gees everyone up when morale is low. Because he wouldn't carry a rifle someone had carved him a long stick, the top of which resembled a bishop's crook. The first time I saw him was in Norway. All the lads were bivouacking up in pairs but I'd got my own little tent. The Padre came wandering across with the Company Commander who suggested the Padre bed down with me. So I said, 'Yeah, come in here with me, Sir.' So we sat there and chatted away – but we'd just had a meal and all I wanted to do was blow wind and burp. So I said, 'Might as well get our heads down then, Sir,' and, lo and behold, the Padre's lying there and rolls over and farts. 'Bloody hell, George,' he said, 'I needed that.' I thought, 'Thank Christ for that!'

We were eventually told that the big push was on. The CO came up with the classic statement, 'We're going to break out of the bridgehead and the bad news is 45 Commando have got to walk!' So we started by going across San Carlos Water in broad daylight in the landing craft, and that was enough to give you grey hairs.

362

Tragically, we learnt later on that day that the Argies had bombed the refrigeration plant and killed six of our lads whom we all knew. It was a bit of a blow, but then again it gave us the resolve and determination to really get on and sort it out. Being the unit's first casualties it put everything on a very personal level. In fact, it was ironic that the majority of people that 45 lost were drivers and chefs.

Then we had the epic march carrying all that kit; it was unbelievable. The weight the guys were carrying was phenomenal. 3 Para were moving in a parallel line with us, but all they had was fighting order. At that stage we didn't know exactly what the situation was going to be. Inbred in us from Norway is the idea that if you get stuck out in the open without sufficient kit, you're in big trouble; so we opted initially to carry all our kit with us. That first day was hell. In my position as Troop Sergeant you've got to be seen and you've also got to be seen to be geeing up the lads as well. I found that every time we stopped for a break the guys were flopping and you really had to get them going even when you were shattered yourself. You had to go around and make sure it was done. In the Marines the relationship between the Troop Commander and the Troop Sergeant is usually that of a team. Ultimately, the decision belongs to 'Sir', but as always, two heads are better than one. The Troop Commander was Lieutenant Chris Caroe who although he had only been with the troop a short time did a good job and was rewarded with a Mention in Despatches.

We eventually stopped just before last light and the CO said, 'Right. Make a wet and get a meal to keep us going.' Then we suddenly got an air raid warning. All the cookers had to be doused and packed up, so nobody had any food and we were bloody hungry. We had to set off again and eventually got to a place between San Carlos and Douglas, which was our objective. We stopped there and all we did was collapse in a big Commando circle, shoulder to shoulder, with sentries up. We just flopped down and the guys slept, and it rained and it rained and it rained! The guys were saturated from head to foot and the next morning the decision came, 'Strip your kit to the bare essentials. All you want is your ammunition and your sleeping bag.'

We always seemed to be on the move. It's an impressive sight to see these companies of men. There they were, hundreds of them, with a recce troop in front, spotting, and the rest of them all spread out across the old plains in Commando formation – two companies up front, one back with HQ, all moving out across miles of terrain. It's very uplifting to be part of that.

So we advanced to Douglas where the Argentinians had just moved out. We proceeded to dig in there. While we were there we came to terms with the reason why we were fighting. A lot of people had said, 'Oh, the Falklands, they're bloody 8,000 miles away. Why should we worry about them? They all speak with Australian accents,' and all this. But arriving in Douglas where the locals had been locked up in sheds and actually seeing their faces when we moved in was very, very touching. Their gratitude and, you know, 'Thank Christ you're here, boys.' That was very moving and I defy anyone to say, if they had a choice, that they wouldn't have gone down there and done it. It's a British colony – we have responsibilities there; as much as we've shirked them over the years, and as political as it was, I still think we did the right thing. I continue to believe that, whatever anyone says.

We tried not to impose on the locals at all, as they'd been treated quite badly. The Argentinians had left the place in an atrocious state. We fanned out and proceeded to dig into this rock-solid ground. But you get an amazing surge of strength if you think there's going to be an aircraft coming over any moment; the guys' arms were going like windmills and we were in – like that.

The next couple of nights we were bloody cold. We had realized how cold it was going to be and as there were big sheep sheds we left fifty per cent in the trenches and fifty per cent in the sheds. We stayed there for about three days and, surprisingly, there was not much moaning. Once again, the old wit and humour. It was so cold, there was always a brass monkey to keep the sentry company!

On the march from San Carlos one of the most pitiful sights was guys actually injured by twisting ankles, etc.; we just had to leave them. If they had a machine gun or something we'd take it off them and say to them, 'Right, you're just going to have to sit here and hope that there's some back-up coming to pick you up.' We left two from our troop and we didn't see them again till we got to Teal Inlet; thankfully, they were fit again and rejoined the troop. But it was a pitiful sight when you're marching along and trudging through bogs and whatnot to see this forlorn creature sitting on the side of the route, with his head in his hands because of a twisted ankle or something. There were guys with twisted backs and cracked collar bones, all through the weight they were carrying. The phenomenal weight – ammunition more than anything else. I wouldn't like to have been sitting there myself, that's for sure, having to drop out through trench foot or frostbite. I'd rather go on and lose my foot at the end. Some guys who had injuries kept going – they suffered, but they kept going. That takes guts. It's hard to tell what motivates a Marine but prior to the Two Sisters and Harriet someone let slip that the Argentinian ration packs each had a small bottle of whisky in them; this may explain the speed of the assaults on those features and also the strange clinking of glass in the fighting orders of the Marines on the march into Stanley.

One guy, John Gillon, really thin but a tough little lad, twisted his ankle on the tussock grass on the way to Douglas. I heard the old click and I said, 'Oh no!' But he jumped up and he said, 'I'm all right, I'm all right.' So I asked if he was sure and he said he was. He shuffled off and I could see he was in pain, so we took as much weight off him as we could. He went all the way, all the way right through the battle and then he got run over by a Land-Rover in Stanley! He was standing there directing prisoners and this crackpot in a Land-Rover zoomed up to one of the parking slots, reversed and sent him flying! He was put into Stanley hospital. I went down to see him and he was lying there, a real sick look on his face, really pissed off. I'm sure it was the gods taking revenge on him because when we were going up Two Sisters I actually got wedged by my kit between some rocks. I was trying to see through these two little bits of rock and I got stuck. We were being mortared at the time and I couldn't get out. My frigging legs were kicking like mad. He was just behind me and I said, 'Get me out! Get me out!' And he was lying there, looking at me, as if to say, 'No fucking way!' Great lad that. We still laugh about it.

From Douglas it was Teal Inlet and once again it was a slog. It was beginning to get tiring by this stage; blokes' feet were a great problem. I think our mountain and arctic training and the mountain boots did help because they gave us support on the rough terrain. Every time we stopped for a day the guys would have their boots straight off and they'd look after their feet or look after each other's feet – powdering them and drying them, putting dry socks on if they had them, or trying to dry out the ones they'd been wearing. If the guys had sleeping bags then they would strip right off and pack the wet kit around them, under their armpits or on their belly or in the groin, so they'd dry out. I didn't have one guy with trench foot in my troop.

We moved to just behind Mount Kent where the conditions were atrocious. We had to cross the big rock runs to get up there, for a start, which was epic. When we actually got there we relieved a company of 42 Commando who'd been flown in by helicopter, and they were in a bit of a state. The Argentinians had left the place in a real mess; they'd shit in the only water supply there. We had to dig positions and build them from rocks. The weather was so horrendous that the wind literally lifted guys up and blew them over. There was nothing we could do except try to hang on to rocks and things. We lost a lot of kit because it was flying everywhere; we were doing our best to fight a war and the elements were hammering us as well. But when everyone got into one shelter, they started singing and laughing because with the howling, there was no way the sound was going to carry anywhere. Next morning, the weather abated and they were raring to go again!

We stayed up there for six days. During that time 3 Troop went forward and had quite an exciting fighting patrol on Two Sisters. Chris Fox also led a recce troop up there and had a bit of a scrap as well. Conditions were bad and they sneaked right in amongst the Argies, but they didn't know how many were there. When dawn broke they found themselves in the middle of a company position of Argentinians and all they could do was make a run for it. So they gave it all they had, quite bloodily, yet Chris Fox was the only casualty – he just nicked the end of his finger. They were really, really lucky because they virtually ran through the position, firing as they went. 3 Troop, led by Dave Stewart who got an MC, also got a few of the enemy and came away without any casualties. So we were making an impact on them.

We had just begun to organize ourselves and get our food together when we were called for a briefing. In characteristic fashion, Captain Gardiner gave us the orders that he'd written on the back of a cigarette packet. We then had to go away and brief the lads. Our orders were to move on our own route, led by 1 Troop, to the righthand peak of the Two Sisters. The other two companies were to move in a different direction to get round to the lefthand peak. We got to the start line and all lined up. It's strange, you feel there's so much you want to say to the guys because you know that this time it was going to be it. Instead of the Argies retreating in front of us, they'd held, and we knew we were going to have to fight them. I'd been with the troop for a long time, I knew them all, and I just wanted to say, 'Well, you know, don't take any unnecessary risks. Take care and bloody good luck,' but I didn't have time. I'd like to think they carried those wishes from me. I went round checking them all beforehand and had a little word with each guy as we were lined up ready to go.

I was apprehensive but that was tinged with a bit of

'Let's get in there, lads, and sort it all out.' I don't know if that's the bloody-minded attitude of the Marines or what. We all knew we were going to go through this hell, and the training that had been drummed into us was eventually going to bear fruit, or otherwise, depending on how it went. I never felt actual fear. I was apprehensive and at certain stages I was worried about the way things were going, but not from a personal point, more from an overall point of view. We were on the foot of Mount Kent, waiting to move up, when I was called with George McMillan and Pete Jolly to see Captain Gardiner. He just got us three Troop Sergeants together and said, 'I've only got one thing to say – whatever happens, mark your dead.' Wherever one of the guys fell he wanted it marked – that was the policy of the brigade. If possible we were to stick their rifle in the ground with a helmet on top, or just stick the rifle in the ground, just so that people following up would realize that he was one of ours, because with some of the modern weapons systems, bodies can be made unrecognizable. All he said was, 'Mark your dead,' and I thought it was a strange remark to say at this stage of the game.

Our objective was the righthand peak of Two Sisters, which has three prominent clumps of rock going up the spur. At this stage we were all carrying a 30 lb Milan missile each, because we had a Milan troop with us. We began scrambling across these rocklands and we were having real problems. We were to attack the top, and the powers that be thought we'd have more rest when we actually got there because we'd be waiting for the other two companies to take their objectives, so we could carry the missiles! As it turned out, we were the only ones who had to fight when we got to the top!

By this stage 42 Commando were already attacking Harriet and the fire that was going down there was phenomenal. I daresay our feature must have looked the same but just at that moment, looking across at Harriet and then across at Longdon, where 3 Para were, you could see the scrapping going on. Then we saw Zulu and Yankee

Companies come under fire on the lefthand peak of Two Sisters; tracer flying everywhere, and I thought, 'Whoops, here we go.' One troop moved off across this big open expanse, trying not to run, trying to be quiet! They were crossing a patch lit by moonlight and you could see the lads sort of starting off nice and slow, then speeding up! They got across the first clump of rocks and to their eternal credit nobody panicked at all. They took the rocks but nobody was there. Across the net came the codeword for 'Objective Taken'.

3 Troop then moved off through 1 Troop and came to their objective in this clump of rocks and they took that without a shot. Just then this lad Gillon turned to me and said, 'Perhaps there's no one there.' And just as he said it, as if it was on cue, this big line of tracer came from the top of our feature – boom, boom, boom, boom, boom – and he just looked at me!

We moved up through 1 Troop, then through 3 Troop, and at this stage there was a lot of Argentinian bodies in the rocks. They had been there since the fighting patrol had hit them about three or four nights previously. It was still dark as we were moving up and they were just sat there, bits and pieces all over the place. I'd seen people killed by gunshot before in Ireland, but I'd never actually seen bits and pieces. It wasn't terrifying; at that stage it was a job to be done and we just wanted to get on with it.

We actually fixed bayonets just before we moved through and a funny glint comes into people's eyes when they've put a bayonet on! It's the old click, and then it's back to Rorke's Drift and parry and thrust. But what else is there to do if your weapon suddenly jams and there's a six-foot-six Argentinian standing in front of you? It's a blade and although the Geneva Convention states that you can't sharpen them, you can ram them in – that's what they're meant for.

As we moved through we weren't actually under fire. 1 Troop had secured their objective, 3 had secured their objective. When our attack went in, they'd all withdrawn to the top, so we moved through 1 and then through 3 and as we came up to the Commander of 3 Troop, Dave Stewart, the initial burst of fire came down. We still had about a kilometre to go up to the top of the feature. I think they sensed someone was there but they couldn't actually pinpoint us so their fire wasn't that accurate. But whoever sighted the positions for the Argies at Two Sisters was a pretty switched-on guy. It meant whichever way we went, we were channelled towards a heavy machine gun.

By this stage we were crossing a bit of open ground and had managed to make our way round the feature. We then crossed an open patch and came under mortar fire. How we got away with it, I do not know. The point section had moved forward – we were moving with one section up, and two back – and as we moved to this open patch, a mortar round came in and landed smack in the middle of three guys. The whole feature was rock but for some reason there was a patch of soft earth and the round hit smack into it. Lance-Corporal Montgomery went down like a bloody ton of bricks – we all went to the ground. Someone shouted, 'Monty's been zapped.' They thought the Section Commander was out of the game because the blast had bowled him right back down the hill. So I grabbed one of the other lads, a foolish move, and we crawled out to drag one guy down who'd been hit in the head. He was all right, just a bit stunned. Then we crawled over to where we expected to find bits of the Section Commander – I mean, we could hear him groaning. The fire was still coming in so we crawled a couple of yards and then – crash! It was about this time that I discovered adrenalin is, in fact, brown. We made ourselves small, crawled a few more yards, and eventually we found him just lying there. I expected him to be a mess, but I was feeling around him and couldn't even find any blood. So we opened his jacket and started to cut away at his shirt – one of these Norwegian shirts which we have to buy ourselves. I put my hand inside, looking for the entry hole – he's lying there groaning and hardly able to breathe – but nothing! I put my hand round the back for the exit hole – nothing. It was too dark to see clearly, but I could feel it was really puffy around his shoulder – and that's all it was! He'd actually been blasted by a sod of earth, the lucky bugger, but he moaned later about his shirt!

We moved off and it was then we came under really heavy fire. To their eternal damnation, the Argentinians opened up too soon. The point section were just cresting a ridge line when they opened up and the guys immediately went to ground. The first volley of heavy machine-gun fire went over their heads, over our heads and landed where Wynne the Padre was. He wasn't happy. He said in his wonderful Welsh voice, 'Here I am, a man of God, and these bastards are trying to kill me. They're bastards, George, they're trying to kill me.' The next day he was all smiles. He said, 'You saved my bloody life last night. Those bastards! How dare they? I'm a man of the cloth!'

Even though they opened up too early the weight of fire was so heavy that we were stuck; we couldn't get over this little hummock. It was coming from heavy machine guns on the top. One was engaging Yankee and Zulu Companies and the other one was engaging us and we were channelled. Everywhere we tried to go the rock channelled you towards these machine guns.

I don't know whether we Marines tend to err slightly on the side of caution rather than throw ourselves into a situation, but we looked for ways round this situation and were trying to figure out a way of getting up amongst these people. To go over the top of these boulders would have been suicidal. Then suddenly the Troop Commander, instead of taking a whole section with him, grabbed three guys and shouted, 'Right! Follow me!' He went shooting off up this gully but I knew every gully led to a machine gun. Off he went, 'Follow me, boys,' zooming up the hill. About ten seconds later he came zooming back down the gully, followed by a hail of tracer. He didn't do that again! Still, we did have a smile! Apart from the two heavy machine-gun positions, single guys would open up with a full magazine of FN, which meant twenty rounds coming in your direction. More than once I felt the old tickle and the old whip of the round passing.

Young Dave O'Connor, who's a rogue, and he'd be the first to admit it because he's always in the shit as a peacetime soldier, suddenly leapt forward with his machine gun, screaming, 'You Argie bastards.' He went over the rocks, totally exposed, yet followed by his number two who carried the ammunition. They dived down on the rock and commenced to open fire at this machine gun. For a couple of seconds it was just our machine gun going bmm-bmm-bmm, and theirs going bmm-bmm-bmm-bmm-bmm-bmm, and then he went into the open under heavy fire, continually engaging this machine gun. That drew their fire for a second and in that second another young lad, barely out of training, jumped up with a 66mm rocket launcher, fired it at their machine-gun position and hit just above. He stayed there in the open, shouting for another which was thrown to him, fired, and it smashed in close to the machine gun. For a split second the fire stopped and we just lifted, off we went. That was the gap we needed to get across the initial ridge and we covered those 150 yards at an incredible pace and managed to get in amongst the rocks. It was then that they started to retreat. They left bodies and they left bits and pieces. Those two brave acts opened the way.

Two of the bodies we found which had tried to crawl away were special forces. The conscripts had legged it; they didn't want to know, basically. They'd put down fire, move, then put down more fire, but all the time they were working back and trying to make their way across to the other peak. We reckoned there was at least a troop and a half on the top of Two Sisters; the weapons that were left behind would indicate that. Initially that position was a company position because there were loads of rifles, rocket launchers, the lot. But they left in a hurry, because all the weapons were still warm.

After we'd taken the machine gun out, there were a couple left further up on the way to the other peak. The guys took them out with grenades and rifles, and the way they did it was amazing. We practise clearing enemy positions just as we practise house clearing; it's a very similar drill, in fact. The grenade goes in first and then, after the explosion, in you go, firing a few rounds into the building. The point section did exactly the same to clear all the little rock positions. The lads up there were working in pairs. One would throw in a grenade, the other would charge in, fire a few rounds, shout 'Clear,' and then move on to the next one. It was so ingrained, and shows that the training does work – it was second nature.

While this was going on I was reorganizing the two rear sections, making sure that all the positions below were clear, because it was very difficult to see. We found afterwards small one-man positions – you could see where one guy had been lying with his stack of magazines firing at us. We made sure the whole of the feature was clear and there weren't any of them left. Before we actually made the initial breach up there, Captain Gardiner had stayed behind the point troop all the time, so when 1 Troop moved up, he was behind them. Then when 3 Troop moved off he went behind them, so he was going forward all the time. He got on the radio and said, 'Send a sitrep. We wanna know what's going on. We've got to take the top of this feature because Yankee and Zulu are getting a bit of hammer.' The Troop Commander said, 'Well, at present we assume there's a troop strength of enemy on the top and we're under quite heavy fire and we're having difficulty moving.' So Captain Gardiner came back, plain as day; he didn't use any call-signs, he just came across in clear speech: 'Well, get up there and kill them then' – that was another of his classic lines – which is what we did.

When we took the top of the feature we immediately came under mortar attack but we knew they weren't going to re-take the top. It was clear that we were all going to succeed, 42 on Harriet, 45 on Two Sisters and 3 Para on Longdon, so we withdrew from the top of the feature to where we couldn't be effectively mortared. It worked, in fact, because it meant that the only artillery or mortar fire we came under was unobserved: they couldn't direct fire onto us. Thankfully, X Company didn't lose anyone in that attack and only suffered one casualty. We were very lucky.

We were then asked immediately to stand by to support the Scots Guards on Tumbledown. But, instead, we sat tight on Two Sisters for three days under constant artillery fire to organize the burial parties and things for the bits and pieces that were left of the Argentinians.

We found an Argentinian officer who'd been killed while pointing. What he was pointing at I don't know. His face was a bit of a mess. He was half standing and had died in that position. Rigor mortis had set in and he was solid. He must have just got up to say, 'Look at that . . .' when, bang! He was hit. The lads had to break his arm to bury him. There was never any occasion of mistreating the remains of the Argentinian dead, but it was a case of trying to get these people buried because they were beginning to smell. We put them in amongst the rocks because we couldn't actually dig in there – it was purely temporary, until we got to Stanley. Then we could clean up and bury them with honours.

After the attack I sat on my own waiting for the sun to come up, and also waiting for the news coming back on Lance-Corporal Montgomery who'd been choppered out. I was having a bite to eat but could smell this cloying, deathly, sickly smell. As it got light, on the rock beside me I saw a big splat of remains and the buckle of an Argentinian marine's webbed belt and what looked like a wrist joint or something – just a little bit of bone with a few tatters of flesh hanging off it. I just sat there, sat there eating. It didn't seem to matter just then.

There was a lot of remains there from people who had been caught by heavy artillery or mortar fire and there were pieces all over the feature. But it could just as easily have been our guys. There was no feeling of hatred for the enemy, just relief that this particular battle was over. There was a light-hearted moment while we were burying some of them. Corporal Frank Melia heard a mortar coming in which must've had his name on it because as it came in, he dived, and the only place to go was in this hole on top of the bodies! The mortar went off really close and a bit of shrapnel carved a neat nick right out of the top of his head. But he survived, and was never nonchalant about mortar fire again.

Wynne-Jones went away on a burial party – a big one back down at Brigade HQ. On his way back, on his own up the Two Sisters, it was just getting dark. We were all sitting there in the gloom when this Welsh voice shouted, 'X Company! X Company! Don't shoot, it's me, Wynne, I've forgotten the bloody password!'

An interesting thing is that after we'd taken Two Sisters I noticed a big down amongst the guys, a big depression. We'd been so psyched up, really, we'd got such a boost from that attack on Two Sisters that the next couple of days were really a big anti-climax. It would have been quite difficult to motivate the guys to back up the Jocks on Tumbledown. I suppose we'd have done it, but there was a big trough – everybody just seemed to go into themselves after the high tension of the night before. It lasted that way for a couple of days.

After the surrender we eventually got on board ship. We were supposed to be on there for twenty-four hours but we eventually ended up being on there for three days, because it had to go round Bluff Cove and other places resupplying detachments. It was then that guys took their boots off and kept them off for the first time in a month and people's feet started to swell.

We went back on the land and commenced guarding. We were allocated a certain amount of housing up in the hill around Stanley which the Argies had left in a state. We cleaned them up as best we could. We managed to purloin a .5 machine gun complete with loads of ammunition which we could present to the skipper of the *Stromness* on the way back.

We were guarding the sheds, full of prisoners, and the poor buggers were really ill. The dog, you know, they had the dog – they'd go and shit in the pit or go and spew in the pit; they were in a right state. We were starting to get it, we were catching it from them. Then young John got run over by a bloody Land-Rover! We were actually going to steal him from the hospital because we knew we were going to be moving off soon and there was no way we were leaving the guy behind. No way. We had it all planned: we were going to sneak down there, burst in, grab him and run for it. But, thankfully, it never came off because he got his discharge!

We were told initially, 'Right, 45s, you're going back on the *Canberra*.' So we kicked up hell about it and the skipper of *Stromness* requested us back on board, but unfortunately he couldn't take us all the way back to the UK. He could only take us as far as Ascension Island.

On the *Stromness* we were messing around with this big .5 and the Captain didn't really know what it was for. Our armourer, Ben Chapnell, got it in working order and draped an X Company flag on it which we'd flown at Sapper Hill. We presented the Captain with this .5 and the guy was dumbstruck. Both companies were there as well and the CO. We also presented him with a green beret. It was really touching because we had such a rapport going. It was a shame he couldn't take us back to the UK.

We flew from Ascension but as we came in to land at RAF Leuchars, the pilot overshot, so we thought, 'Christ! That's close.' We could see the control tower level with us. He gave it the old big throttle back and he said, 'I'll just go round and try that again, gentlemen!' We were all sitting there thinking we've come all this way to die in a bloody plane crash! We landed at three in the morning and there was a pipe band to greet us and about 100 people from the RAF camp – but no wives. General Stuart Pringle, who'd once commanded 45, was standing there. He shook hands and spoke with every man, which meant a great deal to us.

All our wives were waiting at Condor Camp. As we drove into Arbroath all the banners were up. So that was it. We had to sit and watch the *Canberra* coming in on television. Zulu Company of 45 led them off and that was very touching. It seemed a shame then that we weren't on it as well.

It wasn't till I sat down with my wife that I realized what

a hard time she'd had with the waiting. With all the ships going down and the definite knowledge that we were going to have to fight, I thought it best, the night before we landed, to write to her. I wrote telling her exactly how I felt about her. I told her that if I should be killed, she's still young, someone else is bound to come along, and that I was sorry if I'd let her down in any way. It's strange how you always wish you had said certain things when it's too late.

She was very distressed when she received it. She'd just heard about the casualties from 45 at Ajax Bay, so morale was a bit low. Then, while she was standing in the kitchen, there was a knock at the front door. We've got one of those bubbly glass doors through which you can just make out a shape on the other side. All she could see was a uniform – she virtually went to pieces on the spot. She opened the door and it was the bloody postman! She really gave me a hard time over that letter, but at least she knew what I felt about her.

I was very proud of what we did down there and particularly proud of the young lads in my company.

Today's youths, the football hooligans, the punk rockers, the spiky-head mohicans and the kids who wear four earrings, people knock them, but from the same walk of life comes the modern Marine or Para. A lot of people say standards in the forces are dropping, and it's not the old school any more, that they don't join up because they want to be Marines or Paras, they join up because they can't get a job. But I feel the standard, the skill, the professionalism, the guts, and the all-round ability of these guys is better than the guys of a few years ago. There was no hesitation: they were taking orders under fire, doing things under fire which you could never have dreamed possible. You'd look at the lads – the average age couldn't have been more than nineteen or twenty – and they're all fresh-faced guys stood there, full of the joys of spring. You call in every morning and there they are. Then suddenly these same lads are in the midst of a firefight, a battle, and some of the things these guys were doing, almost totally unnoticed, were incredible. It's very moving when you see that – very moving.

Captain Ian Gardiner

Royal Marines

At midday on Friday, 2 April, 45 Commando was due to go on Easter leave. At five o'clock that morning I was informed by telephone that the unit had been recalled. If the Argentinians had really done their homework, they would have invaded the day before: nobody would have believed it. It was a pretty peculiar feeling being called to war by telephone from one's bed. The next half-hour was spent scratching around like a hen in a shed trying to find my sleeping bag, but I was in camp by 06.00, ready to go almost anywhere. It was with some awe that we all read the signal ordering us to prepare for amphibious operations in the South Atlantic.

We had to wait for a week. During that time we trained, zeroed our weapons, packed, unpacked and packed again. We listened to the news hourly and wondered if it was all real. Reality appeared in the shape of a corporal who had fought with 8901 (commanded by Mike Norman) and had been captured on the Falklands. His quiet description of the battle and his experiences were listened to with great interest. There was little doubt in my mind that we would have to fight. It was time to go in any case. Prayers were being said in church for my safety while I was still planting lettuces!

We flew from RAF Leuchars to Ascension Island on 13 April. After two weeks there, training in earnest, we embarked on RFA *Stromness* and sailed on 7 May. The ship's officers, led by Captain Dickinson, were helpful and co-operative to a man and we considered ourselves lucky with such a harmonious partnership. We came to think of *Stromness* as a great grey mother who provided us with all we needed. We grew to love her.

We were now fully committed to the idea of landing and fighting, and our training programme reflected this. Physical training was difficult due to lack of space, and little information was available. Our only source of news was the BBC and it became evident during the final rumblings of the UN negotiations that we would be sent in to land soon.

On the morning of 20 May, I was on the bridge when the CO was summoned to read a signal. He turned to me and said, 'We're off.' There was no more to be said. All plans had been made, all briefings finalized, all kit checked: we had been set up in every way to go and do a job. Now we had been given the job. The process was complete. Down in the mess deck that evening the atmosphere was not unlike a rugger changing room before the match, each man going about his business, preparing himself, dressing, packing, loading magazines; quiet determination was everywhere.

Early next morning the time came for us to muster at our assault stations. I think this moment was one of the worst of the whole campaign: we were about to make the transition from comfort to discomfort, relative safety to danger, from comparative certainty to the complete unknown. We climbed over the guardrail, down the scrambling net, and crammed into the landing craft. We were now passive, helpless creatures subject to whatever our luck might bring. I wanted to do something, to say something that might suggest that we had some control over what might happen to us. I have often suspected that one of the elements of successful leadership is the ability to amuse the men, to entertain them. One can do this in a number of different ways. One can do it by jumping them over cliffs; one could try shooting every second Marine and I daresay that would tend to keep their attention. I tried it by playing the mouth organ to them. People are drawn towards harmless eccentricity, although playing the mouth organ hardly qualifies one as a maverick. We are, in the main, a music-less lot and it is not every day that a Marine is serenaded by his Company Commander in a landing craft sailing to war. Scots regiments enjoy a huge advantage in this respect and, being a Scot, I keenly missed the sound of the pipes. Their sound can have a remarkable polarizing effect on morale in a battle: terror to one's enemies and courage to one's friends, even to unbelievers!

So the greater part of 45 Commando was in three small boats sailing up what closely resembled a Scottish sea loch, surrounded by unsecured land. It needed just one machine gun or one wide-awake pilot and things would not have gone well for us. But they never came. Once landed, we secured our objective unopposed and quickly deployed to the hills. We were over the most vulnerable part and now in our element. For the first, and not the last time, fortune had smiled on us.

It was a beautiful day. We tramped off, feeling a lot better. We consolidated our positions on the ridges above Ajax Bay and dug like little moles. That night, we froze. Next morning I heard a chilling description of HMS *Ardent* burning and sinking stern first. The shock of actually being at war was beginning to sink in. I was to see things in the next few days that I thought I would never live to see, and hope I never see again.

The serious bombing started that day, 22 May. Several times throughout the day Skyhawks appeared and tried to bomb the large number of ships in San Carlos Water. That evening two frigates limped in, one of which was the *Antelope* who came in under her own steam a little later. She was making smoke, rather dirty, wispy smoke, unusual for a Type 21 frigate, and had a hole either side of her hull forward of the funnel, but her 4.5 gun traversed, depressed and elevated so she certainly had the power to fight. We were completely unprepared, therefore, for the huge explosion that erupted from her soon after sunset. A large lump of superstructure flew through the air as the explosion ripped through her, just forward of the Seacat radar, aft of the funnel. From the magnitude of the explosion and the speed of the fire that followed, it became evident early on that there was no saving her.

By now, although the sun was down, all was bright as day. A number of helicopters had very quickly taken off from HMS *Fearless* or *Intrepid* and illuminated the rescue with their underslung lights. Much bravery was done that night. A number of secondary explosions were taking place and yet the helos continued to fly. I could see the crew quite clearly, in their orange immersion suits, through my binoculars. There was no question of panic and all appeared very orderly as landing craft came alongside, completely disregarding their own safety. Soon almost all the crew were off. Aft of the funnel, the ship was well ablaze. Suddenly about a dozen men appeared on the port waist aft of the bridge. One brave, nameless, landing-craft coxswain came alongside and took them off from a ladder. It was a most impressive rescue.

I watched fascinated while *Antelope* burned through the night. I had been shown round her in Hamburg, yet here she was, dying before my eyes. I can understand why sailors, and particularly captains, get emotional about their ships. She carried on burning and exploding throughout the night until soon after first light when her back broke and she folded in the middle and sank like a tired old lady sitting down in a deckchair. She went quite slowly in a cloud of steam. Her bow remained visible for some hours, still anchored to the bottom.

The Ajax Bay air show was not finished. Again waves of Mirages and Skyhawks came in. I saw two aircraft positively crash. One Mirage struck by a Rapier missile immediately trailed heavy smoke and soon smashed into the side of a hill; a cheer went up from the troops on the hillside that would have done credit to Hampden Park. But it was nothing to the roar of approval as a Skyhawk, coming in very low over the water and in full view of us on the hill, was struck by something, flipped over on its back and plunged into the water with an almighty splash. Ironically enough, he finished very close to the spot where

Antelope had disappeared two or three hours before. How the pilot had time to eject, I don't know, but he did and we saw his parachute coming down. He was rescued by a small raiding craft.

At this stage I began to wonder at the morality of feeling elated when one sees aircraft with men inside them crash into sides of hills, but I suppose that men whose lives are threatened are entitled to express their relief when they see those that would kill them get their come-uppance. We were watching a gladiatorial contest of the highest order. Those pilots were extremely brave and very skilful. They came back again and again in the full knowledge of the hazards they were running. They pressed home their attacks with vigour, skill and determination and achieved a number of notable successes. They could have won the war for the enemy if it had not been for the outstanding performance of our Harriers and the amazing Sea Wolf missiles. The men of the Royal Navy covered themselves with glory on those days.

The walk from Port San Carlos to New House, some twenty kilometres, was the worst of my life. The weather was not too bad, but the ground was boggy. Where it was not boggy there were strong lumps and tufts of grass and whichever way one stood on them, even in daylight, one stood a good chance of turning one's ankle. In places it was pretty steep, but all faded into insignificance compared to the cursed weight we carried. The Marines were magnificent. We lost the first man after 200 yards and about six more over the next few hours. The rest went on with great stoicism and good humour until two o'clock the following morning. I was immensely proud of them. Marching in darkness was much worse than in daylight, and for those at the tail end of the line of 600 men bumping and stumbling through the black night, life must have been hell. I was fairly preoccupied with trying to keep people together, but by the time we leaguered up, I was near my wits' end.

At 2 a.m. I gave the order to bed down without erecting bivouacs. This was a bad mistake because it rained during the early morning and the plastic bags in which our sleeping bags were stretched did not keep the water out, so our sleeping bags were soaked. The last citadel of a man's morale is his sleeping bag; the comfort and resource it offers is amazing. When you were being shelled, or heard bombing close by, it was an instinctive, automatic reaction to wriggle deeper into the 'green slug'. So at 5 a.m. when I woke to find my bag and self soaked, then my morale was at its lowest.

After mentally weeping for an hour I noticed the rain was not so heavy. 'Aha,' I thought, 'if it stops I can get up and stamp around in the wind and start getting things dry.' As the rain faded away, I began to gather my shattered spirits. The rain stopped. I waited ten minutes, just enjoying not getting any wetter; the rain started again. I pulled the sodden bag over my head and smoked a cigarette. It was the last barrier between me and desperation. But one hardened. Colder and more bitter nights followed and it was not the last time my citadel was breached.

The men who survived that march stuck it right through to the end and morale got higher as we moved east. We refined our methods of living in this inhospitable place to such a degree that by the end we were like animals and almost preferred it out of doors. We could have lived in the wilds indefinitely on what we carried in our fighting order. Never let it be said that we had come to the end of our endurance by the time we reached Stanley or that the weather would have beaten us. We could have gone on for ever.

On 9 June, Lieutenant David Stewart, 3 Troop Commander, was given a mission to harass the enemy and inflict casualties. He prepared his patrol well and I never saw an operation so well founded. He had an artillery observer and engineers to deal with wire and mines, and the best communications I could give him. His men were champing at the bit and I had high hopes for his success. My only fear was the lack of cover presented by the bright moonlight. As I bade them farewell at one o'clock in the morning, I had a last-minute feeling of horror. I could see them with the naked eye for 300 yards and with binoculars for up to half a kilometre. But the enemy never saw them until they were upon them.

The troop moved to the southern end of the Two Sisters feature, a rock which was to be my company's objective during the brigade attack. There, with considerable skill, they crossed open moonlit ground and inserted themselves into the bottom of the position. They killed two men on sentry at very close range and in the subsequent firefight killed another five. They were engaged by at least three machine guns from different positions and had to fight their way out against an enemy of superior numbers defending ground of his own choosing. Our artillery did not arrive until they had 'withdrawn' across the open ground which they had earlier crossed. With bullets ripping up the bog around them, they skirmished backwards, running like hell to get to the nearest decent cover across the river, 1,000 yards away. By the grace of God, no one was hit.

By any standard this was a successful patrol and, it so happened, had considerable bearing on the success of our subsequent operations. In the same way that 2 Para's attack at Darwin and Goose Green set the tone for the rest of the campaign, so did this patrol and others like it establish our moral dominance. If this was what thirty men could do, the Argentinians would not wish to linger when 600 came, supported by artillery. Three nights later we put this theory to the test.

Before last light, we conducted rehearsals on a nearby crag conveniently similar to our objective. We then relaxed and ate a meal. We moved off, all 150 of us, about one hour after last light. The Chaplain, Wynne-Jones, came with us. He brought up the rear with extra medical stores. I was sufficiently apprehensive to say to him quietly as we gathered to do our final checks, 'Pray for our souls, Vicar.' 'I won't need to,' he said, 'I won't need to.' His presence had a curious effect. X Company did not have many who would have professed allegiance to any formal religion but to have this man of God in our midst was a wonderful source of comfort. How much of it was his personality and how much was the idea that his presence somehow lent an air of legitimacy and respectability to our endeavours, I do not know. His presence was most beneficial and the Marines thought the world of him. He told me afterwards that he had chosen to come with my company because he reckoned we would take the most casualties. Had he mentioned this at the time, I would have agreed with him, although I may not have thanked him for this encouragement.

It is not easy to describe one's feelings before one is committed to battle. Fear certainly plays a part but it is not fear of death itself. It is more a sadness about the grief that will follow one's death among one's family. As a Company Commander responsible for the lives of some 150 men, I felt pretty lonely in that hour when our preparations were complete and before we moved off, but I am prepared to bet that each individual felt just as lonely. I was surprised to find 'the loneliness of command' spread as far down the chain to company level. The commander shares the isolation of the widow. Friends may be sympathetic and kind but the pure loneliness of the circumstances are shareable with nobody. I found that I didn't actually want anyone to speak to me. I spent my hour smoking a cigar and preparing myself to accept whatever disasters the night might bring – in a single word, praying.

The march to the forming-up point from which we were to start our assault was a near-nightmare. I had not appreciated how much the man-packing of the Milan would slow us down. Instead of covering the relatively easy ground, which had been recce'd, in about three hours, thus giving us an hour to spare, we took six hours. A piece of rock or a small stream that a man in normal fighting order would never have noticed became a major obstacle to a man carrying his own kit plus a 30lb round of Milan ammunition. We had something like forty rounds and the company was constantly being split. To make matters worse, my route recce team manifestly failed to take us the easiest route. We eventually got there by cutting the Gordian knot and taking the most direct route, but not before we had stumbled and cursed our way over rocks and cliffs for half the night. I even managed to lose half the company on two occasions which meant further energy and time wasted going back to look for them. I lost one man, a key signaller, who became ill in the middle of it all – we had to despatch him to a nearby artillery battery – and one man knocked himself out falling thirty feet over a cliff-like slope. How he wasn't flattened by the weight of his kit I will never understand! When he was 'resuscitated' he was very brave and trudged on.

It had been planned that radio silence would be imposed until the assault. I broke this almost immediately we left base. Had I not, we could still be there trying to find each other. I was also able to inform the CO of our predicament and that the plan had changed yet again! By the time we reached the forming-up point two hours late, we were 150 very fed up and tired men. But it is miraculous where the reserves of energy can come from. I explained briefly to the Colonel on the radio what the position was. To my great relief he put me under no unreasonable pressure and said simply, 'Carry on as planned. I will do nothing until I hear from you.' As a result of his patience, I was able to turn round to my commanders and say, 'Put the last six hours right behind you, make your final preparations in your own time, and when you are completely ready, let me know and we will go.' I suppose the first lesson every soldier who ever goes to war learns is that nothing ever goes to plan. Although this shouldn't discourage one from making a plan, the leader who succeeds is the one who can keep his aim in mind and pick up the bits, stick them together and be ready to mend that when it breaks again! On this occasion, ten minutes later, 150 men were as good as new and the assault began.

The worst point of all was the crossing of the open ground. As we approached we could see the tracer from a heavy machine gun arcing across towards a neighbouring hill from the top of our objective. I watched the leading elements, the Company Sergeant-Major and 1 Troop, get to the river and then I lost them. It was with my heart in my mouth that I then committed 3 Troop to the open ground, and followed close after them. That left only 2 Troop secure in the forming-up position, but by then 1 Troop would almost be in the rocks the other side! James Kelly soon told me what I had begun to hope against hope for: he was secure in his objective and had met no opposition. I despatched David Stewart's troop through 1 Troop and followed him up to the rocks myself. To my astonishment and relief, he reported his objective was clear and asked permission to exploit. I thought this was a good idea as it would save time. If he met something, 2 Troop with Chris Caroe could go through him. He was by now half-way up the 1,500-metre-long feature, and he soon ran into opposition. Two machine guns on the top of the ridge had seen him. Any attempts to close with them drew fire from the northern feature, which was by now being attacked by Z and Y Companies. I decided to pull him back, wallop the place with mortars and artillery, and send in 2 Troop.

While 2 Troop were moving up, I decided to see what the Milan could do. This meant Milan-firing at night without the benefit of nightsights, at extreme range over our heads – and we were at the nether end of the range! But the Milan Troop, attached from 40 Commando, did what was required and accurately gauged our relative positions from the machine-gun tracer.

It is an extraordinary thing having a Milan rocket fired over your head. We could see it coming, quite slowly, towards us, making a curious spluttering noise, quite unlike what I expected. It sounded almost friendly. We all involuntarily ducked, but it must have passed about thirty feet above us, and when it hit, it produced a most satisfactory bang.

Soon 2 Troop were ready and Chris Caroe had given his orders, but although mortars had given me one barrage of eight rounds, I could not get any artillery at all at the critical moment. Because we had been late in arriving on the objective, the batteries were now all engaged on other targets; nobody's fault, just another change of plan. I asked mortars to repeat their mission and ordered Milan to fire another two rockets. The rockets came but the mortars then failed me; their base plates had disappeared into the soft ground and were only able to support us with one solitary mortar. So, without artillery or mortar support, Chris Caroe took his men up the hill.

It was an impressive performance. Not only were the enemy now using an anti-tank weapon, but they were lobbing the odd artillery shell over too. Caroe's men picked and clambered their way round, up and over the rocks towards the enemy position. It was almost like fighting in a built-up area, like fighting in street rubble, in a town that had been bombed. Two men would cover while one man jumped over. It was leapfrog all the way. They actually got on top but were forced off it by artillery and took our only casualty. Lance-Corporal Montgomery and Marine Watson were both some five feet from a shell when it exploded. It picked them up and threw them several yards. Montgomery had dislocated something in the shoulder and Watson was unhurt, if just a trifle deaf! Lucky X-Ray! When I saw the ground next day my heart missed a beat. It was much more rugged than I had envisaged and had I known where I was sending Caroe's lot I would have had serious doubts about their chances – but I would have had no alternative as there was only room for one group at a time.

The setback to the progress of 2 Troop was only temporary and they soon reapplied pressure on the machine-gun posts. Eventually they prevailed and we were secure on our objective.

My HQ was still being shot at in a desultory fashion by a half-hearted rifleman. We ignored him. We were safely established in the rocks and if he was going to be daft enough to be around in the approaching daylight, he deserved what was coming to him. But the shelling began more seriously now and that was unpleasant. They were only using two guns, but over thirty-six hours some forty or fifty shells landed among our positions. Fortunately we received no casualties, but it is a disagreeable business being shelled, even in this somewhat intermittent manner. We had a good opportunity to make something of a study of this.

The irony is that if there is not too much noise elsewhere, one can hear the enemy gun go off and then the whistle as the shell comes your way. More often than not, one only hears the whistle. But the longer you can hear the whistle, the further away from you it is going to land. If a shell is coming really close, you get about a two-second warning; and if it is going to hit you, you get none at all! During a lull, I got out of the rocks to have a pee and a look round. I hadn't finished when I heard the dreaded whistle and a shell hit the ground at the same time as I did. A healthy chunk of rock landed on my back. I measured the distance afterwards: it was nineteen paces. I gather that it became something of a mischievous fashion among the Marines to whistle at their fellows during their more vulnerable moments!

I reached the top of the feature at first light. When I looked back down the ridge and realized what we had done, my spine froze. Potentially, the position was impregnable. If they had held it the way we would have held it, we would never have got them out. The exertions of the night and the previous day, and the realization of our enormous good luck, now began to have their effect. I felt physically and mentally drained. I personally was very glad at this stage that we were now too late to move on to attack Tumbledown as had originally been planned. Two attacks in one night might have been pushing our luck somewhat.

I thought long and hard about what must have happened on that position during the two days between David Stewart's patrol and our attack. I believe that as a result of the hammering they took, the enemy command structure had broken down and the weaker members, who must have been in the majority, fled. A hard cadre of some twenty men had stayed behind and fought, and they were brave men. Those who stayed and fought had something. I for one would not wish to face my Marines in battle.

Our relief did not prevent us taking advantage of our good fortune. We found a prodigious amount of ammunition, weapons and food on the position. Watching Marines go through the enemy camp was strongly reminiscent of a family of tinkers picking over a Corporation rubbish tip. When it became known that each Argentinian ration pack contained twenty fags and a lot of whisky, a large number of men could be seen going about their business with bulging pockets and big grins on their faces.

We found seven dead on the position and we buried them *in situ*. I supervised the burial of an unidentified officer and sergeant who had both been shot at close range, probably by 3 Troop on 9 June. We put them in a shallow grave, marked the spot carefully and made a record to submit to the authorities. I said a few words in prayer.

Two days later, as we were advancing up Sapper, rumours started filtering through about a surrender. Late in the evening we heard for sure that it was all over and that the Belgians had beaten them 1–0 in the World Cup!

On 16 June we walked into Stanley. It was an emotional hour and I can recall few prouder experiences. We marched to the pier where I smoked the cigar I had been saving for this occasion. After a few moments, I had the feeling that the numbers in my company had diminished somewhat. To be more precise, they had all but disappeared. 'Where are the men, Sergeant-Major?'

'Come with me, Sir,' and CSM Bell took me by the hand, metaphorically speaking of course, to join the company. As if in answer to a Royal Marine's prayer they had homed in on a pub called the Globe Hotel and we found ourselves in a smoky, wooden, barn-shaped room. One hundred and fifty Marines, unshaven, dirty, tired, stinking, and very lightly boozed. Every man with a can in his hand – God knows who was paying – and in company with a number of very nice, appreciative civilians (clearly with no sense of smell), urging us to go down to the airport and machine-gun the prisoners. Not a moment to be forgotten in a lifetime.

I saw and heard of much courage on the Falkland Islands, but courage manifests itself in many ways. Certainly that which lets a man fix a bayonet and go over the top is courage. However, I don't always think that it is necessarily pure courage or pure gallantry that drives a man into doing such things. In many instances it is desperation. The courage I hold in highest esteem is the courage which is fortitude in adversity. Given the physical circumstances surrounding the campaign, I think that every man who actually started and finished down there showed a great deal of courage. I also bow to the courage of the commanders who had to make plans and decisions under great pressure. I bow to the courage of the Brigade Staff, the intelligence officers who had to get information and disseminate it knowing that men would live or die on the quality of their staff work.

Courage is what? What does it take for a man to do something? There are some men for whom it is nothing to go and die in battle. They are supported by something else, by religion or by a cause. I think they are wrongly attributed with courage. I think courage is what fills the gap between what you would prefer to do and what you actually do. To measure courage, measure the stress that people have to undergo to do what they do and still keep a cheerful face and achieve their aims. Courage is coping with stress, and the people who are under the greatest stress of all are the people who are ignored: one's parents, one's family. It's very easy for a man to be brave once, to be classically brave, to fix his bayonet and charge. I only fought once. Ask David Stewart and 3 Troop or 2 Para what it's like to fight a second time. Speak to the Naval Gunfire Observation Teams, some of whom fought four or five times. Charles Moran in his *Anatomy of Courage* talks of each man having a reservoir of courage, rather like a cistern: one can draw from a cistern but it will need topping up; you can't draw on it indefinitely. I am not sure

391

I subscribe entirely to that theory but certainly it is more difficult to be brave a second time round.

Although it is almost impertinent to compare our adventure with something like the Somme, I believe I have had a glimpse of the sort of moral strength that made our forebears continue despite knowing their chances were poor. Remember, the fact that we had got off lightly only became apparent after we had won. Until then, the prospect for every man of having his block knocked off was real enough.

13/14 June

Assault on Tumbledown Mountain

Major John Kiszely

Scots Guards

Military Cross

On the night of 13/14 June 1982, on the Island of East Falkland, the 2nd Battalion Scots Guards attacked well-entrenched enemy positions on the craggy ridge feature of Tumbledown Mountain, seven kilometres to the west of Port Stanley. Major Kiszely was commanding the leading company as they neared the last phase of the assault.

Despite heavy artillery fire from our own guns, the enemy continued to fight back. Major Kiszely immediately appreciated that direct action was essential to maintain the momentum of the attack. Under fire and with a complete disregard for his own safety, he led a group of his men up a gully towards the enemy. Despite men falling wounded beside him he continued his charge, throwing grenades as he went. Arriving on the enemy position, he killed two enemy with his rifle and a third with his bayonet. His courageous action forced the surrender of the remainder. His was the culminating action in the battalion successfully seizing its objective.

Major Kiszely, by his outstanding leadership and heroic example, was an inspiration to his men. His bravery and courage under fire were of an exceptionally high order.

On the way down there on the *QE2* I squared off everything in my life – all the things that mattered. I wrote to my parents saying you won't be hearing from me for a bit, but I'll be all right – same with the girlfriend. I told them I was not actually going to write to them any more. Wrote to the bank manager, wrote to the solicitor, stockbroker – squared everything off and got my will all sorted out with my lawyer. Therefore, as a bachelor, when I got down there I had everything squared off at home, so I had cut myself off from everything that was happening in the rest of the world, and found it easy; I don't think a married man could do that. When the situation arises and you think there's a chance in the next ten minutes or quarter of an hour that you are going to die, most people think of their wife and children and the people who depend on them and everything else, but I did not think that at all.

It crossed my mind, quite seriously, that I might be killed when we lay for a long time before our artillery could register, receiving shit coming in – I mean, really very close; and I don't know whether it was Argentinian or British because it's immaterial – it comes down, it explodes beside you. I suppose over twenty yards was the nearest, which of course hits your head, the blast of it, the noise. It's rather like a light at night, when it's pitch black and you see a light, you don't know if it is a very bright light a long way away or a tiny little pencil beam very close – it's like that with artillery shells. There's the tremendous bang and a crash and you're blinded and deafened and shaken – now that could be a mortar bomb landing five yards away or a 155mm landing thirty yards away.

Where I was lying there was a platoon beside me, and several times a great crump of shells would land down and I thought, 'Christ! It's wiped out the whole platoon'. I shouted down to them, 'Sergeant Jackson, who did that hit, who's it killed?' and he said, 'Don't worry, Sir, we're all right.' When the shit was coming down really heavily, I thought there was at least a fifty per cent chance, without being optimisic or pessimistic or anything else, that I was going to be killed. I thought then, 'Have I told the Company Second-in-Command the right frequency – you know, is he going to know where to come? Did I give him the right map?' All the things like have I got my air ticket with me? That sort of thing, whereas I think a married person in that situation would start thinking about his wife, his children, his loved ones.

The youngsters were very brave. For example, this young Platoon Commander, 2nd Lieutenant James Stuart, who was only nineteen, had arrived in my company straight from Sandhurst in April. There he was a month later in the Falklands. He was aged nineteen, green behind the gills, and within the first five minutes of coming under fire he'd had his Platoon Sergeant killed – Platoon Sergeant dead in his arms – this other man killed, two other people wounded and his Company Sergeant-Major shot in the hand. But he did extremely well, this young boy. In many ways it was a proof of the system. You think, how could someone like that possibly cope? You know, he's way out of his depth, obviously very frightened, but knew what he had to do and got on with it. Right the way through the night he commanded his platoon, really under fire all the time, clearing right the way through Tumbledown. But you know, a young boy like that, I just wonder when I was nineteen whether I could have done that. You think, could I have done it? An adult experience for a teenager. And yet he commanded his platoon right the way through it, with all these disasters. Just imagine having your Platoon Sergeant being shot right beside you! When you come to a platoon, the Platoon Sergeant's a pretty key guy, keeps you straight, says, 'Look, Sir, don't do that, best do it this way.' When that is taken out of your life and disaster is all around you, you think – why me? I think he related quite closely to the casualties at the time too. It hit him. He came up on the air to me and said, 'What do I do?' So I just talked in a very calm matter-of-fact voice and said, 'Well done, one or two things are going wrong, but it's not a disaster. You're doing well, keep plugging on with it and we'll be up alongside you again. You're winning through, well done, keep going.' He probably thought I was mad, but he went on doing it, and did a bloody good job. He soon steadied them down. He got a Mention in Despatches.

I found it very odd when I was on the other end of the radio set when he was saying all these things like 'Platoon Sergeant dead' and the other platoons were reporting men killed. Then in the platoon beside me the Platoon Sergeant was taken away, wounded with shrapnel from these shells that were coming down, and then they had another man shot through the head. And when all these casualty reports came in to me, all within the space of about half an hour, I remember thinking, 'I know these lads, they are boys who I am like a father to and who are very close to me.' Now, thinking back on them, and indeed before, if someone had said to me that Guardsman Sterling was not going to come back from this campaign I would have been in tears – you know, he was practically a boy, who I knew extremely well – or that Sergeant Simeon was going to be killed, I wouldn't have believed it, I'd have wanted to leave the Army. Yet at the time, you know, you haven't any feeling; they're murdering these boys, and you're not feeling anything. Afterwards I thought I must be a bit odd not feeling any emotion for them. Looking back on it, perhaps that's how it should be and that if you are over-emotional about it you start making unbalanced decisions. But it shocked me in that I didn't know that about myself.

Afterwards, I did feel emotion, especially when I was writing letters to their wives or mothers who I knew. I started to write these letters the night after Tumbledown was taken. I wrote them in the sheep-shearing sheds at Fitzroy by an oil lamp on a scruffy airmail form with a biro. I felt I wanted to sit for a bit and think of each of the seven blokes who had been killed in the company and have each letter right from the heart, so it took me about three or four hours to write each one. It was over a couple of days that I wrote them, late into the night. I thought what awful letters I had written and yet, when I went back to visit their relatives in their homes, they'd practically framed those letters. I suppose it's because they were absolutely truthful and straight.

There is, thank God, a lighter side to war. For example, Guardsman Shaw was carrying the magazine for his rifle in his breast pocket when he was shot in the chest. He was thrown ten yards back and said to himself, 'Fuck me! I'm hit, but where's the blood? Why aren't I dying?' The magazine had actually stopped the round – lucky boy! That was First World War stuff! You know, you read these things and you think that's rubbish, that never happens, but it does.

I was hit myself in the pouch. The bullet went into the pouch, through the bayonet scabbard with a neat hole in it, and then into my compass. I thought that something had hit me but I didn't know what it was – I didn't think I'd been shot at all. Afterwards, at first light, we were looking things over when one of the lads said, 'You've had a lucky escape there – look at that!' I took out my compass from its pouch and the bullet was still inside it. I've still got the bayonet scabbard with the hole in it.

We had been pinned down at the foot of Tumbledown for two or three hours because the Argentinians' positions were so strong and they couldn't be moved. They were the troops of the 5th Marine Battalion who were highly professional. 2 Para's great thing was that you fire an anti-tank weapon at the enemy sangar and if it doesn't kill them they're out with their hands up as fast as possible. I had spoken the day before Tumbledown to a 42 Commando who had been on Mount Harriet the night before. He was a Troop Commander picking up some stuff, so of course I got this bloke to one side and said, 'Come on, tell me, what's the score? What happens? What's it like? What did you do? How did you do it?' He said the same thing as 2 Para, you know, 'Get the big guns on them, 84mm and anti-tank weapons firing at their sangars and you've got it made. . . ' I then went back to my company and said exactly the same to them, but when we tried that, it didn't work. So there was a bit of a crisis of confidence; the boys were thinking: 'Is the boss spinning us a line or what?' And I thought, you know, 'Shit, what's the matter, why isn't this happening with us as well?' We were getting quite close hits with these anti-tank weapons, but they were staying there and firing back.

We couldn't advance until the artillery was actually on target but it's a very complicated process bracketing the rounds to come down directly on the target, especially at night. It's easy on Salisbury Plain, you have a demonstration of artillery and the target is on the ground and if it doesn't hit it you bracket to the left and then bracket forward and back. Here, the artillery was saying, 'A ranging shot is coming over in ten seconds.' Then ten seconds later the rounds are falling absolutely everywhere, some falling on top of you. When you know it's your own side's rounds, it's not a lot of fun.

This shelling went on for over an hour and we'd already been pinned down for an hour before that, but at the time it seemed much shorter. Time, however, was ebbing away fast and I was getting anxious, because not only had our attack got to be completed by first light, but the other company also had to complete its objective by first light. The Gurkhas then had to pass through and take out Mount William and the Welsh Guards had to take out Sapper Hill, all this before daylight.

I knew there was big pressure on. I also knew that to get up and go forward without the artillery managing to get the enemy's heads down first was total suicide. We wouldn't have achieved it with heavy casualties – we wouldn't have achieved it, full stop! They were giving out a lot of machine-gun fire and until we could get the artillery rounds on target to keep their heads down, we couldn't move. So there we were lying there with all the shit coming in, all this artillery, until eventually, and only two hours before first light, the rounds at last registered on target.

I said to the Platoon Commander, Alastair Mitchell, 'Look, the rounds are on target now, so put in a platoon attack on the first ridge two or three hundred yards ahead of us.' I thought when I told him that, 'This could be goodbye Alastair Mitchell.' But they achieved it because the enemy's heads were down. As the artillery stopped they rushed straight in and managed to sort out the enemy. We moved forward to join Mitchell's platoon which was 300 yards up the hill. As I got to the ridge where they were busy finishing clearing the position, I saw this next ridge about two to three hundred metres up, with no activity on it, because the Argentinians' heads were still down. I thought, 'Hell, if we can get up there, that's another ridge taken.' I looked around and there was a platoon down to my right sorting out their objective so I realized that all I had to do was to get them going at right angles up the hill instead of carrying on down to the right. I also realized that only I could do that because I was the only one that could see the ridge. I started rather over-involving myself in the platoon's battle and got the ones nearest to me by shouting at them and grabbing them, saying, 'Come on!' But only about a dozen heard me. In the meantime, I had run on to the next ridge only to find myself totally alone because those who were coming on had either lost direction or were going other places, and some were kneeling down, shooting, keeping the enemy's heads down. But eventually, in ones and twos, they found me.

It was absolutely pitch black and we couldn't see anything. However, we got to this next ridge and sorted out three or four sangars that were there. Then again I looked up, and there was this other ridge about 200 metres ahead and I thought, 'We've done it once, we'll do it again!' The same thing happened, except this time, of the twelve or so that were with me, one was shot dead and another was shot in the chest and we had also taken some prisoners. So we had to leave somebody with them and somebody had to stay with the wounded man, so the number was whittling down. After we had done this about three times and actually got up to the crest, there were only six people with me. I didn't realize it was the top. I thought it was another false crest until we got on to it and looked down, and there below us, about half a mile away, were the lights of Port Stanley! I thought in my own mind that Stanley would be blacked out – not a bit of it. You could see the street grids, the street lights, cars going up and down the roads; it was absolutely surreal! So much so, that I stood absolutely stock-still with these other six people beside me, gaping in amazement that we'd done it, we'd got to the top of Tumbledown, we'd achieved our mission!

Just at that moment a machine gun opened up and three of the six who were with me were shot. Entirely, utterly my fault. There's only one person to blame for that and that's Kiszely.

I had seven people at the top of the hill, three of whom were wounded, which meant that three of the others would have to look after them. This also meant there was only one man actually looking out for the enemy, which made us very vulnerable for a counter-attack as their machine gun was only 100 yards away.

The Platoon Commander, Alastair Mitchell, was shot in the shoulder and thigh and I was beside him patching him up and at the same time trying to drag him into cover. I didn't know it at the time, but Alastair only had a flesh wound in the thigh. I thought he was badly injured so the first thing I had to do was to rip his trousers to get at the injury. How do you rip a trouser leg? Well, obviously you've got to cut it with a blade. However, my bayonet was jammed on my rifle, and I couldn't find his rifle to get his bayonet. I had a knife which I always carry tucked away, but I couldn't get at it. So there I was, desperately trying to get this knife out and all the time there was this chap bleeding to death because I couldn't cut his trousers! Bloody daft situation. In the end I grabbed a bayonet off someone else's rifle and cut the trousers open and patched him up.

We were all doing this first aid job while Guardsman MacKenzie was guarding us. I said to him, 'You watch out.'

'Sir,' he said, 'I haven't got any ammunition.'

'What!' I said. 'What a fucking time to run out of ammunition.' He had an SMG, all the others had SLRs. 'How long have you been without ammunition?'

'Since the bottom of the hill, Sir.'

'Did you know that?' I said.

'Yes, Sir.'

'Well, why did you come on up with me if you had no bloody ammunition?'

'You asked me to, Sir.'

What a brave man! He was an extraordinary chap, because right at the bottom of the hill, when I'd gone forward and said, 'Come on, come on with me,' I'd found myself with nobody with me. So I'd shouted out, '15 Platoon, are you with me?' There was no reply. So I thought 'Kiszely, you've really blown it this time.' I shouted out again and this voice right beside me said, 'Aye, Sir, I'm with you,' and it was MacKenzie, who had no ammunition! Amazing boy. There was this lad, without any ammunition at all who had decided he was going to come because he was there, and because the Company Commander was asking. So there we were at the top, him without any ammunition, so we swapped weapons. I said to him afterwards, 'You brave bastard!' He just looked at me with a big grin on his face. I suppose I probably owe my life to him. Somebody like that, perhaps it happens in every regiment, but to me he personifies the Guards. Somebody else would think that what he did was stupid, which of course it was. To go up the hill with no ammunition was to make a walking figure-eleven target of yourself. He was also a radio operator, so he obviously thought he was needed, so on he went. It's the strength of our system; we have many weaknesses in our system and other people have many strengths compared with us, but his sort of action shows some of our strength.

One of the strengths of the British Army is the regimental system and the competitiveness of it – you know, 'Fuck the Paras, and the Green Jackets, and the Marines – we are the Guards.' They in turn are saying, 'Fuck the Craphats, we're the Paras.' Sometimes that gets out of hand. Occasionally, like anywhere else, in the Falklands there was unfounded criticism for the sake of being competitive. But I don't think there ever was between us and 2 Para. I think we had a very good relationship with 2 Para. Their victory at Goose Green represented to us something that we very much admired; it set an example. It appeared that they had achieved the most fantastic thing in the most fantastic style. They had very little artillery support, it was the first major contest of the war and it really set the standard for the rest. In the same way H. Jones set a standard of bravery; it was like a gauntlet being thrown down to other officers. In a way, 2 Para threw the gauntlet down to the rest of us and said, 'Match that.' That's what Goose Green meant to me. It was a good, tactical victory; hard fought, bloody good. 2 Para set an example to us and, I guess, everybody else in the Falklands, even if they didn't actually say so at the time. But they felt it subconsciously.

I think everybody learnt something about themselves on Tumbledown; some with shame, some with pride, some with surprise. I learnt a lot about myself and about my judgements of other people. I tend to form first impressions and yet after Tumbledown I really was quite ashamed of one or two initial judgements I had made of people in my company. This was particularly so of people who were just attached to the company. These were people like Officers' Mess barmen, somebody out of the Clothing Stores, out of the Quartermaster's Stores, or an odd clerk. I thought, 'Hell, fancy having to carry them.' There was Lance-Corporal MacColl who was a clothing storeman, aged about forty-five, and I thought, 'I don't want him.' I told the Commanding Officer that I'd rather not have him on Tumbledown, but I had to take him. I put him in charge of some stretcher-bearers. Then, to my amazement, I saw him going forward three or four times to pick up casualties and bring them back. He was standing right in the open, knowing that he had to get forward. People were screaming at him, 'For fuck's sake get down!' But he knew he had to get up there because Sergeant Simeon was dying and nothing was going to stop him getting to him. When I saw how brave he was I felt ashamed. He was a quiet self-effacing man. He earned his Mention in Despatches many times over.

Fear is infectious; but what I never realized until Tumbledown is the fact that, in exactly the same way, courage is also infectious. In those first few moments when the bullets are flying around and everybody is lying down, looking around to see what the bloke next door is doing or what the Platoon Commander is doing, you realize that probably nobody has done this before. They are questioning themselves, you know, how do you behave, what are you meant to do, what's the etiquette? If the first thing they see is people being scared, people running away, people not lying there with a rifle looking out for the enemy but lying hiding, cowering under a rock, they will do that as well. If, however, they see people doing courageous things, they will think this is obviously what one is meant to do in battle, and so they will do it too. Now that's something that surprised me, and I was very lucky because in my company, and absolutely nothing to do with me, that's what caught on, because people like Corporal MacColl were seen doing very brave things early in the battle. People who under other circumstances might have lain behind the rock were doing very brave things right the way through the battle. Courage caught on – it was absolutely contagious.

Lieutenant Robert Lawrence

Scots Guards

Military Cross

On the night of 13/14 June, on the Island of East Falkland, the 2nd Battalion Scots Guards attacked well-entrenched positions on the craggy ridge feature of Tumbledown Mountain, seven kilometres west of Port Stanley. Lieutenant Lawrence and his platoon were amongst leading elements in the assault.

As they came up to an area of prominent rocky crags they came under intense fire from an enemy machine-gun position. Lieutenant Lawrence, to the fore throughout, immediately led an attack. Throwing grenades onto the enemy's position as he went, he continued in the heat of the firefight to exhort his platoon to follow him in the assault. His attacking group destroyed the enemy.

Firm on that position, he gathered up a handful of his men and began to work his way along the ridge to engage an enemy sniper. As they closed and just before he could attack, Lieutenant Lawrence was severely wounded.

His actions were an outstanding example of leadership under fire and courage in the face of the enemy.

Tumbledown was divided into three parts – G Company, Left Flank, and Right Flank at the end part. We followed on and then got onto G Company's first third. Virtually nothing seemed to happen whilst we were going across; this was mixed in with the fear of, 'Oh God, what are we doing out here in the open?' even though it was dark. Every now and again we would be thinking completely the opposite, 'Oh God, there's going to be no one there. It's all been one bloody great waste of time.' So I approached Tumbledown with dreadfully mixed-up emotions and it was bloody cold, bloody freezing.

We learnt that G Company had come on and not met anyone. Then firing started and fighting seemed to be going on quite heavily in front and it was obvious that Left Flank had come across some fairly aggressive resistance. There was also quite a lot of firing coming from Mount William on our right. I could see a lot of tracer and starlight shells in the air but we were very detached from it and had little to do with the battle at that stage. Then the odd round started to come close from this Argentinian nutter who seemed to be trying to take on the company on his own. He held us up for a considerable time.

Because we had been under very little fire, everyone was very excited. All the time we were waiting, it was bloody cold and when it gets that cold, it's bloody difficult to do anything. You reach a certain level of cold and you really think, 'This is it.' That's when my Platoon Sergeant Jackson really helped. He was going round kicking the boys and making me kick them, which was keeping me going as well. I am sure he realized it.

We got up and we started moving through, but became disorientated in the dark. I sat down behind a rock for half an hour whilst I listened; then we moved forward and heard that Left Flank had a lot of casualties and all sorts of problems and they had been stopped by a machine-gun post. It all started for me there.

We moved up and came across Left Flank who were in a line across the top of the mountain. I met John Kiszely – eyes gleaming, loving every minute of it! It was all very exciting. I started to enjoy it then, because we were going to do something; the cold didn't bother me any more. John briefed us and as he was getting poor back-up from artillery he told us he needed our help to take out the machine-gun post. It seemed a very impressive post and wasn't going to fall that easily. He told us where it was and we decided on a right-flanking attack.

We began moving down the gully to the right and I suddenly realized the problem of doing a righthand attack was that we couldn't tell exactly where the enemy were. So I got on the radio to James Dalyrumple, the other Platoon Commander, and said, 'Could you put down some fire to tell us where they are?' The fire he put down showed us where they were and also that our back-up fire wasn't that effective, it wasn't hitting home. Anyone shooting at you is effective to some extent, but you soon learn that bullets going within three feet of you aren't worth worrying about. It's the bullets that are coming within six inches of you that make you think, 'Oh God.'

We started putting down fire as we moved in and the machine-gun post were retaliating fairly strongly, so my platoon ended up being pinned down. I then started crawling forward with a phosphorus grenade, away from my platoon, towards the enemy. I hadn't told my Sergeant I was going to do this, it just tended to happen – at that stage the ball was rolling and I wanted to keep it going. I didn't have time to brief everyone, I just screamed it out.

I got close enough to lob in a grenade but because we

hadn't done a lot of work with these grenades, I didn't really know how bloody tough the pins were to get out – they should have been prepared beforehand but we hadn't done it. So there I was, trying to pull the pin out, but it wouldn't come, so I had to crawl back and get one of my corporals to hold the pin while I held the grenade and pulled it out! I then crawled up again with the grenade in my hand holding down the safety valve! As I crawled up, I really thought, 'This is it. It's all over,' because I had my platoon behind firing over my head at the Argentinians, the Argentinians in front of me firing towards my platoon, and the remainder of the Left Flank and 1 Platoon firing from my left. I had three-way bullets, not to mention anything that ricocheted off the rocks – all this and a grenade without a pin in!

I approached the rock, which I knew would give me cover when I threw the grenade, and the closer I got to the rock the more ricochets were coming off. At one stage I was screaming at the platoon to reduce their fire. I don't know whether they did or not, but I got behind the rock and I threw the grenade and then I was screaming for my platoon to come on. This was probably the most fantastic thing I have ever seen in my life because they all did: every single man got up and went in so mad, without thinking, that the Argentinians must have thought we were out of our brains and crazy – we just ran over that machine-gun post.

Having been told at the beginning that there was only one machine gun in it, we then found that there were three and another one further back. The machine-gun posts were at the base of a large crag of rocks and there was still firing coming from the other side. Although we had defeated them on this side it suddenly occurred to me that we had our first enemies in our hands and they weren't giving up that easily. We'd got their marines and they were not going to stop. I had spoken to some Paras a couple of days beforehand and they said, 'Get within 200 metres and they'll give up. Hit them with an anti-tank weapon and the bunker will drop out.' Well, it just didn't happen. We really had to fight for it. The problem was that we had our first enemy and the boys were fascinated: they had their chance to tie them up, take their kit off them, drag them around, and threaten them – all natural things if you are fighting an enemy – but we were still being fired at from the other side of the rocks. So I said, 'Come on, we can't stop here. We have got to get on.' I ended up gripping a couple of people, one of whom was Guardsman Pengelly who won a Military Medal.

We went across the Stanley end of Tumbledown and as we were stepping round the corner of some rocks the air burst! Everything around us went bam-crack. Everything just went up. We were bowled straight backwards and I thought, 'Fuck this – dear me – that's not a good idea.' But we traced our steps back. On the way, Pengelly realized that there was firing coming from the top of the rocks. I saw him climb up the rocks and I thought, 'Right – he's doing his job, I must get on and do mine.' You can't stop to observe each other, you have all got to do your bit. Basically, once he started going up the rocks I left him. I think it was seconds after that that he was hit – it was all very fleeting.

I grabbed two or three other people, including Sergeant McDermott and Corporal Renny, and we went round the other end of this small rock, because there were snipers there. We started skirmishing down – the classic one man down, another man runs down, first man up, etc. It really was like being on a range in Wales when we were training and waiting for the target to flip out! It was all grass and there were large rocks with hundreds of places where people could hide. We were going along like James Bond waiting for someone to appear from behind a rock. It seemed ironic that we should be doing this because when you go to the cinema you say to yourself, 'It would never be like that in real life,' but surprisingly enough it was. It really was like being in the *OK Corral* waiting for a guy to appear from behind a post – you would draw on each other. I felt it shouldn't be like this, it should be more organized, and yet it wasn't.

As we went through I found a guy lying face down and I thought, 'Is he dead or isn't he?' I didn't have any ammunition left at that stage, but I had a bayonet on my rifle; I hadn't used it and it is the ultimate in fighting when you use it. So as I went past him I stuck the bayonet into the back of his arm – God knows why I did it, I think it was just because he was there, and it was a quick way of finding out whether he was alive or not. I stuck it into the back of his arm. It obviously hurt him a great deal, and he suddenly swung round and he bust my bayonet, so I ended up finishing him off. But had I left him, he might have sat up afterwards and shot me in the back. I wish I had kicked him in the face to see if he was alive; it seems I used the bayonet unnecessarily, and I regret that.

We skirmished through and took out some snipers. At this time McEntaggart got shot a couple of times, but when he got hit in the back of his arm he said, 'Excuse me, Sir, I think I've just been shot.' I couldn't believe it! I thought, 'Well, you know if you've been shot – you must do!' He turned his arm and I could see that a high-velocity round had just nicked his arm and had obviously numbed him. I then felt a shot go very close to my face and thought, 'They must be behind us,' because McEntaggart had been shot from there. We looked and we couldn't see them. I was impatient to go and finish them off, because in my opinion there would be a second wave coming from the machine-gun post, cleaning up after us. Unfortunately, that didn't happen and that was really why I got hurt. Some of our own people should have been coming down cleaning up in case we'd missed someone or hadn't properly killed everyone.

I turned and carried on and I must have only gone about five yards when suddenly it felt as if I had been hit. I carried on running three steps and then my legs collapsed underneath me and I thought, 'I've been hit by something.' I didn't think it had penetrated me because I felt that that would be more of a piercing pain, whereas this was like being hit by a cricket bat really, really hard. Sergeant McDermott came running to help me and I could feel the blood running into my ears and eyes and I realized that it had pierced me. They took off my beret and I started losing a lot of blood. They put field dressings on and dragged me back out of the open but all the time we had these rounds coming in. At one stage, Sergeant Bates, our medical sergeant, was lying on top of me with Sergeant McDermott, trying to keep me warm, when an artillery round came in and landed within four feet of us. It didn't go off but buried itself in the soil. We were very lucky, because all three of us could have disappeared had it gone off.

When I was first hit, and after I'd got over the initial pain, and because it was bloody sore all the time, I started worrying about my boys. I was desperately scared that I had led them into something that they wouldn't be able to handle and they'd all be killed. So I was asking where the hell my team was, and what had happened to them; who was hurt and who wasn't. After that, because of the loss of blood, I started getting very cold and I was desperately keen to know where the helicopter was, and I started worrying about that.

After I'd been lying there two and a half hours, Sam Drennan, who got the DFC, came forward under heavy fire. He used to be a colour-sergeant in the Scots Guards and had transferred to the Army Air Corps. I think he'd disobeyed orders to get us out and crossed the line to come and get us, because he'd heard that a number of Scots Guards had been wounded and that an officer had been shot and was dying.

When I got to Fitzroy they graded the casualties and worked on those they could save. I was there, fully conscious, for three and a half hours at the back of the queue because they thought I was just going to die and there was no point in working on me. I was awake for all of that. My brain was hanging out; you can't really strap it in with a first field dressing because it makes it too dry. Every time it came out someone put it back in! You can't, of course, stop the blood flowing – I lost about five and a half pints. But I kept sitting up and talking to people,

411

which upset them tremendously, and I was conscious all the time. I thought I was dying. People say how brave I was, being awake and suffering all that pain, but I was more frightened of dying. If I had gone to sleep, I probably would have died – that was another reason why I lived, because I didn't lose consciousness. But I would say I was more of a coward because I was frightened of dying than a hero and brave about being able to live with it. I was buggered if I was going to die of it. I was too frightened to die. I wasn't angry. It was just that I couldn't believe it, I couldn't really understand it. When I found my arm and leg and the whole of the lefthand side of my body didn't work, it didn't worry me. Had someone said, 'If we cut off your left arm, your head will stop hurting,' I would have let them. My head was so bloody sore that my arm and leg just didn't matter at all. I couldn't believe the pain I was in. I could feel the morphine ampoules hanging round my neck but I knew I wasn't allowed to use them because it was a head injury. That was bloody annoying.

When I went in for my first operation in Fitzroy, they cut off my smock. I didn't mind that, but I'd laced my boots in a certain way ever since I joined the Army, in the theory that if you cut a particular lace you can just pull the boot off, but they cut down the side with this bloody great pair of scissors, and I was furious! They then cut off all the rest of my kit and a white phosphorus grenade fell out into the operating theatre, which caused a few panics at the time! I found it very amusing. Then they found a Colt 45 in my smock which I had taken off an Argentinian I had killed. The surgeon said to whoever he was handing it to, 'It's loaded but it's not made ready.' I thought to myself, 'Well, he knows what he's talking about,' which reassured me, which was stupid, of course, because it didn't matter whether he knew anything about pistols so long as he knew how to do surgery! But I suppose I was reassured, as a soldier, by the fact that if he knew what he was doing with weapons, he must know how to deal with a scalpel. When he took it away I stuck my hand straight out and said, 'Can I have it back, please?' He said, 'No. Don't worry, I'll give it to so and so and you'll be able to get it afterwards.' I never did, of course, because they wouldn't allow us to have any weapons at all. But I sat and complained that they were taking this Colt 45 that I wanted so dearly!

I've lost the use of my left arm, and my left leg is bad, but I'm able to get about. The brain surgery causes me periods of black depression but at least I'm alive. I had to fight hard when I came back to England for everything I wanted – I think that was one of the things that kept me going.

My time in the Army was something I really enjoyed and I was most disappointed when I realized how badly hurt I was and that I'd never be a soldier again. I think I was always a bit of a cowboy and I think cowboying is a very healthy thing – it makes people more interested in what they are doing. If they get enjoyment out of being wet and living in holes in the ground, then that's to be encouraged.

My father was in the RAF and so was my grandfather so I was determined to have a service life. From the moment I joined the regiment, I had a ball. I suppose I'm military shit really; I love the Army, I love weapons and loved everything we did, all the jungle warfare and the courses. I never found it difficult to lead. I was one of those nuts who run in without thinking, which isn't the recommended thing to do. But I loved jumping in and saying, 'Come on, boys, follow me.' I was an experience hunter. It seems ironic that my careers master at my school, Fettes, who was also in charge of the College Cadet Force, threw me out of that and told me I wasn't disciplined enough for any kind of service life and that I should avoid the forces at all costs!

But that's all over now and I'm adjusting to it, though every now and again I think, 'Fuck this.' It makes me angry. I used to like dancing and playing silly buggers. All my life I've done it. I remember at Warminster climbing out of the back of one guy's car and into another car as we were speeding along. In Borneo I climbed out of the passenger window of a car over the roof and in through the front with the driver. I used to enjoy doing stupid things – that was me.

A lot of people who are depressed just sit and think and become morbid and upset. When they are happy those problems are still there. So the answer is: don't think about them! Just get on with it!

Captain Samuel Drennan

Army Air Corps

Distinguished Flying Cross

During the night of 13/14 June 1982, on the island of East Falkland, the 2nd Battalion Scots Guards attacked well-entrenched enemy positions on the craggy ridge feature of Tumbledown Mountain, seven kilometres to the west of Port Stanley. A pilot, Captain Drennan flew his helicopter in direct support of the battalion.

In the assault the battalion was subjected to continuous, accurate enemy small-arms and artillery fire. Despite this, Captain Drennan repeatedly volunteered to fly forward to evacuate very seriously wounded casualties who required immediate medical attention and who could not have survived movement on a stretcher over the extremely rough ground of Tumbledown. In order to reach the wounded in the battalion's front line, on at least three separate occasions he had to move to exposed, forward slope positions in full view of the enemy. He was personally responsible for the evacuation of sixteen casualties from Tumbledown under extremely difficult conditions. Flying under fire, over difficult mountainous terrain, in extremely turbulent winds and heavy snow showers, Captain Drennan repeatedly put his own life at risk. His complete disregard for his own safety undoubtedly saved many lives.

His conduct was courageous and outstanding and inspired his fellow pilots. Captain Drennan's was a superb individual contribution to the successful outcome of the battle, carried out at great personal risk.

I was on the *QE2* because I was a very late arrival, having joined the squadron on the day they sailed from Southampton. I'd done a quick Scout refresher course. I was not a war reinforcement, but they wanted another officer, and I happened to be available. I had to do the refresher course because I hadn't flown a Scout for almost two years. So I did the course, got all my kit and reported to the squadron on the day they sailed.

Corporal Jay Rigg, my air gunner and co-pilot, and I arrived in the Falklands on 1 June, just after the battle for Goose Green, so we were latecomers, really. Being aviators, we went to all the places of interest where things were happening, so we got acclimatized very quickly. We had to start off doing recces in Lafonia to check for enemy there and the Army Air Corps on its own captured seven Argentinians there. That was our first aggressive contact with the enemy. We'd seen prisoners before, at Goose Green, where there were hundreds of prisoners everywhere, bodies being buried, and all sorts of things happening. I'd been in hostile situations before, both in Ireland and Rhodesia, but this was the first all-out shooting war that either of us had been involved in. I'd joined the Army in 1964 and had been training all these years, and eighteen years later I came into my first real war. And, thank God, it proved that all the training over the years does in fact pay off.

We were doing all sorts of things from the time we landed until the final push, one of which involved us in taking out suspected observation positions in the high ground to the north of Goose Green. They also reckoned there were Exocets on a place called Lively Island so three Scouts were sent to take them out, but we never found them. Up until the night of Tumbledown we were flying every day. We flew sixty hours in fourteen days, which is about two months' flying normally, in a squadron. But we got used to it, got used to each other, and into a routine. Some days we never stopped the engine from about half an hour before dawn until half an hour after dark. We would go on board a ship for fuel, or have a 'hot refuel' when we refuel the aircraft without stopping the engines; then we could get out and have a pee or sometimes a cup of coffee. It was particularly good on the back of some of the ships which were crewed by the Chinese hands in all their flashproof gear. One man used to keep giving us a can of Coke and others used to give us a mug of Bovril, but the ace man was the one who gave us little rice balls! They'd got such smiles on their faces when they gave these things to us; they felt they were doing something – they were giving us food, doing their part. They kept us going a lot of times, when we were hungry and tired. They couldn't speak a word of English but they understood. For the rest of the day we used to live on Dextrose tablets.

We had twenty-four-hour ration packs which consisted of tinned mince or chicken supreme which we could have hot or cold. After we got settled at Fitzroy we had one of our men open all the packs and pile all this stuff into the pot and heat it. It was pretty tasty.

When we went on the back of any ship, they'd give us as much fresh food as they could spare. We couldn't get eggs, but if they had a spare loaf or two, because they had their own bakery, they'd give it to us. We found sailors very generous and helpful people and many of our aircrew formed firm friendships with them.

By the time of the Tumbledown battle Jay and I had developed an extraordinary rapport – a tremendous trust. When we were flying towards Goat Ridge, out of the half-darkness came this voice: 'Do you know where you're going?' I replied, 'Trust me, for God's sake, trust me.' And he did. I believe that was a most important moment for both of us, because if I'd mucked it up then, he would never have trusted me again – there would always have been a tension.

From the day we arrived we were really preparing for

the big push on Stanley. We were to assist the Scots
Guards on Tumbledown which I was glad about because
they are my old regiment. I'd left them a Colour-Sergeant.
On the night that Tumbledown started we'd been lying
there in our sleeping bags, trying to keep warm all night,
hoping that our lads wouldn't get a pasting. We were in an
old wooden garage with the wind whistling through,
waiting for the call. We got more and more tense as the
night progressed. Inside I nursed a little bit of jubilation,
because I thought, 'The infantry are not getting a pasting.
They must be really kicking the arses of the Argentinians,
without great expenses in casualties.' Then we were called
to go and pick up an injured Gurkha and a Scots
Guardsman from the side of Tumbledown.

Although we were about fifteen miles from
Tumbledown, as we moved to our briefing we could see it
all going on – it really looked and sounded like a big Guy
Fawkes night. We were briefed by the Squadron
Commander, and told that things were not terribly healthy
up there, but would we like to give it a go? He knew
exactly what the score was, and he knew it was a bit risky.
He was wearing his worried face! There was no order to
go. He said, 'Look, this is the score. The baddies are here,
they're resisting fiercely, but we've got a casualty here and
one there, who are both badly hurt and need to come out.'
The aircraft were sitting outside ready to go. It was pitch
black, no moon, and we didn't have nightsights. It was
going to be an interesting night!

So off we went to Tumbledown. We went up to the
RAP and went past that to Goat Ridge. From there we had
a look, and on one side was the Gurkhas' mortar platoon,
dug in in holes in the ground. Previously a Navy helicopter
had got that far and the Gurkhas had put a mortar straight
through his rotor blades without touching a blade. On
that, the Navy gave up – they wouldn't go any further.
They've got big helicopters, and without a doubt they
would have been hit. We didn't go forward of the
Gurkhas' mortar platoon because they'd probably have
scared us too. So we went round the other side and we

looked over the ridge and Jay pointed out where the first casualty was. I realized that no helicopter had been that far forward on Tumbledown. The Argentinians then opened fire on us. That was the first time anyone had fired at us – but it was not to be the last!

My big fear wasn't getting hit by a shell, because if you get hit by a shell, you die and that's the end of the story. But if you see a missile heading towards you, and you can tell by the smoke, that is rather worrying but you can avoid it if you're fast. So I said to Jay, 'If you see a missile, give me a shout,' which was greeted with raised eyebrows and a wry smile – apparently something had just passed by our tail and I hadn't seen it!

The first one we stuck our neck out for was a Gurkha. I went quite slowly down the side of this hill, at about fifty knots, because I'd decided that if we saw the smoke track of a missile coming towards us I'd put the aircraft on the ground bloody quickly because I'd rather break the aircraft by dumping it than have the missile impact blow us to a thousand bits.

Jay was keeping his eyes open; in fact, I think he had his visor down to stop his eyes from popping out! I was concentrating on missing the rocks on the way down and all the time there were puffs of smoke where shells were landing, which was quite spectacular – some were quite close to us. But because you're rather cocooned you rarely believe one is actually going to hit you – you daren't.

We found the Gurkha and they lifted him into the pod. We were using pods, like coffins, on the side of the helicopter, so we could get more casualties in. The back was open, because Jay was in and out all the time loading and unloading casualties. We could have had a pod on the left but it was taking minutes extra to turn the aircraft round to get back, so we didn't bother. I was just sitting there. I had nothing else to do. I was watching all this activity conducted by Jay around the aircraft, helping the Gurkhas to get their injured mate into the aircraft. I was just looking round, and there was a little puff of a shell landing here and a little puff there, and I thought, 'Christ,

I hope there's not a little puff here soon.' I was worried about the Scots Guardsman that we had to pick up as well, because I couldn't see him anywhere. We didn't know it at the time, but he was in a minefield; we'd been told that this chap would be brought to the same position as the Gurkha. Suddenly we saw this soldier on the horizon with his rifle signalling to us, so we went across and landed. We didn't know it was a minefield, but logic dictated that that was a good place to put one! I'd got plastic armour underneath my seat, so if I'd hit a mine, it would have to go through the aircraft and the armour on the floor and on my seat before it blasted a hole in me and I might have survived. Not so Jay: he was on the skid! If we'd hit a mine he'd have got killed. It was probably a good thing we didn't know. But that's the way it goes. It was our job to pick up this soldier and we did.

We then lifted off, turned round and went like a bat out of hell for the safety of the ridge behind Tumbledown. We didn't waste any time worrying about missiles and things, we were just going as fast as the Scout would go. We went zooming over the top and simultaneously we gave a great cheer because we were safe! We went whizzing back to the MDS (Main Dressing Station) where the two casualties went to the surgeons straight away. We were elated: we had broken the duck, lost our virginity! We'd managed to get in and get out again without getting killed. Then the floodgates opened.

We were authorized to return to the same area to start taking out Scots Guards casualties. We weren't nervous – we were totally eager. In fact, it was like we had ants in our pants. I couldn't stay still. I thought about Jay at this point, because I could have been taking him to his death. But he knew we had a job to do. He said to me, 'Think of your own self bleeding to death on a mountainside, and people saying, "I'm not going to come and get you." That wouldn't do.'

I thought of those poor wounded – some of them had been lying there for a number of hours. Some had died, some were dying. What moral alternatives did we have?

The answer is we had no alternatives. We went and did the job for which we were paid, and upon which these soldiers, and their families, were relying.

We went whizzing back out, accompanied by Sergeant Ian Roy and his mate, Corporal Johns, who started from the back of Tumbledown. We stopped off at the RAP, where the doctor and the medical assistants were. I came across an old friend of mine, Colour-Sergeant Archie Baird. We go back many years, to 1965, and I said, 'Hello, Archie. How's it going?' He said, 'Not so good,' and turned back to the doctor and spoke about one of the men who was lying injured in the middle of the battlefield. 'He's gone into a deep coma, and it looks like he's had it.' Both Jay and I sparked at the same time and thought, 'No, he bloody hasn't.' I said to Archie, 'Where is he?' and he said, 'Well, he's with Right Flank.' The significance of that escaped me at the time. I said to Jay, 'Right, wait for the grid reference and I'll run down and start the aeroplane.'

Where we had to get to was right at the front end of Tumbledown. Jay pointed out where it was on the map and I looked down and all hell was going on down there. We looked at each other and resolved we were going to go; it was one of those unsaid things.

We went past the Gurkha mortars and over the hill. We went to the same position as we'd been earlier – we knew we could get in and out of there without getting killed – and then we sneaked along the northern side of Tumbledown until we got to the friendly side of the ridge which was shielded from enemy machine-gun fire. We couldn't actually land because it was too steep so I dropped off Jay, who went half-way up the mountain to see what was happening rather than risk us being blown out of the air. He came across some Gurkhas lurking there, who apparently said to him something to the effect, 'Don't go round there. The enemy are there.' I saw Jay running back so I hovered and Jay came up underneath the aircraft and grabbed hold of the skid. I didn't have time to wait for him to climb in – he pulled himself up to the chest and then reached over and grabbed the inside of the door stanchion and pulled himself in. He was a bit breathless because he'd run a long way up the side of this hill to speak to these chaps. It only took a couple of minutes but it seemed like a lifetime, because we knew that people were up on the hill waiting for us, and there was no way they were going to get out except for us.

We didn't take the advice of the Gurkhas because we assumed we were going to survive! We had a look over this hill where shells were landing and making rather large bangs – it was quite pretty! We looked at each other as if to say, 'Well, shall we give it a whirl?' But there was no point in saying it because we both knew we would. We went along the side of the mountain and were speaking to the company concerned on the radio, and I could tell they were slightly disbelieving; the chap wasn't convinced that we were actually going there. I think he thought we'd got the call-sign wrong. He'd probably been told about the advice given to us, not to proceed beyond a certain grid reference. It was sound advice and very wise. The point was, this sort of advice is given to people at the time, and if you judge that the situation warrants disregarding that advice, you're quite free to do so providing you can justify it later, should the occasion arise. If we'd gone forward and got shot out of the sky, I'd have been branded the biggest twerp ever. But the motivation was high, because we knew there were people there. We also knew that the stretcher parties could not get back, because some of them had been killed by mortar. Therefore these people could not get back and survive. So, at the bottom line, we had no choice.

We flew along the side of the mountain and identified where these people were. One stood up – a brave boy – so we could actually see where they were and then we just went straight for them. We got in behind a rock and noticed there weren't too many Scots Guards about. It was obviously not too healthy a spot. We were looking right down on Port Stanley and it was the first time I'd seen it, and it was quite spectacular really. There we were, sitting on top of this mountain, looking over the edge at Port Stanley, and on the mountain just to our right were Argentinians who I later learned were having a real go at us with their machine guns. It was very much like a Second World War movie! Apparently the rounds were coming cracking over the top and some were bouncing off rock, but they never got us, thank God.

As we landed Jay jumped off, doing his Audie Murphy bit; we were both high on adrenalin by then. We landed on this steep slope and before I knew what happened, Jay had gone. He was out and he was loading these injured soldiers, one into the pod and one inside. They were being carried to us by the Scots Guards, big hairy soldiers looking after their wounded comrades with such tenderness and affection that it brought a lump to my throat. All the time the bullets were cracking over the top. I got a false sense of security because I was just sitting there while Jay was doing all the work. The longer we stayed there the closer the bullets got.

In my days in the police force in Dumfriesshire many years ago, one of my colleagues was a chap called Jack Oakes, whom I hadn't seen for years. Yet, there he was, standing there with all this fire coming down. He's the Pipe Sergeant of the regiment, but he was here in his secondary role as a medic. It was great to see him there, solid as a rock. He came in the front of the aircraft and we were doing the old sign-language bit. He was saying that he had a few more casualties who should come on this trip, so, with nods of the head and thumbs up, I promised that we would come back – if we survived to come back. He said, 'Okay then.' He was out there, the rest had sensibly gone by this time, but Jack was still there. He was very concerned about his men and was making sure that we were coming back. He's a very conscientious person and a brave man. I gave my word, and that meant a lot to him.

We had two casualties, both badly hurt. We managed to get Lieutenant Bob Lawrence into the back to be looked after by Jay, and the other one, with severe chest and gut injuries, we put in the pod. Unfortunately Bob Lawrence was badly placed in the aircraft and had his head, which had a bullet lodged in it, very exposed to the bitter cold air. Jay had this young lad's injured head on his knee. Unbelievably, he was still conscious and looking up at Jay and muttering. Jay put his furry hat on Bob Lawrence's head to protect him, but it flew away. Bob Lawrence then tried to get up, but fell down, so Jay pulled him round a bit and put his body in front of him. We were very determined this brave lad wasn't going to die because even with injuries of such severity he was still fighting to live.

We didn't bother with stealth. We dived over the side, gave a great cheer, and sunk down the side of this mountain as fast as the Scout would go, and as soon as we got past Goat Ridge, we were safe again! We'd got the casualties out – and thankfully they both lived.

When we got back the Scots Guards control station called up on the radio and said, 'Will you go to a different location to pick up some casualties?' I said, 'No, because I've promised call-sign 1 (which was Jack's) that I'll go back there.' We had to go back, Jack was relying on us; so were the other people, but they would have to wait just a short while longer.

All the casualties were delivered to the surgeons at Fitzroy which was a twelve-minute round trip from Tumbledown, and we went as fast as the Scout would travel. We dropped the casualties off and came straight back and got another two, went back to the hospital, which was an old shack, a so-called Community Centre, and refuelled. Our aircraft technicians were there waiting. By the time we'd touched down, these blokes, who were used to working under the rotors, were unloading the casualties and carrying them out in no time. It was really tremendous.

After the first lift a reporter got into the aircraft. He wanted to get up to Goat Ridge, which is near Tumbledown, to find out what was going on, and full marks to him. At least he had courage. But we were very impatient at the time because we knew there were other casualties to collect; we'd seen the state of the lads we'd already brought back, and knew that we had to get back – and get back bloody quickly. Anything that distracted us from that provoked immediate anger. This poor chap, who was doing his job and doing it very well, jumped in and we both resented it and said so.

After three trips to the nasty area we'd taken out six of Jack's casualties but there were more along the really dangerous side of the ridge – the side of the ridge open to gunfire from Mount William, where there was no protection. We went back again to Jack's pick-up point and got the last one in on the litter on the side. I got my thanks from Jack at the end of the war, in Ajax Bay. I was walking along when I heard the haunting sound of bagpipes. It was coming from a shed. I went inside and there was Jack. We didn't say a word; he just put the bagpipes under one arm, came forward and shook my hand.

After we'd picked up the last of Jack's casualties we still had a spare space in the back and I was damned if we were going to go back without filling it. So we hopped over the ridge because that was the only way of getting the other casualties out. We had to go along the really nasty side of the mountain and pick them up.

We were nipping in among the rocks, more or less a 'bring out your dead' situation – we were like a tumbrel. In fact, they brought out their living and stuck them in the back. We nipped back and forward a few times and on one of our trips we saw Major John Kiszely, whom I've known for years, who just smiled, which was nice. He probably thought, 'What are you doing here, you maniac?' He's a good egg, and a fine officer. I was very pleased to have helped his boys in particular, because they'd taken a hammering, but in the best British tradition they'd really got in there and shown the Argentinians a bit of cold steel.

We got some injured out near him and by now we were getting quite cocky, because we knew there had been a lot of activity trying to knock us down, but we'd survived, possibly because of a mixture of adrenalin and good camouflage. It was amazing, really, because the adrenalin takes you to such a high; I felt full of zing and vigour, like I rarely feel. I know Jay was the same because he was in and out of the helicopter loading the wounded and looking after them on the way back like a man possessed. It was quite incredible. Neither of us had slept all night, but then neither had those lads who were fighting and we weren't going to stop until they did.

We went back again to pick up some more casualties. I decided, after consultation, that we would go round the front of Mount Harriet because we'd never been that way. So we went whizzing round the front, going very fast, when over the radio came this voice that sounded like an exasperated mother talking firmly to a naughty boy. He said, 'Hello, Two Charlie. This is Zero. You're being shot at – again.' Just as if to say, 'If I get hold of you, I'm going to smack your arse!' So I realized that I'd made a mistake in coming that way. I started to do the old jigging-around bit so it would give us a fair chance of getting missed. The fact was, they'd missed us when we were closer to them, so there was no reason to suspect they were going to hit us now, when we were about another 500 metres away. But at the time I thought it was a stupid decision of mine – Jay also thought that, but he said something stronger than stupid! But it had saved about two minutes, and, to my mind, two minutes might mean the last gurgling breath of some poor soldier who'd got his blood running out of him. So I was prepared to chance it.

As we got closer to Tumbledown I heard over the radio that they'd found a soldier who had been severely injured, and asked me if I'd go in again. We'd been knocking the hell out of our aircraft for two hours and they hadn't killed us, so we thought, 'Let's get him out, let's go.' When we got there this poor lad was really in a bad way. He'd obviously got separated from his platoon, got badly shot up, fallen behind some rocks, and had been lying there for some hours before he was found. You could put someone in those rocks and you could search all day and not find them. But they'd found him, almost on his last gasp, and the doctors with the battalion had done a miraculous job in keeping him alive. We got him on board and he was just lying there, like a rag doll covered in gore, looking up at Jay with big, frightened, staring eyes. He was in a terrible state. Although it was freezing cold Jay took off his gloves and held his hand really tight. This poor lad was really holding on – as if he was holding on to his life. I kept looking back at him, thinking, 'Jesus Christ – I hope he makes it!' All the time he never let go of Jay's hand. Those terrible, big, staring eyes had gone into a look of death. I thought, 'He's never going to make it,' but I'd underestimated just how fast a Scout can go, because that time she flew very fast indeed. When a man's blood is ebbing out of him, every second is vital until the doctors get a needle into him. The decision to take that short cut, hairy as it was, probably saved his life.

But saving him wasn't just speed, I'm sure of that. Indelibly printed in my mind is Jay holding this dying lad's hand. He looked as if he was willing his strength to go from him into the other guy – and this lad did survive. Jay, who was twenty-one at the time, told me later that he was determined that he wouldn't let him die. He said, 'To see a guy the same age as me, with so much life left in him, dying – I couldn't let that happen!'

When we got that lad back, we knew there were no more serious casualties. I couldn't clasp Jay to my breast and say 'Well done' because I was strapped to the aeroplane! So we trundled back to Tumbledown and landed there, where they told us they'd seen white flags. I remember I jumped down and hugged Jay and the medic. I thought we could relax, but some Argentinians thought otherwise and took a few shots at us. But we knew we'd won and that we could slowly wind down – we'd been on the go for two hours. It had been frantic, equal to sprinting for two hours. We got so wound up and so keen that everything should go right and that we'd get there in time and get the casualties out. When the white flags were hoisted and all the baddies were running away, I couldn't believe it. I just said, 'Thank Christ for that.' I thought it was miraculous because we'd realized that we couldn't go on indefinitely with what we were doing; the risks were so great, they would have to hit us soon; the law of averages said that we'd get knocked down eventually. We were trying every trick in the book to avoid getting knocked down and they never hit us, not once. They certainly tried hard enough. We knew that there had been a lot of activity going on, but we didn't actually know fully how much. I was told a couple of days afterwards that they'd really had a good go at us from Mount William. They knew we were going to come back but they didn't know exactly where we were going to pop up; but I don't know how they missed us. I like to think that we used a bit of skill and cunning, the technique of flying an Army helicopter very close to the ground against a decent backdrop. But sometimes we had to expose ourselves to get the boys, and then they had a really good go at us. The lads on the ground told me that they could tell when we had arrived because there was a crescendo of gunfire from the front end of the mountain! We weren't totally oblivious to the fact that it was very unhealthy to be there!

We then started to take out the less seriously wounded. We were taking life easy, just picking up the people with small shrapnel wounds and things. One chap was very dazed, as shell-shock or explosive victims are, and I sat him in the back of the aircraft. We couldn't strap him in but we made sure he was all right and then we went rounding up more casualties. All the time we were stopping and picking up these lads, this chap was sitting in the back of the Scout. As we picked up the last one I looked round and he'd gone – he'd absconded. I found out later that he went back to his comrades.

You've got to work yourself up into a sense of antagonism towards your opposer or else you can't do anything unspeakable to him, and I had done this. I didn't like Argentinians, and I wouldn't admit to myself that they were the same as us; you can't, else you can't do warlike things to them. About an hour after the war had ended and we had finished taking out all the casualties, I felt drained, and I'm sure Jay did as well, because he'd been far more energetic than I had. I felt drained and I also felt a deep resentment towards the Argentinians. Near us was a row of our lads who were dead, lying under a tarpaulin, with their feet sticking out. Young men – never to laugh again. I was thinking of them when I was brought an Argentinian casualty who was obviously in great pain as he'd been badly shot up. He was just an eighteen-year-old lad, of peasant stock. He looked bewildered and terribly afraid. He'd got big brown eyes – I shall never forget them, they were staring out like chapel hat pegs. He was obviously terrified that these British swines were going to do terrible things to him, but all we were going to do was take him straight away to a surgeon where he'd get exactly the same treatment as our boys. He was well strapped up, so Jay put him on the litter, but the noise of the helicopter rotors and all the rest of it must have really scared him. He was in a hell of a state, so Jay just leaned over and pinched his cheek and gave it a gentle shake and a pat. This lad's whole face lit up with relief and all the anger and resentment which I felt against him evaporated in an instant. It was great, because that purged my system completely. You can't allow yourself great humanitarian feelings when people are trying to kill you, but, when the battle is over, it's like after a boxing match – you're all friends together. And I felt like that; I felt like reaching out and touching this chap and reassuring him, but I couldn't because I was strapped in, so I looked over at him and gave him a big wink. He must have seen this unshaven creature in a green hat, in the driving seat of a helicopter, winking at him and he smiled again. Jay then lowered the lid on him and we whizzed him off with the same urgency as our guys. After all, the war had ended and this soldier was in a bad state. We landed and when we took the lid off the litter, there was this lad looking terribly afraid again. It's not a pleasant experience in the Scout litter but Jay gave him another quick pinch of the cheek and a pat and a thumbs up and he was all right. You couldn't really speak to him because of the noise. I'd never seen a happy casualty before, but this bloke looked happy. That really gripped me.

The day they surrendered we continued doing our various flying tasks until night came: a pitch-black, horrible, moonless night with horizontal snow. When we went in to our old shack, snowflakes were coming in through the slats. I thought, 'Christ, it's not a nice night for flying.' I hoped I wouldn't have to fly, but about 10:30 the Welsh Guards called up on the radio and said they'd got a Guardsman on Sapper Hill who had a perforated ulcer and was in terrible pain; the doctor had said that if he wasn't brought out, the chances were that he would die. We were top of the pile so it was our turn to go.

We were worried not only about the weather but also about the Argentinians who hadn't handed in their weapons by this stage, and were very, very jumpy. So we taped over the lights in the aircraft with masking tape so there'd just be this droning sound in the sky but they wouldn't be able to see us. The snow had stopped but the night was horrible: it was black and filthy. The only way we could find Sapper Hill was by using the light from a few fires around Stanley and the lights of an Argentinian hospital ship anchored just off Port Stanley. We flew along the coastline and the only way we could tell it was the coast was the luminescence of the waves hitting the shore. We were not only having difficulty seeing but were being buffeted by very strong winds. Then, to make matters worse, our radar altimeter went unserviceable, so we couldn't tell how high we were or where we were above the ground! We could tell roughly from the pressure altimeter, but the radar altimeter is the one which tells exactly how high you are. Somehow, everything seemed against us. The war was over, they'd signed the surrender, yet here we were on this vile night, travelling almost blind.

We flew along and found the area of Sapper Hill, but we couldn't identify it specifically. There were fires all over the place, but we couldn't see the landing lights. Normally, at night, they put out a 'T' in lights, but we couldn't see this. So we couldn't go in to land. We tried to get in for about an hour and eventually we lost radio contact with them. Things were not going right. At last I saw a winking light down below, and assumed it was them trying to signal us. We went down into a low hover to find it was the indicator on a tracked vehicle! But no Welshmen.

By now we were experiencing intermittent snowstorms and we were getting a bit weary. We took off again, heading west. I had kept a good mental plot of where we were. But shortly after we'd taken off Jay said to me, 'There's a mountain ahead!' And I said, 'No, there isn't. We're going to miss it.' I thought we were about 200 metres further north than we actually were, but because he couldn't see anything he'd been keeping a damn good mental plot. He turned out to be dead right. Suddenly, he was screaming at me, 'There's a mountain ahead, you cunt!' I slammed on the landing light and coming towards us at an alarming rate was sheer wall-to-wall rock. I took frantic evasive action and somehow – and I'll never know how – I managed to swerve to the side of it. I thought then, 'Jesus! Thank God I trust my partner. Why did I not trust him a few seconds earlier?' I'd trusted him implicitly during the course of all that activity during the battle, through which we'd both come unscathed, and yet I'd doubted him at a vital moment. I thought I was right but I was wrong; terribly, almost fatally, wrong. We headed out to sea for a bit of a breather, because we were both trembling. Jay started to apologize for the terms he'd used to attract my attention to the fact that we were about to get killed. I recall vividly saying, 'Please don't apologize. You were absolutely right. I am exactly as you described me.'

After the war had finished, after going through all that we'd been through together, imagine my stupidity killing us both. In fact, we got back, having not picked up the casualty, and I decided that Jay had had quite enough. He'd just saved our bacon, and I couldn't waste such a partner. Jay had worked himself to the bone; he was absolutely tremendous. In fact, if I'd been the guy who was dishing out the gongs after this little escapade, I'd have given him one the size of a dinner plate, because he really was quite something. He went into that war as a young man of twenty-one and he came out of it a very mature man. I saw him change from a youth to a man in a matter of minutes. He was terribly brave and I shall never forget him standing on the skid at 140 miles an hour in a horrid gale of freezing cold, sub-zero temperatures, looking after these poor wounded who were almost dead. He did it and he did a fantastic job.

Mick Sharp, who's a Warrant Officer and a very experienced aviator, decided to come with me and have another go at getting this casualty out. We went back and this time we had radio communications and after a few attempts we managed to get in and find him, but he was in a very bad way. At the time we took off there was a really bad snowstorm – the snow was horizontal. Had we thought about self-preservation we'd have stayed there until the storm had passed, which might have taken thirty minutes. But by then this chap could have stopped gurgling in the back – he'd have probably been dead. Because the wind was so strong the only way we could take off was hover-taxi over the top of Sapper Hill and take off from the top. We went to the top and took off and hit such a bump of turbulence that it toppled my main artificial horizon in the aircraft, so I lost my main reference and I could see nothing but pitch black. All I could do was fly by my emergency artificial horizon, which is a tiny little thing. I said to Mick Sharp, who was in the back trying to calm down this groaning soldier who, because of his pain, was making a lot of noise, 'I've lost my main horizon, Mick.' He, knowing just what that meant, reacted so calmly – it was incredible. He just sat in the back of the aircraft, looking after the soldier, chatting away, keeping me from doing anything silly. Because I didn't want to hit anything I flew out to sea and waited. I thought, 'What else are they going to throw at me tonight?'

The chap groaning in the back kept putting me off. I was flying on instruments over the sea with no way of being recovered by radar, or any other assistance. We had to find our own way back to our base at Fitzroy. I got my instruments working properly again, but by now we were in a thick snowstorm. I turned back and found the coast by looking vertically downwards because there was no horizontal vision at all. I saw this faint luminescence off the shore, and I knew where we were then, so I turned left and flew along the coastline. I was flying on instruments, looking vertically down, out of my right eye, past my right foot, to keep following this luminescence. We seemed to be going well when suddenly we lost it in a really thick patch of snowstorm. I could see nothing. I thought, 'If there's anyone up there, look after me, because I really need you badly.' I said to Mick, 'I've lost it.' I meant I'd lost the shoreline, but I thought instantly that had I been sitting in the back and the pilot had told me he'd lost it, I'd take it to mean he'd lost control. So I hastily reassured Mick, but there was not a squeak from the back – all he was doing was trying to keep the casualty quiet and give me the radar altimeter readings. He was just calling 150, 140, 150, 130. The figures were so erratic because of the turbulence; we were up and down like a whore's drawers. But Mick was so calm, he was just sitting there as if he was on a Sunday outing; it was like having a stabilizer in the back. He is a very, very brave man, because I was scared out of my wits, and I was flying the thing! Eventually, I found the coastline and we managed to get back. People were a bit worried at the other end that we were not going to succeed. They knew we'd got the casualty but they were worried that we wouldn't get back because we were in real trouble. I'd never been so frightened in all my life. It was horrifying.

I find there are very, very few things which frighten me now, compared to how scared I was on that night – not the flying about with people shooting at me, but that one frightening, terrifying night in the dark. All my experiences before and since pall into total insignificance compared to that.

The Falklands experience has made me review my priorities considerably and things which were important to me before the Falklands are of total insignificance now. I'm a different person, I think, because my priorities are so different. I'm far more relaxed than I used to be. I used to be terribly ambitious, and now I've found that ambition is totally irrelevant. I look and see that I've got arms and legs, I can see, and I'm very thankful for that, and life is much, much sweeter now.

I think we all hope that when it comes to the test that we're going to find reserves of whatever is required. As military people, we all train for war, and hope it never comes, but we train for it seriously. I think we all have this nagging doubt in the back of our minds that when it comes to the crunch, when our life's on the line, are we going to be shrinking violets or are we going to find the depths of courage required to do our jobs, and do them properly? That is something which has always been in the back of my mind, and I'm relieved that I've actually been put to the test and passed. I'm sure nearly everyone else passed as well. I don't want to do it again, but I've looked inside myself to see what was there and I wasn't too ashamed of what I found. I can look at myself in the morning, when I'm having a shave, and not feel guilty.

Command at Sea

Rear-Admiral John Woodward

Royal Navy

Knight Commander of the Bath

At HQ the business is cool-headed management. You are into careful planning and the assessment of chances; you have to disengage from the battle cries and the hot lead. You are always hearing first-hand reports of damage and disaster, and your job is to distance yourself because they are naturally highly emotive, almost confusion factors. If you don't distance yourself you can become frightened and distressed, and that will cloud your judgement. Despite your cares, you have to calculate the odds, the gains and the losses.

The decisions I liked least were when I had to send friends in harm's way when, of course, I couldn't go in myself; they were very uncomfortable. I remember ringing up the Captain of *Alacrity*, Commander Craig, on the secure telephone to ask him to go through Falkland Sound at night. Before landing in San Carlos we needed to find out what was going on there, how difficult the passage would be by night, and whether the opposition had laid any mines. I said, 'I want you to go into the Sound, have a look round and keep them on their toes. If you find anybody, do what seems necessary. Come out the northern end and be back offshore with the battle group by dawn.' I wasn't going to tell him about the mines; I dissembled because I never wanted to put the frighteners on my captains any more than I had to. But Craig, bless him, saw through me straight away: 'Oh, I expect, Admiral, you'd like me to go in and out of the northern entrance several times before I come home?' Realizing I'd been rumbled, I replied, 'Well, that's quite a good idea, but why do you suggest it?' And he said, 'I imagine, Admiral, that you want to find out if there are any mines in the northern entrance.' 'Oh,' I said, 'it's funny you should mention it, but we would be very glad to know and we'll do our best to bail you out later if we can.' I thought it was a bloody brave thing to do: a small ship, thousands of miles from home, on his own and knowing damn well the risks involved, which in this case were high. I had already assessed that there was no other way to do the job, and, probably, so had he. He had seen instantly what I wanted and had accepted it with humour. Fortunately, it all turned out well.

Throughout the campaign I was surrounded by such men, whom I knew and could trust, and by men who also knew me, and one of the good things when doing the cool planning bit was knowing that others were doing it too.

Most days on *Hermes* my life settled into a routine, albeit a routine I'd never done before. With the management of a large force you're trying to build a picture of everything that's going on, and there was a mass of periodically repeated tasks to do in a fairly routine manner. You have to follow everything that's going on in order to find the odd thing because it's the odd feature that you're going to have to deal with. You must be ready for the unexpected that can come at you from nowhere, as it did to the poor old *Sheffield* in three and a half minutes flat. I was often encouraged to go off and visit the other ships, but I never felt that was part of my job. I always thought that things could go wrong very quickly and to be absent from my place of duty on *Hermes* wouldn't be too sharp. For instance, I remember when *Sheffield* got hit and the information came into our Ops Room, where we all were, one or two people were very badly shaken. Voices were raised and getting louder and one said, 'Come on, Admiral, you must do something!' I had to say, 'No. Leave it to the people on the spot. There's one frigate already there with a helicopter, and another frigate on the way. All we need to do is tell the chap who's there first to take charge of the on-scene action. If we get involved with the tiny detail we'll only bring the operation to a grinding halt.'

On that occasion there had been a near-panic reaction; people were pressing me to do something, when all we had to do was sit cool and calm. Panic is infectious. I've always been conscious that the way the Captain performs his duty is vital to morale. Unlike a land force leader, you're comforted by the familiarity of your surroundings and the danger may be less immediate, but even when you're 100 miles away from where it's actually happening and you're sitting in a large tin box with a low light, people still need to turn to the place where the boss is sitting to see what's written on his face.

The Ops Room on *Hermes* was about fifteen feet by fifteen feet with fairly low lighting in order that we could see the various radar screens and monitors. I had a funny little cabin just down the passage, about nine feet by nine, with a little bunk, a tiny table and a shower: a cell, really. About twenty people worked in the Ops Room checking the data with a Group Warfare Officer on watch, doing the minute-to-minute management of the battle group. Normally, comparatively junior officers would have held that position, which would have meant calling the Admiral every few minutes to take a decision. I thought that I was likely to be down south for a long while and that if called to make decisions that any Captain could make I would be running around all the time and incapable of doing the long-term thinking or planning. So I chose to change the system and co-opted Captain Buchanan and Captain Woodhead for the job. They worked twelve hours on and twelve hours off from late April until July and did marvellously well. Both Captains were friends of mine and had worked with me before, so it was a very easy relationship, for me, anyway! I don't know how I would have got through without them.

I wasn't physically tired but, like everybody else, I was mentally tired from the strain. I realized that I could go on for a couple of months without any real exercise because

I'd done that before, and I made a point of keeping myself as rested as I could. You can remain alert and in good, decisive, reactive condition for very long periods as long as you look after yourself, almost cocoon yourself. When I'd done it before, I didn't sleep for more than forty-two minutes at a stretch, and that was once in two months. You can only do it easily if you're used to it. You have to discipline yourself.

I used to find when I got back to my cabin after being in the Ops Room I'd sit down and say, 'Well, what about writing a letter home, or reading a book, or watching a chat show on the internal television?' Then I'd say to myself, 'Now, hang on a minute. Just think through yesterday again, or the day before. Think through what you intend to do next week and whether there is any way you can find a solution for that problem which has proved intractable so far. Just remember you're here to do a job. Go over and over things again.' So, in the end, even had it gone wrong, I would have been able to say to myself, 'Well, I did give it the absolute maximum amount of thought and time I possibly could. If in the end my solution was found wanting, well, so be it, it was wanting, but it wasn't for lack of effort.'

As manager of the organization, there are lots of things you have to keep to yourself – you live with your responsibilities. I found my diary a great safety valve. You can get rid of the steam and hassle of the day and you feel better when you've done it. But no one should take too much notice of what's written; often it's just the steam. I think my diary was my main outlet for my feelings.

On the way south we didn't know we were going to war, but we might have been, so there were a lot of conflicting requirements on what I said. I had to convince the workforce, my own blokes, that we could do a good job and we had a good chance – you don't tell anyone they're going to lose, even if you think they are. Then there was the opposition: the message I wanted to pass on to the Argentinians was one of determination, efficiency and confidence. Bearing in mind the national characteristics of

440

the Argentinians, I was slightly more pushy in what I said to them; my own workforce may not have been able to take it, but the opposition probably needed it. Then there was the home market to consider, ranging from the Prime Minister to the man in the street – they all wanted to hear something.

In the face of such demands and constraints the only safe answer was to say nothing but, of course, you're not allowed to do that. As a consequence I got variously interpreted and variously misunderstood. I most regret being reported as saying, 'What I expect is a walkover.' I know that sometimes you think you've said one thing and it's heard as something else, and I accept entirely that Brian Hanrahan, a bloody good, objective journalist, reported it the way he heard it. But what I actually meant was something very different: I said I would much prefer a walkover, in the sense of a tennis match where your opponent doesn't turn up and you're given a 'walkover'. The press had a field day, *Private Eye* talking about the 'jumpy little bugger' saying 'it's going to be a walkover'. That caused a lot of trouble back home and I had to live with the repercussions for a while.

Obviously PR is important, but at the time I had rather more worrisome things on my mind. The thing is, it's not my trade. If I were an actor or a politician it would be different, but I hated the publicity, and still do. Going from Captain of a ship to Admiral of a whole group of ships means you go from being a bit-part actor to the lead, where all the lights are on you and the microphones are everywhere. I'm not a stage sort of person. I've always preferred to do my business from the edge. I therefore found the change to being an Admiral and, indeed, an internationally known one, extremely difficult. I'd been rather pitchforked into the front of the limelight business.

Some of the men were very apprehensive about the probability of actually going to war. It was the biggest fleet of British ships to sail since South Korea and, of course, most of us had not seen active service before. I joined the Navy in 1946 at the age of thirteen and a half but I didn't go to sea until I was seventeen and a half. The first time I'd really had to face the fact that I might have to go to war as part of my profession was during the Suez crisis in 1956. Up to then the Navy had been a way of life rather than a job where you might get killed in action. I had to try to explain this commitment to a lot of young people on the way south. One man's contract had expired a few days after we sailed, but as a fully trained man, I told him we had to keep him: one trained man was worth ten volunteers. He took it very well. Professionals have no choice other than to go along, and I must say that during the campaign I never had to exhort people to do things. There were always too many willing to go – I had to hold them back.

As we went further south there was a strong sense of time pressing, because the whole operation could only last for a limited period. We knew we hadn't got a forward base and therefore we would eventually run out of everything. I reckoned my ships were going to fall apart by the end of June, especially the aircraft carriers because we had none to replace them. We had replacements for most other things, such as frigates and destroyers, but we also were short of Sea Wolf systems and Sea Harriers; our force for long-range air defence was thus a very limited asset. For various reasons we actually couldn't have a landing force in before about mid-May and we had to be finished by 1 July, so there could only be a six-week period for the land battle. It was quite a close thing, as it turned out, because, of course, we finished in mid-June. Fortunately, Sea Harriers were quite plentiful because we didn't lose them, which was a relief, and the carriers continued satisfactorily, with *Hermes* running for over three months and *Invincible* for more than four. But the destroyers and frigates were really falling apart by the end, because they were the workhorses. On the last night, 13/14 June, I agreed to give General Moore four ships for Naval gunfire support for the land forces, and unfortunately, because of damage and wear and tear, I think only one ship managed to turn up. Air defence systems were also badly affected by weather and action damage: on 14 June only about one-eighth of the systems were available to us. If the opposition had found us then, we'd have been in a very poor way.

I would say there was one really low moment in the campaign. This was 25 May, which is the big Argentinian naval day; their aircraft carrier is even named after it. I wrote in my diary, 'They will probably do something today.' Then, later in the day, I wrote, 'Well, they don't seem to have done much, maybe we'll get away with it.' That was my mistake. Within the hour they got the *Coventry*, and shortly afterwards the *Atlantic Conveyor*.

As for the *Belgrano*, enough has been said on that subject to satisfy anyone, I'd have thought, but personally I have always been of the same view as the Argentine Admiral Lombardo, who effectively called it the fortunes of war and no more or less than he would have done in the same circumstances.

The finest example of straight calm in the face of extreme anxiety that I can recall was shown by Bill Canning, the Captain of the *Broadsword*, at the time of the sinking of the *Coventry*. He was on one of the high-frequency radios telling me about the situation as the attack occurred. I was about one hundred and ten miles away listening to what was effectively a running commentary. He was telling me what he was doing and suddenly said, 'I'm going to stop for a moment – something's happened.' There was a twenty-five-second pause and then he came back and continued describing what was going on, in exactly the same voice. During that break two bombs had passed straight through the stern of his ship. Remarkable cool – he just carried on in the same calm voice, even when the *Coventry* was hit seconds later by the next wave of aircraft.

Another facet of character occurs to me. I don't much like talking about the campaign, and perhaps I should have known better than to ask one of my COs, long after the war was all over, what was the single, most important lesson he had learnt down there. I immediately added,

'No, don't answer that.' But he said, 'No, I will. I learnt to cry.' A fantastic thing for a young commander to say to his Admiral; an honest and a very courageous thing to say. I think a lot of people did learn to cry – it is, after all, a very important thing to learn.

I took a particular interest in the SAS raid on Pebble Island since I always felt, rightly or wrongly, that it was one of 'my' operations. It went very well despite some major difficulties and was completed in a very short time. One of the features was that it was rehearsed, very professionally prepared, in five days flat. It's most unusual to go into an unreconnoitred area, working against aircraft not seen before on the ground and destroy eleven in the middle of the night in a gale. It was a great success story – the biggest single disaster for the Argentinian air force. Later I flew out to Pebble Island in a Sea King and the memory of it is still very clear. Green fields similar to the north-west of Scotland, lovely cold, bracing wind, and there in the middle of this peaceful scene those eleven aircraft, looking almost undamaged until you got close. The bombs the SAS used had blown their centres out, absolutely wrecking them as far as flying was concerned but leaving the rest of the aircraft largely intact. They created, especially the Pucarás which looked like praying mantises, a surreal and uncomfortable image. Everything was fresh, brisk and clean apart from this dead, deserted machinery – quite symbolic.

The day after the surrender I landed on board *Fearless* on the way to meet General Moore at Port Stanley. General Menendez was on board and I was asked whether I would like to meet him. I decided I didn't wish to. I could easily have become extremely angry; the temptation was to say, 'What a bloody waste of time and valuable lives and limbs! Why couldn't you have bloody well given in on 3 April?'

In Port Stanley General Moore suggested we went down to the airstrip to have a look at all the prisoners. The General and I, his Colonel, his Chief of Staff and a young subaltern armed to the teeth all packed into a car and we drove right onto the airstrip. It was the first time I had seen the Argentinians at close quarters, which was ironic, and it was a nervous moment; 5,000 men were there and we had only one properly armed bloke. I found myself a bit reluctant to unlock the car door but the General leaped out and off we went for a walk down the runway. He was quite right, they were docile, and I felt more than a litle foolish.

Up until March 1982 I never dreamed we'd go to war with Argentina. The whole emphasis of the armed forces is to be so patently good enough that it is not worth the candle for the opposition to take action against you. That's the thesis, the underlying precept of our lives. The concept of deterrence is important, and in the history of that funny little war we did in fact fail it. We withdrew HMS *Endurance* and it was read by the Argentinians as the final pull-out. They thought, 'There are only forty-odd Marines left, and as long as we don't kill them, the job will be done.' You can't entirely blame the Argentinians for not being deterred, but at the time we could not find it in our hearts to believe that the removal of the *Endurance* was of any real significance. But that's the danger with deterrence – you don't know when the balance is being tipped until it's too damned late.

Glossary

A number given after a name, e.g. Roberts 32, identifies which Roberts is meant in a unit which may have many men with the same surname. A number given after a rank, e.g. Warrant Officer 2, denotes Class 2.

amtrack – amphibious tracked vehicle
ASW – anti-submarine warfare
Augusta 109 – troop-carrying helicopter used by the Argentinians
BAOR – British Army of the Rhine
BC – Battery Commander
bergen – infantry backpack containing mess kit, sleeping bag, etc.
Blowpipe – hand-held wire-guided ground-to-air missile
Bomb Alley – San Carlos Water
bug out – vacate a place in a hurry
CAP – combat air patrol; hence capping, i.e. patrolling
casevac – casualty evacuation
chaff – radar-reflecting tinsel to deter homing missiles
Chinook – large twin-rotor helicopter with a lifting capability of up to 10 tons, used by both the British and the Argentinians
CO – Commanding Officer
Cobra – anti-tank rocket
CQMS – Company Quartermaster-Sergeant
CSM – Company Sergeant-Major
cud – countryside
84 – tube-launched 84mm anti-tank rocket. Also known as Carl Gustav
endex – end of exercise
EOD – Explosive Ordnance Disposal

Exocet – multi-role guided missile
FIDF – Falkland Islands Defence Force
FN – Belgian-manufactured automatic rifle
fragged – injured or killed by a fragment of artillery
FST – Field Surgical Team
Gazelle – British-built reconnaissance and attack helicopter
GPMG – general-purpose machine gun
GR3 – RAF Harrier version designed for ground-attack role
Harrier – British vertical take-off and landing strike aircraft
helo – helicopter
Hercules – American-built C-130 transport aircraft, used by
    both the British and the Argentinians
IV – intravenous
LAC – Leading Aircrewman
LSL – landing ship logistics. Lightly armed troop-carrying
    ship equipped for helicopter operations, RFA manned –
    e.g. *Sir Galahad, Sir Tristram*
Lynx – British-built armed helicopter
Matra – French 68mm ground-to-air rocket
Mirage – French-built fighter-bomber, used by the
    Argentine Air Force
MoD – Ministry of Defence
NAAFI – Navy, Army and Air Force Institutes. The
    organization that provides canteens and shops for
    British military personnel
NCO – non-commissioned officer
negligent discharge – unintentional firing of a weapon
NGLO – Naval Gunfire Liaison Officer
NGSFO – Naval Gunfire Support Forward Observation
O(Orders)Group – a meeting at which a unit's officers are
    briefed by the commander
OC – Officer Commanding
OP – observation post
Op – operation
Operation Corporate – code-name for the Falklands
    campaign
Operation Paraquat – code-name for the recovery of South
    Georgia
pan – aircraft parking area

PCT – Parachute Clearing Troop

PO – Petty Officer

POW – prisoner of war

Pucará – twin piston-engined ground-attack aircraft, used by the Argentine Air Force

Puma – Anglo-French-designed medium-lift helicopter, used by the Argentinians

RAMC – Royal Army Medical Corps

RAP – Regimental Aid Post

Rapier – British-built ground-to-air missile system with a four-missile launcher

reverse slope – the slope of a hill that has the summit between you and the enemy, i.e. the slope away from the enemy

RFA – Royal Fleet Auxiliary/Royal Field Artillery

RMO – Regimental Medical Officer

RQMS – Regimental Quartermaster-Sergeant

R & R – rest and recuperation

rubber dicked – caught out, cheated

SAM – surface-to-air missile

sangar – a protective stone wall built by troops

SAS – Special Air Service

SBS – Special Boat Squadron. A Royal Marine small craft Commando unit

Scimitar – light tank armed with a 76mm gun and with excellent cross-country capability

scoff, as in 'make a scoff' – prepare food, get a meal ready

Scorpion – light tank armed with a 30mm automatic cannon and with excellent cross-country capability

scott, as in 'go out for a scott' – take a look, have a scout round

Scout – British Army communications helicopter

Seacat – sea-to-air medium-range missile

Sea Harrier – Harrier version fitted with Blue Fox radar

Sea King – Naval anti-submarine helicopter, capable of carrying 20 men

Sea Wolf – short-range low-level sea-to-air missile

second dickie, as in 'to fly second dickie' – to fly as co-pilot

Sidewinder – American-built, heat-seeking air-to-air missile fitted to Sea Harriers

sitrep – situation report

66/66 LAW – light anti-tank weapon. American-built short-range anti-tank rocket carried by infantry

SLR – self-loading rifle

SMG – submachine gun

SNCO – senior non-commissioned officer

SNEB – an aircraft-launched rocket system

SS-11 – air-to-air or air-to-ground missile fitted to British helicopters

star/starlight shell – an illumination shell

Sunray – radio code-name for a commanding officer

Super Etendard – French-built, single-seater naval attack aircraft used by the Argentinians

TA – Territorial Army

tab/tabbing – Parachute Regiment vernacular for a long, tough walk

TAC 1 – a division of Tactical Headquarters

Tigercat – British ground-to-air missile

2I/C – Second-in-Command

UKLF -United Kingdom Land Forces

u/s – unserviceable

UXB – unexploded bomb

Vulcan – British four-jet long-range bomber, can carry up to twenty-one 1,000lb bombs

Wessex – British troop-carrying helicopter

wet, as in 'make a wet' – make a hot drink

WO – Warrant Officer

WRENS – Women's Royal Naval Service

Zulu time – Greenwich Mean Time

yomping – Royal Marine vernacular for a long, tough walk

Index

455

457

A SELECTION OF BESTSELLERS FROM SPHERE

FICTION

DUNN'S CONUNDRUM	Stan Lee	£2.95 ☐
GOLDEN TALLY	Pamela Oldfield	£2.95 ☐
HUSBANDS AND LOVERS	Ruth Harris	£2.95 ☐
SWITCH	William Bayer	£2.25 ☐

FILM & TV TIE-IN

BOON	Anthony Masters	£2.50 ☐
LADY JANE	Anthony Smith	£1.95 ☐

NON-FICTION

THE FALL OF SAIGON	David Butler	£3.95 ☐
THE AMBRIDGE YEARS	Dan Archer	£2.50 ☐
THE SUNDAY EXPRESS DIET BOOK	Marina Andrews	£2.50 ☐
THE PRICE OF TRUTH	John Lawrenson and Lionel Barber	£3.50 ☐

All Sphere books are available at your local bookshop or newsagent, or can be ordered direct from the publisher. Just tick the titles you want and fill in the form below.

Name _____

Address _____

_____

_____

Write to Sphere Books, Cash Sales Department, P.O. Box 11, Falmouth, Cornwall TR10 9EN

Please enclose a cheque or postal order to the value of the cover price plus:

UK: 45p for the first book, 20p for the second book and 14p for each additional book ordered to a maximum charge of £1.63.

OVERSEAS: 75p for the first book plus 21p per copy for each additional book.

BFPO & EIRE: 45p for the first book, 20p for the second book plus 14p per copy for the next 7 books, thereafter 8p per book.

Sphere Books reserve the right to show new retail prices on covers which may differ from those previously advertised in the text or elsewhere, and to increase postal rates in accordance with the PO.